third edition

readings in auditing

J. Herman Brasseaux, Ph.D., C.P.A.

Professor of Accounting and Chairman
Department of Accounting
Louisiana State University in New Orleans

John D. Edwards, Ph.D., C.P.A.

Professor of Accounting
Northeast Louisiana University

Published by

SOUTH-WESTERN PUBLISHING CO.

A02

CINCINNATI   WEST CHICAGO, ILL.   DALLAS   PELHAM MANOR, N.Y.
BURLINGAME, CALIF.   BRIGHTON, ENGLAND

PREFACE

This book contains a compilation of articles and materials designed to give a stimulating analysis of issues of current concern in the examination of financial statements by the independent auditor and in the issuance of audit reports. Emphasis was placed on the inclusion of materials which highlight, not only the basic essence of the audit function, but also the boundary and horizons of the profession.

Determination of change in any field evokes controversy. Accordingly, the belief that the student of auditing should be aware of the challenges in his profession provided a constant guide in assembling the articles.

This edition stresses current developments and hence most of the items included are new to the third edition. A broad cross section of the literature in auditing is again represented in this collection of readings.

The materials in this volume are intended to serve as a supplementary reference to the text in a first course in auditing. The added insights and current exposure which these readings provide should enrich and broaden the perspective of students in a first course. Instructors in advanced and graduate courses in auditing should find that the topics covered in the individual selections complement discussions regarding the auditing function and its dynamics.

Each part and section is introduced by a short editorial comment which attempts to give continuity and coherence to the various selections.

Sincere appreciation is expressed to the authors of the materials included in this edition. This volume was made possible only as a result of the significant contribution to auditing literature by these authors and their consent to the use of their articles. We also wish to thank the publishers and their editors for their cooperation in making the materials available for this book.

Professor James T. Johnson, co-editor of the first and second editions, has relinquished his role due to his retirement from active teaching. His counsel and encouragement have been very valuable to us in preparing this edition.

J. Herman Brasseaux
John D. Edwards

CONTENTS

v

PART ONE

Evolution and Nature of
The Audit Function

An understanding of the nature of the audit function requires an appreciation of the historical development of auditing. Auditing objectives and techniques are in a continuous state of change and the student of auditing must be aware of the current "state of the art" and should ponder prospective extensions in the audit function to determine direction as well as appropriateness of change.

The first two articles by R. G. Brown and H. W. Bevis were selected to give the reader a feel for the major forces which have helped to shape the audit function as it is presently understood. Mr. Nurnberg in the third selection surveys the implications to the public and to the auditors of extending the audit function in several important areas. Extensions of the audit function are treated in greater depth in Part Five.

1. Changing Audit Objectives and Techniques*

A review of the history of auditing provides a basis for analyzing and interpreting the changes which have taken place in audit objectives and techniques. Even more important, this review reveals a significant recent trend toward increased reliance on internal controls and a decrease in detailed testing. Auditing in the future will probably consist primarily of a procedural (or system) review, with the analysis of effectiveness of internal controls providing the major basis for the procedural appraisal. Several arguments seem to support this view:

1. Rising costs in public accounting and the consequent additional emphasis on economy and effectiveness.

2. Requests received by the auditor from management, owners, and other parties-at-interest for additional information.

3. The increased complexity of the business enterprise resulting in geometric compounding of data control problems.

4. The development of new communication and information systems and introduction of extremely reliable data processing machines.

It is interesting to view present auditing objectives and techniques in terms of their evolution, as tabulated on page 3.

ANCIENT TO 1500

Prior to 1500, accounting concerned itself with governmental and family units. The use of two scribes who kept independent records of the same transactions was designed to prevent defalcations within the treasuries of the ancient rulers. A secondary objective was assurance of accuracy in reporting. Inventories were periodically taken to prove the accuracy of the accounting records; auditing was not relied upon for this function. The "hearing" of accounts during the time of the Roman Empire was also primarily concerned with preventing fraudulent acts by the quaestors.

Subsequent to the fall of the Roman Empire, auditing developed hand-in-hand with the Italian City States. The merchants of Florence, Genoa

---

*From *The Accounting Review*, Vol. XXXVII (October, 1962), pp. 696–703. Reprinted by permission of the American Accounting Association.

†R. Gene Brown, Ph.D., CPA, is Vice-President, Syntex Corporation, Palo Alto, California.

Period	Stated Audit Objectives	Extent of Verification	Importance of Internal Controls
Ancient– 1500	Detection of fraud	Detailed	Not recognized
1500– 1850	Detection of fraud	Detailed	Not recognized
1850– 1905	Detection of fraud Detection of clerical error	Some tests, Primarily Detailed	Not recognized
1905– 1933	Determination of fairness of reported financial position Detection of fraud & errors	Detailed and Testing	Slight recognition
1933– 1940	Determination of fairness of reported financial position Detection of fraud & errors	Testing	Awakening of interest
1940– 1960	Determination of fairness of reported financial position	Testing	Substantial emphasis

and Venice used auditors to assist in the verification of the accountability of the sailing-ship captains returning from the Old World with riches bound for the European Continent. Auditing was primarily fraud-preventive during this era.

The audit of the City of Pisa in 1394 was designed to test the accounts of the governmental officials to determine whether defalcation had taken place. Accuracy was sought in most of these cases, but only insofar as it might indicate the existence of fraud. Mr. L. Fitzpatrick commented on the early audit objective as follows: "Auditing as it existed to the sixteenth century was designed to verify the honesty of persons charged with fiscal responsibilities."[1]

A review of the literature pertaining to the early history of auditing reveals nothing concerning the existence of internal controls (or indeed

---

[1] L. Fitzpatrick, "The Story of Bookkeeping, Accounting, and Auditing," *Accountants Digest*, IV (March, 1939), 217.

accounting systems). Early auditing techniques consisted almost exclusively of a detailed verification of every transaction which had taken place. As an audit procedure the concept of testing or sampling was unknown.

1500 TO 1850

There is little in the period of 1500 to 1850 which would distinguish audit objectives from earlier times. Auditing was expanded in scope to include the earlier manufacturing activities arising during the early days of the Industrial Revolution. Audit objectives were still directed to detection of fraud, achieving more importance as it became common for owners to be separated from management and their capital investment. Detailed checking was still the rule and the accepted approach.

However, rather significant changes in attitude occurred during this period. The first was the recognition that an orderly and standardized system of accounting was desirable for both accurate reporting and fraud prevention. The second important change was a general acceptance of the need for an independent review of the accounts for both large and small enterprises.

Examples of this latter attitude are found in the English Companies Act of 1862 as well as certain bookkeeping texts of that era.

> The fundamental principles of Double Entry are as infallible in their application to every species of accounts as their operation is extensive; in practice, however, they are exposed to all the moral and mental imperfections of the accountant: They are neither exempt from the defects of ignorance— the errors of indolence — or the practice of fraud, — and frequent and careful investigations on the part of the proprietor himself are scarcely sufficient to render him secure from such evils.[2]

> ... the Italian Method, by a double entry of Debtor and Creditor, by way of eminence, is now always distinguished by the appellation of Bookkeeping as being of all others the most perfect, the most elegant and the most satisfactory, either for the Merchant's own information ... or otherwise for the inspections of others. . . .[3]

The recognition of the importance of a standardized system is also well covered in Jackson's book.

> In conducting of business, Order and Method contribute very much to lighten the care, facilitate the despatch and ensure the success thereof. The advantages of regularity are not more sensibly experienced by the extensive trader, in any part of his transactions, than in the orderly stating and keeping of his books of account.[4]

---

[2]B. F. Foster, *Commercial Bookkeeping* (Philadelphia: Perkins & Marvin, 1836), p. 4.
[3]William Jackson, "In the True Form of Debtor and Creditor," *Jackson's Book-keeping* (New York: Evert Duyckinck, Daniel Smith and Others, 1823), p. iii.
[4]*Ibid.*

The understanding that internal control was a desirable product of an accounting system came sometime after this. It was not specifically identified with any audit processes. The strength or weakness of the accounting system, and thereby of internal control, did not influence the amount of detailed checking accomplished.

1850 TO 1905

The fifty-five years following 1850 encompassed the period of greatest economic growth in Great Britain. The large-scale operations that resulted from the Industrial Revolution provided the impetus necessary to bring the corporate form of enterprise to the foreground. As management passed from individual owners to hired professionals, the owners in absentia became concerned over the proper protection and growth of their capital investment. The time was ripe for a profession of auditing to emerge.

Shortly after the middle of the nineteenth century, teams of stockholders, making periodic visits to the corporations, attempted to verify the recorded data. It soon became evident that a reliable audit required specialized training. This recognition, coupled with the suggestions for auditing in the Companies Act of 1862, increased substantially the demand for trained accountants who could perform professional, independent audits.

Internal control was recognized as existing in standardized systems of accounting, but little attention was paid to it in auditing. Little interest was shown in any systems of controls for assets other than cash. The built-in control inherent in double entry accounting was often the only cross check recognized as significant for all accounts. Because of this, the audits during the period 1850 to 1905 usually involved rather complete reviews of transactions and the preparation of corrected accounts and financial statements. This was inefficient, expensive, and did not satisfactorily provide for strengthening of weak areas in subsequent periods. The need for changes in the accounting system to improve the accuracy of reported amounts and reduce the possibilities for fraudulent acts was obvious. As the accounting system and the organizational structure were strengthened, the technique of sampling became accepted practice for auditors.

The implementation of testing as an auditing procedure can be traced to the last ten years of the nineteenth century. By 1895 there was evidence of sampling in Great Britain. In the London and General Bank case of that year, the following statement was made by the presiding judge:

> Where there is nothing to excite suspicion, very little inquiry will be reasonable and quite sufficient; and, in practice, I believe business men select

a few cases haphazard, see that they are right and assume that others like them are correct also.[5]

The new technique of sampling was not peculiar to English auditing; it also appeared in the United States about this time:

> With the rapid growth of American business following the Spanish-American war, the increase in size of many enterprises and the auditing of larger concerns, there developed the necessity for making the audit one of selected tests of the accounts rather than an endeavor to examine all of the transactions of the period.[6]

Evidence of sampling in auditing can also be seen in one of the pre-1900 New York CPA Examination Questions which asked, "In an audit where an exhaustive detailed examination . . . is not stipulated or practicable, what examination is necessary to assure . . . general correctness?"[7]

One would expect to see some evidence of a change in audit objectives during this period which would account in part for the acceptance of the new technique of testing. Techniques implement objectives; a change in techniques normally results from a corresponding change in objectives. However, in the literature relating to auditing in this period, there is no argument to support this assumption. The primary objective of auditing was still the detection of fraud; the reason that the auditor switched from detailed verification to testing was simply because he could no longer check every transaction of the evergrowing corporate entities.

Prior to 1905, a natural basis for deciding to limit the amount of testing to be done in auditing would have been the improvements in accounting systems, and consequently in internal controls, which existed in the larger corporations. Surprisingly, it was sometime later, during the period 1905 to 1933, that auditors realized the importance of internal controls and the relation of strengths and weaknesses therein to their testing programs. The first true recognition of internal control as a foundation for deciding on the amount of detailed verification to be done appeared in the American version of Dicksee's *Auditing*, ". . . a proper system of internal check [will] frequently obviate the necessity of a detailed unit."[8]

Despite this statement in a leading auditing book of the era, detailed testing was still the rule. Testing did exist, but was limited in application. This same book summarized the audit objectives at that time as follows:

The object of an audit may be said to be three-fold:

---

[5]E. D. McMillan, "Evaluation of Internal Control," *The Internal Auditor*, XIII (December, 1956), 39.

[6]Walter A. Staub, *Auditing Developments During the Present Century* (Cambridge: Harvard University Press, 1942), p. 10.

[7]C. A. Moyer, "Early Developments in American Auditing," *Accounting Review*, XXVI (January, 1951), p. 5.

[8]Lawrence R. Dicksee, *Auditing*, ed. Robert H. Montgomery (New York: Ronald Press, 1905), p. 54.

1. The detection of fraud.
2. The detection of technical errors.
3. The detection of errors of principle.[9]

1905 TO 1933

The auditing objectives and techniques of Great Britain formed the basis for the development of the American auditing profession in its early years. However, in the ten years after the turn of the twentieth century, the American auditing profession progressed independently of its origins. The objectives and approach of the British auditors were found to be unsuitable for American business. British audits designed to discover defalcations did not continue long into American auditing. The first major American work on auditing characterized this change in objectives in this manner:

> In what might be called the formative days of auditing, students were taught that the chief objects of an audit were:
>
> 1. Detection and prevention of fraud.
>
> 2. Detection and prevention of errors, but in recent years there has been a decided change in demand and service.
>
> Present-day purposes are:
>
> 1. To ascertain actual financial condition and earnings of an enterprise.
>
> 2. Detection of fraud and errors, but this is a minor objective.[10]

Accompanying this change in objectives was a rather significant change in techniques. The transition from British to American auditing was characterized by a change from detailed verification to testing. Auditors decided that ". . . it was not necessary to make a detailed examination of every entry, footing, and posting during the period in order to get the substance of the value which resulted from an audit."[11]

The literature of this period began to recognize more fully the importance of internal control and its relation to the extent of audit testing to be done. An English book published in 1910, *Audit Programmes*, pointed out that the first step in any audit was to "ascertain the system of internal check."[12]

Typical of the American authors' treatment of this subject were the following:

> Systems of operating accounts and records should be formulated with a single guiding principle — that they must furnish means of control.[13]

---

[9]*Ibid.*, p. 22.

[10]Robert H. Montgomery, *Auditing Theory and Practice* (New York: Ronald Press, 1912), p. 13. This identical statement appeared in the second (1923), and the third (1927) editions.

[11]Frank G. Short, "Internal Control from the Viewpoint of the Auditor," *Journal of Accountancy*, 70 (September, 1940), 226.

[12]E. V. Spicer and E. C. Pegler, *Audit Programmes* (London: H. Foulkes Lynch & Co., 1910), p. 4.

[13]F. R. Carnegie Steele, "The Development of Systems of Control," *Journal of Accountancy*,

Where there is a satisfactory system of internal check, the auditor is not expected, and should not attempt, to make a detailed audit.[14]

If the Auditor can satisfy himself that the work of record keeping is done in such a way as to furnish a system of internal check . . . he can accept the results [of the system] as being correct, subject to tests. . . .[15]

Unfortunately, the literature was far ahead of actual practice. The auditor continued to expand his use of the technique of testing, but his decision as to the extent of testing was not directly tied to an appraisal of internal controls. This direct relationship was not to come until some years later. The stated audit objectives changed; the techniques changed; but the attitude of the auditor was slow to change.

The adoption of sampling procedures probably represented the most important development in auditing during the early 1900's. Account analysis was done, but this seems to represent no departure from the point of view of the detailed auditor's, merely a substitution in the quantity of the work formerly done.[16]

1933 TO 1940

The period encompassed by 1933 and 1940 is interesting not only because of the influence of the New York Stock Exchange and various governmental agencies on auditing, but also because of the relative confusion that existed regarding audit objectives. At the inception of this period some writers were beginning to discount the significance of detection of fraud as an objective of auditing while others emphasized its importance. By the end of the eight years there was a fair degree of agreement that the auditor could not, and should not, be primarily concerned with the detection of fraud. This attitude was undoubtedly influenced by the McKesson Robbins case.

This transition in attitude is well demonstrated in successive editions of Montgomery's Auditing text during this period which stated: "An incidental, but nevertheless important, object of an audit is detection of fraud." (Fifth Edition, 1934, page 26.) "Primary responsibility . . . for the control and discovery of irregularities necessarily lies with the management." (Sixth Edition, 1940, page 13.)

Prior to 1940, uniform agreement as to audit responsibility for the detection of fraud did not exist. Other authors had stated: "It is well

---

4 (October, 1913), 282. This excellent article was the first on the subject of internal control to appear in an American professional accounting magazine. Most of Mr. Steele's comments could be lifted verbatim from context and be as timely today as they were in 1913.

[14]Montgomery, op. cit., p. 82.

[15]DeWitt Carl Eggleston, Auditing Procedure (New York: John Wiley & Sons, 1926), p. 19.

[16]Moyer, op. cit., p. 7. It is interesting also to note that an auditing text published in 1919, Auditing Procedure, by William B. Castenholz made no mention of internal control or check, yet suggested that less than detailed testing was permissible.

established that one of the main objects of an audit is the detection and prevention of fraud."[17] "The partial checking, or testing of a group of items is firmly established in audit procedure as a means of discovering the presence of fraud."[18] ". . . in the testing process, the auditor has a powerful weapon against fraud — one perhaps more potent than has heretofore been realized."[19]

The question of the importance of fraud detection during this period was a relative one; most authors agreed that the normal audit was primarily concerned with determining the fairness of reported financial statements but disagreed as to the role of tests designed to detect fraud.

Despite the disparity in defining audit objectives, there was nearly uniform agreement on audit techniques. By this time, testing was the rule, not the exception. The degree of testing decided upon was largely dependent on the effectiveness of internal control. Fairly typical of the acceptance of internal control as the basis for testing decisions are these three quotations:

> The first step to take when planning an audit by test methods consists of a thorough investigation of the system on which the books are kept. . . . It is not the auditor's sole duty to see that the internal check is carried out but to ascertain how much it can be relied upon to supplement his investigations.[20]

> It has been the accepted practice of public accountants to consider the adequacy of the system of internal check in determining the extent of the examination required.[21]

> . . . audits consist largely of samplings, tests and checks. Their value depends on what are known as "internal checks and controls." Auditors are supposed to satisfy themselves that these internal checks and controls are adequate and, if they are, not to make a more complete examination.[22]

1940 TO 1960

Audit objectives and approach changed only slightly between 1940 and 1960. Emphasis continued to be placed on the determination of the fairness of financial statement representations with a corresponding deëmphasis on fraud detection. This was the attitude expressed by the American Institute of Certified Public Accountants and most accounting writers. Officially the Institute was on record as follows:

---

[17]L. F. Foster, "Internal Check," *Accountants Digest*, 1 (March, 1936), 236.
[18]Lewis A. Carman, "The Efficacy of Tests," *American Accountant*, 18 (December, 1933), 360.
[19]*Ibid.*, p. 366.
[20]Anonymous, "Test Methods in Auditing," *Accountants Digest*, 1 (March, 1936), 240.
[21]Victor H. Stempf, "Influence of Internal Control Upon Audit Procedure," *Journal of Accountancy*, 62 (September, 1936), 170.
[22]Johnson Heywood, "Are Auditors Hard of Hearing?", *Nations Business*, January, 1940, as reviewed in *Accountants Digest*, 5 (March, 1940), 203.

> The primary purpose of an examination of financial statements by an independent Certified Public Accountant is to enable him to express an opinion as to the fairness of the statements. . . .
>
> The ordinary examination incident to the issuance of an opinion respecting financial statements is not designed and cannot be relied upon to disclose defalcations and other similar irregularities.[23]

However, many audit techniques in this period were specifically designed to assist in the detection of fraud.

In addition to this disparity between stated audit objectives and certain techniques used in implementing those objectives, there was some disagreement in the literature as to the auditors' responsibility for performing tests to disclose fraud. Typical of the prominent accountants who accepted the position of the Institute with reservations was Samuel J. Broad: "The discovery of error and irregularities is still an objective [of auditing], but not the primary one."[24] Considering the importance placed on fraud detection in the history of auditing and the disagreement in the literature as to the subject, it was not surprising that much of the general public viewed the auditor as a detective.

1960 TO DATE

In "Statement on Auditing Procedure Number 30," published in the January 1961 *Journal of Accountancy*, the American Institute's Committee on Auditing Procedure undertook a clarification of the position quoted above from the 1951 Codification. The general comments at the outset of Statement 30 serve primarily as a reaffirmation of the official Institute attitude communicated in the earlier Codification. In the latter paragraphs of the more recent Statement the Committee becomes somewhat more specific. They state that the auditor

> . . . recognizes that any fraud, if sufficiently material, may affect his opinion on the fairness of the presentation of the financial statements, and his examination made in accordance with generally accepted auditing standards gives consideration to this possibility.

And further,

> When an independent auditor's examination leading to an opinion on financial statements discloses specific circumstances which arouse his suspicion as to the existence of fraud, he should decide whether the fraud, if in fact it should exist, might be of such magnitude as to affect his opinion on the

---

[23]American Institute of CPA's, *Codification of Statements on Auditing Procedure* (New York: A.I.C.P.A. 1951), pp. 11, 12.
[24]Broad, *op. cit.*, p. 39.

financial statements. If the independent auditor believes that fraud may have occurred which could be so material as to affect his opinion, he should reach an understanding with the proper representatives of the client as to whether the independent auditor or the client, subject to the independent auditor's review, is to make the investigation necessary to determine whether fraud in fact has occurred and, if so, the amount involved.

It is somewhat questionable whether this statement has provided the proper solution. Another look at current auditing objectives is necessary. The objective of the independent review of financial statements is the expression of an opinion as to the fairness of the representations included in those financial reports. In order to be in a position to form a professional opinion regarding the financial statements, the auditor must do sufficient work so as to be reasonably assured that there are no errors of commission or omission of sufficient materiality to misstate reported amounts. This is necessary regardless of the source of those errors. To deny responsibility for testing to determine if material fraud may exist because of any consideration of time or cost involved or because of the difficulties of detection is to reduce the value of the professional opinion.

The suggestion that a portion of the testing be shifted to the client creates many new problems. In line with generally accepted auditing standards, the auditor must determine that the client personnel performing the work are technically equipped and proficient, maintain the necessary independent attitude, and exercise the same professional care that the auditor himself would use. Further, it could be easily argued that in order to meet these professional standards, the auditor must actively supervise such tests and not confine his interest to a post-test review. Short of this, if material fraud is suspected there is little justification for rendering an opinion on the fairness of financial statements.

Additional clarification relative to professional responsibility as to testing for defalcation is necessary. This can be accomplished best by a redefinition and restatement of audit objectives. Such a redefinition must include audit responsibility for performing tests designed to disclose all material misstatements of financial statements, whatever the source. Only then can the auditor's opinion be accorded the respect it deserves.

For some reason whenever the subject of fraud detection arises, special rules for audit responsibility are felt necessary. This is an unduly defensive position to assume. There is no reason why the general rules governing audit responsibility in other areas cannot incorporate material fraud. As to any possibile material misstatement of financial statements it must be emphasized that the auditor's responsibility is to *perform tests* in line with generally accepted auditing standards designed to detect the possibility for such misstatements. The auditor is not responsible for detecting gross fraud, for example, but cannot and should not disclaim responsibility for *testing* for it within the course of his normal examination. That this is an existent consideration within most engagements few auditors will deny.

The final paragraph of Auditing Procedure Statement Number 30 is related to this argument:

> The subsequent discovery that fraud existed during the period covered by the independent auditor's examination does not of itself indicate negligence on his part. He is not an insurer or guarantor and, if his examination was made with due professional skill and care, in accordance with generally accepted auditing standards, he has fulfilled all of the obligations implicit in his undertaking.

Despite the existence of differences in opinion as to audit objectives, there is widespread general acceptance of the approach wherein the review of internal control is the starting point of the audit and the results of that review the basis for determining the extent of testing required.

> In more recent years the independent auditor has gradually changed from a program of detailed auditing to one of test and analysis. It is no longer practical in large or even medium-sized companies to examine in detail the increased volume of transactions; nor is it necessary in view of the improvements in the organization of the clients' accounting and allied internal operations.[25]

SUMMARY

In most professions it is rather difficult to predict the future, but there are some significant trends revealed by the history of auditing which should carry forward into succeeding years. Interpreted in line with changing audit objectives and techniques these trends seem to indicate:

1. The first and foremost audit objective will remain the determination of the fairness of financial statement representations.

2. Reliance on the system of internal controls will increase. The audit will be primarily a system of audit of procedures. Detailed testing will take place only insofar as it is required to detect irregularities, errors, or to evaluate the effectiveness of the internal controls.

3. Since the fairness of the financial statement representations is affected by all material misstatements, there will be acceptance of the general responsibility of the auditor to perform tests to detect material defalcations and errors if they exist. This will be incorporated as a supplementary audit objective.

---

[25]Victor Z. Brink, "The Independent Auditor's Review of Internal Control," *Journal of Accountancy*, 73 (May, 1942), 430.

The evaluation of internal control effectiveness is destined to become the most important part of the auditor's program for evaluating fairness of financial statement presentations. The four conditions cited at the start of this article offer support to this conclusion. Auditing in the future will place a greater emphasis on system control techniques designed to insure reasonable accuracy and less emphasis on what has happened in the past. ". . . the modern audit . . . has shifted from a review of past operations to a review of the system of internal control."[26]

---

[26]Oswald Nielsen, "New Challenges in Accounting," *Accounting Review*, XXXV (October, 1960), 584.

2. The CPA's Attest Function in Modern Society*

Herman W. Bevis†

The attest function results in the expression of an opinion by an independent expert that a communication of economic data by one party to another is fairly presented. Discharge of the function lends credibility to the representation and increases reliance upon it. The opinion implies (if it does not so state) that the data presented are appropriate for the purpose of the representation, that there is objective evidence underlying the data, and that the judgments exercised in interpreting the data are such as to justify the opinion.

What social need does the attest function fulfill in modern society? What is the attest function's probable and potential future course? What part does the CPA play in it now; what is his future role? Discussing these questions is the purpose of this paper. It may be well to set the stage for the discussion, however, by first defining some of the terms.

"Economic data" consist of "material serving as a basis for discussion and inference pertaining to the management of the affairs of a government or community with reference to the source of its income, its expenditures, the development of its natural resources, etc."[1] The attest function is most frequently applied to data of individual political or economic units which, in the aggregate, make up a government or community. Economic data, which include economic activity and position, relate to resources — their source, nature, quantity, accumulation, allocation and exhaustion. The data can be expressed in various quantitative terms, including monetary. Although the attest function has in the past usually been utilized primarily in connection with monetary data, the subsequent discussion of its elements will indicate that there is no basis for an exclusive relationship. On the contrary, the function is applicable to economic data expressed in any quantitative terms.

The term "attest function" has been deliberately chosen for this discussion in preference to some such term as "independent audit function." One reason is that the latter may still be interpreted by some laymen as applying to a process of meticulous detailed checking, searching for fraud,

*From *The Journal of Accountancy*, Vol. 113 (February, 1962), pp. 28–35. Copyright (1962) The American Institute of Certified Public Accountants, Inc. Reprinted by permission of the AICPA.

†Herman W. Bevis, CPA, is a retired senior partner of Price Waterhouse & Co.

[1]See definitions of "data" and "economic" in Webster's New International Dictionary — Second Edition (Unabridged).

etc. Moreover, the term "attest function" (the root of which means to bear witness) seems particularly descriptive of the independent auditor's relationship to data communications. While in the minds of some the term may be narrowly associated with "truth" or "facts," as used here it is also considered applicable to expressions of judgment.

The CPA as a trained observer of economic activities, relationships and status is the most appropriate agent to discharge the attest function. His competence has been identified by a state authority. His position as independent auditor, which involves a peculiar responsibility to third parties, is not assumed by those in private employment. Other "auditors" (e.g., revenue agents, bank examiners, etc.) are affiliated with the users of data and their objectives and scope of activity are different from those involved in the discharge of the attest function. While the CPA's attest function is most frequently encountered in opinions on financial statements submitted to investors and creditors, as has already been indicated its use is not and should not be so confined.

The remainder of this paper is divided into three principal parts: first, a review of the present utilization of the attest function in this country and abroad and a catalog of some questions which arise from the review; second, a close look at the social purpose of communications of economic data and of the attest function related thereto, in the hope that these fundamentals will help answer some of the questions and point the way to the CPA's potential for future contributions to society; and, finally, an enumeration of some of the potential areas of expanded service and possible areas of action by CPAs to accomplish their full social purpose.

The Use of the Attest Function Abroad

The writer has corresponded with associates in a small sample of countries abroad in an attempt to assess the degree to which the attest function has been locally developed elsewhere. By "locally developed" is meant the use of the function in connection with enterprises financed by capital generated within the country and managed by its citizens. Enterprises financed from another country, say the United States, are not necessarily dealt with, since the use of the function in connection with these enterprises would generally follow the custom in the U.S. The writer's observations resulting from a review of this correspondence are set out below.

The use of the attest function in other English-speaking countries — Australia, Canada and England — appears to be more extensive than in the U.S. It is applied to communications of financial data to investors by a greater variety of issuers because of statute or custom. Beyond that, it seems almost instinctive that reports from those handling other people's money be attested. Taxing authorities frequently call for the attested report to stockholders. There seems to be a widespread consensus as to appropriate standards for the measurement and communication of financial data.

Among Italy, France, the Netherlands, Switzerland and West Germany there are widespread differences in the manner and extent to which the attest function is both called upon and discharged. Statutory requirements for its use vary from all-inclusive to none. The dictates of custom show a wide range. In some cases, the independent auditor's opinion on financial statements is furnished to management but not used by the latter to add credibility (the end purpose of the attest function) in reports to investors. There is sometimes a disparity between statutory requirements for widespread application of the function, and the obviously inadequate qualifications required of those bearing the independent auditor designation or the clearly inadequate number of those who are unquestionably qualified. The consensus as to standards appropriate for communications of financial data seems to be far less clear than in the English-speaking countries.

The review of the attest function's role abroad suggests that the following are among the factors which have influenced its development and use:

Making for greater use	*Making for lesser use*
Widespread ownership of enterprises	Ownership concentrated in few hands, even for large enterprises
Highly industrialized society	Some industry, including a few large organizations, but most productive capacity resting in small units
Industry mostly privately owned, and mostly regulated by competition	Government participation greater through regulation and, sometimes, ownership
Accounting standards for reporting to stockholders and creditors fairly well developed and applied	Little consensus as to accounting standards for reporting to stockholders and creditors

Since all of the factors enumerated above making for greater use are descriptive of conditions in the United States, it is pertinent to turn to that country.

USE OF THE ATTEST FUNCTION IN THE U.S.

The CPA's attest function, although widely employed in the United

States, has an uneven usage. The following summary demonstrates this in connection with major types of communications of economic data:

Reports to stockholders. Attest function required for commercial and industrial companies in communications via the SEC and certain stock exchanges. Also required for electric, gas and certain other utilities but not for railroads and insurance companies (although used voluntarily by some of the latter).

Used unevenly by banks, to a fair extent by unlisted and unregulated widely owned companies and to a lesser extent by narrowly owned companies.

Reports to creditors. For long-term indebtedness: If registered with the SEC, the use of the attest function follows along the lines of reports to stockholders; its use in reports to bond trustees and institutional bondholders varies and is frequently confined to ratios, current asset levels and other selected data; it is rarely used for bond issuers which are governments or their instrumentalities.

For short-term indebtedness, such as to commercial bankers, the requirement for use appears to depend upon the policy of the institution and to vary from a rigid requirement of all borrowers, to borrower's option.

Reports to regulatory and supervisory authorities. Use of the attest function appears to vary by industries, or laws from which the authority derives, and the differences may derive partially from historical accident.

Reports to taxing authorities. The attest function is not legally required nor voluntarily used. (The CPA's participation in tax return preparation, and settlement of taxes, is presently more in the nature of advice and assistance rather than the discharge of the attest function.)

Reports by Governmental bodies to taxpayers. The attest function is used to a limited extent by municipalities and counties, and perhaps to a somewhat greater extent by Governmental authorities and instrumentalities.

Internal reports. The attest function is used to some extent by owner-managed companies, the degree appearing to vary proportionally to the size of the enterprise. For the large public companies, it is used in a few cases — mostly for subsidiaries or branches abroad or otherwise remote from the headquarters of the organization.

Considering the attest function's purpose and its significance to the user of financial and other economic data, the discrepancies in the above recital seem curious. This is particularly true in view of some of the trends which are in evidence.

As stated at the outset, the purpose of the attest function is to lend credibility to the representations of one party to another. The use of the function is increasing sharply. More and more of those handling other people's money are realizing that the attest function of CPAs may relieve them of responsibility which they would otherwise have to assume.[2]

The expansion of use of the attest function for small businesses is gaining impetus from the requirements of creditors.[3] There are signs that commercial credit grantors are now scrutinizing audited financial statements of prospective borrowers in addition to merely ascertaining their credit ratings. Credit agencies have been giving consideration to indicating in their reports whether or not financial data presented have been audited by CPAs and what kind of opinion has been issued. The emerging influence which the attest function is exerting in modern society seems clear. Yet its use is still uneven. Why?

REASONS FOR UNEVEN USE OF THE FUNCTION

Probably at least one or more of four causes explains the nonuse of the attest function where a useful purpose could be fulfilled:

1. The user of data believes he can satisfy himself sufficiently as to the data's credibility.

2. There is the mistaken impression that the attest function is being discharged.

3. Users may be ignorant as to the role and value of the function.

4. The user feels that the independent auditor either does not comprehend, or does not subscribe to, the accounting standards which he considers appropriate for the data he desires.

Under the first point, users undertaking the responsibility for satisfying themselves as to data's reliability and conformity to standards suitable to them include:

The owner-manager of an unaudited enterprise
The directors of an unaudited enterprise
Commercial lenders who consider that their intimate knowledge of
the borrower's enterprise, and appraisal of the character of owners

---

[2]John L. Carey, "The Next 50 Years," *The Ohio Certified Public Accountant*, Winter, 1959, pp. 7–14.
[3]Robert E. Witschey, "What's Ahead for the Accounting Profession," *Massachusetts CPA Review*, October 1959, pp. 22–35.

and management, are either more important than financial data or
an assurance as to reliability of data, or both

Federal, state and local taxing authorities

Some Governmental regulatory or supervisory authorities

Each of these users, to the extent that he satisfies himself as to data he
receives, does so only with regard to his own needs. Data suitable for his
purposes are not necessarily appropriate or adequate for other purposes
or for other groups of people.

Regarding the second point, many users of financial data, even some
directors and members of management, believe that the attest function is
being discharged in their enterprises by examiners from banking, insurance,
public utility and other supervisory or regulatory authorities. This notion
persists notwithstanding the disclaimers of the authorities themselves that
their field of interest is narrower than that required to discharge the attest
function for data directed to stockholders and other users. For example,
whereas bank examiners primarily concern themselves with liquidity of
assets looking toward the protection of depositors, the CPA reporting to
stockholders is basically interested in a fair presentation of all financial
data bearing on position and results.

Why have some users of data remained ignorant of the role and value
of the attest function (point three above)? Perhaps, because of indiffer-
ence, lack of education or complacency, they don't comprehend fully the
part the CPA plays in the scheme of things. It is true that both the usefulness and the limitations of, say, conventional financial statements to investors can be best appreciated only with some knowledge of the techniques
and judgments underlying them; this is also true in varying degree for communications of other economic data. With such knowledge, the importance of the attest function becomes clear. Whether the educational process is difficult or not, it assumes paramount importance if the CPA is to
make his full contribution to society in satisfying expanding needs for the
attest function.

The fourth reason given above for nonuse of the attest function has to
do with accounting standards. It seems probable that the fact that accounting standards can — and should — vary according to circumstances and
needs of issuers and users of data has gradually become obscured. What
seems to have disappeared from view even more is that review of the appropriateness of accounting standards is an integral part of the attest function.

The foregoing discussion suggests that it may be well to re-examine the
nature and purposes of communications of economic data, and to dwell
particularly on the role of standards in connection with them. Perhaps this
exercise will give some guidance to the CPA in adapting to future calls on
the attest function.

WHY ARE ECONOMIC DATA COMMUNICATED?

A satisfactory system for communicating financial and other economic data is an essential condition for the accumulations of capital from widespread sources in single enterprises — i.e., for a successful industrial economy. Persons having an interest in resources are in various stages of remoteness from them and from the factors which affect them. The greater this remoteness, the greater the need for communication of data. Thus, the small-plot, one-crop farmer can obtain most of the economic data which he needs regarding his changing resources through his physical senses. The individual with extensive farming operations managed by others throughout the world needs many more communications of data. If the latter enterprise is owned by inactive investors, or borrows money, then the receipt of data by investor or creditor becomes even more important. In fact, without assurance of reliable economic data, the remote investor or creditor probably would not supply capital to the enterprise. (The extent of the remoteness also indicates the need for *internal* communication of data.)

The complexity of the resources involved and the events affecting them also evoke communication of economic data. The carnival medicine man needs little communication beyond the information furnished by his physical senses to assess the trend in his resources. On the other hand, the owner of a drug store stocking thousands of different items, and buying and selling on credit, needs a considerable amount of economic data before he can assess the trend in his resources — even if he handles every transaction personally. Thus, the necessity for measuring and communicating economic data can exist in complex situations even though the element of remoteness is absent.

The same elements of remoteness and complexity call for communications of data in connection with regulations, taxes and many other social functions.

The number of economic interrelationships among the units of a society multiplies the communications of economic data. In a primitive agrarian economy, these are few. At the other end of the scale is the highly industrialized United States with its combination of free enterprise, private capital, high rates of taxation, some degree of regulation or supervision over selected economic units, and a national policy of economic growth without severe fluctuations.

Within the United States, the communications of economic data are enormous in scope and quantity. Besides investors and creditors, those to whom a large corporation might direct such communications would include: Governmental regulatory or supervisory authorities, Federal and state; taxing authorities, Federal, state and local; military, other Governmental and private customers where cost is a factor in determining price; courts, in a variety of issues where economic data are pertinent; legislative committees and commissions; suppliers and credit agencies; insurance companies for claims; public and industrial associations and agencies for economic statistics; royalty recipients; labor unions; employees; parties to legal contracts and covenants; and the general public. The small business communicates to fewer parties, of course, but the quantity still looms large to it. Every year the four million business organizations operated in this country create and communicate a vast quantity of economic data. Here are a few examples:

> Over twelve million American investors are receiving reports from one or more of 5,000 publicly held companies. About two-thirds of these investors hold securities listed on the New York Stock Exchange.
>
> In a recent year, over 990,000 corporate income tax returns were submitted to the Federal Government.
>
> Under just *one* regulatory statute, the Securities Exchange Act of 1934, over 12,000 annual and other periodic reports were filed by issuers with the SEC in a recent year.

To repeat, satisfactory operation of a highly industrialized society, with its complex of interrelated units, requires the measurement and communication of an extraordinary scope and quantity of economic data.

KEYS TO SUCCESSFUL DATA COMMUNICATIONS

Before economic data can be communicated, they must be measured. The whole process of measurement and communication constitutes the accounting function. The end purpose of the function is to convey information to someone in such manner that he may utilize it in formulating judgments and making decisions. Naturally, all rules of basic communication apply.

In any successful communication, a meeting of minds must exist between issuer and user as to the meaning of terms. Before there can be a meeting of minds in the communication of financial and other economic data, these are among the conditions that must be satisfied:

1. The issuer and user of economic data must have an understanding as to standards for measurement and summarization.

2. The issuer must have the requisite knowledge and skills to carry out the antecedent steps leading up to, and to prepare, the communication.

3. There must be absence of bias in the communication (to the extent humanly feasible).

4. The communication must be intelligible to the user.

The importance of the last three conditions is patent; the matter of standards, being more complex, will be examined further. (It will be noted that all four conditions suggest a role for the attest function.)

AGREEMENT ON ACCOUNTING STANDARDS

Whenever data regarding the quantity of and changes in resources are required for a continuing enterprise, conventions must be established to guide the measurement. Many of these conventions are mere assumptions as to the future and, being such (since the future cannot be accurately foretold), cannot be said to have precision. If periodic reports during an organization's existence (say, of net income) were not required, the assumptions would be unnecessary; the former being required, however, the assumptions are unavoidable. These are the accounting standards — underlying the measurement of economic data communicated — regarding which it is important that issuer and user have a meeting of minds.

There is sometimes a difference of objectives between the issuer and user of data which has a direct bearing upon standards chosen. Where this is known, the attest function cannot be fully discharged until issuer and user come into agreement. (However, the CPA may still be helpful either in isolating and identifying areas in which the two parties must come into agreement or in seeing that the issuer communicates sufficient information that the user may revise the data according to his own standards.) A few illustrations will demonstrate the point.

Income taxing authorities may well be inclined, from considerations of fiscal policy, toward standards for the measurement of annual net profit which result in the earliest possible reporting thereof for taxation. Issuers of data (taxpayers filing tax returns) may be inclined to the opposite. Taxable incomes may be increased or decreased, from considerations of social or economic policy, for all or selected groups of taxpayers, through the adoption by legislative or taxing authorities of standards for measuring net profits which achieve that end. Taxpayer issuers of data may or may not agree with the objectives or the standards suitable for reaching them. Where issuers and users of taxable income data differ as to important standards for their measurement, the standard is usually established by law as interpreted by the courts.

Standards are established under legal authority with judicial interpretation for the measurement of financial and other economic data communicated by utilities to regulating authorities. The regulatory objective is essentially to limit net profit to a fair return on invested capital. Both legislative and regulatory bodies are subjected to conflicting social, economic and political pressures from consumers, investors and managements. The choice among accounting standards for determining net profit or invested capital is sometimes strongly influenced by the dominant pressure. If the issuer of data — the utility — differs as to standards promulgated for his use, again the final authorities are the legislatures and the courts.

The supervisory authority of a banking or insurance institution has as his primary objective the protection of depositors or policyholders. Accounting standards which measure readily realizable assets at minimal amounts, and maximize liabilities, are the most suitable for the objective. The fact that the collateral effect of application of these standards might be distortion of, say, net profit reported to stockholders is outside the field of primary interest of the authority.

Some other important users of financial data, their principal objectives and the basis upon which they would judge the appropriateness of accounting standards, would include:

User	Objective	Standards desired to measure
Short-term creditor	Repayment of loan at maturity	Minimum prospective cash flow, or net assets readily realizable in cash, or both
Government purchasing nonstandard material	Allowance to supplier of specified rate of profit on contract costs and/or on capital employed	Minimum costs allocable to contract or capital associated with it
Purchaser of a business based upon equity or earnings	Lowest purchase price	Minimum equity or periodic earnings

One of the most important groups of users of financial data consists of long-term stockholders in public companies. The standards involved in the measurement and communication of data to this group assume great importance in the private enterprise system. The greatest interest of these users of data is the periodic net profit of their enterprise. The accounting standards appropriate for this purpose are essentially the same as those for measuring the extent to which each such privately owned unit has achieved the objective which society has established for it: to create resources in excess of those exhausted — to create economic values — which is another way of saying "to make a profit."

Long-term stockholders in publicly owned companies, unlike most of the other users of data, are largely inarticulate as to the standards most appropriate for their purposes. The role of enunciating these has largely fallen to the American Institute of Certified Public Accountants, acting formerly through its committee on accounting procedure and presently through the Accounting Principles Board.

It will be obvious that standards appropriate for measuring and communicating economic data to satisfy the needs of the long-term stockholder are not all necessarily the most appropriate to meet the needs of the income taxing authority, the regulatory or supervisory body, nor of the other data users which have been mentioned. A crying need exists to clarify the appropriate areas for the application of the many sets of standards which are in use today for the measurement and communication of financial and other economic data. This is also a condition precedent for full utilization of the CPA's attest function.

PROPER DISCHARGE OF THE ATTEST FUNCTION

It might be well at this point to recapitulate the principal conditions which must be met for the attest function to be effective. There must be:

1. Economic data measurable in quantitative terms (such as money, material, labor and time) for which a communication need exists.

2. Standards for measurement and summarization of economic data which are acceptable to the user and practicable of application by the issuer of such data. The attester must be able to satisfy himself that the standards are appropriate for the user's needs if the latter has not participated directly or through representatives in formulating them; if the user has so participated (as, say, in income taxation), the attester must be satisfied that issuer and user are in agreement.

3. Competent evidential matter supporting the economic data, on the nature and validity of which the attester must be able to pass judgment. By examination of such evidential matter, he must be able to satisfy himself as to whether or not established standards for measurement and communication of economic data have been properly applied or complied with. The attest responsibility includes ascertaining that there are no important

distortions of data due to bias, ignorance or human error.

4. Agreement by the issuer to disclose all data and other information needed by the user to formulate his judgments and make decisions.

5. Readiness to accept a format for the communication which is comprehensible to the reasonably knowledgeable among the users.

6. Practicability of adequate timeliness in the communication to suit the user's purpose.

7. Independence, objectivity and reliability on the part of the attester.

8. Requisite knowledge and skills on the part of the attester in all important phases of the measurement, substantiation and communication processes which are involved. This includes the exercise of due professional care.

9. Familiarity, on the attester's part, with the purposes of the communication, including appreciation of the user's needs.

These conditions are being satisfied, and the attest function is being discharged, on a constantly widening scale.

POTENTIAL FUTURE OF THE ATTEST FUNCTION

The imaginations of many have ranged wide as to potential new areas in which the CPA's attest function would be valuable in that all requirements for its utilization exist. Here are some possible areas for the attest function which have been proposed:

1. Attestation of Federal income tax returns.[4]

2. Certification to business planning (prospective accounting). Since budgetary control already is oriented to the prospective view, it is suggested that this would be as excellent an avenue as any to commence auditing's new future in this field of business planning.[5]

3. The CPA could become a representative of the courts as referee in resolving issues in litigation turning on accounting questions.[6]

4. Congress has been considering independent audits of unlisted ("over-the-counter") companies.[7]

5. Various legislation or proposed legislation involving optional provisions for independent audits involve banks, credit unions, insurance com-

---

[4]Robert E. Witschey, *The Journal of Accountancy, op. cit.*
[5]Oswald Nielsen, "New Challenges in Accounting," *The Accounting Review,* October 1960, pp. 583–589.
[6]J. S. Seidman, "What is the Future of the Accounting Profession?" *The Journal of Accountancy,* March 1959, pp. 29–36.
[7]John L. Carey, "The Next 50 Years," *The Ohio Certified Public Accountant,* Winter, 1959, pp. 7–14.

panies, local Government units, labor unions, and trustees of charities, hospitals, nonprofit associations and educational institutions.[8]

6. Audits involving attestation to industrial and/or economic statistical compilations.[9]

7. Use of independent auditors by Government.

The last item merits some elaboration. All signs indicate that the Federal Government will spend, or control the expenditure of, a larger percentage of the gross national product in the years to come. This expansion will result in large measure from the challenge of communism, long-term foreign aid programs, housing, urban and rural redevelopment, education, unemployment benefits, public transportation, old-age security, etc.

Because of this amplified scope of activities, the Government is almost certain to require submission of financial data by an increasing number of private and quasi-private organizations for several basic purposes:

1. To develop acceptable cost data for purposes of Government defense procurement contracts and renegotiation.

2. To provide some protection for Government funds advanced to organizations in the form of loans, grants, insurance, etc.

3. To aid the Government in determining compliance with regulatory statutes (such as those affecting stock-issuing corporations, labor unions, etc.).

4. To afford a basis for the regulation of and/or the setting of rates to be charged by regulated companies (e.g., banks, gas, electric, transportation, insurance and communications companies).

Naturally, it is the public welfare which decides whether or not greater use should be made of the CPA's attest function by the Government. Several sound reasons exist for advocating the use of the function:

1. Regulated areas frequently involve private and quasi-private enterprises which historically have relied on independent auditors. Government "examinations" which ignore the auditor's work result in needless and costly duplication of effort.

2. The independent audit will often provide more useful and reliable information for regulatory purposes than the limited government "examination."

3. Since CPAs are geographically dispersed, substantial economies can be realized by using them at the site of regulated enterprises rather than dispatching Government examiners from a limited number of centers.

---

[8]*Ibid.*

[9]William A. Campfield, "Professional Accounting at the Crossroads," *The Illinois Certified Public Accountant*, Spring, 1961, pp. 1–6.

4. The CPA is not directly affected by the political problems confronting the Governmental agency staff.

5. More than twenty agencies of the Government already use independent auditors (REA and SBIC programs being the best examples).

Because of these and other factors, the accounting profession is entitled to encourage the greater utilization of independent auditors by the Government.[10]

Recently, there have been appearing in professional literature suggestions that the CPA will in due course be undertaking "management audits" and reporting thereon to third parties. These suggestions have coincided with observations by Berle and others as to the concentrations of economic power in the nonowner managers of public companies where the only protection against abuse of this power is a "public consensus." The thought is advanced that society has a growing desire that there be an "accounting" by these managements in nonfinancial as well as financial terms for the authority assumed and responsibilities undertaken — and that enlightened managements themselves would welcome this means of discharging the obligations which they have assumed.

It may well be that the future will see the CPA's services so utilized. However, any such challenges must be reviewed carefully against the conditions under which the attest function makes its contribution: a representation which is communicated; acceptable standards for the measurement and communication; relevant evidence available for examination by the independent auditor; etc. All these may come in the nonfinancial, noneconomic areas. They are not here yet.

CONCLUSIONS

The attest function in the United States and other highly industrialized nations of the free world serves an essential purpose in modern society by adding credibility to financial and other economic data via the measurement, substantiation and communication processes.

Discharge of the function in the U.S. is confined largely to the CPA, because of his professional knowledge, skills, stature and other qualifications — including the characteristics of independence, dependability and objectivity.

The social importance of the attest function and the changing economic environment strongly suggest the expansion of its use. To bring this about, it would seem important that these things be done:

---

[10]The American Institute as early as 1957 supported Federal legislation providing for independent audits of employee pension and welfare funds. (John L. Carey, "The CPA in a Changing World," *The Illinois Certified Public Accountant*, Winter, 1957–58, pp. 4–10.)

1. Educate issuers and users of economic data as to the attest function's purpose, role and value. (This includes eradicating any mistaken impressions held regarding the functions being discharged.)

2. Inform the public and the CPA as to those areas in society where the attest function, although not presently performed, would fulfill a social need.

3. Cultivate judgment in selecting appropriate accounting standards for diverse economic units, issuers, users or purposes, and proper application of the standards chosen. (Included is the development of new or alternative accounting standards where needed.)

The responsibility for these projects lies squarely on the accounting profession.

3. The Independent Auditor's Attest Function: Its Prospects for Extension*

Hugo Nurnberg†

The attest function results in the expression of an opinion by a second party that a representation by a first party to a third party is fairly stated; discharge of the attest function lends credibility to the representation, hence increases the reliance a third party may place on it.[1] The second party must be independent of the first party and competent in gathering and evaluating objective evidence sufficient to conclude whether the representation is fairly stated; the first and third parties must concur on, and the second party must be knowledgeable in, the purpose, adequacy, timeliness, and format of the representation and the standards of measurement underlying it. Representations involve communication and communication is imperfect if the first and third parties do not concur on these elements, for they will have different perceptions of the same thing. For similar reasons, attestation is imperfect if the second party is not knowledgeable in these elements.

Discharge of the attest function adds credibility to representations of corporate management to outside parties. For the most part, only the representations included in published annual financial statements are presently covered by the independent auditor's attest function, although they are not the only representations of corporate management to outside parties. Suggestions have been advanced to extend the attest function to other representations of corporate management. This paper examines the prospects for such an extension.

SUGGESTED AREAS OF EXTENSION

Perhaps the most obvious and feasible extension of the attest function is for more economic entities to publish financial statements accompanied by an opinion of an independent auditor. Indeed, there

*From *The New York Certified Public Accountant* (October, 1971), pp. 727-732, 783-788. Reprinted by permission of the New York State Society of Certified Public Accountants.

†Hugo Nurnberg, Ph.D., is Associate Professor, Department of Accounting and Financial Administration, Michigan State University. The author is indebted to Alvin A. Arens (Michigan State University), Max Block (New York State Society of Certified Public Accountants), John B. Farrell (Price Waterhouse & Co.), Gardner M. Jones (Michigan State University), Carl L. Nelson (Columbia University), and Joseph L. Roth (Price Waterhouse & Co.) for helpful comments. Any errors, of course, are the responsibility of the author alone.

[1]Herman W. Bevis, "The CPA's Attest Function in Modern Accounting," *The Journal of Accountancy*, CXIII, No. 2 (February, 1962), pp. 28-35, esp. pp. 28, 33.

is a trend in this direction by privately-owned companies that have not published such statements, notably banks and insurance companies, and by nonprofit entities such as local governmental units, labor unions, hospitals, charities, credit unions, and educational institutions. Other possibilities include requiring an opinion of an independent auditor on interim financial statements, tax returns, cost reimbursement claims, and information reports filed with public agencies.

The attest function may also be extended by altering the content of the financial statements covered by the auditor's opinion and by extending the coverage of the opinion itself. Suggestions have been made to extend the attest function to the following representations: financial summaries and highlights; statements in terms of dollars of constant purchasing power; statements in terms of current values; schedules of sales and earnings by lines of business, broad industry groups, product lines, geographical markets, or customers; schedules of wages and salaries, management compensation, advertising expenditures, plant and equipment expenditures, and research and development expenditures; statistics on units produced and sold, unfilled purchase and sales orders, productive capacity, index of selling prices, patents received, and natural resource reserves; data on customers, suppliers, employees, officers, directors, and shareholders; and descriptions of cost behavior under different conditions, methods used to allocate overhead, terms of government contracts, activities among affiliated companies, and relations with financial institutions.

Conceivably, the auditor may also attest to the absence of fraud; to the absence of conflicts of interest by employees; to compliance with terms and conditions of contracts; and to compliance with laws and regulations. Another possibility is to have the auditor attest to the adequacy of internal controls — not just accounting controls, but also administrative (or management) controls. Perhaps the most remote suggestions for extending the attest function include evaluating management's past performance and reviewing its budgets and long-range plans. Nevertheless, these suggestions follow logically from previous considerations.

FEASIBILITY OF EXTENSION

Although the desirability of extending the attest function may only be conjectured, the feasibility of extending it to the above areas may be evaluated more conclusively. For this purpose, it is useful to distinguish between reporting and auditing. Expanding upon a comparable distinction between accounting and auditing offered by

Mautz and Sharaf,[2] reporting involves the measurement and communication of business events and conditions as they affect a given entity; auditing involves a review of these measurements and communications for propriety. In order for this review to be meaningful, standards must be available to evaluate the professional performance of the reviewer and to indicate accepted requirements of performance to outsiders who have occasion to judge or evaluate the review and rely on the representations.

The ten generally accepted auditing standards[3] largely define professional performance of ordinary examinations of financial statements. It is postulated that an extension of the attest function requires an extension of these standards or the development of comparable standards. Accordingly, in the remainder of this paper, the feasibility of extending the attest function is considered within the context of these ten standards.

ATTESTATION OF INTERIM FINANCIAL STATEMENTS

The major conceptual impediment to extending the attest function to interim financial statements relates to the periodicity constraint: it is unclear whether the income of an interim period should be determined independently of the income of the other interim periods and the year as a whole, or as a preliminary and partial estimate of the income of the entire year.[4] But a similar periodicity constraint pertains to annual financial statements without precluding their attestation. Extending the attest function to interim financial statements should follow the resolution of this conceptual question. Obviously, time and cost problems cannot be ignored, for the former may delay the auditor's report for an unacceptable period and the latter may be too burdensome. Perhaps both problems could be mitigated by using a negative assurance type of report for interim statements and a standard short-form report for annual statements.

ATTESTATION OF FINANCIAL STATISTICS AND OTHER DATA IN ANNUAL REPORTS

As noted previously, suggestions have been made to extend the attest function to financial summaries and highlights, schedules of

---

[2]Cf. Robert K. Mautz and Hussein A. Sharaf, *The Philosophy of Auditing,* American Accounting Association Monograph No. 6 (n.p.: The Association, 1961), p. 14.

[3]American Institute of Certified Public Accountants, Committee on Auditing Procedure, *Statements on Auditing Procedure No. 33,* "Auditing Standards and Procedures" (New York: The Institute, 1963).

[4]Gordon Shillinglaw, "Concepts Underlying Interim Financial Statements," *The Accounting Review,* XXXVI, No. 2 (April, 1961), pp. 222–31, esp. p. 224.

sales and earnings by lines of business, schedules of particular expenditures, production and sales statistics, and similar items. These representations often appear in annual reports, but are only occasionally covered by the auditor's opinion. Nevertheless, they pertain to past events that are considered by the auditor in the course of his examination of conventional financial statements. For example, financial summaries and highlights are abstracted from audited financial statements; production statistics are examined while auditing inventories and cost of goods sold.

Extending the attest function to financial statements in terms of dollars of constant purchasing power or current values presents a different situation. Both types of statements also pertain to past events. The major impediment to extending the attest function here involves the first reporting standard: both types of statements are not in accordance with generally accepted accounting principles.

Except for statements in terms of constant dollars or current values, all of these representations on past events should articulate with conventional financial statements based on historical cost. Accordingly, these representations may be included in the conventional financial statements or footnotes thereunto and covered by the standard short form opinion. Alternatively, they may be excluded from the conventional financial statements or footnotes thereunto and, together with statements based on constant dollars or current values, covered by an expanded or separate opinion. An important reporting problem would be to identify which data are attested by the auditor and which are not.

ATTESTATION OF TAX RETURNS, COST-REIMBURSEMENT CLAIMS, AND INFORMATION REPORTS

Tax returns, cost-reimbursement claims, and information reports filed with public agencies are prepared in accordance with directives that differ from generally accepted accounting principles. How does this affect the attest function? Recall that the reliability of financial statements is attested to within the context of generally accepted accounting principles. Can auditors attest to the reliability of tax returns, cost-reimbursement claims, and information reports filed with public agencies within the context of the directives underlying their preparation, and is this extension of the attest function desirable?

Support for extending the attest function to these items is based in part on the assumption that duplication of effort could be eliminated. Thus, the same records are often examined by both independent auditors in conjunction with the rendering of an opinion on financial statements and by auditors of one or more governmental agencies. If a single, comprehensive audit could be performed more efficiently and economically by independent auditors than could two or more separate audits by different auditors, then there is good reason to consider extending the attest function.

Although the elimination of duplicate efforts is desirable, a significant number of accountants who responded to a recent survey opposed extending the attest function to these items especially to tax returns.[5] A possible reason for these objections is the belief that independence may be impaired if the auditor also advises his clients on how to reduce taxes, increase cost-reimbursement claims, and appear in a more favorable light before public agencies. That is, independence is impaired if the auditor is called upon to attest to his own work. But a somewhat comparable situation arises with respect to management services; independence may, but need not be impaired, if the auditor advises his clients how to operate the business. Thus, the possibility of impaired independence is not unique to extending the attest function to tax returns, cost-reimbursement claims, and information reports.

But particularly with respect to tax returns, because tax laws and regulations are highly technical and taxes are self-assessing, accountants function more as advocates than as attestors. In ambiguous situations, just what would attestation mean and to what extent could the government rely on it? Extending the attest function to tax returns appears unlikely, not so much because of the possible impairment of independence, but because the tax laws and regulations are too ambiguous for attestation to have significance. The recent trend to extend the attest function to cost-reimbursement claims and information reports is explained perhaps by the fact that directives underlying their preparation are less complex than tax laws and regulations.

ATTESTATION OF FREEDOM FROM FRAUDS AND CONFLICTS OF INTEREST

Frauds. At one time, a major purpose of an independent auditor's ordinary examination of financial statements was to detect fraud as well as attest to the fairness of financial statements, but this is no longer true. Today, the official position of the profession is that the purpose of an ordinary examination of financial statements is not to detect

---

[5]See Frank J. Imke, "The Future of the Attest Function," *The Journal of Accountancy,* CXXIII, No. 4 (April, 1967), pp. 51–58, esp. pp. 54–58.

fraud, although the detection of fraud may result; rather, the detection of fraud depends principally on adequate internal control. In effect, management is primarily responsible for detecting fraud because management is responsible for instituting adequate internal control. The accounting profession contends that an auditor is responsible for detecting significant fraud only to the extent of knowledge acquired in the course of his examination, provided his examination is made in accordance with generally accepted auditing standards and is not limited by the client as to scope.

Nevertheless, the public still regards the detection of fraud as a chief function of the independent auditor. It is questionable whether he can absolve himself of responsibility for detecting fraud by a simple declaration to this effect, particularly when it was once an important part of his duties.

If the auditor were to search for all possible frauds, his examination would be so extensive that its cost would be prohibitive. Cheaper, although not necessarily better protection, is afforded individual clients by good internal control coupled with fidelity insurance. But it does not follow that examination for fraud by the independent auditor is undesirable. In some instance a client may find that it is less expensive to insure against losses, and then recover from the insurer if a loss occurs, than to pay for a more extensive audit or, alternatively, for a more elaborate internal control system. But someone must pay for every shortage and defalcation. For a particular client, insurance may reduce losses; for business society as a whole, it merely spreads them over a larger base. The early detection of fraud minimizes this social cost.

Conflict of interest. Closely related to if not part of the detection of fraud is the detection of conflicts of interests. Auditors have always been concerned with the possibility of conflicts of interest by management. This concern received renewed impetus in the early 1960's concurrent with the discovery of such conflicts in the managements of several leading corporations. Indeed, recent reporting practices disclose that management itself is taking the initiative and making disclosures on company-management relations. The feasibility of attesting to the absence of conflicts of interest is partly demonstrated by the experience of Scandinavian auditors, who regularly report whether stockholders have a basis for legal action against management for breaching fiduciary responsibilities.[6]

---

[6]Edwin C. Bomeli, "Management Review by Scandinavian Accountants," *The Journal of Accountancy,* CVI, No. 1 (July, 1964), pp. 33–37.

Recommendation. Attesting to the absence of fraud and conflicts of interest is one way the auditor can increase his service to society. But what would such an attestation mean? Obviously, an auditor could not attest to the total absence of fraud and conflicts of interest. Accordingly, any attestation should take the form of a negative assurance. What is needed is a clear and forthright statement of the responsibility the auditor can and should accept for the prevention and detection of fraud and conflicts of interest. This is clearly preferable to allowing the public's confusion about it to continue.

ATTESTATION OF COMPLIANCE WITH CONTRACTS, LAWS, AND REGULATIONS

The auditor may also be called upon to attest to compliance with terms and conditions of contracts and with laws and regulations. Indeed, auditors already issue reports attesting to compliance with loan agreements, bond indentures, rental and royalty payment agreements, and certain laws and regulations.

The continuing trend toward more complex business agreements and greater governmental regulation will necessitate an increasing volume of reports on compliance; many of these reports will be attested by independent auditors. A recent survey revealed that public accountants are more favorably disposed than controllers to extending the attest function to compliance with laws and regulations.[7] A major advantage of this extension is the elimination of duplicate work by independent auditors and government employees. Auditors already are involved in determining compliance with contracts, laws, and regulations insofar as noncompliance may adversely affect financial position and results of operations; attesting to compliance is a logical extension of this involvement.

The criteria for preparing a representation on compliance are often readily forthcoming from the related contracts, laws, and regulations. But the feasibility of extending the attest function to such representations is another matter. First, there are the legal questions as to what compliance means and when does it exist. Second, there is the question of the auditor's competence in legal matters. Although the independent auditor is not an attorney, he must have a general understanding of the legal implications of his client's operations. He is routinely concerned with ascertaining the existence of unrecorded liabilities, and relies in part on information from a client's attorney and a letter of representation from the client's management. Similar sources of

---

[7]Imke, *op. cit.*, pp. 55–57.

information, supplemented by an auditor's observation during the examination of financial statements, may be a suitable basis for an audit report, perhaps in the form of a negative assurance, attesting to compliance with contracts, laws, and regulations.

ATTESTATION OF ADEQUACY OF INTERNAL CONTROL

The second standard of field work requires the auditor to study and evaluate the existing internal control as one means of setting the scope of his examination. For many years, auditors have formally concluded on the adequacy of internal control in their working papers, and have made oral or written suggestions to clients recommending improvements. A logical extension of this practice is for auditors to report to outside parties on the adequacy of internal control.

What has impeded the auditor from reporting on the adequacy of internal control:

> First, there is really no such thing as an overall evaluation of internal control. An auditor views internal control in terms of specific types of errors and irregularities which may occur. . . . Unless internal control is excellent in every respect, generalizations about the adequacy of the overall system are extremely difficult to make. Strengths in one area of internal control do not normally offset weaknesses in another area. . . .
>
> Second, . . . there is the incomparability of an opinion on the financial statements taken as a whole and an opinion on the internal control system taken as a whole. Weaknesses in internal control can have a potential material impact on operations, but their materiality cannot be evaluated in the same manner that a known dollar amount of error can be with respect to the financial statements taken as a whole. . . .
>
> Third, there are many inherent limitations on the effectiveness of any system of internal control. Certain actions are not subject to control within the scope of internal control systems. Control procedures that depend primarily on the separation or incompatibility of duties can be circumvented by collusion. Management officials who are charged with administering the internal control system are in the position to perpetuate intentional errors and irregularities. . . . Perhaps the most critical inherent limitation is the fact that . . . there are many possibilities for error arising from misunderstandings, mistakes, carelessness, distraction or fatigue.
>
> Finally, . . . reports on internal control create a significant possibility of unwarranted and misleading inferences on the part of users.[8]

---

[8]Douglas R. Carmichael, "Opinions on Internal Control," *The Journal of Accountancy,* CXXX, No. 6 (December, 1970), pp. 47-53, esp. pp. 48-49.

In other words, at present there is an absence of guidelines for field work and reporting standards for expressing an opinion on internal control. Thus, the auditor who renders an opinion is exposing himself to an undefined responsibility.

Attesting to the adequacy of internal control perhaps is facilitated if the attestation is limited to accounting controls. Recall that in the course of an ordinary examination of financial statements, the auditor is primarily concerned with accounting controls which bear directly on the reliability of the financial records. Attesting to the adequacy of internal control is a more logical extension of present auditing practice if the attestation covers only those controls that affect the reliability of the financial statements.

But of what relevance is this attestation to outside parties? None, apparently, because this attestation is already the essence of the auditor's opinion on annual financial statements. Attesting to the adequacy of internal accounting control may provide additional assurances as to the reliability of presently unaudited interim financial statements. However, extending the attest function directly to interim statements is a better way of providing such additional assurances.

It follows that to be meaningful, an attestation of the adequacy of internal control must include administrative controls as well as accounting controls. But administrative controls relate mainly to operational efficiency and adherence to managerial policies and only indirectly to the reliability of financial data. Accordingly, attesting to the adequacy of internal control inclusive of accounting *and* administrative controls involves attesting not only to the reliability of financial data but also to the adequacy of management itself.

ATTESTATION OF ADEQUACY OF MANAGEMENT PERFORMANCE

Agreement is lacking as to the precise meaning of the term *management audit* and there is no explicit theory of *management auditing* within the context of the attest function.[9] It is unclear who should perform management audits and for whom the audit report should be prepared. Thus, a management audit involves a comprehensive and constructive examination of an entity or one of its components, such as a division or department — its plans and policies, its financial controls, its methods of operation, its use of physical and human resources — in order to evaluate the effectiveness of management in

---

[9]Harold Q. Langenderfer and Jack C. Robertson, "A Theoretical Structure for Independent Audits of Management," *The Accounting Review*, XLIV, No. 4 (October, 1969), pp. 777–787, esp. p. 777.

carrying out assigned responsibilities and accomplishing specified objectives; a review of the system of internal control inclusive of administrative controls as well as accounting controls is clearly envisioned in a management audit.[10] But whether it should be performed by internal auditors or independent auditors and whether the resulting report should be prepared only for management or also for interested outside parties remains subject to controversy. Internal auditors have long performed management audits to assist management, and independent auditors have provided the same service either as part of an ordinary examination of financial statements or as a separate management service engagement; in both cases, the resulting reports are prepared exclusively for management. Presently, there is widespread interest by outside parties in also receiving these reports, particularly if attested by independent auditors.

Obviously, a management audit for outside parties differs from one designed to assist management itself. The credibility of information on management performance for outsiders would be enhanced if attested to by an independent expert. If independent auditors do not accept this challenge, management audits for outside parties may be performed by other independent experts.[11] Accordingly, within the context of the attest function, the major controversy pertains to audits of management performance by independent auditors reporting to outside parties. In turn, this controversy centers on the question of feasibility.

Independence. For attestation to be meaningful, the auditor must be independent. Questions concerning the independence of auditors providing management services are applicable to auditors performing management audits to assist management, because management audits to assist management are broadly conceived management service engagements. But management audits for outsiders differ from management audits to assist management. Undoubtedly, to maintain his independence, the auditor must not become involved to any significant extent in the management function itself. More relevant, however, the management audit for outsiders is a third party attest function and not a management service engagement. Accordingly, any questions concerning the auditor's independence

---

[10]Cf. Mary E. Murphy, *Advanced Public Accounting Practice* (Homewood, Ill.: Richard D. Irwin, Inc., 1966), p. 323; William L. Campfield, "Trends in Auditing Management Plans and Operations," *The Journal of Accountancy*, CXXIV, No. 1 (July, 1967), pp. 41-46, esp. p. 42; John C. Burton, "Management Auditing," *The Journal of Accountancy*, CXXV, No. 5 (May, 1968), pp. 41-46; and Corinne T. Norgaard, "The Professional Accountant's View of Operational Auditing," *The Journal of Accountancy*, CXXVIII, No. 12 (December, 1969), pp. 45-48.

[11]See American Institute of Management, *Management Audit Questionnaires: (Fact-Gathering for the Management Audit)* (New York: The Institute, 1961).

in the management audit are comparable to questions concerning his independence in the financial audit. The possible impairment of independence is not unique and does not preclude attesting to the adequacy of management performance.

Competence of auditor. The second standard of field work requires the auditor to evaluate internal control as one means of setting the scope of his examination. Even for ordinary examinations of financial statements, if internal control is interpreted broadly to include administrative controls as well as accounting controls, the question arises whether the auditor's responsibilities under this standard extend beyond his area of competence.[12] The question of competence is still more pressing if the auditor also attests to the adequacy of internal control per se and management performance.

In recognizing these problems, the AICPA Committee on Auditing Procedure notes that the independent auditor must be qualified to practice as an auditor, not as a functionary performing the activities under his examination.[13] Because of this limitation, which is common to internal auditors as well as independent auditors, one writer contends that the competence of both is limited to evaluating procedures and controls but not overall operating efficiency.[14] The results of a simulation study support this suggestion:

> The student auditors had never played the game. Nor were they . . . knowledgeable managers. . . . Yet they were able to look at the decision-making process and the organization of these firms and were able to make . . . discerning and useful evaluations and . . . recommend improved methods for operating the firms. . . . In short, . . . concentration on *methods* rather than on *results* allowed them to function effectively and to substantiate their conclusions and recommendations.[15]

Others expect that independent auditors will develop the skills needed to evaluate not only procedures and controls but perhaps overall operating efficiency also.[16] Indeed, the competence of independent auditors to perform audits of management performance is currently being developed in the management service divisions of the larger firms.

[12]Mautz and Sharaf, *op. cit.,* p. 145.

[13]American Institute of Certified Public Accountants, Committee on Auditing Procedure, *op. cit.,* p. 10.

[14]John A. Edds, "The Auditor's Responsibility beyond the Financial Audit," *The Canadian Chartered Accountant,* LXXXVII, No. 6 (December, 1965), pp. 406–409, esp. p. 407.

[15]Neil C. Churchill and Richard M. Cyert, "An Experiment in Management Auditing," *The Journal of Accountancy,* CXXI, No. 2 (February, 1966), pp. 39–43, esp. p. 42.

[16]Joseph W. Dodwell, "Operational Auditing: A Part of the Basic Audit," *The Journal of Accountancy,* CXXI, No. 6 (June, 1966), pp. 31–39, esp. pp. 38–39; and Paul E. Cloutier. "The Management Audit," *The Canadian Chartered Accountant,* LXXXIV, No. 3 (September, 1966), pp. 178–181, esp. p. 181.

In conclusion, the problem of competence does not preclude extending the attest function to audits of management performance; any lack of competence is rectifiable once standards of competence are defined.

Standards of management performance. If the attest function is extended to the adequacy of management performance, reporting on the adequacy of internal control may well be the first step. However, it is extremely difficult to evaluate a system of internal control in its entirety, as one student of the problem notes;[17] the individual parts of a system of internal control have not been enumerated in a manner that facilitates the rendering of a piecemeal opinion on their effectiveness.

The problems inherent in evaluating a system of internal control in its entirety also pertain to evaluating management performance. Can management performance be satisfactory but not excellent? Are standards available to serve as criteria for the preparation of a report on management performance, consistent with an extension of the first generally accepted standard of reporting? Do individual aspects of management performance lend themselves to piecemeal opinions? Will the opinion clearly indicate the character of the auditor's examination and the responsibility he is undertaking in his evaluation, consistent with an extension of the fourth generally accepted standard of reporting?

If an audit of management performance is to be conducted in the same manner as a financial audit, a set of generally accepted principles of management must be available as criteria for evaluating performance, and management must be willing to be evaluated by them. Most accountants oppose attesting to the adequacy of management performance precisely because of the present absence of practical and meaningful criteria that are generally accepted.[18] But some presume that this problem may be resolved by using "accepted principles of management" to audit the "*processes* of managerial decision-making and control . . . not the *results* of managerial decisions."[19] On the other hand, others suggest that the auditor will be called upon to appraise the results, not the qualities of management;[20] and still others contend that he may be called upon to evaluate either processes *only* or processes *and* results.[21]

---

[17]Carmichael, *loc. cit.*

[18]See Imke, *op. cit.,* p. 55; and Norgaard, *op. cit.,* p. 48.

[19]Churchill and Cyert, *op. cit.,* pp. 41–42. Italics in original.

[20]Williard E. Stone, "Depth Auditing: (Appraisal of Management Performance)," *The New York Certified Public Accountant,* XXI, No. 8 (August, 1961), pp. 521-528, esp. p. 525.

[21]Burton, *op. cit.,* pp. 42–43.

Despite the extensive controversy on the subject, it is unclear whether an evaluation of processes is more or less important than an evaluation of results. It is also unclear whether criteria for evaluating processes are more readily available or will develop faster than criteria for evaluating results. But criteria will be developed in response to the need for an extension of the attest function to management performance, much as generally accepted accounting principles developed in response to a comparable need to attest to the fairness of financial statements.

Due to the present absence of a set of generally accepted principles of management to serve as criteria for evaluating performance, a report on management performance should emphasize comprehensive disclosure. The report should also indicate the nature of the auditor's examination and the degree of responsibility he is taking, consistent with an extension of the fourth generally accepted standard of reporting.

Verifiability. Should management make representations on its own performance which are subject to examination and attestation by the auditor, or should the auditor make his own evaluative representations on management performance? Although the former is fully analogous to the attestation of financial statements, the latter may be more feasible.[22] But assuming that a management audit does in fact involve attesting to representations by management on its own performance, can sufficient evidence be obtained to afford a reasonable basis for an opinion on these representations, consistent with an extension of the third generally accepted standard of field work? Can the auditor satisfy himself to the fairness of these representations?

Mautz and Sharaf contend that ". . . any assertation having a basis of corporate action and planning can be subjected to useful verification and confirmed or negated by more or less convincing evidence."[23] But compelling evidence is available to support only a limited number of financial statement propositions and, for a great many other propositions, the mind of the auditor is not compelled but only persuaded of the reliability of the assertion at hand. Moreover, auditing exists within a framework of economic usefulness that requires a balancing of cost with benefit; it may be unreasonable to incur substantial cost to ascertain the absolute truth of certain representations.

This concept of evidence also pertains to management's representations on its own performance, but differs on the subject matter of

---

[22]Thomas G. Secoy, "A CPA's Opinion on Management Performance," *The Journal of Accountancy*, CXXXII, No. 1 (July, 1971), pp. 53-59, esp. p. 57.

[23]Mautz and Sharaf, *op. cit.*, p. 192.

evidence. Representations in financial statements may be evaluated in terms of a set of generally accepted accounting principles; representations on management performance cannot be evaluated in terms of a set of generally accepted principles of management, for no such set possesses a comparable degree of acceptance. Perhaps representations on the adequacy of processes and controls are more readily verifiable than representations on the adequacy of results. But both of these are basically like the types of representations included in financial statements; they are either assertions of past events, assertions of the existence of physical and nonphysical qualities, or mathematical assertions. Given the type of assertion, the type of evidence generally available for judging its reliability is derived from the nature of that assertion; similarly, the technique for obtaining audit evidence is derived from the nature of the evidence.[24]

Although somewhat speculative, these considerations are supported by the findings of a simulation experiment in which student auditors documented reports on management performance ". . . with the same quality of evidence as any other audit statement or disclosure."[25] Thus, it appears that the auditor can satisfy himself concerning representations by management on its own performance.

ATTESTATION OF REASONABLENESS OF BUDGETS

In order to serve as an audit of management performance, a suggestion has been offered that the ordinary examination of financial statements should be enlarged to include an analysis of management's expectations for the coming year in the form of a pro-forma income statement, a pro-forma balance sheet, and a pro-forma funds statement; a comparison of the audited financial statements for the current period with the pro-forma statements prepared at the beginning of the period; and the use of a long-form type of report in which the differences between expectations and actual results are explained and evaluated.[26]

Publishing plans and expectations would require management to do a considerable amount of careful planning and forecasting. But what would prevent management from publishing overly optimistic or pessimistic plans?

---

[24]Cf. Robert W. Clarke, "Extension of the CPA's Attest Function in Corporate Annual Reports," *The Accounting Review,* XLIII, No. 4 (October, 1968), pp. 769-776, esp. p. 771.

[25]Churchill and Cyert, *op. cit.,* p. 42.

[26]James R. Wilkinson and Lloyd D. Doney, "Extending Audit and Reporting Boundaries," *The Accounting Review,* XL, No. 4 (October, 1965), pp. 753-756, esp. p. 753.

There could be some temptation for management to make a very conservative estimate for the coming year in order that the eventual comparisons of goals with realizations might be favorable. However, this temptation would be balanced or largely offset in most cases by the desire of management to present information in the projections which would encourage stockholders, present and potential, to invest or to continue their investments in the firm.

Conversely, an over-optimistic forecast would certainly be tempered by the realization that a comparison of goals and achievements would be made at the end of the period by the independent auditor.[27]

However, deviations from the budget do not always indicate poor performance or forecasting abilities; on occasion, drastic changes in plans are made in response to unanticipated changes in the business environment. When actual results deviate significantly from projections, an accompanying explanation should be provided.

The comparison of actual results and original projections as of the beginning of the current year should be reported in close proximity to projections for the upcoming year, perhaps together with the actual results of the preceding year. Particularly if attested by an independent auditor, these additional disclosures would enable interested outside parties to more readily evaluate management's plans for the future and compare management's past plans with its actual accomplishments.

Problems in publishing and attesting to budgets. The publication of budgets is challenged on the grounds that they are not reliable, not that they are not relevant. The reliability of budget data is questioned because of the problems inherent in any attempt to predict the future, whether by management or by the auditor, and because of the problems of verifying the reasonableness of predictions. Although the usefulness of budget disclosure is unquestionable, its implementation must be supported by effective budget auditing in order to assure the initial reliability of the data.[28] For this purpose, it becomes crucial to develop a set of generally accepted budgeting principles and a set of generally accepted budget-auditing standards so that firms and auditors have frameworks to rely upon in developing budgets and in performing budget audits.

What is involved in auditing budgets? Ijiri, a noted authority on the subject, suggests that audits of budgets are similar to one auditor's review of another auditor's conclusions:

---

[27]*Ibid.*, p. 754.
[28]Much of the following discussion parallels Ijiri. See Yuji Ijiri, "On Budgeting Principles and Budget-Auditing Standards," *The Accounting Review*, XLIII, No. 4 (October, 1968), pp. 662–667.

[In] evaluating auditors' work, what is significant is whether the auditors' inferences are "reasonable" or not. This is exactly the point that partners of a CPA firm check when they review audit working papers prepared by field auditors. That is, the auditors' task in reviewing audits made by others (namely, audits on audits) is to see whether original auditors' inferences are "reasonable"; patently their task is not to make such inferences by themselves.

Similarly, in preparing budgets the management must make inferences on various factors in the future based on clues that are available at the time of the prediction. Therefore, the essential of budget audits lies in checking whether the inferences that the management made in preparing the budgets are reasonable or not.[29]

Establishment of budgeting principles. For this purpose, budgeting principles and budget-auditing principles have been suggested. Budgeting principles may be divided into two parts, one concerning the prediction of events, the other concerning the recording of events. The latter relates to the ordinary accounting procedures followed after certain events are predicted according to the former. If budgets are to be reported in the form of pro-forma financial statements, the predicted events may be recorded in accordance with generally accepted accounting principles and procedures. Although it is possible to set up a different set of accounting principles and procedures for recording predicted events, budgeted and actual amounts would not be comparable unless the conventional financial statements were also prepared in accordance with these principles and procedures.

Two basic principles govern the prediction of events: make the inference process explicit and consistent. The consistency principle is divided into internal consistency and external consistency. Internal consistency relates to the data internal to the firm that are used in budgeting. It has two aspects: historical consistency, that is, consistency between current estimates and estimates made in the past; and current consistency, that is, consistency among current estimates. External consistency relates to consistency of budget estimates with estimates of industry and general economic factors.

Establishment of budget-auditing standards and procedures. In addition to budgeting principles, a set of budget-auditing standards and procedures must be developed to define methods of examining budget working papers and related evidence which support the inferences concerning forecasted amounts as well as the extent of the examination, and to provide reporting standards for budget audits.

---

[29] *Ibid.*, p. 664.

Specifically, budget-auditing standards and procedures should indicate the extent to which auditors are asked to check internal and external consistency of budget estimates; and they should indicate the types of budget-audit reports that auditors are supposed to provide.

Consistent with an extension of the second general auditing standard, the auditor must be independent, hence must not participate in the budgeting function either by making predictions or by recording them. The budget must remain a representation of management. The auditor's report on a budget should indicate whether the examination conforms to budget-auditing standards and procedures. Moreover, consistent with an extension of the generally accepted standards of reporting, the auditor's report should indicate whether the budget is prepared in accordance with budgeting principles and procedures consistently applied. Budget disclosure should be adequate so as not to mislead.

The development of budget-auditing standards will not be quick and easy. Perhaps for this reason, several writers suggest limiting severely the attestation of budgets. For example, one suggests attesting to ". . . the existence of a budget system, its comprehensiveness and the care that was evidenced in its preparation";[30] others suggest that the attestation should involve only ". . . a procedural test in advance . . . and . . . a comparison of the budgeted figures against the documented results," together with an evaluation of evidence supporting explanations of significant differences between actual and budgeted amounts.[31] But still others suggest attesting only to the reasonableness of budgets.[32] Obviously, the auditor cannot vouch for the accuracy of the projections in the sense of guaranteeing the results. Indeed, the AICPA Code of Professional Ethics prohibits the auditor from doing this.[33] But the Code does not prohibit the auditor from having his name associated with a profit forecast, provided there is disclosure of ". . . the source of the information used, or the major assumptions made, . . . the character of the [audit] work performed . . ., and the degree of responsibility he [the auditor] is taking," including a statement that the auditor is not vouching for the accuracy of the forecast.[34]

When do budgets appear reasonable? One writer, Roth, suggests that the auditor ". . . can appraise the reasonableness of the relation-

[30]Stone, *loc. cit.*

[31]W. W. Cooper, N. Dopuch, and T. F. Keller, "Budgetary Disclosure and Other Suggestions for Improving Accounting Reports," *The Accounting Review,* XLIII, No. 4 (October, 1968), pp. 640–648, esp. p. 646.

[32]Wilkinson and Doney, *op. cit.,* p. 755; and Clarke, *loc. cit.*

[33]American Institute of Certified Public Accountants, *Code of Professional Ethics* (New York: The Institute, 1970), p. 4.

[34]*Ibid.,* p. 23.

ships of income, costs, and expenses based on clearly defined assumptions,"[35] hence stresses what Ijiri calls internal consistency among current estimates. Ijiri implies that reasonableness also requires external consistency of budget estimates with industry and general economic factors. Thus Roth implies that the auditor should evaluate the calculation of estimates but need not evaluate the specified assumptions on which they are based, consistent with the Code of Professional Ethics, whereas Ijiri implies that the auditor should evaluate both.

Experience in Great Britain and Ireland. Although the latter is more difficult, it is nevertheless feasible. For many years in Great Britain and Ireland, prospectuses or similar documents have included profit forecasts. Moreover, it has been a well-established practice for independent auditors in Great Britain and Ireland to take considerable pains to satisfy themselves that the forecasts are prepared on reasonable bases and are fully documented. Since 1969, these auditors have been required to report on profit forecasts included in prospectuses issued in connection with merger or takeover transactions. The auditors' reports must be included as part of the prospectuses; the forecasts continue to be considered representations of the directors.[36]

The auditors do not vouch for the ultimate accuracy and realization of the forecasts; their responsibility is confined to reviewing the accounting bases and calculations and verifying that the forecasts have been properly computed from the underlying assumptions and data and are presented on a consistent basis.[37] In discharging this responsibility, the auditors must satisfy themselves that the forecasts are consistent with the given economic, commercial, marketing, and financial assumptions which underlie them; they should also satisfy themselves, insofar as they are able, that the assumptions appear realistic and that those of importance are clearly set forth in the prospectus.[38] It has been suggested that existing auditing practice in the United States would not be altered significantly by adopting comparable reporting requirements on profit forecasts.[39]

---

[35]Joseph L. Roth, "The Role of the Auditor," *Corporate Financial Reporting: Conflicts and Challenges,* ed. John C. Burton (New York: American Institute of Certified Public Accountants, 1969), pp. 245–258, esp. p. 256.

[36]See John P. Grenside, "Accountants' Reports on Profit Forecasts in the U.K.," *The Journal of Accountancy,* CXXIX, No. 5 (May, 1970), pp. 47–53, esp. p. 48.

[37]Institute of Chartered Accountants in England and Wales, The Council, *Miscellaneous Technical Statement S 15,* "Accountants' Reports on Profit Forecasts" (London: The Institute, 1969), pp. 1–7.

[38]Grenside, *op. cit.,* p. 51.

[39]John J. Willingham, Charles H. Smith, and Martin E. Taylor, "Should the CPA's Opinion Be Extended to Include Forecasts?," *Financial Executive,* XXXVIII, No. 9 (September, 1970), pp. 80–82, 88–89, esp. p. 89.

It seems apparent that budgets will be published eventually:

> While managements now generally refrain from predicting future results
> or releasing information about their budgeted earnings, a more sophisticated
> generation of investing public may demand this additional data. Corporate
> officials may be faced with the alternatives of furnishing it, reluctantly,
> or admitting that they do not have sufficient confidence in their plans
> for future periods to commit themselves publicly to them.[40]

And once budgets are published, auditors will be called upon to attest
to them. The attest function will be extended to budgets as the need
for attestation is demonstrated.

CONCLUSION

The attest function results in the expression of an opinion by the
attestor that certain representations by management to outside parties
are fairly stated. Discharge of the attest function adds credibility to
these representations, hence increases the reliance outside parties may
place on them. There is enough evidence of the value of the attest
function to justify considering its extension to all representations
where the possibility exists for adding credibility. This paper has
examined the prospects of such an extension.

Extending the attest function has been repeatedly called for by
many report users who presently rely to an increasing extent on unaudited data. This trend toward increased reliance on unaudited data
is not desirable. If report users rely on unaudited data in large part,
why not rely on unaudited data for all of their needs? Surely, the
reliability of both types of data is equally desirable. If the reliability
of presently unaudited data is not attested by auditors, perhaps some
other independent experts may preempt this function.

But the attest function should not be extended merely to protect
the self-interests of auditors who have been virtually the only ones
to perform this function. Conversely, it should not be limited merely
to limit responsibility in view of the spate of lawsuits involving alleged
negligence by auditors. The basic question is whether to extend
service to society. As Mautz and Sharaf note, a profession exists,
not to compensate its members, but to serve society while its members concurrently earn a livelihood.[41] Report users need data not
presently included in financial statements covered by the auditor's
opinion. A review by an expert would add to the reliability of this

---

[40]Joseph L. Roth, "What's Ahead for the Auditor?," *The Journal of Accountancy,* CXXVIII,
No. 2 (August, 1969), pp. 60–62, esp. p. 62.

[41]Mautz and Sharaf, *op. cit.,* p. 239.

data. It may be argued that the auditor already has an implied responsibility to review certain ostensibly unaudited data, because his name is already associated with this data. Thus, consistent with the emphasis on service to society, the attest function should be extended in part because the public may already believe it to be more encompassing that it really is.

Certain questions on reporting remain to be resolved. In particular, the placement of the attestation and any accompanying data in the report requires study. Obviously, auditors must be willing to experiment with different formats.

In the future, the attest function will be performed in an environment characterized by increasingly sophisticated information users requiring additional assurances as to the credibility of the information. There is little doubt but that the attest function will be extended to meet these needs, much as it has been extended in the past.

PART TWO

The Auditor

The personal attributes which the auditor possesses or should possess have rightly received a great deal of attention from the auditing profession. The profession's generally accepted auditing standards call upon the auditor to be competent, to maintain an independent state of mind, and to bring an appropriate degree of professional care in the performance of his task.

A profession's code of ethics announces to society the motivation for and the type of behavior which can be expected from the members of such a profession. A socially approved code of conduct inspires confidence on the part of laymen only when the actions of the members of the profession actually exemplify that code.

The auditor's position is perhaps unique because of his role as an intermediary between the client and third party users of financial statements. This judicial-like relationship demands complete independence in mental attitude in all dealings with the client. When performing related, though not auditing, services such as management consulting or tax consulting, the question may arise as to the role of independence in these related services as well as the impact, if any, of these services on auditing independence.

The ultimate bounds of the auditor's responsibility to the public are, of course, determined by the courts. The extent of legal liability has been redefined and broadened in recent years and the eventual impact on the auditing profession and its function is still being pondered. No student of auditing should fail to give the matter of legal (and hence social) responsibility his most serious attention.

SECTION A

Ethics and Ethical Behavior

Ethics and ethical behavior are as essential as they are elusive. E. B. Wilcox provides a discourse on reasons why a person or a group will want to be and act ethically. In the second article T. G. Higgins and W. E. Olson present reasons for and the rationale of the restatement of the AICPA Code of Ethics. The restatement of the Code represents a major change in the format and content of the rules of professional ethics. For the first time, the Code, effective March 1, 1973, will contain a series of ethical essays stated in a positive rather than negative form. The third selection includes the ethical essays entitled the "Concepts of Professional Ethics," the "Rules of Conduct," and the AICPA Council Resolution of May 6, 1969, relating to professional corporations.

In the last selection, J. C. Burton reports on some current issues involving ethics and financial reporting which were examined in a recent symposium.

---

4. *Ethics: The Profession on Trial** Edward B. Wilcox† ‐

Ethical responsibilities are difficult to define principally because we don't know what ethics mean — nor why anyone should feel responsible about them. Ethics — sometimes (although not helpfully) described as

---

*From *The Journal of Accountancy*, Vol. 100 (November, 1955), pp. 72–79. Copyright (1955) by the American Institute of Certified Public Accountants, Inc. Reprinted by permission of the AICPA.

†Edward B. Wilcox (deceased) was a partner of Lybrand, Ross Bros. & Montgomery.

the science of morals — has baffled the great minds of all times. The bafflement is not hard to explain. The great minds have attacked this problem by attempting to find a solid premise on which to erect a logical structure. This seldom works outside of a textbook on logic. When physical science was a branch of philosophy and its conclusions were reached by deduction in ivory towers, it got nowhere. Progress began when the scientists went into the laboratory and out in the world to learn what was happening. In our own field, attempts to erect a structure of accounting principles by deductive logic based on some arbitrarily selected premise proved sterile. Usefulness has followed only from research into the needs and purposes which accounting must serve. A review of ethical systems shows this same pattern.

The challenge to the student of ethics is to find the answers to two questions: what is desirable behavior, and why would anyone want to act that way.

The great ethical systems have tried to answer these questions but with only modest success. They have suggested that what is desirable is to be found in an abstract principle of absolute goodness, in divine commands, in universal maxims or hedonism, or in the worship of nature. They have sought to explain the desire to behave ethically in terms of man's better nature, or eternal reward, or rationality, or pleasure, or fulfillment, or conscience, or social approval. Always these systems of ethics have sought to create a logical structure pleasing to the architectural eye, but always in some part unrelated to the way people behave.

It is not really difficult to answer the two questions posed by a contemplation of ethics if we abandon the predilections of the ivory tower.

Desirable behavior is that which produces the greatest good. The good may be large or small; it may affect only the doer of an act, or one other person, or a few others, or all persons. It may affect some favorably and others unfavorably and in varying degrees. It is not easy to measure the consequences of many acts, and the attempt to do so requires effort, intelligence, knowledge, and understanding. Today, in view of the unprecedented interdependence of all people, this is more difficult than ever before. An understanding of what is ethical behavior, therefore, requires application of the hard and painful process of honest thinking based on a large fund of information.

As to why a man would want to behave ethically, the best answers in the classical systems are conscience and social approval. These do not help him to know what to do, because consciences have varying backgrounds and society approves of various things at different times and in different places. Wise uniformity of conscience and social approval would be helpful. The committee on accounting procedure of the American

Institute of Accountants mentioned something like that in its 1954 re-statement and revision of Accounting Research Bulletins — the kind of uniformity in which different authorities working independently on the same case should reach the same conclusions — and there may some day be developed consciences among men and accepted views in society which will be good guides to ethical conduct.

Group consciousness

Today, however, the problem of creating a desire to behave ethically is more difficult than simple reliance on the vagaries of individual con-sciences or on the widely divergent areas of social approval. There must be inculcated in each person an informed and expanding group conscious-ness — and an identification of himself with others. Society must learn the lessons to be derived from the history of community living, so that individuals will learn to find their greatest satisfactions in desirable behavior. Many do that now. If this were universal, the consciences of all men and the social approval they naturally desire would lead to the greatest good. Thus the two questions cannot be answered as separate questions. Each depends in part on the other.

It may seem that general ethics is too vague to have much relationship to professional ethics — and that professional ethics is a special matter, related distantly, if at all, to general ethics. Exactly the reverse is true. Professional ethics is a special application of general ethics, and is an excellent example of it. An understanding of the rules of professional conduct of the accounting profession, and the nature and direction of their evolution, depends in large part on the grasp of a sound and useful approach to general ethics. Some of the confusion that has existed on this subject is due to the absence of just this understanding.

A profession can be recognized in several ways. It is heavily influenced by the service motive rather than entirely by the profit motive. Its practice involves judgment and the acceptance of responsibilities to others. Fitness for it requires special knowledge and skills not ordinarily possessed by laymen. It follows that those who rely on a profession must do so without being able to check or test the quality of the service on which they rely. And from this it follows that the practitioner of a profession could for a time at least betray those who depend upon him. Obviously, the greatest good is to be achieved if he does not betray them.

Public accounting is such a profession — especially, although not exclusively, when the accountant is expressing an opinion on financial statements. Those who rely on the statements are well served if they are not betrayed, and so are the accountant himself and his client. It may sometimes seem that the accountant and his client might benefit by deceiving others, but even if this were so in a specific case it would not constitute the greatest good. So it follows that professional ethics which spurns betrayal constitutes good general ethics. The fact that the practitioner himself is one of the beneficiaries of his own conduct does not detract from its ethical value; rather it adds that much more to it.

The subjects of false and misleading statements and independence relate most closely to this fundamental aspect of the ethics of the accounting profession, and are most clearly examples of good general ethics. In expressing opinions on financial statements, the accountant adds credibility to them in the eyes of those who read them. These are the people who must not be betrayed if the greatest good is to be achieved. To avoid betrayal the accountant must be independent of his client, and the statements he approves must be usefully informative and not misleading. This much is clear.

THE COMPETITIVE ELEMENTS OF PRACTICE

What sometimes seems to be a different aspect of professional ethics in accounting relates to such things as advertising, solicitation, and competitive bidding. In the view of some people, these matters affect only the accountants themselves in their relations with each other, and do not affect any larger group.

If this were true, then the greatest good could be measured by the effect on the accountants themselves. If they were all better off by agreeing not to advertise or compete, it would clearly be good ethics to refrain. However, it is difficult to believe that these actions do not affect others. Clients might argue rather persuasively, and some do, that they could cut the costs of auditing if accountants would compete. It could follow from this argument that agreements among accountants not to compete constitute bad ethics. Clearly the greatest good resulting from any act or its omission cannot be judged unless all of its effects are taken into consideration.

THE ESTABLISHMENT OF CODES

Since ethics consists of an intelligent seeking of the greatest good, it can reasonably be asked why professions should draft codes or rules of conduct for themselves.

One answer might be to restrain the evil ones from wrongdoing; but that is not an effective answer. In any case, it has more to do with why people behave ethically or would ever elect to do so, than with the definition of good behavior.

There are two compelling reasons for codes of professional ethics. The first of these arises from the need for intelligence, wisdom, and understanding in deciding what is desirable conduct. The obligations of a profession are complex and far reaching. The areas of behavior which will achieve the greatest good for all concerned, without unduly hampering or restricting the activities and development of the profession, are not easy to define. No one is more fitted to attempt this difficult definition than the members of the profession itself. Thus, the profession has an ethical obligation to pool its joint wisdom and competence in its own field, and to define the kinds of behavior in that field which will lead to the greatest good. This joint pooling of understanding furnishes to each member of the profession greater wisdom as a guide to conduct than he, alone, could be expected to have.

THE RELIANCE OF THE PUBLIC

The second compelling reason for written and published codes of professional ethics is that they benefit those outside the profession who rely on it. Obviously, the services of a profession will be of greatest value if the recipients of those services know the extent of reliance they may safely place on them. If the readers of financial statements know that a CPA is independent, they are thereby enabled to obtain the maximum benefits from statements accompanied by his opinion. Conversely, if they know that he is not a guarantor of the statements, they will not be misled into excessive reliance. Widespread public knowledge that professional accountants have accepted a code of ethics and, furthermore, knowledge of what it says, help those outside the profession to understand the value of the services on which they rely, even though in each individual case they cannot check or measure that value.

These considerations indicate a general pattern to which codes of professional ethics should conform. They should prescribe conduct which enhances justifiable public confidence. Appearance of evil must be avoided as well as evil itself, as in the matter of ownership of a client's securities. The rules laid down must be sufficiently clear to be understandable and to facilitate compliance in good faith, and yet sufficiently general in their terms to avoid the possibility of apparent violations more technical than real, or conversely to create loopholes for evasion. Some parts of a code are appropriate to specific definitions while others can only refer to broad areas of behavior in general terms. And the codes must be evolutionary in nature, related to the greatest good, and subject to alteration as the needs and conditions of the community served by the profession change. The ethics of the accounting profession exemplify these considerations.

ARE WE ETHICAL?

"I can easier teach twenty what were good to be done," said Portia, "than be one of the twenty to follow mine own teaching." Apparently we in the field of professional accounting have trouble enough in deciding what is good, but to the extent that we have made the decision, it may be asked how well we follow our own precepts.

If we are to be honest, and a fairly useful maxim of ethics tells us that we should be, we must admit that we don't know. There has been no Dr. Kinsey to go among us with a staff of interviewers trained to elicit embarrassing admissions. If we judge by the cases that come before committees on ethics, state boards, the Securities and Exchange Commission, and the Treasury Department, we can take some pride in the record. The known failures are not overwhelming in numbers. But we know that some violations are never reported. In the areas of solicitation and advertising there is a widespread (and I think regrettable) disposition not to complain. In the areas of auditing and financial reporting there is occasional grumbling at published statements that appear questionable but are never formally challenged — though it should be recognized that this grumbling is sometimes based on inadequate information. It must be assumed, therefore, that the violations of our codes of ethics are in excess of known cases.

There are, however, two factors which should be mentioned in judging the quality of ethical behavior of accountants:

1. The violations which most readily escape notice are those of the least turpitude. The serious offenses are more apt to be brought to light. A review of the complaints brought against accountants indicates that they deal mostly with solicitation and advertising, seldom with anything more derelict than honest mistakes or unintentional negligence, and almost never with deliberate fraud.

2. Accountants have achieved considerable prestige in the public mind. This could not have been acquired and maintained if it were not merited to a high degree by performance. It may, therefore, reasonably be concluded that the performance of professional accountants conforms in large measure with their established standards of ethics.

From another standpoint, the question of how ethical we are can be judged by the published codes themselves. These codes embody agreements on areas of behavior; they do not reflect the best that anyone can conceive. To the extent that they fall short of the best that we know, they are imperfect — and to that extent, the public accounting profession is imperfect. Every advance in the development of our codes of ethics has had to overcome reluctance on the part of some. Today, as mentioned earlier, there are areas regarding independence, competitive bidding, and changes of auditors in which the reluctance of many members of the profession has not yet been overcome. Yet, in spite of these imperfections, the growth and development of accounting codes has been remarkably rapid and demonstrates a keen awareness of their importance.

THE PROFESSION ON TRIAL

Related to the content of the published codes is the effectiveness with which cases of violations are handled by trial boards and committees on ethics.

When an accountant is on trial before his colleagues, the profession itself is on trial even more significantly than is the accused member. It is in these procedures that the profession demonstrates the seriousness with which it regards its own rules. If friendship or pity were to influence judgment, the accused member might escape censure but the profession would find itself guilty of a kind of fraud. There have been instances when something like this seems to have occurred, but they are rare and not recent. The seriousness with which the American Institute's trial board and most state society committees discharge their unpleasant duties testifies to a genuine respect for the ethics of the profession.

Attempts to judge the ethical status of public accountants are necessarily concerned with its limitations, and contemplation of limitations inevitably appears discouraging. It shouldn't. When a steel bar is tested in a laboratory, it is subjected to a load until it breaks. That tells the limitation of its strength. But the fact that it breaks is not failure. Its strength is the load it carried before the breaking point. That is the way to regard the ethical standards of the accounting profession and their observance in practice. Recognition of limitations in the rules of conduct, their observance, and their enforcement, as they exist today, not only give cause for considerable pride in our profession. They also give eloquent promise of further progress.

WHY BE ETHICAL?

If we ask why an accountant should be or would want to be ethical, we might find an easy, though not too glorious, answer in the fear of penalties. If he violates standards set by state boards, the Securities and Exchange Commission, or the Treasury Department, he may be deprived of his living or at least a part of it. The cynical will say that the pocketbook is the only part of the human personality capable of feeling pain. But it is implicit in this answer that the crime consists in getting caught, and fear of penalties is no more ethical than keeping your hands off a hot stove. It does not explain why an accountant would want to be ethical.

An equally unsatisfactory answer is that the accountant values his good name and fears disgrace. It is probably true that the sense of shame felt by an accountant who has been found guilty of a violation of ethics causes him greater pain than the attendant loss of revenue. If this were not true, respondents before trial boards and committees on ethics of professional societies would not be greatly concerned. The most that these bodies can do is to expel the member, and that need not impair his income. Yet the fact is that respondents in these cases protest vigorously and are often crushed in spirit when found guilty, even if the penalty is no more than a reprimand. If the concern of the accused is over no more than loss of face, it is not much more ethical than concern over loss of income. The crime still consists in getting caught. However, the discomfiture at being branded as unethical comes, in part at least, from conscience and from an inner desire to be the kind of person who can live at peace with himself. These considerations get close to the soundest and most lasting reasons why anyone would want to be ethical.

People cannot be classified as simply good or bad. Those who regard ethics as hopeless because you can't change human nature, don't know human nature. Modern psychology has taught us that there is not an eternal war within us between the beast and the angel. The basic drives so easily recognized in the child — the needs for love, respect, freedom, security, and achievement — are the drives of the man. They constitute human nature and they are neither good nor bad. They can be channeled in either direction. They are forces which can either serve or destroy. It is early training, good social environment, and expanding group conciousness of the individual, and the identification of himself with others, that will direct these forces into ethical channels. To achieve this for society in general, we must learn the slow lessons of community living over and over until they are imbedded in all men.

For the professions, and specifically for public accountants, these lessons are not so slowly learned. The accounting profession offers satisfactions of basic needs which can be attained by useful conduct. The opportunities for prestige in a responsible profession lead naturally to the assumption of related obligations. The wise self-interest of the accountant leads him to the satisfactions and gratifications that come from ethical behavior. He will be rewarded in so far as he is useful and contributes to the merited prestige that he shares. He will identify himself with the ever-expanding group that he serves which has no limit other than the limit of all mankind. And he will find that his own desires are most fully gratified when he disciplines himself to be the kind of person he can be proud of being — when he can know that the satisfactions he enjoys are his because he is worthy of them. Any person intelligent enough to be a competent professional accountant is intelligent enough to see this — and that is reason enough why professional accountants want to be ethical.

ETHICAL DUTIES AND OPPORTUNITIES

In meeting his ethical responsibilities, the professional accountant is, in a larger and truer sense, grasping his ethical opportunities.

Responsibility connotes duty which — however commendable it may be — has the same lack of charm as a debt. But the ethics of his profession offers the accountant more than that. It offers him the greatest opportunity for fulfillment and gratification. He has sound reason within himself to want to be ethical, to exemplify the code of his profession, to work constantly for the betterment of that code, and to encourage his colleagues toward the same goal. In grasping these opportunities by meeting responsibilities, the accountant serves others, but he also best serves himself. He has done this in the past. He does it now in good measure. There is every reason to believe that he will continue to do so in the future — and, with the passing years, that he will learn to do it better, more wisely, and more usefully.

5. Restating the Ethics Code: A Decision for the Times*

Thomas G. Higgins
Wallace E. Olson†

The accounting profession has recently come under a barrage of criticism.

Some may be inclined to regard such criticism as a natural manifestation of the increased visibility of the profession's role — suggesting that the cause is not so much a matter of inferior performance as it is a failure to communicate our accomplishments. Others may contend that a great deal more than the mere application of effective publicity techniques will be required if the profession is to satisfy the rising expectations of the public.

Regardless of how one evaluates the nature and seriousness of the criticism, it seems clear that now, more than ever, the conduct of all CPAs must be exemplary. While a code of ethics, no matter how logical or inspiring, will not guarantee that such conduct will be attained, a code is vital to the process of professional self-discipline. Members must have a clear understanding of the requirements and underlying philosophy of ethical behavior if they are to be motivated to perform in a manner which will maintain the confidence of a discerning public.

A PROPOSED NEW CODE

Recognizing the significance of a well-developed code of ethics, the Institute's division of professional ethics launched an intensive review of the present Code in 1967. The review was conducted by a special committee on Code restatement formed within the division. As a result of four years of nearly continuous work, a new Code was presented to the Institute's governing body early in May (1972). Council approved the proposed revised Code for submission to the

*Reprint of Thomas G. Higgins and Wallace E. Olson, "Restating the Ethics Code: A Decision for the Times," *The Journal of Accountancy* (March, 1972), pp. 33-39. Copyright (1972) by the American Institute of Certified Public Accountants, Inc. Single copies of the updated article may be obtained from the Institute, 666 Fifth Avenue, New York, NY 10019.

This article, which was published in the March 1972 issue of *The Journal of Accountancy*, has been updated to recognize changes in the proposed restated Code which were approved by Council at its May 1972 meeting and to comment on the omission of the rule against competitive bidding which results from a civil antitrust suit brought by the United States against the Institute.

†Thomas G. Higgins, CPA, is a member of the Institute's Code Restatement Committee and is a retired senior partner of Arthur Young and Company. Wallace E. Olson, CPA, is the executive vice-president of the American Institute of Certified Public Accountants.

membership. The restated Code will be discussed, but not acted upon, at the Institute's annual meeting in Denver in October (1972) and then submitted to the membership for vote. A two-thirds majority of the members voting is needed for passage.

The authors of this article served on the special committee. They may thus be accused of bias in contending that the Code revision confronts the profession with a kind of watershed decision. Yet at least two circumstances testify to the exceptional importance of the decision to be made.

First, the Code is a main foundation document of the profession; for while the charters and bylaws of the American Institute and other accounting societies, plus the statutes pertaining to accountancy in all the states, set the bodily structure of the profession, it is the ethical concepts that infuse the body with spirit. Indeed, as suggested earlier, it is agreement on ethical concepts and adherence to them by an overwhelming majority of practitioners that transform a vocation into a profession.

Second, the Code restatement committee would never have come into being if a significant number of practitioners had not found the present Code inadequate.

The reasons for dissatisfaction became apparent when the Code restatement committee began analyzing it section by section, rule by rule, often word by word.

In many cases, for example, key terms are used without being defined, so the intent of a statement is not explicit and the way is open to differing interpretations.

The present Code contains no reference whatever to generally accepted auditing standards.

With ten years having passed since the Code had any sort of overall examination and updating, pronouncements by technical committees have obsoleted some of its parts.

Changes during the past decade — the expansion in scope of practice, the increased use of computers, adoption of the corporate form of organization by some practice units and other developments — have had ethical implications outside our previous experience.

THE PRESENT NEGATIVE CODE

The greatest deficiency of all in the present Code, however, is that it is entirely negative. It deals only with those things which, if done by a member, will make him liable to penalty. This approach inevitably results in defining the bottom limit of acceptable conduct. It does not hold before the practitioner, or reveal to the public, the goal of excellence at which the profession must constantly aim.

The proposal to revise the Code will undoubtedly create some misgivings because all of us tend to have ambivalent feelings about change. That is, we often find change interesting and even pleasing in superficial instances, such as women's fashions, but are uneasy if it seems likely to affect our work or living habits. Yet we also know that any organization which fails to perceive the changes taking place in its environment (or, perceiving them, refuses to accommodate to them) can be threatened with extinction. The accounting profession should be determined to avoid that old mistake of neglecting to adjust to new conditions.

Early in its deliberations, the Code restatement committee applied itself to determining what ought to be retained as good and continuingly pertinent in the existing Code, what should be dropped because of being repetitive or inconsistent, what required sharper definition or clearer language, what needed to be added to fill gaps and keep the document attuned to the times. To this end, it studied the published codes of accounting societies throughout the world, and those of all state CPA societies and boards of accountancy. It also studied the ethical rules of the major professions practicing in this country.

STRUCTURE OF THE PROPOSED CODE

The committee decided that the product of its efforts should not only set forth standards of conduct but should present them in a format and with sufficient background as to bring out the underlying rationale. Accordingly, the proposed new Code consists of three distinct sections:

- An *essay* discussing in philosophical fashion the concepts from which the rules of conduct flow and why these concepts are integrally important to the profession.
- The *rules* of conduct, infraction of which would make a member liable to discipline; since this is the basic operative section, the eventual vote of the membership will pertain to this section only.
- *Interpretations* of the rules, which will explain their application and scope. They will take the place of the present opinions of the ethics division.

The concepts discussed in the essay section are presented under five headings: independence, integrity and objectivity; competence and technical standards; responsibilities to clients; responsibilities to colleagues; and other responsibilities and practices. These ethical principles are broad guidelines as distinguished from enforceable rules. Members will not be subject to discipline for failing to attain the aspirations set forth in the essay.

The second section consists of 15 rules, a list of definitions and a statement on applicability of the rules.

The rules are grouped under the same five headings used in the essay, thus indicating the relationship between concepts and rules. The latter are to have the same status as those in the present Code in that they establish the fundamentals of behavior and form the basis for disciplinary action. As stated above, this is the only section of the Code that would require adoption by the membership through vote by mail ballot.

The definitions in this section provide guidance as to the intent with which certain words and phrases are used throughout the Code, thus avoiding ambiguities found in the present Code. As an illustration, the "practice of public accounting" is defined as holding oneself out to be a CPA or public accountant and at the same time performing for a client one or more types of service rendered by public accountants. In the past, application of ethical rules as they relate to a member offering accounting services to the public has not depended on whether he holds himself out as a CPA. This fact has caused some confusion as to the member's responsibilities when he abandons the formal practice of accountancy to establish, for example, a data processing service center or a consulting activity. Under the definition, such a member would not be subject to the rules relating to accounting practitioners, *so long as he does not represent himself as being a part of the profession.*

The statement on the applicability of rules declares that they apply to all services performed in the practice of public accounting, including tax and management advisory services, except (1) where the wording of the rule indicates otherwise and (2) that a member who is practicing outside the United States will not be subject to discipline for departing from any of the rules so long as his conduct is in accord with the rules of the organized accounting profession in the country in which he is practicing. The latter exception is modified by another proviso: that where a member's name is associated with financial statements in such a manner as to imply that he is acting as an independent public accountant and under circumstances that would entitle the reader to assume that United States practices were followed, he must comply with the proposed rules on auditing standards and accounting principles.

The applicability statement also establishes three fundamental norms:

- That a member may be held responsible for compliance with the rules by all persons associated with him in the practice of public accounting who are under his supervision or are his partners or shareholders in the practice,
- That a member engaged in the practice of public accounting must observe all the rules of conduct, but that a member not so engaged must observe only the rule which states that no member may knowlingly misrepresent facts, and the rule that states that no member may commit an act discreditable to the profession, and
- That a member must not permit others to carry out on his behalf, either with or without compensation, acts which, if performed by a member, would constitute a violation of the rules.

Although the conditions stated above seem self-explanatory, the question has been raised as to whether all partners of a firm should be held responsible for the acts of an offending member. It has to be recognized that a partner is legally responsible for the acts of his partners and of those employees under his supervision, and the wording of the rule simply recognizes this existing legal fact. It seems only reasonable to apply this legal standard in an ethical sense to those partners who may share a direct responsibility for the member's act through their positions in the management of the firm.

Provision has also been made for *interpretations* of the rules to be issued by the ethics division as guidelines on the scope and application of the rules. The interpretations, which will not themselves be enforceable, will take the place of the present opinions of the ethics division. The division has adopted interpretations of the proposed rules to replace the present opinions upon adoption of the restated rules. These interpretations are included in the proposed Code so that members will understand how it is intended that the proposed rules will be construed.

INDEPENDENCE

Since some of the more complex ethical questions in our profession have to do with independence, it is understandable that a substantial part of the proposed new Code — the essay, the rules and the interpretations — deals with this subject.

The first rule of the new Code (Rule 101), in fact, is concerned with independence. It is the result of a natural evolution of the profession's statements on the subject. In 1947, the Council of the American Institute officially defined independence as "an attitude of mind, much deeper than the surface display of visible standards." The rules at that time concerned themselves with independence in fact. However, in 1962, members of the Institute adopted the present rule on independence, which requires that an auditor be independent not only in fact but in appearance as well. The rule then specifies certain relationships with a client — certain financial interests, or service as a director, officer, key employee, promoter, underwriter or voting trustee — that would cause a member to be considered lacking in independence when he is expressing his opinion on financial statements.

The ethical considerations in the proposed Code further refine the concept of independence in appearance by specifying that independence is the ability to act with integrity and objectivity, and that certain relationships with a client would cause third parties to question the ability of an auditor to act with requisite impartiality. Without doubt the concept of independence should not be interpreted so loosely as to permit relationships likely to impair the CPA's integrity or the impartiality of his judgment, nor so strictly as to inhibit the rendering of useful service when the likelihood of such impairment is remote. Therefore, the committee proposes a rule in which three additional prohibitions would be added to those contained in the present rule. These are: (1) any joint closely held business investment with a client or any of its management which is material in relation to the member's or his firm's net worth; (2) any loan to or from a client or any of its management; and (3) service as a trustee for any pension or profit-sharing trust of a client, or service as a trustee or executor for a deceased client where the trust or estate has a direct or material indirect financial interest in a client. The committee recognizes that the latter proscription may cause inconvenience to some members. Accordingly, provision is made that it will not become effective until two years after adoption of the new Code.

The restated Code makes clear that these examples are not meant to be all-inclusive. It also makes clear that the proscription as to loans from a client does not apply to the following types of loans from a financial institution, made under normal lending procedures and terms: loans which are not material in relation to the net worth of the borrower, home mortgages, or other secured loans made under normal terms. A firm's guarantee of repayment of a partner's unsecured loan will not cause it to be considered "secured" under this exception.

The independent rule in the present Code contains an exception for nominal directorships in non-profit organizations. An interpretation of the proposed independence rule clarifies the exception by providing that when a member is asked to lend the prestige of his name to a nonprofit organization as a director, he will not be considered lacking in independence so long as he does not participate in management decisions and the board itself is sufficiently large that a third party would conclude that his membership was purely honorary.

Sometimes it is asked whether a CPA's independence may be impaired by his providing bookkeeping or data processing services for an audit client. An interpretation of the proposed independence rule states that the auditor does not necessarily lose independence under such circumstances, but it lays down four conditions which he must meet to avoid the appearance that he is lacking in independence. These conditions in summary are:

1. The auditor must not have any relationship with the client which would impair his integrity and objectivity.
2. The client must accept the responsibility for the financial statements as his own and, when necessary, the auditor must discuss accounting matters with the client to be sure that he has the required degree of understanding.
3. The auditor must not assume the role of employee or of management — thus he should not consummate transactions, have custody of assets or exercise authority on behalf of the client.
4. The auditor, in making an examination of financial statements when he has performed accounting services, must conform to generally accepted auditing standards — the fact that he has processed or maintained certain records does not eliminate the need to make sufficient audit tests.

How important is the *appearance* of independence in the case of management advisory services and tax practice? The essay states that while a CPA need not appear to be independent in performing such services, it is desirable that he avoid the relationships proscribed in Rule 101.

INTEGRITY AND OBJECTIVITY

The second rule in the revised Code — a new one — deals with integrity and objectivity and makes three points: that no member, whether in public practice or not, may knowingly misrepresent facts; that no member engaged in the practice of public accounting, including the rendering of tax and management advisory services, may subordinate his professional judgment to others; and that a member engaged in tax practice may resolve doubt in favor of his client as long as there is reasonable support for his position.

COMPETENCE

The rule on competence, also new, states that a member must not undertake any engagement which he or his firm cannot reasonably expect to complete with professional competence. A related interpretation states, in substance, that a member who accepts an engagement implies that he has the necessary competence to complete it according to professional standards; that, while a member may have the basic knowledge needed to complete an engagement, additional research or consultation may in many cases be necessary during the course of the engagement; and where a member has doubts that he can complete the engagement with professional competence, even with additional research or consultation, he should suggest the engagement of someone competent to perform the needed service, either independently or as an associate. It should be noted, however, that while the need for competence is stressed, the CPA who accepts a professional engagement does not assume a responsibility for infallibility.

AUDITING STANDARDS

It comes as a surprise to many to learn that the technical standards rules in the present Code do not mention generally accepted auditing standards. And while present Rules 2.02 and 2.03 are condensations of Statement on Auditing Procedure No. 33, the status of the SAPs themselves is unclear. A proposed new rule entitled "Auditing Standards" would take the place of present Rules 2.01, 2.02 and 2.03, and would require that a member not permit his name to be associated with financial statements in such a manner as to imply that he is acting as an independent public accountant unless he has complied with the applicable generally accepted auditing standards promulgated by the Institute. Thus the new rule would incorporate the ten generally accepted auditing standards approved by the membership in 1948 and 1949.

It should be noted that the proposed rule applies only when a member permits his name to be associated with financial statements in such a manner as to imply that he is acting as an independent public accountant. Consequently, a member in industry signing a financial report in his capacity as a treasurer or controller of a corporation would not be required by the rule to comply with generally accepted auditing standards as they relate to practitioners. However, it would be improper in any event for him to be associated with misleading financial statements.

Some members have also questioned how the auditing standards rule would apply to unaudited financial statements. SAP No. 38 makes it clear that CPAs may be engaged to assist a client in the preparation of financial statements which have not been subject to sufficient auditing procedures to permit the CPA to express his opinion. While not all the generally accepted auditing standards would apply in such circumstances, SAP No. 38 requires, under the generally accepted standards of reporting, that the CPA disclaim an opinion and provides sample language for such a disclaimer. Of course, if in addition to the aforementioned scope limitations, a member is also lacking in independence, he would disclaim for lack of independence pursuant to SAP No. 42, without describing any reasons for lack of independence or limitations in scope.

ACCOUNTING PRINCIPLES

Another proposed rule provides that a member must not express an opinion that financial statements are presented in conformity with generally accepted accounting principles if there is any departure from an accounting principle promulgated by the body designated by Council to establish such principles which has a material effect on the statements taken as a whole, unless the member can demonstrate that due to unusual circumstances the financial statements would otherwise have been misleading. In such cases, the member's report must describe the departure, its approximate effects (if practicable), and the reasons why compliance with a principle would have resulted in a misleading statement.

In this connection, readers will recall that in 1969 a proposal to amend Rule 2.02 of the present Code to require disclosure of departures from APB Opinions failed by a fraction of a percent to achieve the two-thirds vote necessary for adoption. The Code restatement committee believes that the proposed new rule is preferable to both present Rule 2.02 and the defeated amendment since the thrust of the new proposal is to require a presentation which, in the auditor's professional judgment, is not misleading. A related interpretation states, in substance, that while there is a strong presumption that adherence to officially established accounting principles would, in nearly all instances, result in financial statements that are not misleading there may be, on occasion, unusual circumstances where the literal application of pronouncements on accounting principles would have the effect of rendering financial statements misleading. In such cases, the interpretation points out, the proper accounting treatment is that which will render the financial statements not misleading.

The proposed rule on auditing standards makes clear that Statements on Auditing Procedure are considered to be interpretations of generally accepted auditing standards and that departures from such Statements must be justified by those who do not follow them. In the case of APB Opinions, members would also have to justify, on the basis of fair presentation, any departures. Thus, while requiring the profession to unite behind the work of its senior committees, the rule would allow for the exercise of professional judgment.

The proposed new Code makes no mention of enforceable technical standards in the areas of tax and management advisory services, but it is anticipated that additional rules of conduct covering these areas of practice will be proposed for adoption by the membership when a body of technical standards has evolved and become generally accepted.

FORECASTS

The rule on forecasts in the new Code — and a related interpretation — does not differ materially from present Rule 2.04 — and Ethics Opinion No. 10 — but makes it clear that a member ought not to vouch for the *achievability* of a forecast with which he is associated (the present rule relates to the "accuracy" of the forecast).

CONFIDENTIAL RELATIONSHIP

The rule in the present Code which states that a member may not violate the confidential relationship with his client has proved inadequate because it does not make clear whether "violate" prohibits any disclosure whatever or only disclosure which would harm the client's interest.

The proposed new rule provides that a member must not disclose any confidential information obtained in the course of an engagement, except with the client's consent. It then states that the rule must not be construed to:

- Relieve a member of his obligation of fair disclosure under the rules relating to auditing standards and accounting principles.
- Affect his compliance with a valid subpoena or summons of a court.

- Prohibit an evaluation of a member's professional practices as part of a voluntary quality review program under Institute authorization.
- Preclude a member from responding to inquiry by the ethics division or Trial Board of the Institute, by a duly constituted investigative or disciplinary body of a state CPA society, or under state statutes.

The rule also provides that members of the ethics division and Trial Board, and professional practice reviewers under Institute authorization, must not disclose any confidential client information which comes to their attention from members in disciplinary proceedings or otherwise in carrying out their official responsibilities. However, this prohibition is not intended to restrict the exchange of disciplinary information between duly constituted investigative or disciplinary bodies.

CONTINGENT FEES

The proposed rule on contingent fees does not differ materially from the present rule but makes clear that it would be improper to render professional services under an arrangement in which a fee would not be charged unless a specified result were attained. Fees are not regarded as contingent, however, if fixed by courts or other public authorities, or, in tax matters, if based on the results of judicial proceedings or findings of governmental agencies.

ENCROACHMENT

The proposed rule on encroachment is essentially a combination of present Rules 5.01 and 5.02 but is more specific. It states that a member must not endeavor to provide any professional service currently provided by another public accountant. A member may furnish service to anyone who requests it but when an audit client of another accountant requests a member to provide professional advice on accounting or auditing matters in connection with an expression of opinion on financial statements, the member must first consult with the other accountant to be sure the member is aware of all the available facts.

When a member receives an engagement by referral from another public accountant, he should not seek to obtain any additional engagement from the client, nor should he accept the client's request to extend his service beyond the specific engagement without first notifying the referring accountant. The rule clarifies the propriety of a member's insisting on auditing any subsidiary, branch or other component of a client which, in his judgment, is necessary to warrant the expression of his opinion on consolidated statements. An interpretation points out, however, that the auditor's exercise of judgment in this regard is subject to review. Thus, insistence on auditing an unreasonably large percentage of consolidated net assets or net income might lead to the conclusion that the auditor's judgment had been made as part of a plan to solicit an engagement which would be a violation of the rule on encroachment. Under another interpretation, the unsolicited sending of firm literature or invitations to seminars which cover services currently rendered to a client by another public accountant would be considered a violation of the rule on encroachment.

OFFERS OF EMPLOYMENT

On offers of employment a proposed rule broadens the present one by requiring notice to a practitioner employer of offers of employment made on behalf of a client. The present rule is silent on this.

DISCREDITABLE ACTS

A rule prohibiting acts discreditable to the profession is included and is identical to present Rule 1.02. While there was sentiment for dropping this proscription, it was felt to be so basic to ethical conduct as to be an imperative in any code.

SOLICITATION AND ADVERTISING

The rule on solicitation, combining the essence of present Rules 3.01 and 3.02, states that a member must not seek to obtain clients by solicitation and that advertising is a form of solicitation. There are 14 interpretations under this rule, dealing with announcements, office premises, directories, business stationery, business cards, help wanted advertisements, firm publications, publications prepared by others, responsibility for a publisher's promotional efforts, statements to the press, participation in educational seminars, solicitation of former clients, soliciting work from other practitioners, and fees and professional standards.

These interpretations contain the substance of a number of opinions on the present Code but are more specific. Under the interpretation concerning newspaper and magazine articles, for example, a member may respond factually when approached by the press for information concerning his firm but must not use such inquiries as a means of aggrandizing himself or his firm. The interpretation adds that while a member cannot control the journalistic use of any information he may give when interviewed, he should notify the reporter of the limitations imposed by professional ethics. The interpretation also prohibits press releases concerning intrafirm matters.

COMMISSIONS

A proposed rule on commissions clarifies present Rule 3.04 on fee splitting and prohibits payment to anyone to obtain a client. It also prohibits receipt of a commission for referring products or services of others to a client. Present Rule 3.04 permits such payments when other practitioners are involved. The new rule does not prohibit payments for the purchase of an accounting practice, or retirement payments to individuals formerly engaged in the practice of public accounting, or payments to their heirs or estates.

INCOMPATIBLE OCCUPATIONS

The rule in the present Code on incompatible occupations is clarified by specifying that a practitioner may not, concurrently with his public practice, engage in any business or occupation which impairs his objectivity in rendering professional services or which serves as a feeder to his practice.

COMPETITIVE BIDDING

The following statement is required to be published with the Code of Professional Ethics pursuant to the Final Judgment in the court decision referred to below:

> The former provision of the Code of Professional Ethics prohibiting competitive bidding, Rule 3.03, was declared null and void by the United States District Court for the District of Columbia in a consent judgment entered on July 6, 1972, in a civil antitrust suit brought by the United States against the American Institute. In consequence, no provision of the Code of Professional Ethics now prohibits the submission of

price quotations for accounting services to persons seeking such services; and such submission of price quotations is not an unethical practice under any policy of the Institute. To avoid misunderstanding, it is important to note that otherwise unethical conduct (e.g., advertising, solicitation, or substandard work) is subject to disciplinary sanctions regardless of whether or not such unethical conduct is preceded by, associated with, or followed by a submission of price quotations for accounting services. Members of the Institute should also be aware that neither the foregoing judgment nor any policy of the Institute affects the obligation of a certified public accountant to obey applicable laws, regulations or rules of any state or other governmental authority.

This statement is included in the proposed restated Code in an interpretation referring to solicitation and advertising — Fees and Professional Standards.

CONCLUSION

In concerning themselves with the details of ethical standards, CPAs must not lose sight of the fact that such standards are central to every profession. Members of a profession undertake to supply society with some service whose performance depends on long training and on skills which are largely intellectual. People turn to professionals not only for service but for advice.

Because of these characteristics of professional work, society provides special recognition to professional practitioners, not just in the form of legal authorization to practice but in terms of a large measure of control by the professional over his own work. In return for this freedom, members of a profession are expected to set high standards of performance and to behave with a high sense of responsibility to client and public.

At some point in the evolution of a profession, therefore, its practitioners form an association for diffusing knowledge among themselves and for governing themselves. To the extent that they fail in self-government, they invite a curtailment in their freedom of action in their sphere of work. Thus a code of ethics bears not only internally on a profession's own affairs but externally on its position in society.

Without overstraining comparison, the code of a profession can be likened to the constitution of a government. So, as the Council and membership of the AICPA approach decision on the Institute's Code, it is perhaps not inappropriate to recall the time in our nation's early history when the states that had lately won independence sent delegations to a meeting to improve the foundation document of their young government. The delegates of Virginia brought to the meeting a message which included these words:

> The Crisis is arrived at which the good People of America are to decide the solemn question whether they will by just and magnanimous Efforts reap the fruit of that Independence which they have so gloriously acquired and that Union which they have cemented with so much of their common Blood, or whether by giving way to unmanly Jealousies and Prejudices or to partial and transitory Interests they will furnish our Enemies with cause to triumph.

With similar sentiment, one may hope that appraisal of the restated Code will be of the document as a whole and not prejudiced by dissatisfaction with some part of it, and that in each member's decision on the casting of his ballot, personal interest will be subordinated to regard for the common weal.

6. Restatement of the Code
of Professional Ethics*

Division of Professional Ethics,
American Institute of
Certified Public Accountants

CONCEPTS OF PROFESSIONAL ETHICS

A distinguishing mark of a professional is his acceptance of responsibility to the public. All true professions have therefore deemed it essential to promulgate codes of ethics and to establish means for ensuring their observance.

The reliance of the public, the government and the business community on sound financial reporting and advice on business affairs, and the importance of these matters to the economic and social aspects of life impose particular obligations on certified public accountants.

Ordinarily those who depend upon a certified public accountant find it difficult to assess the quality of his services; they have a right to expect, however, that he is a person of competence and integrity. A man or woman who enters the profession of accountancy is assumed to accept an obligation to uphold its principles, to work for the increase of knowledge in the art and for the improvement of methods, and to abide by the profession's ethical and technical standards.

The ethical Code of the American Institute emphasizes the profession's responsibility to the public, a responsibility that has grown as the number of investors has grown, as the relationship between corporate managers and stockholders has become more impersonal and as government increasingly relies on accounting information.

The Code also stresses the CPA's responsibility to clients and colleagues, since his behavior in these relationships cannot fail to affect the responsibilities of the profession as a whole to the public.

The Institute's Rules of Conduct set forth minimum levels of acceptable conduct and are mandatory and enforceable. However, it is in the best interests of the profession that CPAs strive for conduct beyond that indicated merely by prohibitions. Ethical conduct, in the true sense, is more than merely abiding by the letter of explicit prohibitions. Rather it requires unswerving commitment to honorable behavior, even at the sacrifice of personal advantage.

The conduct toward which CPAs should strive is embodied in five broad concepts stated as affirmative Ethical Principles:

---

*The Restatement was submitted to the AICPA membership and approved. Copyright (1972) by the American Institute of Certified Public Accountants, Inc. Reprinted by permission of the AICPA.

Independence, integrity and objectivity. A certified public accountant should maintain his integrity and objectivity and, when engaged in the practice of public accounting, be independent of those he serves.

Competence and technical standards. A certified public accountant should observe the profession's technical standards and strive continually to improve his competence and the quality of his services.

Responsibility to clients. A certified public accountant should be fair and candid with his clients and serve them to the best of his ability, with professional concern for their best interests, consistent with his responsibilities to the public.

Responsibilities to colleagues. A certified public accountant should conduct himself in a manner which will promote cooperation and good relations among members of the profession.

Other responsibilities and practices. A certified public accountant should conduct himself in a manner which will enhance the stature of the profession and its ability to serve the public.

The foregoing Ethical Principles are intended as broad guidelines as distinguished from enforceable Rules of Conduct. Even though they do not provide a basis for disciplinary action, they constitute the philosophical foundation upon which the Rules of Conduct are based.

The following discussion is intended to elaborate on each of the Ethical Principles and provide rationale for their support.

INDEPENDENCE, INTEGRITY AND OBJECTIVITY

A certified public accountant should maintain his integrity and objectivity and, when engaged in the practice of public accounting, be independent of those he serves.

The public expects a number of character traits in a certified public accountant but primarily integrity and objectivity and, in the practice of public accounting, independence.

Independence has always been a concept fundamental to the accounting profession, the cornerstone of its philosophical structure. For no matter how competent any CPA may be, his opinion on financial statements will be of little value to those who rely on him — whether they be clients or any of his unseen audience of credit grantors, investors, governmental agencies and the like — unless he maintains his independence.

Independence has traditionally been defined by the profession as the ability to act with integrity and objectivity.

Integrity is an element of character which is fundamental to reliance on the CPA. This quality may be difficult to judge, however, since a particular fault of omission or commission may be the result either of honest error or a lack of integrity.

Objectivity refers to a CPA's ability to maintain an impartial attitude on all matters which come under his review. Since this attitude involves an individual's mental processes, the evaluation of objectivity must be based largely on actions and relationships viewed in the context of ascertainable circumstances.

While recognizing that the qualities of integrity and objectivity are not precisely measurable, the profession nevertheless constantly holds them up to members as an imperative. This is done essentially by education and by the Rules of Conduct which the profession adopts and enforces.

CPAs cannot practice their calling and participate in the world's affairs without being exposed to situations that involve the possibility of pressures upon their integrity and objectivity. To define and proscribe all such situations would be impracticable. To ignore the problem for that reason, however, and to set no limits at all would be irresponsible.

It follows that the concept of independence should not be interpreted so loosely as to permit relationships likely to impair the CPA's integrity or the impartiality of his judgment, nor so strictly as to inhibit the rendering of useful services when the likelihood of such impairment is relatively remote.

While it may be difficult for a CPA always to appear completely independent even in normal relationships with clients, pressures upon his integrity or objectivity are offset by powerful countervailing forces and restraints. These include the possibility of legal liability, professional discipline ranging up to revocation of the right to practice as a CPA, loss of reputation and, by no means least, the inculcated resistance of a disciplined professional to any infringement upon his basic integrity and objectivity. Accordingly, in deciding which types of relationships should be specifically prohibited, both the magnitude of the threat posed by a relationship and the force of countervailing pressures have to be weighed.

In establishing rules relating to independence, the profession uses the criterion of whether reasonable men, having knowledge of all the facts and taking into consideration normal strength of character and normal behavior under the circumstances, would conclude that a specified relationship between a CPA and a client poses an unacceptable threat to the CPA's integrity or objectivity.

When a CPA expresses an opinion on financial statements, not only the fact but also the appearance of integrity and objectivity is of particular importance. For this reason, the profession has adopted rules to prohibit the expression of such an opinion when relationships exist which might pose such a threat to integrity and objectivity as to exceed the strength of countervailing forces and restraints. These relationships fall into two general categories: (1) certain financial relationships with clients and (2) relationships in which a CPA is virtually part of management or an employee under management's control.

Although the appearance of independence is not required in the case of management advisory services and tax practice, a CPA is encouraged to avoid the proscribed relationships with clients regardless of the type of services being rendered. In any event, the CPA, in all types of engagements, should refuse to subordinate his professional judgment to others and should express his conclusions honestly and objectively.

The financial relationships proscribed when an opinion is expressed on financial statements make no reference to fees paid to a CPA by a client. Remuneration to providers of services is necessary for the continued provision of those services. Indeed, a principal reason for the development and persistence in the professions of the client-practitioner relationship and of remuneration by fee (as contrasted with an employer-employee relationship and remuneration by salary) is that these arrangements are seen as a safeguard of independence.

The above reference to an employer-employee relationship is pertinent to a question sometimes raised as to whether a CPA's objectivity in expressing an opinion on financial statements will be impaired by his being involved with his client in the decision-making process.

CPAs continually provide advice to their clients, and they expect that this advice will usually be followed. Decisions based on such advice may have a significant effect on a client's financial condition or operating results. This is the case not only in tax engagements and management advisory services but in the audit function as well.

If a CPA disagrees with a client on a significant matter during the course of an audit, the client has three choices — he can modify the financial statements (which is usually the case), he can accept a qualified report or he can discharge the CPA. While the ultimate decision and the resulting financial statements clearly are those of the client, the CPA has obviously been a significant factor in the decision-making process. Indeed, no responsible user of financial statements would want it otherwise.

It must be noted that when a CPA expresses an opinion on financial statements, the judgments involved pertain to whether the results of operating decisions of the client are fairly presented in the statements and not on the underlying wisdom of such decisions. It is highly unlikely therefore that being a factor in the client's decision-making process would impair the CPA's objectivity in judging the fairness of presentation.

The more important question is whether a CPA would deliberately compromise his integrity by expressing an unqualified opinion on financial statements which were prepared in such a way as to cover up a poor business decision by the client and on which the CPA had rendered advice. The basic character traits of the CPA as well as the risks arising from such a compromise of integrity, including liability to third parties, disciplinary action and loss of right to practice, should preclude such action.

Providing advice or recommendations which may or may not involve skills logically related to a client's information and control system, and which may affect the client's decision-making, does not in itself indicate lack of independence. However, the CPA must be alert to the possibility that undue identification with the management of the client or involvement with a client's affairs to such a degree as to place him virtually in the position of being an employee, may impair the appearance of independence.

To sum up, CPAs cannot avoid external pressures on their integrity and objectivity in the course of their professional work, but they are expected to resist these pressures. They must, in fact, retain their integrity and objectivity in all phases of their practice and, when expressing opinions on financial statements, avoid involvement in situations that would impair the credibility of their independence in the minds of reasonable men familiar with the facts.

COMPETENCE AND TECHNICAL STANDARDS

A certified public accountant should observe the profession's technical standards and strive continually to improve his competence and the quality of his services.

Since accounting information is of great importance to all segments of the public, all CPAs, whether in public practice, government service, private employment or academic pursuits, should perform their work at a high level of professionalism.

A CPA should maintain and seek always to improve his competence in all areas of accountancy in which he engages. Satisfaction of the requirements for the CPA certificate is evidence of basic competence at the time the certificate is granted, but it does not justify an assumption that this competence is maintained without continuing effort. Further, it does not necessarily justify undertaking complex engagements without additional study and experience.

A CPA should not render professional services without being aware of, and complying with, the applicable technical standards. Moreover, since published technical standards can never cover the whole field of accountancy, he must keep broadly informed.

Observance of the rule on competence calls for a subjective determination by a CPA with respect to each engagement. Some engagements will require a higher level of knowledge, skill and judgment than others. Competence to deal with an unfamiliar problem may be acquired by research, study or consultation with a practitioner who has the necessary competence. If a CPA is unable to gain sufficient competence through these means, he should suggest, in fairness to his client and the public, the engagement of someone competent to perform the needed service, either independently or as an associate.

The standards referred to in the rules are elaborated and refined to meet changing conditions, and it is each CPA's responsibility to keep himself up to date in this respect.

RESPONSIBILITIES TO CLIENTS

A certified public accountant should be fair and candid with his clients and serve them to the best of his ability, with professional concern for their best interests, consistent with his responsibilities to the public.

As a professional person, the CPA should serve his clients with competence and with professional concern for their best interests. He must not permit his regard for a client's interest, however, to override his obligation to the public to maintain his independence, integrity and objectivity. The discharge of this dual responsibility to both clients and the public requires a high degree of ethical perception and conduct.

It is fundamental that the CPA hold in strict confidence all information concerning a client's affairs which he acquires in the course of his engagement. This does not mean, however, that he should acquiesce in a client's unwillingness to make disclosures in financial reports which are necessary to fair presentation.

Exploitation of relations with a client for personal advantage is improper. For example, acceptance of a commission from any vendor for recommending his product or service to a client is prohibited.

A CPA should be frank and straightforward with clients. While tact and diplomacy are desirable, a client should never be left in doubt about the CPA's position on any issue of significance. No truly professional man will subordinate his own judgment or conceal or modify his honest opinion merely to please. This admonition applies to all services including those related to management and tax problems.

When accepting an engagement, a CPA should bear in mind that he may find it necessary to resign if conflict arises on an important question of principle. In cases of irreconcilable difference, he will have to judge whether the importance of the matter requires such an action. In weighing this question, he can feel assured that the practitioner who is independent, fair and candid is the better respected for these qualities and will not lack opportunities for constructive service.

RESPONSIBILITIES TO COLLEAGUES

A certified public accountant should conduct himself in a manner which will promote cooperation and good relations among members of the profession.

The support of a profession by its members and their cooperation with one another are essential elements of professional character. The public confidence and respect which a CPA enjoys is largely the result of the cumulative accomplishments of all CPAs, past and present. It is, therefore, in the CPA's own interest, as well as that of the general public, to support the collective efforts of colleagues through professional societies and organizations and to deal with fellow practitioners in a manner which will not detract from their reputation and well-being.

Although the reluctance of a professional to give testimony that may be damaging to a colleague is understandable, the obligation of professional courtesy and fraternal consideration can never excuse lack of complete candor if the CPA is testifying as an expert witness in a judicial proceeding or properly constituted inquiry.

A CPA has the obligation to assist his fellows in complying with the Code of Professional Ethics and should also assist appropriate disciplinary authorities in enforcing the Code. To condone serious fault can be as bad as to commit it. It may be even worse, in fact, since some errors may result from ignorance rather than intent and, if let pass without action, will probably be repeated. In situations of this kind, the welfare of the public should be the guide to a member's action.

While the Code proscribes certain specific actions in the area of relationships with colleagues, it should be understood that these proscriptions do not define the limits of desirable intraprofessional conduct. Rather, such conduct encompasses the professional consideration and courtesies which each CPA would like to have fellow practitioners extend to him.

It is natural that a CPA will seek to develop his practice. However, in doing so he should not seek to displace another accountant in a client relationship, or act in any way that reflects negatively on fellow practitioners.

A CPA may, of course, provide services to those who request it, even though they may be served by another practitioner in another area of service, or he may succeed another practitioner at a client's request. In such circumstances it is desirable before accepting an engagement that the CPA who has been approached should advise the accountant already serving the client. Such action is indicated not only by considerations of professional courtesy but by good business judgment.

A client may sometimes request services requiring highly specialized knowledge. If the CPA lacks the expertise necessary to render such services, he should call upon a fellow practitioner for assistance or refer the entire engagement to another. Such assistance or referral brings to bear on the client's needs both the referring practitioner's knowledge of the client's affairs and the technical expertise of the specialist brought into the engagement. The rules encourage referrals by helping to protect the client relationships of the referring practitioner.

OTHER RESPONSIBILITIES AND PRACTICES

A certified public accountant should conduct himself in a manner which will enhance the stature of the profession and its ability to serve the public.

In light of the importance of their function, CPAs and their firms should have a keen consciousness of the public interest and the needs of society. Thus, they should support efforts to achieve equality of opportunity for all, regardless of race, religious background or sex, and should contribute to this goal by their own service relationships and employment practices.

The CPA is a beneficiary of the organization and character of his profession. Since he is seen as a representative of the profession by those who come in contact with him, he should behave honorably both in his personal and professional life and avoid any conduct that might erode public respect and confidence.

Solicitation to obtain clients is prohibited under the Rules of Conduct because it tends to lessen the professional independence toward clients which is essential to the best interests of the public. It may also induce an unhealthy rivalry within the profession and thus lessen the cooperation among members which is essential to advancing the state of the art of accounting and providing maximum service to the public.

Advertising, which is a form of solicitation, is also prohibited because it could encourage representations which might mislead the public and thereby reduce or destroy the profession's usefulness to society. However, a CPA should seek to establish a reputation for competence and character, and there are many acceptable means by which this can be done. For example, he may make himself known by public service, by civic and political activities, and by joining associations and clubs. It is desirable for him to share his knowledge with interested groups by accepting requests to make speeches and write articles. Whatever publicity occurs as a natural by-product of such activities is entirely proper. It would be wrong, however, for the CPA to initiate or embellish publicity.

Promotional practices, such as solicitation and advertising, tend to indicate a dominant interest in profit. In his work, the CPA should be motivated more by desire for excellence in performance than for material reward. This does not mean that he need be indifferent about compensation. Indeed, a professional man who cannot maintain a respectable standard of living is unlikely to inspire confidence or to enjoy sufficient peace of mind to do his best work.

In determining fees, a CPA may assess the degree of responsibility assumed by undertaking an engagement as well as the time, manpower and skills required to perform the service in conformity with the standards of the profession. He may also take into account the value of the service to the client, the customary charges of professional colleagues and other considerations. No single factor is necessarily controlling.

Clients have a right to know in advance what rates will be charged and approximately how much an engagement will cost. However, when professional judgments are involved, it is usually not possible to set a fair charge until an engagement has been completed. For this reason CPAs should state their fees for proposed engagements in the form of estimates which may be subject to change as the work progresses.

Other practices prohibited by the Rules of Conduct include using any firm designation or description which might be misleading, or practicing as a professional corporation or association which fails to comply with provisions established by Council to protect the public interest.

A member, while practicing public accounting, may not engage in a business or occupation which is incompatible therewith. While certain occupations are clearly incompatible with the practice of public accounting, the profession has never attempted to list them for in most cases the individual circumstances indicate whether there is a problem. For example, there would be a problem of incompatibility if a practicing CPA were to sell insurance or securities because these occupations involve solicitation and promotional activities which might be used to promote a public accounting practice. Moreover, they might, under some circumstances, jeopardize the CPA's independence.

Paying a commission is prohibited in order to eliminate the temptation to compensate anyone for referring a client. Receipt of a commission is proscribed since practitioners should look to the client, and not the others, for compensation for services rendered. The practice of paying a fee to a referring CPA irrespective of any service performed or responsibility assumed by him is proscribed because there is no justification for a CPA to share in a fee for accounting services where his sole contribution was to make a referral.

Over the years the vast majority of CPAs have endeavored to earn and maintain a reputation for competence, integrity and objectivity. The success of these efforts has been largely responsible for the wide public acceptance of accounting as an honorable profession. This acceptance is a valuable asset which should never be taken for granted. Every CPA should constantly strive to see that it continues to be deserved.

RULES OF CONDUCT

In the footnotes below, the references to specific rules or numbered Opinions indicate that revised sections are derived therefrom; where modifications have been made to the present rule or Opinion, it is noted. The reference to "prior rulings" indicates a position previously taken by the ethics division in response to a specific complaint or inquiry, but not previously published. The reference to "new" indicates a recommendation of the Code Restatement Committee not found in the present Code or prior rulings of the ethics division.

DEFINITIONS

The following definitions of terminology are applicable wherever such terminology is used in the rules and interpretations.

Client. The person(s) or entity which retains a member or his firm, engaged in the practice of public accounting, for the performance of professional services.

Council. The Council of the American Institute of Certified Public Accountants.

Enterprise. Any person(s) or entity, whether organized for profit or not, for which a CPA provides services.

Firm. A proprietorship, partnership or professional corporation or association engaged in the practice of public accounting, including individual partners or shareholders thereof.

Financial statements. Statements and footnotes related thereto that purport to show financial position which relates to a point in time or changes in financial position which relate to a period of time, and statements which use a cash or other incomplete basis of accounting. Balance sheets, statements of income, statements of retained earnings, statements of changes in financial position and statements of changes in owners' equity are financial statements.

Incidental financial data included in management advisory services reports to support recommendations to a client, and tax returns and supporting schedules do not, for this purpose, constitute financial statements; and the statement, affidavit or signature or preparers required on tax returns neither constitutes an opinion on financial statements nor requires a disclaimer of such opinion.

Institute. The American Institute of Certified Public Accountants.

Interpretations of rules of conduct. Pronouncements issued by the Division of Professional Ethics to provide guidelines as to the scope and application of the Rules of Conduct.

Member. A member, associate member or international associate of the American Institute of Certified Public Accountants.

Practice of public accounting. Holding out to be a CPA or public accountant and at the same time performing for a client one or more types of services rendered by public accountants. The term shall not be limited by a more restrictive definition which might be found in the accountancy law under which a member practices.

Professional services. One or more types of services performed in the practice of public accounting.

APPLICABILITY OF RULES

The Institute's Code of Professional Ethics derives its authority from the bylaws of the Institute which provide that the Trial Board may, after a hearing, admonish, suspend or expel a member who is found guilty of infringing any of the bylaws or any provisions of the Rules of Conduct.[1]

The Rules of Conduct which follow apply to all services performed in the practice of public accounting including tax[2] and management advisory services[3] except (a) where the wording of the rule indicates otherwise and (b) that a member who is practicing outside the United States will not be subject to discipline for departing from any of the rules stated herein so long as his conduct is in accord with the rules of the organized accounting profession in the country in which he is practicing.[4] However, where a member's name is associated with financial statements in such a manner as to imply that he is acting as an independent public accountant and under circumstances that would entitle the reader to assume that United States practices were followed, he must comply with the requirements of Rules 202 and 203.[5]

A member may be held responsible for compliance with the Rules of Conduct by all persons associated with him in the practice of public accounting who are either under his supervision or are his partners or shareholders in the practice.[6]

A member engaged in the practice of public accounting must observe all the Rules of Conduct. A member not engaged in the practice of public accounting must observe only Rules 102 and 501 since all other Rules of Conduct relate solely to the practice of public accounting.[7]

A member shall not permit others to carry out on his behalf, either with or without compensation, acts which, if carried out by the member, would place him in violation of the Rules of Conduct.[8]

---

[1] Bylaw Section 7.4.
[2] Opinion No. 13.
[3] Opinion No. 14.
[4] Prior ruling.
[5] Rules 2.01, 2.02, 2.03 and prior rulings.
[6] New.
[7] New.
[8] Opinion No. 2.

INDEPENDENCE, INTEGRITY AND OBJECTIVITY

Rule 101 — Independence. A member or a firm of which he is a partner or shareholder shall not express an opinion on financial statements of an enterprise unless he and his firm are independent with respect to such enterprise.[9] Independence will be considered to be impaired if, for example:

A. During the period of his professional engagement, or at the time of expressing his opinion, he or his firm

1. Had or was committed to acquire any direct or material indirect financial interest in the enterprise;[10] or

2. Had any joint closely held business investment with the enterprise or any officer, director or principal stockholder thereof which was material in relation to his or his firm's net worth;[11] or

3. Had any loan to or from the enterprise or any officer, director or principal stockholder thereof.[12] This latter proscription does not apply to the following loans from a financial institution when made under normal lending procedures, terms and requirements:

   (a) Loans obtained by a member or his firm which are not material in relation to the net worth of such borrower.

   (b) Home mortgages.

   (c) Other secured loans, except loans guaranteed by a member's firm which are otherwise unsecured.[13]

B. During the period covered by the financial statements, during the period of the professional engagement or at the time of expressing an opinion, he or his firm

1. Was connected with the enterprise as a promoter, underwriter or voting trustee, a director or officer or in any capacity equivalent to that of a member of management or of an employee;[14] or

2. Was a trustee of any trust or executor or administrator of any estate if such trust or estate had a direct or material indirect financial interest in the enterprise; or was a trustee for any pension or profit-sharing trust of the enterprise.[15]

The above examples are not intended to be all-inclusive.

---

[9]Rule 1.01 ("shareholder" added to recognize corporate practice).
[10]Rule 1.01.
[11]Prior rulings.
[12]Prior rulings.
[13]Opinion No. 19.
[14]Rule 1.01 (present Rule 1.01 uses the phrase "key employee").
[15]Prior rulings. In order that a member may arrange an orderly transition of his relationship with clients, section B2 of Rule 101 relating to trusteeships and executorships will not become effective until two years following the adoption of these Rules of Conduct.

Rule 102 — Integrity and objectivity. A member shall not knowingly misrepresent facts, and when engaged in the practice of public accounting, including the rendering of tax and management advisory service, shall not subordinate his judgment to others.[16] In tax practice, a member may resolve doubt in favor of his client as long as there is reasonable support for his position.[17]

COMPETENCE AND TECHNICAL STANDARDS

Rule 201 — Competence. A member shall not undertake any engagement which he or his firm cannot reasonably expect to complete with professional competence.[18]

Rule 202 — Auditing standards. A member shall not permit his name to be associated with financial statements in such a manner as to imply that he is acting as an independent public accountant unless he has complied with the applicable generally accepted auditing standards* promulgated by the Institute. Statements on Auditing Procedure issued by the Institute's committee on auditing procedure are, for purposes of this rule, considered to be interpretations of the generally accepted auditing standards, and departures from such statements must be justified by those who do not follow them.[19]

Rule 203 — Accounting principles. A member shall not express an opinion that financial statements are presented in conformity with generally accepted accounting principles if such statements contain any departure from an accounting principle promulgated by the body designated by Council to establish such principles which has a material effect on the statements taken as a whole, unless the member can demonstrate that due to unusual circumstances the financial statements would otherwise have been misleading. In such cases his report must describe the departure, the approximate effects thereof, if practicable, and the reasons why compliance with the principle would result in a misleading statement.[20]

Rule 204 — Forecasts. A member shall not permit his name to be used in conjunction with any forecast of future transactions in a manner which may lead to the belief that the member vouches for the achievability of the forecast.[21]

---

[16]New.
[17]Opinion No. 13.
[18]New.
*Ten generally accepted auditing standards are listed in Appendix A, page 90.
[19]New (replaces Rules 2.01-2.03).
[20]New (replaces Rules 2.01-2.03).
[21]Restatement of Rule 2.04.

RESPONSIBILITIES TO CLIENTS

Rule 301 — Confidential client information. A member shall not disclose any confidential information obtained in the course of a professional engagement except with the consent of the client.[22]

The rule shall not be construed (a) to relieve a member of his obligation under Rules 202 and 203, (b) to affect in any way his compliance with a validly issued subpoena or summons enforceable by order of a court, (c) to prohibit review of a member's professional practices as a part of voluntary quality review under Institute authorization or (d) to preclude a member from responding to any inquiry made by the ethics division or Trial Board of the Institute, by a duly constituted investigative or disciplinary body of a state CPA society, or under state statutes.[23]

Members of the ethics division and Trial Board of the Institute and professional practice reviewers under Institute authorization shall not disclose any confidential client information which comes to their attention from members in disciplinary proceedings or otherwise in carrying out their official responsibilities. However, this prohibition shall not restrict the exchange of information with an aforementioned duly constituted investigative or disciplinary body.[24]

Rule 302 — Contingent fees.[25] Professional services shall not be offered or rendered under an arrangement whereby no fee will be charged unless a specified finding or result is attained, or where the fee is otherwise contingent upon the findings or results of such services. However, a member's fees may vary depending, for example, on the complexity of the service rendered.[26]

Fees are not regarded as being contingent if fixed by courts or other public authorities or, in tax matters, if determined based on the results of judicial proceedings or the findings of governmental agencies.[27]

RESPONSIBILITIES TO COLLEAGUES

Rule 401 — Encroachment.[28] A member shall not endeavor to provide a person or entity with a professional service which is currently provided by another public accountant except:

1. He may respond to a request for a proposal to render services and may furnish service to those who request it.[29] However, if an

---

[22]Restatement of Rule 1.03.
[23]Prior rulings.
[24]New.
[25]Restatement of Rule 1.04.
[26]New.
[27]Rule 1.04.
[28]Restatement of Rule 5.01.
[29]Rule 5.01.

audit client of another independent public accountant requests a member to provide professional advice on accounting or auditing matters in connection with an expression of opinion on financial statements, the member must first consult with the other accountant to ascertain that the member is aware of all the available relevant facts.[30]

2. Where a member is required to express an opinion on combined or consolidated financial statements which include a subsidiary, branch or other component audited by another independent public accountant, he may insist on auditing any such component which in his judgment is necessary to warrant the expression of his opinion.[31]

A member who receives an engagement for services by referral from another public accountant shall not accept the client's request to extend his service beyond the specific engagement without first notifying the referring accountant, nor shall he seek to obtain any additional engagement from the client.[32]

Rule 402 — Offers of employment. A member in public practice shall not make a direct or indirect offer of employment to an employee of another public accountant on his own behalf or that of his client without first informing such accountant. This rule shall not apply if the employee of his own initiative or in response to a public advertisement applies for employment.[33]

OTHER RESPONSIBILITIES AND PRACTICES

Rule 501 — Acts discreditable. A member shall not commit an act discreditable to the profession.[34]

Rule 502 — Solicitation and advertising. A member shall not seek to obtain clients by solicitation.[35] Advertising is a form of solicitation and is prohibited.[36]

Rule 503 — Commissions. A member shall not pay a commission to obtain a client, nor shall he accept a commission for a referral to a client of products or services of others.[37] This rule shall not prohibit payments for the purchase of an accounting practice[38] or retirement payments to individuals formerly engaged in the practice of public accounting or payments to their heirs or estates.[39]

---

[30]New.
[31]Opinion No. 20.
[32]Rule 5.02 restated to include prior rulings.
[33]Rule 5.03, "or that of his client" added.
[34]Rule 1.02.
[35]Rule 3.02.
[36]Rule 3.01.
[37]Restatement of Rule 3.04.
[38]Prior rulings.
[39]Opinion No. 6.

Rule 504 — Incompatible occupations. A member who is engaged in the practice of public accounting shall not concurrently engage in any business or occupation which impairs his objectivity in rendering professional services or serves as a feeder to his practice.[40]

Rule 505 — Form of practice and name. A member may practice public accounting, whether as an owner or employee, only in the form of a proprietorship, a partnership or a professional corporation whose characteristics conform to resolutions of Council.[41]   (See Appendix B, page 91.)

A member shall not practice under a firm name which includes any fictitious name, indicates specialization or is misleading as to the type of organization (proprietorship, partnership or corporation).[42] However, names of one or more past partners or shareholders may be included in the firm name of a successor partnership or corporation.[43] Also, a partner surviving the death or withdrawal of all other partners may continue to practice under the partnership name for up to two years after becoming a sole practitioner.[44]

A firm may not designate itself as "Members of the American Institute of Certified Public Accountants" unless all of its partners or shareholders are members of the Institute.[45]

APPENDIX A

GENERALLY ACCEPTED AUDITING STANDARDS
as adopted by the membership in 1948 and 1949

General standards

1. The examination is to be performed by a person or persons having adequate technical training and proficiency as an auditor.

2. In all matters relating to the assignment, an independence in mental attitude is to be maintained by the auditor or auditors.

3. Due professional care is to be exercised in the performance of the examination and the preparation of the report.

---

[40]Restatement of Rule 4.04.
[41]Rule 4.06.
[42]Prior rulings.
[43]Rule 4.02.
[44]Prior rulings.
[45]Rule 4.01.

Standards of field work

1. The work is to be adequately planned and assistants, if any, are to be properly supervised.

2. There is to be a proper study and evaluation of the existing internal control as a basis for reliance thereon and for the determination of the resultant extent of the tests to which auditing procedures are to be restricted.

3. Sufficient competent evidential matter is to be obtained through inspection, observation, inquiries and confirmations to afford a reasonable basis for an opinion regarding the financial statements under examination.

Standards of reporting

1. The report shall state whether the financial statements are presented in accordance with generally accepted principles of accounting.

2. The report shall state whether such principles have been consistently observed in the current period in relation to the preceding period.

3. Informative disclosures in the financial statements are to be regarded as reasonably adequate unless otherwise stated in the report.

4. The report shall either contain an expression of opinion regarding the financial statements, taken as a whole, or an assertion to the effect that an opinion cannot be expressed. When an overall opinion cannot be expressed, the reasons therefor should be stated. In all cases where an auditor's name is associated with financial statements, the report should contain a clear-cut indication of the character of the auditor's examination, if any, and the degree of responsibility he is taking.

APPENDIX B

The following resolution of Council was approved at the spring meeting of Council on May 6, 1969:

RESOLVED, that members may be officers, directors, stockholders, representatives or agents of a corporation offering services of a type performed by public accountants only when the professional corporation or association has the following characteristics:

1. *Name.* The name under which the professional corporation or association renders professional services shall contain only the names of one or more of the present or former shareholders or of

partners who were associated with a predecessor accounting firm. Impersonal or fictitious names, as well as names which indicate a speciality, are prohibited.

2. *Purpose.* The professional corporation or association shall not provide services that are incompatible with the practice of public accounting.

3. *Ownership.* All shareholders of the corporation or association shall be persons duly qualified to practice as a certified public accountant in a state or territory of the United States or the District of Columbia. Shareholders shall at all times own their shares in their own right, and shall be the beneficial owners of the equity capital ascribed to them.

4. *Transfer of Shares.* Provision shall be made requiring any shareholder who ceases to be eligible to be a shareholder to dispose of all of his shares within a reasonable period to a person qualified to be a shareholder or to the corporation or association.

5. *Directors and Officers.* The principal executive officer shall be a shareholder and a director, and to the extent possible, all other directors and officers shall be certified public accountants. Lay directors and officers shall not exercise any authority whatsoever over professional matters.

6. *Conduct.* The right to practice as a corporation or association shall not change the obligation of its shareholders, directors, officers and other employees to comply with the standards of professional conduct established by the American Institute of Certified Public Accountants.

7. *Liability.* The stockholders of professional corporations or associations shall be jointly and severally liable for the acts of a corporation or association, or its employees — except where professional liability insurance is carried, or capitalization is maintained, in amounts deemed sufficient to offer adequate protection to the public. Liability shall not be limited by the formation of subsidiary or affiliated corporations or associations each with its own limited and unrelated liability.

In a report approved by Council at the fall 1969 meeting, the Board of Directors recommended that professional liability insurance or capitalization in the amount of $50,000 per shareholder/officer and professional employee to a maximum of $2,000,000 would offer adequate protection to the public. Members contemplating the formation of a corporation under this rule should ascertain that no further modifications in the characteristics have been made.

7. Symposium on Ethics in Corporate Financial Reporting*

John C. Burton†

Corporate financial reporting in the United States is almost certainly the best in the world. Most corporate financial officers have grown up in a climate where full and fair disclosure is normal business practice, and the reports of an overwhelming majority of publicly held corporations reflect a conscientious effort to tell the corporate story "like it is," at least within the framework of the conventional accounting model.

Despite this generally salutary record, a number of situations have existed in recent years which gave evidence of less than good faith reporting, and these cases have received notoriety far out of proportion to their number. Similarly, there have been cases of less than totally professional practice in the auditing and analytical use of financial information which have been brought to public attention either through the courts or by regulatory authorities.

In addition, there have been criticisms of the basic accounting model and its application in some circumstances where it was not felt to describe business activities adequately, and there have been several suggestions that the historical accounting approach did not present sufficient information on which to base investment decisions.

In the light of these challenges, the four principal organizations professionally involved in corporate financial reporting concluded that a discussion of ethics in reporting would serve a useful purpose in identifying the relevant issues in this changing area and in considering them jointly.

Accordingly, leading members of the American Institute of CPA's, the Financial Analysts Federation, the Financial Executives Institute and the Robert Morris Associates gathered at Absecon, New Jersey, in mid-November for a two-day symposium. Also present were representatives of the Securities and Exchange Commission, the New York Stock Exchange and the legal profession.

Three years previously, the same four organizations sponsored the first Seaview symposium on conflicts and challenges in corporate

---

*From *The Journal of Accountancy* (January, 1972), pp. 46-50. Copyright (1972) by the American Institute of Certified Public Accountants, Inc. Reprinted by permission of the AICPA.

†John C. Burton, Ph.D., CPA, is Chief Accountant, Securities & Exchange Commission, Washington, D.C.

financial reporting (see *J of A*, Jan. 68, p. 33, for summary report), and from that meeting came significantly improved communication among the groups.

OBJECTIVES OF THE SYMPOSIUM

The second symposium, like the first, was not designed to produce any legislative result. No formal group report was contemplated or issued. The objective of the program was to provide a forum where ideas about ethics in reporting could be discussed and new ideas for the improved performance of the reporting process could germinate. In this connection, a number of background papers were prepared which were read by the participants in advance of the meeting. The symposium itself, after a keynote address by Dr. Clarence Walton, president of The Catholic University of America, was devoted entirely to discussion under the leadership of five academicians.

This report, therefore, can represent only an outline of the important areas covered, an identification of those areas where apparent consensus existed and a discussion of the various points of view expressed where these views differed. As in any interpretation, the reporter's senses may perceive things differently than some of the other participants, and this report therefore does not constitute an approved summary.

Later in the spring, an edited transcript of the discussions will be published, together with the background papers and the texts of two cases written to focus discussion of some of the issues. This will represent a far more comprehensive summary of the ideas and points of view expressed.

KEYNOTE REMARKS

The stage for the discussions was challengingly set by Clarence Walton in his keynote remarks. He developed the changing philosophical views concerning the role of the corporation and its management in society, starting with the representationalist view which held that the corporation and its management represented the stockholders and were responsible to them alone; this was the historical and legal view of the entity. In contrast, he identified the trusteeship concept which implies that a corporation holds a franchise from society and that management must therefore take a view of a larger universe that transcends stockholder interests. This latter concept which he perceived as dominant today has implications for both business and reporting decisions and these were considered frequently in the discussions at the symposium.

Within this framework, he also identified the essential criteria of an ethical system. These included freedom of choice, the assumption of rationality, a system of sanctions so that rewards and punishments are attached to ethical effort, and a monitoring system with the ability to exercise sanctions. These criteria also were returned to frequently in the consideration of the ethical system associated with financial reporting.

RESPONSIBILITY FOR REPORTS

The first substantive ethical issue to be considered by the group was the possible conflict of interest between the decision-making role of management and the financial reporting role. In two of the background papers, authors had suggested that there was an ethical problem arising from this joint role that management plays since it could not impartially report on its own achievements. The possibility of an outside "public reporter" was considered, and the public accountant was generally felt to be the most likely to fill this role if it developed. A substantial majority of the group, however, felt that the responsibility for reporting on corporate activities should remain with management subject to the review of the independent auditor as to the fairness of the financial statements. This conclusion was based on the ground that management reporting had largely worked well, that an outside reporter could not possibly be as fully aware of the activities of the business as could management and that even the establishment of the public accountant as public reporter would not assure the absence of ethical conflict due to the fee relationship existing between the auditor and the corporation.

Most participants seemed to agree that altering the basic structure of responsibility for reporting would represent an overreaction, and perhaps an ineffective one, to the small number of cases in which unethical and misleading reporting had occurred. Such a solution would require a definition of who was responsible for a firm's information system and what legal responsibilities would fall on the public reporter, both difficult problems. Substantial additional reporting expense would also probably be incurred if this responsibility were turned over to an outside party, and considerable doubt was expressed as to whether any benefits gained would warrant this cost.

While there were still a few participants who believed that auditors would not have to expand their work substantially to become public reporters and that their independent professional outlook would significantly improve the quality of reporting, the majority seemed to feel that a more modest change in the outside auditor's responsibility would mend the few situations where reports failed to reflect the reality of the firm's activities. The suggestion was made that if the auditor accepted responsibility for and attested to the fairness of financial reports rather than simply to their conformity with generally accepted accounting principles, most of the dramatic cases of using an accounting formula to misstate results would be eliminated.

TIMELINESS AND INTERIM REPORTS

This discussion led to consideration of the timeliness of disclosure and the extent to which reliance on a public reporter or increased responsibility for public accountants would delay corporate reports to the public. Financial managers felt that the potential for delay was considerable if outsiders were to have either primary or audit responsibility for interim reports. Analysts emphasized the need for reliability in quarterly reports and felt that auditors should be associated with them in some fashion even if a full audit opinion were not included. They felt, and the auditors present seemed to agree, that the acceptance of some audit responsibility for interim reports should not require large amounts of additional audit work or any substantial delay in the publication of results. No clear consensus was reached in this area.

"FAIRNESS" AND ACCOUNTING PRINCIPLES

The suggestion that auditors be made responsible for fairness of statements as well as conformity to generally accepted accounting principles led to a discussion of both the definition of fairness and the definition of accounting principles. Here a major controversy arose. One part of the group essentially harked back to Dr. Walton's hypothesis that an ethical system required a dimension of freedom to be operative. From this, it was argued that the rigorous and detailed definition of accounting principles would tend to eliminate ethics from the reporting process and lead to "letter of the law" reporting which would not reflect the realities of the business in some cases. This group seemed to prefer to define fairness in terms of professional judgment about the adequacy of reports in reflecting economic reality, and by implication to prefer a common law approach whereby accounting propriety would be defined through a series of case decisions about appropriate accounting under various factual situations as compared to the Roman law approach where a fixed code of principles would be developed with the intent of solving problems in advance through detailed proscription.

On the other hand, a significant group argued that when you isolate fairness from generally accepted accounting principles, you have nothing; without defined principles, fairness becomes a purely subjective term and not subject to analysis or enforcement. This group argued that the route to improved reporting was a more comprehensive and specific definition of accounting principles which would then represent fairness as generally agreed upon by an authoritative professional body.

After considerable discussion, a consensus seemed to emerge that brought together these views. It was generally felt that the definition of acceptable accounting principles was a step toward fairness of presentation, and that the comparability of various statements which resulted was part of that fairness. At the same time, it seemed to be felt by most participants that a total definition of accounting principles that would meet subjective ethical canons of fairness was not possible due to the diversity of situations existing in the economic world. While such steps as defining accounting principles by industry might be useful, there remained an overall criterion of fairness which could be applied on a common sense basis by a professional accountant which could not be totally supplanted by any institutional or legislative means. Thus, the idea that auditors express an opinion on such overall fairness as well as conformity with established principles retained substantial support. At the same time there was general agreement that the process of definition taking place in the Accounting Principles Board should be continued.

PUBLISHED FORECASTS AND FINANCIAL REPORTING

Another major subject considered at some length in the symposium was whether or not the publication of historical financial statements constituted sufficient financial disclosure by corporations. In this connection the group addressed itself to the comment of one of the paper preparers that one principal objective of good corporate reporting to the financial community is the minimization of surprise. There

seemed fairly general agreement with this proposition and its implementation led to a discussion of the role of published forecasts in
financial reporting.

This topic had been discussed at the first Seaview symposium
and at that time there seemed general distrust of the whole idea. In
three years a significant change in viewpoint could be detected.
Among the participants, the analysts seemed generally in agreement
that public forecasting was an idea whose time had come, while corporate executives, although not agreeing that regular published forecasts were the right answer, did concur that financial management
had a responsibility to avoid surprises and that the publication of
explicit forecasts was one of the ways of meeting this responsibility.
Several executives, however, preferred the approach of giving assistance to analysts so that their forecasts were not too far away from
reality as currently perceived by the corporation.

There was considerable debate as to the appropriate form for
forecasted financial data. Some people seemed to advocate a full
set of projected financial statements for a period of time into the
future while others suggested a more general forecast of a range of
earnings per share and the identification of the crucial events which
management anticipated occurring in subsequent periods.

There was considerable dismay expressed over the potential legal
liabilities that might accrue in any scheme requiring the publication
of explicit forecasts as a regular part of financial reporting. In this
connection Commissioner James Needham, of the Securities and Exchange Commission, commented that the Commission was rethinking
its historical opposition to the publication of forecasts in registration
statements and other published documents. He also indicated that
he recognized that consideration of the problems of liability was an
important part of the rethinking of this and other proposed adjustments in financial reporting.

There was some discussion as well regarding the role of the auditor
in corporate forecasts and reference was made to Great Britain, where
the auditor does associate himself with forecasts but does not take
responsibility for the assumptions on which they are based. Auditors
indicated that they were thinking seriously about their possible role
in this area but there seemed to be no strong sentiment among the group
that an auditor's attestation would add significantly to the reliability
of a forecast.

While it was apparent from the discussion that total agreement was
far from being achieved on the subject of published forecasts, there was
considerably greater feeling in favor of some form of forecasting

than had existed three years before. In considering appropriate steps to take to build on the discussion at Seaview, there was general agreement that one logical step was to pursue the forecasting issue in a systematic fashion at a subsequent meeting of representatives of the four sponsoring organizations. Such a meeting might be charged with the responsibility of developing recommendations for the SEC and the public as to the forms public forecasting might take and the risks associated with it, including the problems of competitive disadvantage, legal liability and behavioral constraints on management touched upon at the symposium.

DEVELOPMENT OF INCREASED PROFESSIONALISM

The papers and the discussions at Seaview also urged the development of increased professionalism both in the preparation and use of financial reports. It was agreed that professional competence in both areas was an important part of the ethical system covering financial reporting, since the basic qualities of honesty and integrity must be placed in an appropriate setting if they are to be operationally effective.

In this connection, it was noted that the AICPA code of ethics requires members to adhere to technical standards and a proposed revision of it greatly expands these requirements. The current codes of ethics of the Financial Analysts Federation and Robert Morris Associates tend to emphasize relationships among members rather than professional competence. It was felt that all three codes might well be supplemented to include definitions of professional objectives and some statements that would define the parameters of competence in each professional area. In addition, standards of performance in the demonstration of competence might be articulated in the codes such that an inadequate effort could be identified and criticized.

It was also observed that the Financial Executives Institute at this point in time did not have a published code of ethics, although representatives of that organization said that one was under consideration. The feeling was expressed that the FEI and the other groups might well consider the development of an ethical code covering all corporate reporting which would be promulgated both to the professionals in the area and to the chief executive officers of corporations who are ultimately responsible for the reports of their enterprises. This code would not replace the codes of individual organizations since they have more than one purpose and specialized interest to consider, but it would blend their joint professional competence in the reporting process.

A SURVEILLANCE SYSTEM

A final area related to professionalism that received considerable attention was suggested by the keynote speaker's reference to the need for sanctions and a monitoring system in connection with any ethical system. The group discussed at some length the need for additional surveillance over ethical practice in financial reporting. Concern was expressed that the temptation to indulge in unethical conduct tended to be inversely related to corporate size and success, and it was felt that any surveillance system would have to include the entire range of public reporting corporations. On the user side, examples of unprofessional use of financial reports would also be difficult to detect.

There was also considerable discussion related to the distinction between ethical and legal standards for defining good practice in the reporting sphere. Some participants felt that only through the development of legal standards and enforcement through the legal process could sound ethical practice be satisfactorily achieved. They pointed out that once ethical standards became norms they would be applied by the courts and would become part of the legal structure of the reporting environment. Recent cases and decisions have supported the view that where professional standards lag behind public expectations the latter may serve as the basis for determining both legal liability and ethical judgments as to what represents the proper course of action.

Those who decided to rely solely upon legal sanctions and the regulatory surveillance system now in existence indicated that they felt a need for an institutional vehicle by which users of financial statements could complain about what they consider to be unethical practice. It was agreed that the accounting profession's institution of practice had not been effective in this area and several analysts believed that there should be some means by which reports that met technical standards but not ethical standards of completeness and economic accuracy could be brought to the public's attention. The Financial Analysts Federation's current procedure of presenting an award to good annual reports was seen as a step in the right direction but a need was also felt for applying sanctions to inadequate reporting as well. Symposium participants seemed sympathetic to this idea, but there were no concrete suggestions for instituting a compliant mechanism, such as a review body or a professional ombudsman. It was pointed out that at present many such reporting deficiencies are brought to the attention of the public through the press, particularly by a few reporters who regularly mention accounting matters in their columns.

SUGGESTIONS FOR THE FUTURE

At the conclusion of the symposium, there was general agreement among the participants that it had been successful in achieving its objectives. Several suggestions were made for the continuation of the communication process among groups. One of these advocated the creation of a Council on Corporate Reporting constituted of four to six representatives of each of the sponsoring organizations, which would meet on a continuing basis to discuss general and specific issues and to make recommendations. Another suggestion was for more frequent symposiums devoted to more specific topics. The consideration of these and other ideas was left to the symposium steering committee for the development of recommendations as to further activities.

Commissioner Needham gave the symposium a charge for future action when he indicated a general recognition of a desire for change in financial reporting and the need for the organizations both to define their respective roles in the process of change and to commit themselves to assume responsibility for a higher level of conduct in day-to-day business affairs. He urged the groups not to wait two or three years for their next symposium, and stated the interest of the SEC in specific recommendations that might arise from this or other joint efforts since he felt that the private sector really has a better capacity than government for dealing with problems of the sort discussed at Seaview.

As was apparent from the objectives of the symposium, its success must be measured not in terms of the specific output but in terms of what follows. The final measure of value must await continuing steps for the structuring of continuity and change in corporate financial reporting.

SECTION B

Independence

Independence is the *raison d'être* of auditing. Yet the auditor finds himself constantly struggling to define precisely and to provide guidelines for the application of independence. Has the profession made significant progress since the turn of the century in providing a clearly formulated statement of independence? Schlosser and others express doubt that progress can be made in settling issues such as the impact of management services on independence until the concept of independence is more fully defined.

In the second article, R. J. Patten and J. R. Nuckols, Jr. consider various solutions to the management services issue and endorse a proposal which declares that the performance of management services for an audit client is incompatible with independence.

The compatibility of tax practice and auditing has not been previously considered a crucial issue by auditors or critics. However, according to W. L. Raby, there may be cause for concern when the auditor also acts as tax advocate for his client. Raby's article points to possible solutions to this problem.

8. An Historical Approach to the Concept of Independence*

Robert E. Schlosser, and Associates†

The concept of an independent audit has begun to enter a very crucial period. Many people have grave doubts that an auditor can be independent when performing various management advisory services for firms which also have engaged him to conduct the audit. While the pro's and con's of this basic disagreement grow, history indicates that there has never been formulated a concept of independence from which the controversy can meaningfully be debated. Thus, it is the purpose of this paper to assemble a summary of this historical development of independence as interpreted by various groups of individuals. As an initial step, it is necessary to identify independence and review its crucial importance.

THE FUNCTION OF THE INDEPENDENT AUDIT

Financial statements are one of the principal ways of obtaining information about a business enterprise. Prepared by management, these statements are relied upon by a great variety of people, including shareholders (present and potential), employees and government agencies. Since management does prepare the statements, however, it is necessary to have some way of insuring that they do perform their function of providing relevant, reasonably accurate and unbiased data in accordance with generally accepted accounting principles. To meet this need, the "independent-audit" was developed.

Through an independent audit it is hoped that the major portion of any possible bias introduced by management will be removed. Thus, the crucial element in the audit is that the person(s) performing the review be free from those influences which would impede his ability to detect and eliminate management bias. This, then, is the essence of independence — an objective viewpoint which is free from influence by an interested party. One can see that this concept is necessary for the audit to perform its function, and that unless the audit performs

---

*From *The New York Certified Public Accountant* (July, 1969), pp. 517–527. Reprinted by permission of the New York State Society of Certified Public Accountants.

†Robert E. Schlosser, CPA, is Director, Professional Development Division, American Institute of Certified Public Accountants.

its function, the financial statements may not satisfactorily discharge their important information-providing responsibility.

Two Concepts of Independence

The concept of independence can be considered in two ways: (1) theoretical, and (2) practical. This is a crucial distinction to be made, because independence is often considered as a state of mind, a viewpoint which is appealing on a theoretical level but defies practical measurement, since it is virtually impossible to look into a person's mind. The failure to make a distinction between these two possible ways of considering the concept may be at the heart of many controversies over the subject. This distinction will be maintained for the discussion in the following sections.

The history of the development of independence will be traced through the points of view of the American Institute of Certified Public Accountants (AICPA), the Securities and Exchange Commission (SEC), and third parties not directly related to these two bodies. All three groups have established positions on this concept which will be compared and contrasted.

The AICPA's View of Independence

The AICPA's definition of independence has not changed over time, though it was not specifically stated until 1947. Independence is and has been, according to the AICPA, a state of mind, an attitude of impartiality concerning the findings which the auditor brings to light in issuing his opinion on financial statements. This state of mind permits the auditor to render a judgment uncolored by any self-interest which may influence his opinion.[1]

The method of assuring that this state of mind existed was to require the auditor to focus his attention on any material misstatements, either omissions or commissions or any material departure from generally accepted accounting principles.

The underlying assumption was that independence would exist if the above rules were satisfied, or, at least if they were not satisfied, no material harm would result. This was evidenced by the Institute's 1947 statement which concludes: "Rules of conduct can only deal with objective standards and cannot assure independence. Independence

---

[1]John Carey, *Professional Ethics of Certified Public Accountants* (New York: American Institute of Certified Public Accountants, 1956), pp. 28–32.

is an attitude of the mind, much deeper than the visible display of standards."[2] In other words, since independence was a state of mind, one cannot establish it in an absolute sense but can only design rules which may be useful in deciding whether there is a high probability that independence does exist. The Institute's revised rules on professional conduct in 1950[3] and 1961[4] did not significantly broaden this concept of independence.

The public image — an element of independence. The revised rules of conduct, published in 1965,[5] coupled with Opinion Twelve,[6] advanced the development of independence from one of rules which estimated a probable state of mind to one of a general and more direct approach. While independence was still considered to be a state of mind in the revised rules, Opinion Twelve added a new and important dimension to determine the existence of independence. This opinion states that

> a member or associate, before expressing his opinion on financial statements, has the responsibility of assessing his relationships with an enterprise to determine whether, in the circumstances, he might expect his opinion to be considered independent, objective and unbiased by one who had knowledge of all the facts.[7]

In other words, the cornerstone of determining the probability of independence existing lies in how the accountant appears to one who has all the facts. For the first time, the Institute freed itself from relying solely upon specific prohibitions and in its place presented a general statement that all factors must be considered in determining the existence of independence, relying especially on the *appearance* of the situation.

There is further evidence for this last point early in Opinion Twelve, where the "reasonable observer's" reaction to a situation is emphasized as the test of the existence of independence.[8] Of course, it must be added that one can never determine a state of mind, but, through Rule Twelve, the Institute attempts to guard against third parties lacking confidence in a specific situation.

From this discussion, we can see that the AICPA was relying basically upon a theoretical definition of independence until it published

---

[2]*Ibid.*, p. 31.
[3]*Ibid.*, pp. 213–216.
[4]American Institute of Certified Public Accountants, "By-Laws: Rules of Professional Conduct" (New York: AICPA, 1961), pp. 15 & 16.
[5]American Institute of Certified Public Accountants, "By-Laws: Code of Professional Ethics" (New York: AICPA, 1965), pp. 30–31.
[6]*Ibid.*, pp. 49–51.
[7]*Ibid.*, pp. 49–50.
[8]*Ibid.*, p. 49.

its 1965 ruling and opinion, at which time it began to deal in a realistic manner with the practical aspects of the concept.

THE SEC'S VIEW OF INDEPENDENCE

In considering the SEC's view of independence, on the other hand, it must be kept in mind that the Commission grew out of the security abuses of the 1920's and therefore has as its primary purpose the protection of present and potential investors. To help insure that companies will not publish misleading information, great emphasis is placed on the validity of financial statements. This emphasis has, in turn, made the concept of independence very important in the eyes of this ruling body. Therefore, it is not surprising to see the idea of independence treated in a very strict and objective manner.

Louis H. Rappaport states, in his book, *S.E.C. Accounting Practices and Procedure,* that the

> SEC emphasizes the specific relationships between an accountant and his client which give rise to a presumption of lack of independence — the SEC will not recognize an accountant as independent if any of the proscribed relationships exist.

Moreover he asserts that "the Institute (AICPA) emphasizes the fact of independence — the state of mind which the word denotes."[9] The question which must be answered here is one of difference. Does the Securities and Exchange Commission have a different view of independence than that of the AICPA, and, if so, how do they differ?

It has already been pointed out that as of March, 1965 the *Code of Professional Ethics* of the AICPA was amended so that Article 1, Section 1.01 is quite similar to Regulation S-X.[10] Even with this change, it still is essential to answer the question at hand, because only then will one be able to assess whether the SEC really had a view of independence different from that of the AICPA.

The part of Regulation S-X dealing with independence is rule 2-01 adopted by the Commission on February 21, 1940.[11]

> (a) The Commission will not recognize any certified public accountant or public accountant as independent who is not in fact independent. For

---

[9]Louis H. Rappaport, *SEC Accounting Practices and Procedures* (New York: The Ronald Press Co., 1966), p. 22.6.

[10]American Institute of Certified Public Accountants, "By-Laws: Code of Professional Ethics" (New York: AICPA, 1965), pp. 30-31.

[11]Security and Exchange Commission, Accounting Release No. 81, *Independence of Certifying Accountants — Compilation of Representative Administrative Rulings in Cases Involving the Independence of Accountants.*

example, an accountant will be considered not independent with respect to any person or any of its parents or subsidiaries in whom he has, or had during the period of report, any direct financial interest or any material indirect financial interest; or with whom he is, or was during such period, connected as a promoter, underwriter, voting trustee, director, officer or employee.

(b) In determining whether an accountant may in fact be not independent with respect to a particular person, the Commission will give appropriate consideration to all relevant circumstances, including evidence bearing on all relationships between the accountant and that person or any affiliate thereof, and will not confine itself to the relationship existing in connection with the filing of reports with the Commission.

Special note should be taken of the wording in paragraph "a" where the words "in fact independent" appear. This paragraph also cites certain criteria for determining the fact of independence while in paragraph "b" it is stated that consideration will be given "to all relevant circumstances." From this Regulation it is difficult to tell what the SEC's concept of independence really is. It is necessary, therefore, to turn to the cases decided under this rule for further information. A useful way to handle this matter is to first consider circumstances directly covered by the law, and then to consider the related issues.

Auditor's financial interest. The first provision of paragraph "a" concerns the direct financial interest or material indirect financial interest in a client or its subsidiaries by the accountant. Here financial interest has been judged in terms of the client's net worth and the accountant's net worth. The interpretation of material is not totally clear, but on at least two occasions 8–9% was considered material. The time of the holding of financial interest should also be noted. The Commission has ruled against independence when the ownership was before, during or immediately subsequent to the audit. The subsequent interpretation is a matter of timing, however, since it has been held that an auditor could certify statements he had audited while he was independent, even though currently he is no longer the auditor nor independent.

Indirect relationship between auditor and client. The indirect relationships of the client and the auditor have also been far reaching. It has been established that the lack of independence of any partner will disqualify a firm, even though he is not working with the particular client. In addition, an accountant has been considered as not independent if his wife, brother, father, uncle, brothers and sisters-in-law or son-in-law had a financial interest in the client.

The second provision encompasses the relationship of the accountant and the client as a promoter, underwriter, voting trustee, director, officer, or employee. This rule applies to *all* employees of the accounting firm, and it is particularly emphasized that no one may make original entries in the client's books and still be independent for auditing purposes. The non-employee clause has also been held to apply to an auditor's son even though he had no connection with the CPA firm itself. This would, presumably, also apply to other members of the auditor's immediate family.

Other flaws. It is also interesting to consider events not specifically covered under the law but still leading to lack of independence. Here one finds such things as conscious falsification of facts, subordinated judgment to client's desires, contingent fees, and incompatible occupation. These latter two factors deserve some additional comment. An auditor cannot make his fee contingent upon any event except the ruling of taxing authorities. Such a situation would imply that the auditor would have an interest in the outcome of his work. Finally, an auditor may not have an incompatible occupation in dealing with a client; a specific case involved here concerned a person who was both an accountant and a lawyer.[12]

As Rappaport points out, the cases are decided after considering a number of circumstances, and it is difficult to know whether one event by itself is determining.[13] One can, however, see how important the SEC considers independence to be, and how strictly the laws have been interpreted.

Importance of state of mind. In spite of the diversity of cases and rulings, a common thread seems to be present. That is, the overriding thought that independence is, in fact, an intangible object, a condition which insures a lack of bias by the accountant. The point was more aptly put in a talk made in 1950 to the AICPA by Donald Cook, a former Chairman of the SEC. He said:

> The independent accountant must combine the impartiality of a judge with the high sense of responsibility of a fiduciary. . . . Though hired and fired by management, he must divorce his mental processes from any bias in their direction when making accounting judgments. Such a standard of professional conduct must be maintained if the auditor's certificate is to be more than a snare and a delusion and the public obligation of the accountant satisfied.[14]

---

[12]These case findings were summarized from Rappaport, pp. 22.12 to 22.40 and Accounting Release No. 81, pp. 32-36. NOTE: All cases discussed through footnote (12) are included in that footnote.

[13]Rappaport, pp. 22.12.

[14]Donald C. Cook, "The Concept of Independence in Accounting," (From an address before the AICPA, October 3, 1950).

One can see over and over again in the cases described above, that to be independent the accountant must be free from those entanglements which might influence his judgment, and thus prevent him from executing his public obligation. One is thus brought to the conclusion that on the theoretical level there is no difference in the concept of independence between the Securities and Exchange Commission and the American Institute of Certified Public Accountants — they are both based on the "state of mind" idea. But, one may then ask, why do the differences between the two bodies seem to exist?

SEC's practical course. While it may be the "proper" state of mind which allows an auditor to discharge his duties to the public, it is extremely difficult to look into a person's mind. Characteristics such as impartiality, responsibility, bias, and integrity are elusive terms and defy measurement as such. However, it was the SEC's responsibility to determine independence in specific instances; thus, it was forced to go to a practical definition of this concept. Since it is not possible to observe a person's thoughts, one must observe his behavior and infer that these are manifestations of his thoughts. Therefore, to determine independence, it was necessary to look not only at actions but also those relationships which would influence actions, and in this way determine the existence of independence.

Certainly it is an imprecise way, but something as crucial as this cannot be left to high and unmeasureable sounding ideals of personal integrity. Admittedly, the legalistic violation approach, per se, has its faults, but in this case, it appears to be the only practical way out of the dilemma. The fact that all relevant circumstances are considered makes this approach a much more valid one, however.

The general conclusion, then, must be there is no difference in the view of independence between the AICPA and the SEC at the conceptual, theoretical level. The differences arise only in the practical notion of independence which occurred because the SEC was charged with the practical responsibility of enforcing this concept. The realization of this may well be implicit in the adoption of the amended code of ethics in 1965 by the AICPA.

THIRD PARTIES' INTERPRETATION OF INDEPENDENCE

Finally, let us consider third parties' interpretation of independence. While the AICPA and the SEC are the instrumentalities charged with the responsibility, among other things, of protecting the investing public, we cannot forget the actual opinions of this public.

For the purpose of this paper, third parties consist of those individuals who are concerned with providing and/or using relevant, timely, and verifiable financial information which is free from bias, but who are not acting as a spokesman for either the AICPA or the SEC. This definition, then, does not eliminate those members of the AICPA or the SEC who express their own individual opinion or findings independently of the body of which they are members, but it does eliminate the "John Doe" (nonpresent or potential investor) who has no conception of auditor-independence and, if asked, would relate his definition merely to a dictionary definition of independence.

Three eras of third-party views. The concept of independence as seen by third parties necessarily is a function of the purpose of an audit, as conceived by these individuals. This in turn can be divided into three eras: (1) Pre-World War I, (2) World War I to the Depression, and (3) Post-Depression.

Pre-World War I views — a hint at independence. Prior to the turn of the century, there were few significant writings on the purpose of having independent audits and, in turn, less (if any) writings on the concept of independence. One can infer, though, some ideas from a few articles written near the end of this first era.

The first of these is Walter A. Staub's 1904 article on the "Mode of Conducting an Audit."[15] Although strictly speaking Mr. Staub should not be considered a third party, his remarks were not necessarily an official position of the AICPA. The significance of this article is not only its early date of writing, but, also, that it won the author a prize at the first International Congress of Accountants in 1904. Mr. Staub considered the object of an audit to be threefold: "(1) detection of fraud, (2) discovery of errors in principle and (3) verification of the mechanical accuracy of accountants." The author's discussion of each of these objectives follows: he spends 65% of the discussion on the fraud element, 25% on the mechanical accuracy, while using only one sentence on the "discovery of errors in principle" aspect. ". . . Owing, however, to its importance, and often its predominating importance, the detection of fraud is conceded a separate place among the objectives on an audit."[16]

Thus, the detection of fraud was the main purpose of the 19th-century auditors. From this it is possible to infer that early auditing-independence had a concept of disinterestedness or "outsiderness," which were those requirements conceived as being necessary in order

---

[15]Walter A. Staub, "Mode of Conducting an Audit," *The Accounting Review* (April, 1943), p. 91.
   [16]*Ibid.*

to detect the presence of any fraud. Historical auditing procedures further indicate that the idea of an "outsider" audit of the books was to detect fraud in that full detail audits were almost always performed.

A second article of importance, a brief one, almost editorial in nature, was written in a 1909 issue of *The Wall Street Journal*.[17] This writing brings forth the factors of integrity and objectivity of this "disinterested auditor."

> Among our firms of public accountants we have not established that high standard and stringent control which so effectively protects the British investor. We are moving that way and we have now firms of accountants who will not on any consideration grant a certificate which does not imply a genuine audit. These houses will not take doubtful business. They say, in effect, "Open all your books, turn over your keys and explain everything before we sign your certificate. This is the only kind of certificate we grant, and the only kind of audit we are willing to make."
>
> This is the proper attitude and no honestly conducted corporation need feel oppressed. There are some corporations still, and far too many of them, whose balance sheet is a farce and whose "accountants' certificate" is not worth the paper it is written on.

From the article, it is evident that prior to this time, it was assumed that an auditor who was independent (he was not on the staff of management) would have no reason to conceal fraud that he discovered. Using this assumption, then, all third party auditors were automatically "disinterested" merely because they were "outsiders."

But as this article brought to light, if the auditor did not stand up to management and say that he (the auditor) will only certify the financial statements if it could be shown there was no fraud, then the fact that an auditor was an "outsider" really meant little.

Thus, one can see being developed the idea of independence in fact (which formed the beginning of the second era). If the auditor was independent, he had the responsibility of maintaining integrity, honesty, and freedom to express his own opinion when certifying a firm's financial statements. In turn, it was brought forth that independence assumes integrity and honesty toward the reporting public and without these qualities the mere presence of "independence" meant nothing. Thus, this new attitude gave interpretation to what independence should mean.

---

[17]*Journal of Accountancy* (September, 1909), p. 382. Reprint of an article from *The Wall Street Journal*, August 7, 1909.

The 1909 article in *The Wall Street Journal* is one of the earliest examples of this new conceptualization of the independence (or outsiderness) of the auditor which formed the beginning of the second era.

The second era — amplification of independence. It must be noted, though, that throughout this second era detection of fraud, through a checking process, still remained the main purpose of an audit, and thus the idea of "outsiders" implying "disinterestedness" still applied. This can be easily seen in two places. One is an article written by A. C. Littleton where he noted the frequency in which the authors of the 1912 edition of *Montgomery's Auditing* used various significant words.[18] The results were as follows:

Rank	Word
1	Ascertain
2	Verify
3	Audit
4	Examine
5	Test
6	Certify

The ranking of these words indicates the necessity of checking the mechanics of statements which, in turn, implies fraud and error detection.

In a 1933 article in the *Journal of Accountancy,* Roger Barton wrote that "it is not customary for railroads to use independent audits, because of their regulation by the ICC which audits the railroad at its discretion."[19] Later in the same article, he stated that "as the situation stands now, however, it is apparent that considerable credit is due America's great corporations for their voluntary and almost unanimous action (except in cases where they come under government supervision) in adopting the practice of independent audits."[20]

The straight-forward implication of this writing is that if a government agency is making sure that the firm's records do not conceal fraud, there is no need for an independent audit. But an underlying concept to this article was that the independence of the auditor did guarantee the honesty and integrity to make audits of such great value that full compliance was advocated.

---

[18] A. C. Littleton, "Vocabularly of Auditing Technique," NYCPA (November, 1947), p. 639+.
[19] Roger Barton, "Independent Audits for Investors," *Journal of Accountancy* (August, 1933), p. 94.
[20] *Ibid.*, p. 98.

One can then summarize this second era by saying that the auditor's primary purpose was fraud detection and to be effective in this function he must not only be "disinterested" in the results of his findings but also have the integrity and honesty to report these findings to the public. Thus, the integrity and honesty aspect of independence was developed during this time.

The third era — the flowering of independence. As we come to the third era, the conceptualization becomes more complex, for the third parties had developed greater sophistication and because of this the concepts of independence as developed by the AICPA, the SEC and third parties became interdependent upon each other.

It can be said that the beginning of this era was started by two significant developments: (1) the SEC's requirements for independent auditors (covered in an above section)[21] and (2) the New York Stock Exchange's requirement for independent audits (required as of 7/1/33 for all listings on the NYSE).[22] The SEC required corporations to be audited by public accounting firms[23] which denotes that the public accountant should formulate generally accepted accounting principles (GAAP) to which the financial statements of these firms should conform.

Thus, at this point, the problem of the formulation of GAAP was thrust upon the accounting profession. This, in turn, created a change in the concept of independence applied to the auditor from one of merely honesty and integrity in reporting fraud detection to one of objective application of accounting principles as well as fraud detection.

Broadened independence concept. Independence was broadened to mean being objective in making sure that the financial statements described the true financial position and results of a firm. Also, since the auditor had the responsibility of applying the newly developed body of GAAP, he had the responsibility of passing judgment on the application of these principles to the firm's financial statements. Thus, we have independence meaning ability and willingness to be objective in passing judgment on the suitable application of GAAP as well as being honest and possessing integrity.

This emerging concept of independence can be detected in an editorial in *The Journal of Accountancy* in 1933:

---

[21]Securities Act of 1933 and Securities Exchange Act of 1934.
[22]Independent Audits Required by New York Exchanges," *The Certified Public Accountant* (February, 1933), pp. 70-71.
[23]Securities Act of 1933 and Securities Exchange Act of 1934.

. . . What the public accountant does is not ex parte. He is kind of appraiser of values of intangible things. He knows the meaning of the accounts which he reviews. He takes the balance-sheet and the profit-and-loss account and the surplus account and all the other financial statements which may be presented to him and he tests what has been done in the keeping of records. He verifies all the vital elements, and then as one who knows the meaning of things he says that he believes the condition to be good or bad or halfway between. He tells the company in his report his expert opinion of what has been done and what is . . . . The public accountant has his impartial status in this great and thrilling game of business. He knows the rules. He knows the players. All the spectators up in the grandstand and on the bleachers will rely on him, if he be a true umpire at heart, to see that the game is conducted fairly and that every one who paid the price of admission shall have a fair deal. The fact of an umpire does not indicate any moral obliquity in any player. An umpire is needed because he can see both sides when often the players, because of their position in the game, can see only their own. . . .[24]

The editorial strongly indicates that the independent auditor is no longer a pencil-pushing fraud and error detector. More importantly, it brings out the "objectivity" concept and even starts developing the "state of mind" concept, when it stated that ". . . if he be a true umpire at heart. . . ."

Two years later, A. C. Littleton wrote an article calling for greater "independence in fact" of the auditors. This article is not one calling for sweeping changes. Instead, it is an expression of the feeling of changes taking place. Discussing the "old" (second era) concept, he said, ". . . He (the auditor) may seek ways of meeting concrete situations without realizing that, while constituting technical 'disclosure,' his phrases may nevertheless fail to carry the necessary message to the reader."[25] He later goes on to advocate that the examination include the following:

a. Examination of the corporate records and accounts to see that the results of the transactions reflect the principles of good accounting.

b. Scrutiny of security contracts, of proposals to change the financial structure and of financial valuations or operations to see that the principles of sound finance were not being violated and that the interest of no class of security holder was (accidentally or by design) being undermined without the latter's knowledge of the real significance of the situation.

---

[24]Editorial, "Why Engage Public Accountants? — Independence is Essential — There Must Be Umpires," *Journal of Accountancy* (September, 1933), p. 196.

[25]A. C. Littleton, "Auditor Independence," *Journal of Accountancy* (April, 1935), p. 286.

  c. Follow up the accounting of new financing to see if the use made of the funds was as stated in the prospectus.

Disclosure would call for the following:

  a. Presentation and certification of a full, clear statement of present financial condition, including a careful indication of the types of security contracts outstanding.

  b. Presentation of full, clear statements of income for the current fiscal period, as well as an analysis of past surplus, and a certification of the earned income of the past three years.

These responsibilities laid upon the auditor would place his trained judgment and skill as an analyst at the disposal, as it were, of the whole investing public. The right of appeal by either party of unsettled issues between auditor and client to the board of financial review for arbitration would further assure the public of sound practices.[26]

The Philosophy of Auditing, written some 26 years after the 1935 Littleton article, brings forth this same idea of objective attitudes:

The meaning of practitioner-independence seems clear. It has to do with the ability of the individual practitioner to maintain the proper attitude in the planning of his audit program, the performance of his verification work and the preparation of his report.[27]

Thus, little by little, this "objective judgment" criteria of independence has developed into the present day idea that independence is a state of mind. As was noted before, the AICPA brought forth this state of mind concept, but one can logically see that it is merely a rewording of the older "objective judgment" concept as developed in the mid-1930's.

IMPLICATIONS

From the review of the various groups' positions on independence, one is struck with their similarity in theory. All the groups view independence, on this level, as an attitude, or state of mind. However, when discussing whether independence exists in a specific factual setting, the groups' similarity of positions disappear. The authors, therefore, submit that the failure to recognize that independence may have both general-theoretical and particular-practical aspects lies at the heart of many controversies on this subject. Before one can

---

[26]*Ibid.*, pp. 287-288.

[27]R. K. Mautz and Hussein Sharaf, *The Philosophy of Auditing* (Menasha: American Accounting Association, 1961), p. 205.

ever meaningfully resolve such issues as whether the rendering of management services impairs an auditor's independence, it is first necessary to resolve this more fundamental issue. What is sorely needed is a "workable" definition of independence which may be applied universally to the various situations which arise, and the key to this problem is to be found in understanding the dual nature of independence.

Pragmatic considerations as well as the flow of theoretical expressions appear to indicate that the AICPA and SEC will base their judgments, basically, on the demands of the public image concept. Thereby, the public interest will be jealously guarded, and this protection will be evident to the public.

To the accounting profession, the subordination of the position that a healthy "state of mind" plus competence assures the necessary independence, to the overriding consideration of public image, will be increasingly acceptable, also on pragmatic grounds.

9. Competence and Independence — The Issue of Management Services*

Ronald J. Patten and
John R. Nuckols, Jr.†

There is a solution to the management services issue which has been plaguing the accounting profession. The solution revolves around the concepts of competence and independence. In this article, the concepts of competence and independence are discussed and the crucial elements of each concept are identified. These crucial elements are then combined into a solution to the management services problem.

THE PROBLEM

What is the management services problem? In reality, there are at least two facets to the problem, one relating to competence and one relating to independence. Each of these will be discussed in this section.

The accounting profession, having been involved with management services for a number of years, is extending its services into areas which, although lucrative in terms of fee potential, are a questionable domain for the accountant. Examples of such areas are market surveys and factory layout engagements. In many instances, a firm of certified public accountants has hired a number of non-accountants (statisticians, mathematicians, psychologists and industrial engineers, to name a few) in order to provide itself with the "in-house capability" that is necessary for a particular engagement or series of engagements. Thus, many of the large CPA firms have become "miniconglomerates." The firms are officially known as firms of CPAs, yet they contain a number of people who are not CPAs, (no new phenomenon), in fact, they are not even accountants (a relatively new phenomenon). Thus, one of the facets of the management services problem is concerned with the scope of services (boundaries, if you will). Necessarily, the concept of *competence* is the focal point of this facet of the problem.

*From *The Louisiana Certified Public Accountant* (Fall, 1970), pp. 20-30. Reprinted by permission of the Society of Louisiana Certified Public Accountants.

†Ronald J. Patten, Ph.D, CPA, is Head of the Department of Accounting, Virginia Polytechnic Institute and State University. John R. Nuckols, Jr., is with the Air Force Audit Agency, Andrews Air Force Base, Maryland.

The other facet of the management services problem relates to the public image of the CPA. The primary function of public accounting is one of bridging the information and credibility gaps which exist between top corporate management and those who are financially interested in the wealth controlled by such management. The CPA is essentially a fiduciary to unknown third parties in his role as "public auditor." Such a role demands the characteristic of independence on the part of the CPA. Independence is the balm which soothes the suspicions of the financial information users and imparts the aspect of credibility to managements' financial reports. The CPA must strive constantly to maintain his independent frame of mind, and must project the image of an independent attestor to third parties. Once the CPA's services extend beyond the attest function and into management services, the independence which is necessary in the attest function is subjected to additional analysis. Thus, *independence* is the focal point of the second facet of the problem of management services.

DEFINITIONAL PROBLEM

What are management services? "Management advisory services by independent accounting firms can be described as the function of providing professional advisory (consulting) services, the primary purpose of which is to improve the client's use of its capabilities and resources to achieve the objectives of the organization."[1] Yet, the preceding description is conceptual in nature rather than definitive in terms of the area of application of management services. No generally accepted itemized list of areas of service is currently available.[2] To some accountants, the absence of such a list is a source of dismay.

At present, management services provided by the accounting profession are expanding rapidly, both in terms of revenue to the profession and in terms of the increasing variety of services rendered.[3] This expansion, in view of the lack of any generally accepted listing of acceptable activities, presents a challenge to the notion of accountancy as a distinct and well defined profession.

---

[1]Committee on Management Services, American Institute of Certified Public Accountants, *Statement on Management Advisory Services, No. 1: Tentative Description of the Nature of Management Advisory Services by Independent Accounting Firms* (New York: American Institute of Certified Public Accountants, 1969), p. 3.

[2]*Ibid.*, p. 4.

[3]Walter G. Kell, "Public Accounting's Irresistible Force and Immovable Object," *The Accounting Review*, XLIII (April, 1968), p. 266.

A profession consists of a limited and clearly marked group of men who are trained by education and experience to perform certain functions better than their fellowman. . . . In general the standards of any profession are menaced if the line of demarcation between it and other activities is not clear, . . . Every man owes it to his profession to indicate clearly what his business is, otherwise he has no right to the benefits accruing to the members of that profession.[4]

THE ISSUE OF COMPETENCE

While the present seemingly unlimited scope of management services would seem to transgress the area of professionalism according to the preceding definition, such a situation also suggests some questions regarding the competence of the CPA to deal on such a technically diversified scale. It is not surprising that the present battle lines regarding the management services question are drawn between the practitioners on one hand and the academicians on the other. Without a direct financial interest in the outcome, it is perhaps easier for the academician to view the problem of management services more objectively. Commenting on the apparent lack of perspective among some practitioners, Mautz and Sharaf write:

In this connection it is interesting to note that many practitioners feel accountants can qualify themselves for this type of work by self-study and professional reading. Although they support the idea that professional training and a qualifying examination are necessary for a person to enter their own ranks as a CPA, they apparently support the somewhat contradictory position that without any further professional training or qualifying examinations they can expand the scope of their professional services in some rather unusual respects.[5]

Another approach to the question of the CPA's competency to render certain management services is provided by Kell. He states that management services may be classified as "accounting services" and "administrative services." Accounting-based services, such as inventory control and budgeting, are defined by Kell as those services which "evolve naturally from the audit engagement and the auditor's familiarity with the client's information system." Kell feels that "the

---

[4]Carl F. Taeusch, *Professional and Business Ethics* (New York: Henry Holt and Company, 1926), pp. 13-14.
[5]R. K. Mautz and Hussein A. Sharaf, *The Philosophy of Auditing* (Menasha, Wisconsin: George Banta Company, Inc., 1961), pp. 219-220.

public *accepts* these services as being logically within the purview and competence of the independent auditor."[6] Administrative based management services are defined by Kell as those services, such as factory layout and market surveys, which are outside the traditional scope of the audit, and which extend beyond the client's information and control system.[7] In summary, Kell would consider a particular management service as appropriate to the independent auditor only if such service were logically related to the client's information system.

The foregoing discussion should not imply that the question of competency to perform management services has received no attention on the part of the CPA-practitioner. Trueblood, although perhaps less pessimistic than Mautz or Kell, expressed the same concern when he wrote:

> There can be no question about the CPA's competence and expertness in all the more traditional phases of the management service function. . . . The only question about the CPA's competence in the management service function relates to the expansion of his knowledge and competence in the newer and more refined measurement methods. . . ."[8]

Likewise, Devore states:

> I think we have to recognize that the performance of peripheral services — i.e., those not "related logically to the financial process or to broadly defined information and control systems" — is raising questions in some quarters, . . . This also raises, . . . the question of competence, . . .[9]

Because of the dynamic nature of public accounting's involvement in management services, many problems and adjustments are to be expected. However, to the extent that the profession is willing and able to perceive its own potential weaknesses, there should be no cause for alarm. The present controversy within the accounting profession regarding the competence of the CPA to provide certain management services is evidence of the profession's continued willingness to face its own problems. From the controversy many suggestions which have been made are as follows:

---

[6]Kell, *The Accounting Review*, XLIII, p. 268.
[7]*Ibid.*, p. 269.
[8]Robert M. Trueblood, "The Management Service Function in Public Accounting," *The Journal of Accountancy*, CXII (July, 1961), p. 41.
[9]Malcolm M. Devore, "Compatibility of Auditing and Management Services: A Viewpoint From Within the Profession," *The Journal of Accountancy*, CXXIV (December, 1967), p. 38. The internal quotation is by Manuel F. Cohen, Chairman of the Securities and Exchange Commission, in a speech at the 1966 annual meeting of the American Institute of Certified Public Accountants.

MICHAEL D. BACHRACH:

1. Increase competency by establishment of a separate and specialized management services department within the accounting firm.
2. Develop a working arrangement with one or more industrial engineering firms.
3. Work out a plan of cooperation with another accounting firm.[10]

WALTER G. KELL:

1. Insert into the Code of Professional Ethics a technical standard for management services.
2. Establish generally accepted standards for management services.[11]

R. K. MAUTZ AND HUSSEIN A. SHARAF:

1. In order to insure proficiency, establish a standard similar to Rule 1 of the AICPA Committee on Auditing Procedure.
2. Construct an acceptable definition of management services.[12]

Many of these suggestions are being utilized already. For example, separate and specialized management services departments do exist in a number of public accounting firms. In addition, Statement on Management Advisory Services No. 1 has been issued under the auspices of the AICPA. This statement describes the nature of management advisory services by CPAs. To the extent that the profession is able to indicate what its activities consist of as far as management services are concerned, public accounting will be able to project as a distinct and reasonably well defined profession.

THE ISSUE OF INDEPENDENCE

Independence is a most important trait as far as the CPA is concerned. The attest function is significant largely as a result of the independence possessed by the CPA. Independence is not only one of the CPA's most important assets, it is also one of his major potential stumbling blocks as far as management services are concerned. Specifically, it is contended by some that the rendering of management services undermines the CPA's audit independence.

---

[10]Michael D. Bachrach, "Co-operation in Services to Management," *The Journal of Accountancy*, CV (March, 1958), p. 37.
[11]Kell, *The Accounting Review*, XLIII, p. 269.
[12]Mautz and Sharaf, pp. 219-220.

Rule 1.01 of the Institute's Code of Professional Ethics provides a useful framework for discussing the present controversy, since much of this controversy has arisen because of the diversity of interpretation given to Rule 1.01 itself. Rule 1.01 reads in part:

> Independence is not susceptible of precise definition, but is an expression of the professional integrity of the individual. A member or associate, before expressing his opinion on financial statements, has the responsibility of assessing his relationships with an enterprise to determine whether, in the circumstances, he might expect his opinion to be considered independent, objective and unbiased by one who had knowledge of all the facts.
>
> A member or associate will be considered not independent, for example, with respect to any enterprise if he, or one of his partners, (a) during the period of his professional engagement or at the time of expressing his opinion, had, or was committed to acquire, any direct financial interest or (b) during the period of his professional engagement, at the time of expressing his opinion or during the period covered by the financial statements, was connected with the enterprise as a promoter, underwriter, voting trustee, director, officer or key employee.[13]

Rule 1.01 is unusual in that while its purpose is to provide guidelines for the measurement of "independence," it declares that such independence is not definable in an exact sense, and that each member or associate must in effect act as judge of his own independence according to his own standards. The problem is compounded when we learn there are actually two kinds of independence with which the CPA must be concerned: (1) independence *in fact* and (2) independence *in appearance*.[14]

Many arguments have been expounded seeking to establish that Rule 1.01 is violated by the CPA in rendering certain management services. Equally strong voices have declared that no conflict between management services and independence, either in fact or appearance, exists in the great majority of cases. Apparently, at least a portion of the controversy has been placed in a state of "quasi-rest" by the AICPA's Committee on Management Services by means of the issuance of Statement of Management Advisory Services No. 3. In Statement No. 3 the Committee concluded that the accountant should assume an objective, advisory posture in his management consulting role. By doing so, the accountant will be placed in a position that will

---

[13]American Institute of Certified Public Accountants, *Code of Professional Ethics* (New York: American Institute of Certified Public Accountants, Inc., 1967), p. 6.

[14]Thomas G. Higgins, "Professional Ethics: A Time for Reappraisal," *The Journal of Accountancy*, CXIII (March, 1962), p. 31.

not impair his objectivity in his other relationships with his client. The accountant, however, should always be alert to the way his role may be viewed by others and not permit himself to be placed in a posture that could cause serious question regarding his objectivity and independence.[15] The value of learning to apply this idea cannot be overemphasized, for should public confidence in the basic integrity and independence of public accounting ever falter, the profession itself might well be doomed.

KEY WORDS IN RULE 1.01

Much of the lingering controversy results from disagreement over the meaning of certain key words in Rule 1.01. For example, what is meant by "a material indirect financial interest?" Who is a "key employee?" Substantial controversy within the profession has also resulted from perceptual differences regarding the public's attitude toward the CPA-auditor-consultant. In short, accountants can agree that the CPA must appear independent to the "reasonable" observer, but they cannot seem to agree on just whom this "reasonable" observer might be. Another area of disagreement between those who think that management services are compatible with the audit function and those who do not is that each side in the controversy is arguing from a different major premise. "Advocates of 'incompatibility' have been satisfied to demonstrate that combined consulting and auditing has the *potentiality* for damaging the auditor's independence, while the advocates of 'compatibility' have demanded absolute proof that independence has been lost."[16]

THE SCHULTE STUDY

Perhaps the most damaging empirical evidence presented so far which would link management services with an apparent lack of independence by the CPA was submitted by Schulte. Schulte mailed questionnaires to four selected groups: (1) research and financial analysts of brokerage firms, (2) commercial loan and trust officers of banks, (3) investment officers of insurance companies, and (4)

---

[15]Committee on Management Services, American Institute of Certified Public Accountants, *Statement on Management Advisory Services, No. 3: Role in Management Advisory Services* (New York: American Institute of Certified Public Accountants, 1969), pp. 28-29.

[16]D. R. Carmichael and R. J. Swieringa, "The Compatibility of Auditing Independence and Management Services — An Identification of Issues," *The Accounting Review*, XLIII (October, 1968), p. 705.

investment officers of domestic mutual funds. On the basis of questionnaires returned, Schulte concluded that 97% of the third parties responding attach a special importance to the CPA's audit independence. Moreover, "nearly half of the financial executives surveyed are concerned about the possible impairment of the CPA's audit independence . . ." while rendering management services to an audit client.[17]

The findings of Schulte have been sharply questioned by Carey and Doherty. Carey and Doherty criticize Schulte's use of the term "management consulting" in his questionnaire. They argue that "nowhere in the questionnaire or the article interpreting it is there a definition of the term 'management consulting.' " The different responses from one answering Schulte's questionnaire. [*sic*] Further, they state that "It is difficult to believe that reasonable observers . . . would see any conflict of interest in the fact that the auditor, in addition to giving an opinion on the financial statements, also applied his technical knowledge and skill to the improvement of management's planning, control and decision-making processes."[18]

One wonders why Carey and Doherty should have so much apparent difficulty in believing that a reasonable observer *might* question the effect of management services on audit independence, when so many CPAs themselves have expressed reservations in this regard. Perhaps, Carey and Doherty mean to imply that those CPAs who do question the compatibility of certain management services and audit independence are rather unreasonable men. Two additional quotations from the Carey and Doherty article are also interesting when considered together. "It is most important not only that the CPA shall refuse consciously to subordinate his judgment to that of others, but that he avoid relationships which would be likely to warp his judgment, even subconsciously, ..."[19] And later in the article: "It may be postulated that the certified public accountant who renders management services will be no less independent *in fact* in his capacity as auditor than the certified public accountant who does not. . . ."[20] One is left wondering how Carey and Doherty arrived at such a conclusion without reference to their previous statement regarding the effect of subconscious relationships on the CPA's judgment. The following statement taken from *The Philosophy of Auditing* would

---

[17]Arthur A. Schulte, Jr., "Compatibility of Management Consulting and Auditing," *The Accounting Review*, XL (July, 1965), p. 589.

[18]John L. Carey and William O. Doherty, "The Concept of Independence—Review and Restatement," *The Journal of Accountancy*, CXXI (January, 1966), p. 41.

[19]*Ibid.*, p. 38.

[20]*Ibid.*, pp. 40-41.

seem to refute the contention of Carey and Doherty that the rendering of management services does not affect the auditor's independence *in fact*.

> Once advice leading to business decisions is given, a mutuality of interest between the consultant and the company begins to develop. . . .
>
> If we grant that independence is a state of mind, we must also recognize influences on one's state of mind that are not always apparent.[21]

Carey and Doherty further illuminate their position with respect to the degree of participation a CPA may exercise in the decision-making process without endangering his audit independence. As a reference point, they utilize the following statistical decision model:

1. Determine the nature of possible decisions.
2. Determine the events which could occur, one of which must occur.
3. Determine the expected profit or loss for each combination of events.
4. Determine the probability of occurrence of each event.
5. Select the act with the highest expected value.

Carey and Doherty contend that "the CPA can freely participate in this process and still be considered independent if he confines his advice to the first three steps." They add: "It is doubtful whether even the fourth step would suggest a conflict of interest to a reasonable observer."[22]

THE CPA AS ADVISOR OR DECISION-MAKER

The preceding statement forces the question, doubtful to whom? It would seem that the fourth step involves the subjective analysis of uncertain future events. While perhaps it is true that the CPA could construct more realistic probabilities than could his audit client, it is possible to divorce the construction of such probabilities from the final decision which ultimately is based on these probabilities? At what point would the CPA cease to act as an advisor and in effect become the decision-maker? A quotation from *The Philosophy of Auditing* again appears to be pertinent:

> Management, of course, is at liberty to accept, modify, or reject a given piece of expert advice. But advice is requested on the premise

---

[21]Mautz and Sharaf, pp. 222-23.
[22]Carey and Doherty, *The Journal of Accountancy*, CXXI, p. 41.

that it will be given rational consideration. . . . Management wants the advice and intends to use it; advice is sought and paid for to be followed, not to be ignored. It seems folly indeed to separate advising and judgment making.[23]

Why is it so important that the CPA refrain from making the final decision? Is it not to insure that no conflict exists between his service to his audit client and his independence from the audit client? If the above line of reasoning is accepted, the advice and the decision are inseparable. The CPA is responsible for both. In these circumstances, is it reasonable to assume that the CPA can objectively audit the results of his own decisions?

WHAT IS AN AUDIT CLIENT?

Another source of conflict may be the term "audit client" itself. The CPA who performs both auditing and management service functions for a single enterprise is likely to refer to the enterprise as his "audit client" in either case. But does he actually serve the same client under these circumstances? Hylton writes:

> It seems that the critical difference between management services and auditing is the identity of the client. While we speak of the business being audited as the "client," in an audit engagement this is actually incorrect. The entire financial community is the *real* client in an audit. Audit reports are circulated wherever the business being audited has any significance. The fact that the auditor has legal and professional responsibility to these "third parties" is well established. The audited business foots the bill, but if this destroys the auditor's independence, his audit is null and void.
>
> In the management services engagement, the client *is* the management of the business.[24]

COMPATIBILITY OF AUDITING AND MANAGEMENT SERVICES

Regardless of the questions which have been raised, management services continue to grow at a rapid rate. Many accountants remain convinced that the effect of management services on their most treasured possession — audit independence — need not be detrimental.

---

[23]Mautz and Sharaf, p. 221.
[24]Delmer P. Hylton, "Are Consulting and Auditing Compatible? — A Contrary View," *The Accounting Review*, XXXIX (July, 1964), p. 668.

Granted, they argue, that "It is of utmost importance to the profession that the general public maintain confidence in the independence of independent auditors. . . ;" nevertheless, everyone is influenced in some way by his physical environment and by the mental impressions which he receives from those around him.[25]   Devore points out that: "Our committee [*ad hoc committee on independence*] recognizes there is no such thing as absolute, pure independence."[26]   Whereas no empirical evidence is as yet available to dispute the findings of Schulte's survey linking the performance of management services by the CPA to an *apparent* lack of independence, those who advocate that the CPA's work in this field is compatible with audit independence point out that no empirical evidence exists which would link the performance of such services by the CPA to a lack of independence in fact.   Devore states that "we have found no substantive evidence that the rendering of management services has, in fact, impaired independence."[27]   Kaufman is equally emphatic:

> . . . CPAs have now rendered millions of hours of management services to their clients. In doing this work, as far as this observer knows, there are no instances in the literature or in regulatory agency records confirming the impairment of independence because of management services activity.[28]

It has also been argued that management services and auditing are compatible since the CPA must be equally objective in performing either function. Carmichael and Swieringa help to put this argument in its proper perspective by pointing out that there are three distinct "phases" of independence:

1. **Professional independence:**
   ". . . an approach and attitude which makes him [the CPA] self-reliant and not subordinate to his client."[29]
2. **Audit independence:**
   "Not only must the auditor refrain from intentionally favoring the client's interests in planning his examination, . . . he must also avoid *unintentional* feelings which might cause him to take such actions."[30]

---

[25]Committee on Auditing Procedure, *Auditing Standards and Procedures*, Statements on Auditing Procedure No. 33 (New York: American Institute of Certified Public Accountants, Inc., 1963), p. 20.

[26]Devore, *The Journal of Accountancy*, CXXIV, p. 38.

[27]*Ibid.*, p. 36.

[28]Felix Kaufman, "Professional Consulting by CPAs," *The Accounting Review*, XLII (October, 1967), p. 719.

[29]Carmichael and Swieringa, *The Accounting Review*, XLIII, p. 698.

[30]*Ibid.*

3. Perceived independence:
   a. The independence of the CPA as observed by a reasonable person who has all the facts.
   b. The independence of the accounting profession as a whole as perceived by the general public.[31]

Returning to the argument that management services and auditing are compatible since both require objectivity, Carmichael and Swieringa observe: "An identification of the issue with the relevant phase of independence does not answer the question for the other vital phases of the auditor's independence."[32]

COMPETITIVE ADVANTAGE

Perhaps the greatest argument in favor of continuing the role of CPAs in the field of management services concerns the "natural" advantages which accountants enjoy in this field over other groups who, conceivably, could render the same services. The natural advantages have been classified by Block into three areas:

1. An intimate knowledge of the client's problems, gained through frequent contact with the client and a basic understanding of the client's information and control systems.
2. A broad base of observation, gained through either a wide degree of diversity or a high degree of specialization.
3. The ability to follow up recommendations and the working out of his installations, with corresponding benefits to the client in terms of accomplishment and cost savings, as a result of interim accounting functions and typically close geographic proximity.[33]

If the public accounting profession should prove unable to resolve the conflicts between management services and the auditing function, the corresponding loss to both the profession and to society as a whole may be judged in terms of these three natural advantages which must then be foregone.

SUGGESTIONS FOR IMPROVEMENT

The preceding discussion, while not designed to take a pro or con view of management services by the CPA, perhaps has illustrated the current scope and wide divergence of opinion regarding the effect of such services on the independence of the auditor. The present

---

[31]*Ibid.*, p. 699.
[32]*Ibid.*, p. 701.
[33]Max Block, "Management Advisory Services—Opportunities and Limitations," *The New York Certified Public Accountant*, XXVIII (February, 1958), pp. 131-41.

controversy regarding the effect of management services on audit independence also has yielded many suggestions which should prove beneficial to the profession.   Some of the suggestions which have been offered are as follows:

MALCOM M. DEVORE:

1. The utilization of "audit committees," desirably consisting of directors who are not officers or employees, to select the company's auditors and to act as a quasi-judicial body in matters relating to the appearance of independence of the CPA in respect to any management service which he may provide.   Such independent committees would in effect serve as "auditors" of the auditors, thus providing even greater assurance to third parties that the auditors were *in fact* independent.
2. Periodic reporting by CPAs to the audit committee concerning all services rendered prior to selection by the committee of the firm's auditors.[34]

WALTER G. KELL:

Kell's clarification of management services into "accounting" and "administrative" services, which was discussed earlier in the section on competence, is equally applicable in the area of audit independence. Kell contends that no conflict exists between the performance of accounting services and audit independence, but that the performance of administrative services might affect such independence.   His recommendations are:
1. The AICPA should officially recognize that management services by CPAs consist of accounting services and administrative services.
2. The rendering of administrative services by a CPA to an audit client should be identified in Rule 1.01 of the Code of Professional Ethics as constituting a relationship which is incompatible with independence.[35]

R. K. MAUTZ AND HUSSEIN A. SHARAF:

1. Below the partnership level, steps should be taken to make more definite the division between auditors and others within the accounting firm.
2. Gradual steps should be taken to separate partners into audit partners and others.

---

[34]Devore, *The Journal of Accountancy*, CXXIV, p. 39.
[35]Kell, *The Accounting Review*, XLIII, p. 269.

3. Once the first and second steps are completed, "profession-wide consideration should be given to the feasibility of dividing each of the large public accounting firms into two parts, the audit staff and the non-audit staff."[36]

Again it can be seen that some of the above suggestions are already being implemented. Audit committees are being utilized to a limited degree and steps have been taken to delineate the auditors and the non-auditors in accounting firms. Yet, the problem of independence has not been solved.

SOLUTION

What is going to come out of all of this controversy? Forecasting the outcome of any activity is a hazardous undertaking to say the least. Yet, primary guidelines are evident. (1) The public accounting profession is too deeply entrenched in the area of management services to withdraw completely. (2) Unless the profession sets its own house in order, the Securities and Exchange Commission may be forced to enter the fray.

In order to remain involved in the area of management services to some extent and at the same time forestall entry of the SEC into the controversy, we submit that Kell has the most reasonable solution in his suggestion to classify management services into accounting and administrative services. The CPAs should then refrain from engaging in the performance of administrative services. Since accounting services can be defined as those services which evolve from the audit engagement and the auditor's familiarity with the client's information system in a natural manner, the CPA should be able to achieve the necessary competence in this broad area. This approach has an additional advantage in that reasonably firm boundaries are established as far as accounting and administrative services are concerned.

This "natural" relationship of the auditor to accounting services should solve the independence problem as well. The cornerstone of determining whether or not independence exists lies in how the accountant appears to one who has all the facts.[37] If Kell's suggestions are implemented and the AICPA does officially recognize the difference between accounting services and administrative services, and rules that the rendering of administrative services is incompatible

---

[36]Mautz and Sharaf, pp. 229-30.

[37]Robert E. Schlosser *et al.*, "An Historical Approach to the Concept of Independence," *The New York Certified Public Accountant*, XXXIX (July, 1969), p. 525.

with independence, the public would probably agree that the auditor should engage in accounting services. This agreement would result in the auditor appearing to be independent in the minds of most observers. Again, the establishment of appropriate boundaries plays a key role. The auditor should confine his work accordingly.

Yet this solution presents problems as well. "Accounting services" is not an absolute concept. As such, it is incapable of precise definition. Thus, a considerable "gray area" will continue to exist. This condition is nothing new to the practice of accountancy. Witness such accounting decisions as selection of the "proper" method of inventory valuation or depreciation. As such the fact that "accounting services" is not an absolute concept does not constitute an insurmountable hurdle.

The time for corrective action is at hand as far as management services are concerned. The ideas of Bachrach, Mautz, Sharaf, Devore, and Kell lend themselves to a feasible solution to the management services problem. The present article has put these ideas together in the form of a viable scheme. Hopefully, the public accounting profession will see fit to seek their implementation.

10. Advocacy vs. Independence in Tax Liability Accrual*

William L. Raby†

On the one hand, the CPA is preparing the corporation's income tax return and is frequently adopting an advocacy role in resolving any questions that arise in connection with the preparation.[1] On the other hand, he is expressing an opinion on the fairness of presentation of financial statements which include as a liability the amount of income tax expense. In this latter role, he is acting not as an advocate but as an independent professional whose responsibility is to third parties rather than to the corporation.[2]

How might the position of the CPA look to outsiders? Perhaps some fictional dialogue would demonstrate. Imagine, if you will, a courtroom scene. An audit partner in a CPA firm which is being sued for negligence has been called as a hostile witness by the plaintiff.

LAWYER: The purpose of your examination was to enable you to express an opinion as to the fairness of presentation of the balance sheet and the income statement of the corporation?

CPA: That is correct.

LAWYER: In making such an examination, what is the relationship of the CPA to the client?

CPA: I don't quite understand your question.

LAWYER: Is the CPA an employee of the corporation? Is he preparing the financial statements for the corporation? Is he determining the numbers that go into those financial statements? Is he trying to assist the corporation in putting the best possible face on its financial transactions? What is his objective and what is his relationship to his client?

CPA: The CPA is making an independent examination. While the client pays the fee, the client cannot dictate the CPA's exercise of

*From *The Journal of Accountancy* (March, 1972), pp. 40-47. Copyright (1972) by the American Institute of Certified Public Accountants, Inc. Reprinted by permission of the AICPA.

†William L. Raby, Ph.D., CPA, is a partner in the executive office of Laventhol, Krekstein, Horwath & Horwath in Philadelphia.

[1]See, e.g., Opinion No. 13 of the American Institute of Certified Public Accountants committee on professional ethics, which allows resolution of doubts in favor of the client "as long as there is reasonable support" for the position taken.

[2]Cerf, Alan R., in *Professional Responsibility of Certified Public Accountants*, California CPA Foundation for Education and Research (San Francisco, 1970), pp. 100-103, discusses aspects of the dual relationship and concludes that the audit function must take precedence in the case of conflict.

his professional judgment. The numbers that go into the financial statement are the client's numbers. What the CPA is doing is expressing his opinion as to whether those numbers fairly present the situation. The audit that is made is for the purpose of gathering sufficient data to enable the CPA to express such an opinion.

LAWYER: Are you aware that the specific liability that triggered the bankruptcy proceeding involving this corporation was the $1 million income tax deficiency asserted by the federal government?

CPA: I am.

LAWYER: Could you explain the way in which your audit was conducted so as to allow you to express an opinion as to the reasonableness of the tax liability provisions that the company had made?

CPA: Well, in a sense the entire audit was related to this, since all of the items that enter into the financial statements also enter into the federal income tax return and the calculation of tax.

LAWYER: Let me be more specific then. Who actually prepared the federal income tax return for the corporation for the years ended March 31, 1966, 1967, 1968, 1969 and 1970?

CPA: Well . . . the actual return was prepared by our audit staff.

LAWYER: You mean, the federal income tax return was not prepared by the corporation?

CPA: That is correct. However, I want to point out. . . .

LAWYER: Just answer the question, please. Now, having established that your firm prepared the federal income tax return, my next question is what audit procedures were followed to determine the reasonableness of the amount of liability shown on that return?

CPA: The return was reviewed by the audit manager, the partner-in-charge of the engagement and even one of the people in our tax department.

LAWYER: I have here a copy of a pretrial deposition taken from the partner-in-charge of your tax department. We can produce him as a witness if you so desire. However, I think we can save that time by asking you whether his statement in this deposition is a fair statement of your firm's policy in reviewing the tax accrual. He stated, "The preparation of a federal income tax return is the first step in an advocacy proceeding. In reviewing a federal income tax return, it is the function of the tax department to determine that no possible tax saving has been overlooked. We are also concerned, of course, that there has been a correct application of the tax law in those areas where the tax rule is clear-cut. And, of course, we do make an incidental check of the mathematical accuracy of the return, the adequacy

of the elections in schedules attached to the return and similar items."
Is this a fair statement as to the review policy of your firm on the income tax return?

CPA: Yes it is. However. . . .

LAWYER: Just answer the question, please. I hand you herewith
a memo dated April 21, 1969, written by the then treasurer of the bank-
rupt, previously introduced as plaintiff's Exhibit 18. I call your attention to the third paragraph of that memo. Would you read it, please?

CPA: (Reading) "Mr. Ex, tax manager of CPA company, pointed
out that the investment credit would likely be available on assets
purchased on or before April 18, 1969, and might be unavailable
for assets purchased thereafter. He opined that a signed purchase
order properly dated would be sufficient to get the credit, and suggested that we review our situation carefully. While he did not come
out and say so, what he obviously meant was that we should get
April 18 backdating on all possible projects such as the Holmes
deal."

LAWYER: Is this the same tax manager who reviewed the corporation's federal income tax return for the year ended March 31, 1970?

CPA: Yes.

LAWYER: What special audit procedures were utilized in checking
the corporation's entitlement to the investment credit claimed on
that return?

CPA: Purchase order and contract dates were reviewed.

LAWYER: And are you aware of the fact that IRS claims that
$70,000 of investment credit was improperly claimed because of back-
dating of documents?

CPA: I am now, but. . . .

LAWYER: Just answer the question, please. Were you aware of the
fact that the IRS might attempt to reallocate all of the income of the
50 corporations to one of the corporations under any of various
theories of the tax law?

CPA: Yes. However. . . .

LAWYER: Just answer the question, please. Were you also aware
of the fact that acquisition of certain of the corporations involved
might be challenged as having a tax reason, and thus the net operating
loss carryovers and investment credit carryovers of those corporations
might not be allowed to this corporation?

CPA: Yes. But. . . .

LAWYER: Just answer the question, please. Were you also aware that
the government might very well argue that intercorporate dividends
resulted from many of the transactions between the corporations

in the group, balanced out by contributions to capital which provide no deductibility? And followed by repayments of those contributions to capital, asserted by the corporations to be repayments of loans, and thus producing still additional dividends and tax deficiencies?

CPA: Yes, but. . . .

LAWYER: Just answer the question, please. Were you aware of the fact that 55 percent of the federal income tax returns that are audited result in deficiencies being proposed?

CPA: Yes, in a general sense.

LAWYER: Did you have any reason to believe that the income tax returns of these corporations would never be audited by the Internal Revenue Service?

CPA: No, although they had not been audited for previous years.

LAWYER: Did the corporation have any substantial amount of taxable income in those previous years for which no IRS audits were made?

CPA: No, it did not.

LAWYER: Did you provide, in determining the tax liability that the corporation put on its financial statements, for any amount to cover the possibility that the Internal Revenue Service might propose and collect additional taxes in the event the corporation's income tax returns were audited?

CPA: No.

LAWYER: Is the amount that was set up as the federal income tax liability the exact amount, to the very dollar, that is shown on the corporation's federal income tax return?

CPA: Yes.

LAWYER: Did you mention in any footnotes to the financial statements that there was a very substantial risk of additional tax deficiencies in large amounts being asserted against the corporation relative to the transactions of the given year and the prior years?

CPA: No. No revenue agent had yet made an examination or made any such proposal.

LAWYER: Do you still contend that in examining this particular item on the financial statements you were functioning as an independent auditor reviewing the amounts which were determined by the client and not by yourself, and applying your best judgment to what would be a fair presentation? Or were you not, at least as to this item, functioning simply as an employee of the corporation, attempting to minimize the corporation's income tax expense and put the best possible face on the corporation's financial statements?

CPA: (No reply)

THE THRESHOLD QUESTION

The question that is posed at the threshold of the discussion might then be: What is the conceptually "correct" amount of federal income tax expense to show on the financial statements for a given period? The answer: That amount of income tax which it is estimated will ultimately have to be paid, whether that payment is made currently, or whether some part of the amount estimated to be due is indefinite as to date of payment.

The deficiencies that are proposed in connection with the audits of corporate tax returns fall into two categories:

1. Those deficiencies which result only from timing differences, such as requiring that tax be paid currently on advance payments of income or reducing the amounts of depreciation allowed in the current year.

2. Those deficiencies which result from matters that are not differences in timing, such as the imposition of a penalty surtax under Section 531, disallowance of officers' salaries in part as unreasonable compensation, the disallowance of interest paid on the basis that it was incurred to carry tax-exempt securities, the utilization of net operating losses in connection with tax-free reorganizations or liquidations of subsidiaries, the classification of gain as capital or ordinary, the personal holding company status of the taxpayer, reallocation under IRC Section 61 or 482, or disallowance of multiple surtax exemptions. (This list is intended to be illustrative and not all-inclusive.)

Timing deficiencies. Should accruals be provided for potential timing differences? For example, if there is a high probability that the current deduction for repairs will be adjusted in a few years by the IRS as a capitalization, should the current year's accrual include provision for this possible future liability? Generally, this would not be appropriate because (1) there is no real liability and (2) the change has no relation to the current year's income. The result of an accrual would be to record a deferred tax debit and a deferred tax credit, having no effect on income and having no net effect on stockholder's equity. This would be similar to accruing future expenses by debiting prepaid expenses, a practice which is not followed. An exception to this general statement would be necessary where working capital would be significantly affected, such as where an adjustment by IRS is imminent, requiring a current tax accrual offset by a noncurrent deferred tax debit, or where it did not seem reasonably certain that the current deficiency would be offset by a future tax benefit.

Differences not due to timing. The major concern of the CPA should, therefore, be with possible adjustments which do not merely involve timing differences. For example, the imposition of a penalty surtax for unreasonably accumulating earnings results in an increase in the income tax expense for the period to which that surtax relates and no offsetting tax benefit in any future year. The possibility of material understatement of income tax expense or of tax liability, in those situations where it is anticipated that the corporation will continue to earn income and pay income tax, will normally arise in situations which fall into this category.

With this as the problem setting, what are the alternatives faced by the CPA in his role as independent auditor when he seeks to evaluate the reasonableness of the tax liability accrual? (In the discussion that follows, it is assumed that deferred taxes arising from APB Opinion No. 11 timing differences will be reflected in all alternatives.)

ALTERNATIVE 1 — TAX RETURN SHOWS LIABILITY

The major justifications for providing a liability amount which is the same as the amount disclosed on the federal income tax return are that (1) the amount of any additional deficiencies would not be material and (2) the provision of a liability that is not explained by specific items of tax deferral can only serve as an invitation to the IRS to more intensively audit the return involved in the hopes of discovering the specific tax items which the auditors have already set up as additional amounts due the government over and above the amounts admittedly due.

One defect in the materiality argument is that most of the practitioners advancing it do not attempt to calculate the amount of any possible income tax deficiencies arising from the transactions of the particular year, and thus are assuming that the possible deficiencies would not be material rather than determining what the amount of deficiencies might be and then resolving that the amount is not material. Certainly, the argument of materiality is not one that should be dismissed, but the use of the concept of materiality to avoid determining whether something is, in fact, material, is an example of a type of circular reasoning which can easily destroy the credibility of the work done by the professional CPA.

The contention that a revenue agent will seize on the amount of the excess tax accrual as an incentive to conduct a more vigorous examination is fiction and not fact. The amount of the excess is shown as a *deferred income tax* liability, and the determination of that amount is a process of estimation and approximation which has nothing to do with the determination of either taxable income or of tax liability. The agent should not be furnished the working papers supporting that calculation, and, if he insists on being provided such work papers, the administrative policy of the IRS in Washington would probably be one of *not* backing him up on his right to see them — absent extremely unusual circumstances.

But even if the IRS would use against the client any accruals in excess of the liability shown on the tax return, this can hardly justify the independent auditor's allowing a material understatement to receive his blessing.

In a majority of the situations in which he is expressing an opinion, the CPA may reach the conclusion that the best amount of tax liability reflected on the financial statements is the amount disclosed on the corporation's federal income tax return for the year. But this does not mean that the amount on the return is the best estimate *because* it is the amount shown on the return. The CPA should approach the question from some other point of view, even though that other point of view may lead him to conclude that the dollar and cent figure shown on the corporation income tax return is a fair presentation.

ALTERNATIVE 2 — REASONABLY CERTAIN

Recognizing that the proper amount of tax liability, in at least some situations, is not the amount shown on the corporation's federal income tax return for the year, the CPA might take the position that the tax liability that should be reflected on the financial statements should be an amount which is sufficient to cover the liability shown on the return plus any additional amounts of tax deficiency which he feels reasonably certain will be asserted and have to be paid.

The conscientious CPA who intends to reflect those material amounts of additional tax deficiency which he feels reasonably certain will be asserted and have to be paid needs a methodology for documenting his analysis. He is going to have to define what he means by "reasonably certain," "probable," or similar language. He is also going to have to find a way of putting down in some sort of quantifiable fashion his professional evaluation of the items that enter into a given year's return.[3]

---

[3]For a specific methodology for evaluating tax controversies, see Raby, *Building and Maintaining a Successful Tax Practice* (Prentice-Hall, 1964), pp. 281-284.

Thus, he may very well want to utilize the methodology to be discussed in the third alternative below, even though he may not be seeking the exact objective discussed in that alternative. In other words, he may want to utilize a subjective probability approach in attempting to determine whether he does feel that it is "probable" that an amount will be asserted.

Where only one or two items are involved, it is quite likely that the analysis made for this alternative and for the next alternative may really be the same analysis and lead to the same conclusion.

ALTERNATIVE 3 — SUBJECTIVE PROBABILITY

The subjective probability approach recognizes that the typical corporate return does result in a tax deficiency or a tax controversy upon being audited, and that the outcome of these audits and of these controversies is usually some sort of a compromise. Thus, the vast majority of taxpayers who contest a proposed deficiency at the Appellate Division level or who docket their cases with the Tax Court wind up reaching a settlement. On the average, these taxpapers pay 30 to 35 percent of the tax originally asserted by the revenue agent.[4]

The approach that the CPA takes as an auditor reviewing a tax accrual has to be different from the approach he takes in preparing an income tax return. In looking at the tax liability from a financial point of view, he is trying to spot any possible issues that could be raised by an examining revenue agent, even though he feels that the taxpayer has a supportable position.

Having ascertained what appear to be some areas where there may be additional potential tax liability in connection with the current year's return, or in connection with his review of income tax returns filed for previous years on which the statute of limitations is still open, how does the CPA arrive at a number which is his "best estimate" of the tax liability? The answer, it is suggested, is that he use his professional judgment, supplemented by the advice of tax technicians, where appropriate, to evaluate the range of alternative outcomes of the tax questions which he has raised.

For example, take the extreme case of a taxpayer who might be exposed to a tax deficiency of a million and a half dollars if net operating loss carry-overs were disallowed, but which is reporting a zero tax liability on the tax returns as filed. The million and a half

---

[4]*Annual Report, Commissioner of Internal Revenue, Year Ended June 30, 1970* (Washington: U.S. Government Printing Office, 1971), pp. 23, 131.

dollars would be sufficient to put the corporation out of business. The CPA analyzes the facts and evaluates the probable outcome of this situation as follows:

Ultimate Liability	Probability	Weighted Value
— 0 —	.6	— 0 —
$ 500,000	.3	$150,000
1,000,000	.05	50,000
1,500,000	.05	75,000
Total		$275,000

The probabilities shown add up to 1.00, of course, and reflect the CPA's best guess (hopefully an informed one) as to the likelihood of the ultimate liabilities indicated. In this situation, the proper tax accrual might be for $275,000 rather than for either 0 or $1,500,000.

Of course, making this estimate is not the end of the matter. Each year, the CPA is expressing an opinion.

Each year, the CPA must review the situation and either conclude that his original estimate is still substantially correct, or that a revised estimate is called for. There might then be a prior period adjustment and the deferred tax liability would be correspondingly increased or reduced.

The real gut question is: What is the position of the CPA if the matter does not work out as estimated and the taxpayer goes to court and loses? Might the CPA, in turn, find himself going to court and also losing? Might it be contended that since he knew there was a potential liability of $1,500,000, he was negligent in not requiring this fact to be revealed in some fashion in the financial statements of year 1?

And the answer to this, I fear, has to be "yes." The CPA is here faced with a choice of unsatisfactory alternatives. At one extreme, he can set up his best estimate and let the matter go at that, justifying his failure to give some sort of footnote warning with the rationalization that it is extremely unlikely that this dire tax result will occur. By so doing, however, he gives no weight at all to the risk aversion schedule of any given reader of the financial statements. A creditor or a stockholder might find even a 5 percent possibility of insolvency equal in weight to the 60 percent likelihood of no deficiency. But he is never given a chance to make any such evaluation. So far as he is informed, there is a $275,000 liability which differs in no material respect from any other fixed dollar debt.

The other alternative is to add a footnote explanation which points out that in the opinion of management it is possible that the IRS might assert tax deficiencies of as much as $1,500,000; that management feels that if such deficiencies are asserted, the position of management will probably be sustained and no deficiencies will finally have to be paid; that, in recognition of the uncertainties attendant upon tax controversies and the fact that most such controversies are settled upon a compromise basis, provision of $275,000 has been made for any such possible deficiencies; and that management believes that this provision is more than adequate. Thus, the financial statements reflect the best estimates possible, while the reader is fully informed as to a significant contingency.

It should be noted that the example used was deliberately extreme. In other instances, the need for a footnote disclosure may not be as great. In case of doubt, the CPA should probably opt for supplementing the tax accrual with a footnote explanation.

The subjective probability approach to estimating a tax liability involves using a methodology which reduces to a quantifiable form a number of judgmental factors which otherwise would not be specifically set down and explicitly analyzed in arriving at a final decision. This approach has the advantage of being understandable to an audience of lay people, such as a jury. Thus, the use of the technique is one which can be explained to people to whom a decision might otherwise appear to be arbitrary in the light of what, in fact, ultimately did happen. It must be remembered that problems that arise in such situations as those involving the tax accrual occur only after the event, and that the perspective of persons trying to evaluate the reasonableness of what was done at the time of the audit is colored by the knowledge they have of what actually occurred. The auditor is battling against this type of "hindsight halo" effect.

The reasoning involved in this subjective probability estimating approach seems consistent with, although not required by, Paragraph 35 of APB Opinion No. 11. In that paragraph, the Board rejects the "liability" method of providing for deferred taxes. The deferred method of tax allocation which is adopted by the Board is only subtly different from the liability method. The difference lies basically in the income determination orientation and the conclusion that the primary focus should be on deferring any temporary benefits of timing differences. As applied to the question at hand, it is probably fair to say that the benefit of taking a deduction which is expected to be disallowed in the future, or the benefit of not paying currently such a tax as the accumulated earnings surtax, which ultimately might be payable in the future, should not be recognized as relieving current income of a charge against it to the extent that it is considered but a temporary benefit. Recognition of a temporary benefit resulting from advocacy position in preparing a tax return would seem to constitute accounting for a contingent asset, which is generally not appropriate under Accounting Research Bulletin No. 50 of the AICPA. As set out in Paragraph 3 of that bulletin, "Contingencies which result in gains usually are not reflected in the accounts since to do so might be to recognize revenue prior to its realization."

Admittedly, there is similarity between a potential tax deficiency and other potential liabilities which are treated as contingent liabilities and not booked. However, the income tax liability is different from any contingent liability situation in at least three respects:

1. The taxpayer has the burden of proof as to what his actual liability should be, whereas other claimants against the client normally have the burden of proof.

2. The liability relationship is a continuing or recurring one as to which estimates of outcome can be made.

3. The independence CPA is, or should be, uniquely qualified to evaluate the tax liability exposure as compared to other exposure where he is relying on the evaluations of others.

The proper time for recognizing the tax saving ultimately resulting from taking an advocacy position in preparing the income tax return would appear to be no later than the year in which the statute of limitations ran on any assessment of a deficiency relative to the item or items involved. At that time, a prior period adjustment would result. If a deficiency was finally paid, then there would be a prior period adjustment in the amount of the difference between the accrual that had been made to cover deficiencies for the year involved and the amount actually determined.

ALTERNATIVE 4 — FOOTNOTE DISCLOSURE

Many CPAs feel that footnote disclosures cure all other reporting defects. Footnotes as to the tax liability include such noncommittal gems as "The company's federal income tax returns have been examined through December 31, 1968, by the Internal Revenue Service." At the other end of the scale are footnotes that disclose that a tax deficiency has been proposed by IRS, the amount thereof, and that the management intends to contest the determination. These latter are often accompanied by "subject to" opinions from the auditors, along the lines of the following:

In our opinion, subject to the outcome of the income tax matters described in Note 5 to the financial statements, the financial statements referred to above present fairly the financial position of ABC Corporation at December 31, 1970, and the results of its operations and changes in financial position for the year then ended, in conformity with generally accepted accounting principles applied on a basis consistent with that of the preceding year.

5. Federal Income Taxes

The company is presently contesting deficiencies in federal income taxes proposed by the Internal Revenue Service for the years 1968 and 1969, in the aggregate amount of $800,000, exclusive of interest. Legal counsel advises that the point in question is one on which there are conflicting federal court decisions and on which further litigation may be required. Consequently, it is impossible to determine the extent of the company's liability, if any, at this time. No provision has been made for this contingent liability.

The first type of footnote is meaningless. If the CPA feels that a contingent tax liability exists which the client is not willing to book, or which is sufficiently uncertain as to its imposition that it is truly contingent, then the contingent liability note should explain the situation.

The second type of footnote is informative as far as it goes. More useful, but seldom if ever provided, is an estimate as to the amount that will be ultimately payable. Such an estimate has the advantage of allowing the reader to evaluate the significance of the tax controversy. Certainly, if the company anticipates that it will be able to settle the tax controversy for $X, and $X is material, this fact is also a material piece of information. More important, the footnote is normally used only after the IRS has appeared on the scene and it is clear that a deficiency will be proposed.

As mentioned, footnote disclosure is frequently coupled with a "subject to" opinion. Such opinions may not be acceptable to stock exchanges in connection with original listing applications, or to the SEC in connection with the filing of registration statements, although they are apparently sometimes acceptable to the SEC in connection with the filing of annual reports on Form 10K. The problem with a "subject to" opinion is that it isn't really the right solution if, in fact, a meaningful estimate of the ultimate liability can be made. The CPA is shifting to the reader of the statement the burden of evaluating the probable outcome of the tax questions involved.

There are those who say that a subjective probability approach is really just pulling numbers out of the air. But from the standpoint of providing the user of financial statements with information that is the best available, it would seem that an estimate based upon the professional judgment of competent tax personnel would be better and more useful than a statement of the maximum possible liability to which the company might be exposed, the opinion of management that it has adopted a defensible position, and an auditor's opinion which is "subject to" the tax footnote and the resolution of any tax controversies indicated therein.

CONCLUSION

If any of the concepts discussed above are accepted, other than the first, it is quite likely that situations will develop where the CPA's role as an independent auditor may conflict with his role as an advocate of his client's tax position.

Four approaches to a solution. The CPA firm is involved in providing tax advice to the corporation, handles the preparation of the tax return in a majority of instances and expresses an opinion as to the reasonableness of these provisions on the financial statements. One possible resolution of the problem is to divorce the CPA from performing all of these separate functions at one time. This may appear to be neat, and theoretically satisfying, but it ignores the reality that the dual relationship has existed for over 60 years, and is not that easily going to be terminated.

Another alternative that might resolve the problem would be to change the relationship of the CPA to the tax return and to the tax planning process. In this resolution, the CPA would become, in effect, a representative of the Internal Revenue Service, conducting an audit that becomes a substitute for such an audit by the IRS. Presumably, in advising clients, he would adopt the most conservative possible position. In fact, this is a solution which has been adopted by at least some CPAs and advocated by many others. They take the position that it is their job to resolve all doubts against the client and to prepare tax returns that will seldom if ever have any deficiencies. If a client appears to be in danger of a penalty surtax for unreasonably accumulating earnings, their solution is to recommend that the client pay out the earnings in the form of dividends, and thus obviate any danger of tax being imposed.

This is what many clients want, for one criterion of an effectively functioning tax department is that when the income tax and other tax returns it has prepared are audited, no material deficiencies are proposed. Any practitioner who has worked extensively with some of the more bureaucratized corporations can testify that this is a performance standard which is widely used by many large organizations. On the other hand, practitioners who have worked with entrepreneurially oriented organizations can also testify that this is not a universal attitude. At the moment, certainly, the attitude of resolving all doubts against the client and the objective of so planning transactions and so preparing returns that no deficiencies can be proposed upon their examination are not universally accepted practices or objectives within the profession. Robert K. Mautz and Hussein A. Sharaf, in their *Philosophy of Auditing*, propose that the practical solution is to divorce auditing from other work.[5] This would presumably mean, in the context of our problem, that the audit staff would not prepare the corporation's federal income tax return; they would instead review the adequacy of the provisions being made by the same firm's tax department. For many accounting firms, tax department preparation of all returns would require substantial expansion of tax departments, and would increase the cost of rendering services to the client. It would thus weaken the profession's dominance of the tax field because there would be less advantage having tax work done by the same firm that did the auditing rather than by tax lawyers. Yet this is probably the most feasible solution — although not a complete one.

Regardless of whether or not the tax department independently prepares the returns and estimates the tax accrual, with review by the auditors, the question still remains of how to live with a dual relationship with the client in a world where the practitioner — presumably an intelligent, well-educated, and conscientious professional man — is desirous of discharging his various obligations with honesty, candor and integrity, and without exposing himself to unnecessary liability suits.

It would appear that the approach of subjectively evaluating the possible issues and their possible outcomes offers an understandable, relatively objective, documentable solution to the dilemma which can and should be adopted now — and is already in use, to some extent, with many firms.

---

[5]"Management requests advice because it expects to use it; the consultant gives it to be used; the consultant knows that he will be judged by the ultimate usefulness of his advice in bringing success to management's efforts.... How then can he claim to be completely independent?" The solution proposed is that "as soon as a given client becomes of sufficient size that there is a substantial public interest in its audited financial statements, we feel a strict separation of auditing and other services should be effected, if not by division within the accounting firm, then by employment of separate accountants for the two types of services." See Robert K. Mautz and Hussein A. Sharaf, *The Philosophy of Auditing* (Menasha, Wisconsin: American Accounting Association, 1961), pp. 222 & 230.

A final comment. The accounting profession is not now being criticized for the way in which tax accruals are handled. Nobody has yet been sued for huge amounts of money. Therefore, it might be argued that there is no problem and thus there is no reason for this discussion. However, if the profession is going to have the status to which it aspires, it is going to have to demonstrate integrity even when no one is looking; if it is going to be viewed as having meaningful standards, these will have to be enunciated before rather than after they are challenged.

If the auditor is to be taken seriously as an independent researcher in entity data, he is going to have to have a concept of what is material and what is significant before, rather than after, he has the numbers in front of him and the client pressures and the time pressures bearing down on him.

Legal Responsibilities

A dramatic increase in the number of litigations involving auditors has occurred since the mid 1960's. Significant changes in the auditor's legal responsibilities have taken place and they promise to have a major impact upon the auditor and the conduct of his examination.

The implications to the profession of recent liability cases are of utmost importance to every auditor. Reiling and Taussig provide a lucid analysis of four major liability cases and present their views as to the real meaning of these cases to the profession. The Continental Vending case is perhaps destined to have the greatest impact and D. B. Isbell, through skillful scrutiny, proposes an outline of the lessons to be learned therefrom.

The accountants' responsibility for unaudited financial statements has not escaped judicial review. Emanuel Saxe, in the last selection of this section, discusses the 1136 Tenants' Corp. case and cites the dangers inherent in write-up work resulting in unaudited financial statements.

11. Recent Liability Cases — Implications for Accountants*

Henry B. Reiling and
Russell A. Taussig†

For the accounting profession, the late 1960's was a time of prosperity and a time of peril. Each year accountants posted new highs in billings and earnings, but at the same time they were reportedly subjected to an unprecedented number of lawsuits. A staff reporter for *The Wall Street Journal* opined that nearly 100 lawsuits were pending against auditors in late 1966.[1] More recently an associate editor of *Fortune* reported that as many claims for damages were filed against accountants in 1968 as in the previous 12 years.[2] While some are skeptical that the volume of cases is so high,[3] it seems clear that there has been an increase in volume of suits filed,[4] that these suits have frequently involved the profession's more prestigious firms and that four cases surfaced which were particularly qualified to capture the profession's attention: *BarChris, Continental Vending, Yale Express* and *Westec.*‡

Many readers are familiar with these cases. Those who are not may refer to Appendix A, page 167, which summarizes the facts, issues and rulings as developed to the date of this article. Litigation is far from over. Indeed, *Yale* and *Westec* have yet to go to trial; nevertheless, enough is known at this time to make a tentative assessment of their characteristics and their potential implications for the public accounting profession. It must be kept in mind, however, that allegations are not synonymous with findings after trial, and lower court

*From *The Journal of Accountancy* (September, 1970), pp. 39-53. Copyright (1970) by the American Institute of Certified Public Accountants, Inc. Reprinted by permission of the AICPA.

†Henry B. Reiling, M.B.A., J.D., is an Associate Professor of Business, Columbia University, New York City. Russell A. Taussig, C.P.A., Ph.D., is a Professor of Business Administration, University of Hawaii, Honolulu, Hawaii.

‡Two additional suits. *Mill Factors* and *Revenue Properties,* were instituted too late to be assessed and possibly commented upon in this article. Both involve very substantial dollar claims and may warrant the reader's attention.

[1] Lee Berton, "CPAs Under Fire," *The Wall Street Journal,* November 15, 1966, p. 13.

[2] Louis, "The Accountants are Changing the Rules," *Fortune* (June 15, 1968), p. 177.

[3] An attorney particularly competent in the area of accountants' liability has expressed this view privately to the authors. On the other hand Mr. Berton informed the authors that his conclusion in *The Wall Street Journal* represented a middle ground of estimates solicited in approximately 200 interviews with members of leading accounting firms, accounting organizations and their attorneys.

[4] It should be noted that accounting is not the only profession experiencing a flurry of litigation. There is a rash of malpractice suits pending against doctors, lawyers, architects and investment bankers. See "Professional Liability and Malpractice," *Federation Insurance Council Quarterly* (Summer, 1967), p. 8.

conclusions can be overturned on appeal. Subsequent developments may affect the tentative conclusions of this article.

In the authors' opinion these cases collectively have the following three significant characteristics:

1. Recent and pending interpretations of federal securities laws appear likely to give plaintiffs not in a contractual relationship with accountants easier access to accountants than was heretofore the case under common law.

2. Judges and juries composed generally of laymen, not experts in the field of accounting, are beginning to render decisions interpreting accounting principles as well as auditing procedures.

3. The responsibilities of officers, directors and other professionals for financial statements appearing in prospectuses and related documents have received judicial comment for practically the first time; the result is a new awareness of responsibilities and risks and a related request for accountants to expand their attest function.

These characteristics raise at least five long-range planning questions for the accounting profession:

1. Must fee structures be adjusted to reflect the greater potential liability which appears to be emerging from recent lawsuits against public accountants?

2. What are the dangers in allowing courts to assume leadership in the pronouncement of accounting principles?

3. How can the accounting profession properly restrict its legal hazards?

4. Should accountants extend their attest function to financial information not now included in certified statements, and certify interim financial statements that are presently unaudited?

5. What are the advantages and pitfalls for accountants in accepting a new role regarding financial statements?

As background for the consideration of these questions let us examine the features of recent cases of particular significance to accountants.

IMPACT OF RECENT CASES UPON RELATIONSHIP OF ACCOUNTANTS TO SOCIETY

Circumvention of Common Law Defenses. Three recent cases, *BarChris, Yale Express* and *Westec* include as plaintiffs third parties who are not in a contractual relationship with the auditor. Until recently, third party actions against accountants generally failed because of the limited scope of legal doctrines available to the plaintiffs. The plaintiffs either had to espouse common law negligence or deceit doctrines, or they had to assert statutory rights available under the Securities Act of 1933 or the Securities Exchange Act of 1934. The common law alternative brought them face to face with *Ultramares Corp. v. Touche, Niven & Co.*[5] or the formidable task of proving fraud[6]; the securities law alternative forced them to assume the uncertainty and risk of pioneering in the interpretation of the statutes.

Judge Cardozo in *Ultramares* held that an accountant was ordinarily liable for negligent misrepresentation solely to the person who retained him, or to the person who was known to be the primary beneficiary of the information. The Court went on to say, however, that an accountant could be held liable by a broader group if his conduct was fraudulent or so grossly negligent as to amount to fraud. A few subsequent cases have imposed liability on this constructive fraud theory, but these cases have been inconsequential. *Ultramares* has been widely followed for more than three decades, and it has effectively blocked negligence actions by third parties under common law. However, the vitality of the common law privity doctrine is once again being tested. Security holders represented by the trustee in bankruptcy are using common law negligence as an alternative theory for recovery in *Westec*. Today the prospects for a successful attack against accountants by security holders are better than in the past; there is evidence that the utility of the privity defense for accountants has begun to deteriorate.[7]

Westec itself may not pose any direct threat to privity. This will become clear only as the facts are developed at trial. Nevertheless, the case is a potentially important barometer of judicial attitude toward privity and the tone of any comment on privity even in dictum must be watched with care and with Holmes' prediction theory of the law[8] clearly in mind. Should the pressures on privity from dictum

---

[5]Ultramares Corp. v. Touche, Niven & Co, 255 New York 170, 174 N. E. 441 (1931).

[6]The conditions under which misrepresentations are fraudulent are set forth in note 51.

[7]A very good discussion of the English and American cases and articles questioning the privity defense is presented by District Judge Pettine in *Rusch Factors Inc.* v. *Levin* 284 F. Supp. 85, 90-93 (1967). Expressing considerable doubt regarding the wisdom of the privity defense in negligence action involving accountants, the Court nevertheless had to stop short of a holding on the subject since the plaintiff in *Rusch Factors* came within the exception to privity available to those whose use is the very end and aim of the audit.

[8]Mr. Justice Holmes defined law as "[t] he *prophecies* of what the courts will do in fact. . . . " [Emphasis added.] Address by Oliver Wendell Holmes, Jr. then a Justice of the Supreme Judicial Court of Massachusetts, Dedication of the new hall of the Boston University School of Law, Jan. 8, 1897, published as "The Path of the Law," 10 *Harv. L. Rev.* 457, 461 (1897). Thus law is a prediction. And precedent constitutes a major but not the only basis for that prediction. See *id.*, p. 457 and p. 467.

and articles continue to mount,[9] and the authors anticipate that they will, the probability of an adverse decision on the doctrine will at some point become sufficiently great that professional practices of individuals and firms should reflect the increased liability risks in advance of any actual adverse holding.

Recent developments also imply an expansion in the legal hazards facing accountants under statutory law. Since passage in 1933 and 1934, the federal securities laws have represented a potentially effective way for litigants to reach accountants when blocked at common law by *Ultramares* or the difficulty of proving fraud. Indeed, aside from the attractiveness of the federal securities laws as the potential means for circumventing common law doctrines, it contains several ancillary features which enhance its usefulness as an alternative legal weapon.[10] However, the securities laws have evolved slowly in areas governing the relationship between accountants and the investing public,[11] and its potential aid to investors has not yet been fully realized. This situation may be changing.

In *BarChris* plaintiffs finally used Section 11 of the 1933 Act[12] against accountants, and in *Yale Express* and *Westec* plaintiffs are testing the utility of Rule 10b-5 promulgated under the 1934 Act[13] as a means of reaching accountants.[14] The outcome of these cases

---

[9]Accountants accustomed to taking the privity defense for granted should also reflect on the fact that it has recently been virtually eliminated from its formerly entrenched position in the product liability area. See Prosser, "The Fall of the Citadel (Strict Liability to the Consumer)," 50 *Minn. L. Rev.* 791 (1966). There are of course many socially significant distinctions between that area and the accountants' liability area, one of the more important of which is the personal injury often attending defective products in contrast to the financial injury that can attend incorrect financial statements. The point is that privity is under attack generally and the mere citation of precedent may no longer be adequate. Accountants' continued insulation from third party negligence claims will in the authors' opinion turn on the marshalling of the social justifications for that insulation.

[10]For example, the 1933 and 1934 Acts reduce the problem of quantifying the amount of damage sustained, and the additional problem of establishing a causal connection between the allegedly improper conduct and the damage.

[11]For example, prior to 1954 the total number of suits brought under the civil sections of the 1933 Act against defendants of all classes totaled only 38, an average of less than two per year. L. *Loss, Securities Regulation*, 989 (Supp. 1955).

[12]Sec. 11 of the Securities Act of 1933 at issue in *BarChris* provides for a civil action for damages against accountants caused by their material errors in a registration statement. The statutory language of Sec. 11 makes it clear that privity is not needed for a successful suit under that section.

[13]The courts have interpreted Rule 10b-5 to permit a civil action for damages caused by fraud and misleading statements made in conjunction with the purchase or sale of securities. This provision reaches conduct which Sec. 11 and Sec. 18 do not.

[14]The following two additional provisions though less important than Section 11 and Rule 10b-5 are also involved in one or more of the four cases treated in this article:

Sec. 18 of the Securities Exchange Act of 1934. In essence it provides for a civil action for damages against any person who makes or causes a fraudulent statement to be made in statements filed with the exchanges or SEC.

Sec. 17 of the Securities Act of 1933. This provision is used to secure criminal indictments and injunctions. It is a general anti-fraud provision, making unlawful any form of fraud, untruth, or omission of a material fact associated with the sale of securities. This provision has not yet produced any case law of special significance to accountants.

and the accompanying legal rationales will probably do much to encourage or discourage other plaintiffs and define the legal environment for accountants during the 1970s.

Although the accountants were held liable for nonfraudulent conduct to third parties not in privity with them, *BarChris* produced no unexpected legal theories or statutory interpretations directly affecting accountants; it was clear from reading Section 11 that a privity relationship was not a prerequisite to recovery and it was also clear that conduct short of fraud would support a recovery. Nevertheless, *BarChris* is likely to have legal significance for accountants. It is the first important case decided under Section 11 and it involved a major firm. The authors anticipate that it may alert potential litigants to a previously little used statutory provision, and similar cases will soon follow.

In the authors' opinion the legal environment surrounding Rule 10b-5 is alive with prospects for an extension of legal doctrines which would increase accountants' risks. The march of cases under the frequently interpreted Rule 10b-5 has steadily enlarged the list of potential plaintiffs and defendants. This expansion has occurred along with the erosion of the privity defense, a common law concept which was judicially appended at an early date to the rule. The question today is whether the erosion of privity is sufficiently advanced and the absence of direct personal gain sufficiently unimportant so that accountants can be reached. Although *Westec* and *Yale Express* are still in the pretrial stage, they both involve 10b-5 and are capable of defining the relationship between accountants and the rule.[15]

Accounting principles. Current cases differ from past ones not only with respect to legal theories used but also with respect to allegations of accounting errors. Plaintiffs increasingly allege violations of generally accepted accounting principles, a marked departure from such classic cases as *Ultramares,* (above), and *McKessen & Robbins,*[16] in which the decisions were based largely on auditing deficiencies. Judges and juries not only are finding deficiencies in the way auditors examine financial records, but also are making statements on accounting principles and the way in which they should be applied.

In *BarChris* the Court ruled that profits on a sale-leaseback should have been eliminated; however, the AICPA statements on accounting

---

[15]Indeed, Judge Tyler in *Yale Express* denied the accountants' motion to dismiss certain parts of the complaint which were premised on 10b-5 though he did so without prejudice to renewal of the motion at trial. Judge Tyler's stress upon the importance of the questions involved and his stress upon the Court's need for further factual and legal development of those questions suggests further important comment will be forthcoming from *Yale Express.* The importance of the case is underlined by the fact that the SEC is participating as *amicus curiae.*

[16]*McKesson & Robbins, Inc.,* SEC Accounting Series Release No. 19 (1940).

principles at the time of the transaction were silent as to the need for eliminating such profits. Publication of Accounting Principles Board Opinion No. 5 resolved the question concerning the accounting for sale-leasebacks. Opinion No. 5 of 1964 provides that ". . . the sale and the leaseback usually cannot be accounted for as independent transactions. Neither the sale price nor the annual rental can be objectively evaluated independently of the other. Consequently, material gains or losses . . . should be amortized over the life of the lease. . . ." However, APB Opinion No. 5 did not exist in 1960, when Bar-Chris entered into the sale and leaseback of its bowling alley. The applicable section of Accounting Research Bulletin No. 43 simply provided that: ". . . in the year in which the transaction originates, there should be disclosure of the principal details of any important sale-and-lease transaction."

Let us re-examine the BarChris sale-leaseback transaction in the light of then existing accounting principles to answer the claims of some commentators that the relevant principles were sufficiently defined before the case was brought to trial. One might advance several reasons to explain why BarChris should have eliminated the profit in its consolidated statements on its sale of a bowling alley to a finance factor after which the alley was leased back by a subsidiary. One might argue that an arm's-length transaction was lacking and the auditor could therefore not attest to the amount of profit on the transfer. One might also claim that management could time the recognition of profit to suit its private needs. Moreover, BarChris still had the use of the property after the sale-leaseback, and to recognize profit portrayed legal form not economic substance. Furthermore, one might argue that recognition of profit violated the ancient principle of conservatism: "recognize all losses, but anticipate no gains." Finally, the overriding doctrine of fairness might be invoked; one might argue profit should be eliminated so that financial statements would fairly present the financial position and results of operations for BarChris.

But the doctrine of fairness is necessarily egocentric. He who espouses it presumes to know the one and only correct interpretation of a given transaction. Unfortunately, fairness like beauty exists in the eye of the beholder. What appears fair to one often appears unfair to another. No one denies the propriety of fairness, but accountants need more explicit guidelines.

A similar comment applies to conservatism. Understatement of earnings can be just as harmful as overstatement. An investor can suffer economic injury from selling a stock on understated earnings as well as he can from buying on overstated earnings. The doctrine of conservatism, a disappearing one,[17] by itself is not sufficient to dictate non-recognition of gain on a sale-leaseback.

It appears that ambiguity as to the definition of the accounting entity existed at the time BarChris entered into its sale-and-leaseback transaction. Furthermore, a review of the pros and cons for eliminating the profit on the BarChris sale-leaseback discloses that reasonable doubt existed as to what was required in accordance with the generally accepted accounting principles circa 1960. In fact, the issuance of Opinion No. 5 would have been unnecessary if the principles regarding sale-leaseback transactions were unambiguous. In rebuttal, one might contend that the principles always existed; and that the opinions were mere codifications of existing practice. This argument runs contrary to fact, however, for the APB Opinions frequently have changed previous accounting methods, as they did with respect to earnings and losses on unconsolidated subsidiaries. It appears to the authors that generally accepted accounting principles for sale-leasebacks were not clearly stated at the time of the BarChris audit, and because of this uncertainty, the Court, perhaps inadvertently, prescribed a method of accounting it considered proper under the circumstances.

Westec is another case in which the Court is asked to consider accounting principles, and to rule on the way in which financial statements should have been prepared.[18] The complaint of Westec's trustee in bankruptcy charges, among other things, that reported earnings for 1964 and 1965 were inflated by the company's improper accounting for several acquisitions. The plaintiff claims that five acquisitions accounted for as a pooling did not meet the established criteria. The handling of these is also attacked on grounds that it was improper to consolidate earnings of companies acquired after the close of the financial period but before release of the period's audit report.[19]

The allegations concerning the acquisition of Seacat-Zapata Offshore Co. illustrate the difficult questions the Court may have to face. Westec's negotiations for Seacat allegedly produced a tentative agreement whereby Westec would acquire Seacat's assets other than $1.5 million cash in exchange for $9.5 million in stock; and Westec would subsequently lease the assets to Zapata, a company which owned 50

---

[17]Maurice Moonitz, *The Basic Postulates of Accounting,* Accounting Research Study No. 1 (American Institute of CPAs, 1961), pp. 46-47.

[18]The description of *Westec* is based on the original complaint of August 23, 1968 filed in U.S. District Court (Houston). It must be remembered that all of the comments concerning *Westec* are based only on allegations. The case had not gone to trial as of February 1, 1970.

[19]The complaint alleges that three acquisitions were consumated on March 26, 1965, the date of the 1964 audit report; it is further alleged that the 1965 audit report was held open until April 28, 1966 to enable three additional acquisitions to be effected for the purpose of inflating 1965 earnings.

per cent of Seacat. The auditors, when asked if pooling could be used, said no. In their opinion the lease of assets prevented pooling since the surviving entity failed the continuity-of-business test. Seacat would have changed from an operating to a leasing company. Although, in the authors' opinion this interpretation is questionable, management was convinced and allegedly asked the auditors for help in revising the terms of the acquisition.

The complaint charges that the auditors then suggested the substitution of a "work contract" for the lease, which in their opinion would permit pooling. According to the terms of the contract, Westec retained legal ownership of the properties and Zapata operated them, receiving as its fee a percentage of profits which rose as profits increased. It was allegedly anticipated that the work contract would produce the same cash flow to both parties as the lease, though it was not a lease[20] and therefore would not prevent pooling. The suggestion was implemented and the auditors approved the use of pooling in the annual reports.

The Seacat aspect of Westec raises three basic accounting questions. Did the work contract differ sufficiently from the original lease to justify pooling? Did the auditors lose their independence by the depth of their involvement? Was it proper to include in the audited statements an acquisition made subsequent to the accounting period in question? In the author's opinion, answers to the first two questions are not available in the accounting literature to date.[21] Nevertheless, the Court must make its rulings, and rulings necessarily rendered in the absence of clear guidelines are fraught with risk for the accountants.

The Court in *BarChris* was confronted with accounting alternatives and, as a byproduct of its decision, a preferred treatment for sale-leasebacks was identified. Alternatives are present in *Westec* and the possibility exists that it will have a similar consequence. This raises the serious question of whether, as a practical matter, judges and juries can avoid selecting amongst alternatives. A related important question is whether accounting guidelines which emerge from the judicial process will be as well conceived as those resulting from the careful method of review and public exposure developed over the years by the AICPA.

Disclosure of privileged information. The plaintiffs in *Yale Express* are asking the Court to decide whether independent accountants, who

---

[20]Should the level of operations have deviated from that which was expected, the work contract would have produced a cash flow higher or lower than the lease.

[21]The Accounting Principles Board has promulgated a statement on this matter. American Institute of Certified Public Accountants, Accounting Principles, Current text, Sec. 1091.13 (1969). Consequently, if the plaintiff is seriously going to urge that retroactive inclusion was wrong, it appears he must argue that the Accounting Principles Board erred in creating the principle, or argue that the Westec situation represented an exception to the principle.

have expressed an opinion on financial statements in a 10-K, must disclose to the public material errors and omissions from those statements which they have discovered during the course of a subsequent management services engagement.[22] The accountants' dilemma arose from the dual responsibilities it assumed. Judge Tyler observed in *Yale Express* that as auditor of the 10-K financial statements its responsibility "is not only to the client who pays his fee, but also to investors, creditors and others who may rely on the financial statements which he certifies. . . . The public accountant must report fairly on the facts as he finds them whether favorable or unfavorable to his client. His duty is to safeguard the public interest, not that of his client. [In the Matter of Touche, Niven, Bailey and Smart, 237 SEC 629, 670-671 (1957).] (Footnotes omitted)."[23]

On the other hand, when the accountant performed the subsequent special study his "primary obligations, under normal circumstances, were to [his] client and not the public."[24] The unique question posed in *Yale Express* is whether the duty to the investing public terminated once the financial statements were certified or alternatively whether a duty to the investing public existed after the certification, which duty dominated the obligation to the client.

The Court deferred until after a trial the question of whether a dominant post-certification duty to investors was imposed by one or more of the following: common law deceit doctrines; Section 18 (a) of the Securities Exchange Act of 1934; and Rule 10b-5. In its ultimate resolution of this question the Court must reconcile the needs of investors for unfavorable financial information against the possible benefits to companies from preserving a confidential relationship between consultants and clients. Should this question eventually go against the accountants, it seems reasonable to anticipate that for companies with less than normal financial strength accountants and clients may find it undesirable to have audits and special studies performed by the same firm.

The threat of criminal action. *Continental Vending* adds the threat of criminal action to the legal hazards of accountancy. In this case, criminal action was instituted against the auditors by the U.S. Attorney for the Southern District of New York. Significantly, crim-

---

[22]The committee on auditing procedure of the American Institute of Certified Public Accountants recently issued Statement on Auditing Procedure No. 41 (October 1969), "Subsequent Discovery of Facts Existing at the Date of the Auditor's Report." The Statement establishes procedures to be followed by the auditor who, subsequent to the date of his report upon audited financial statements, becomes aware that facts may have existed at that date which might have affected his report had he then been aware of such facts.

[23]*Fischer v. Kletz*, 266 F. Supp. 180, 184 (S.D.N.Y. 1967)

[24]*Id.*

inal actions against accountants, particularly major firms, have been infrequent in the past.[25]   Instead, incidents of alleged wrongdoing and substandard accounting practices have been resolved by administrative proceedings within the SEC[26] or in civil suits brought by the injured parties.

The severity of the government's decision to pursue a criminal charge — particularly since the accountants were not alleged to have benefited directly from their wrongdoing — leads one to speculate as to its motivation. Perhaps an analogy to the antitrust area is valid. When the government sustains a judgment against a company for an antitrust violation, that judgment can be used to establish a *prima facie* case by a private party allegedly injured by the violation.[27] Considerable help is given to the private litigant. A violation of the law is tentatively established, substantially reducing the risk of an unsuccessful suit. The prospect of a criminal suit as well as a civil suit makes a company more willing to acquiesce to a consent decree or some other settlement short of prolonged litigation. Perhaps the government is attempting to facilitate civil suits by resorting to criminal action. The criminal judgment would not have *prima facie* civil power,[28] but evidence would have been gathered and much of the rationale for a civil case would have been developed. Alternatively, where civil suit has already been instituted, as in *Continental,* the threat of criminal action might encourage prompt settlement.[29]

Expanded responsibilities.   Last but not least significant of the characteristics of the cases under review is that they result in a pressure

---

[25]Diligent research has uncovered no other criminal prosecution where the motive of personal gain was so lacking and the argument for conformity with generally accepted accounting principles so strong.

[26]The SEC brings disciplinary or "disbarment" proceedings against accountants under Rule 2 of its Rules of Practice. Those rules provide in part as follows:
"(e) Suspension and Disbarment. The Commission may deny temporarily or permanently, the privilege of appearing or practicing before it in any way to any person who is found by the Commission after notice of any opportunity for hearing in the matter
    (1) not to possess the requisite qualifications to represent others, or
    (2) to be lacking in character or integrity or to have engaged in unethical or improper professional conduct." 17 Code Fed. Reg. Sec. 201.2.

[27]15 U.S.C. Sec. 15 (1964).

[28]The successful securities law plaintiff cannot recover treble damages as could his counterpart in the antitrust area. See *Globus v. Law Research Service, Inc.,* 418 F.2d 1276 (2d Cir. 1969).

[29]The prospect of criminal action is particularly threatening to accountants because of its potential impact on their professional lives. AICPA Bylaws 7.3.1, as amended February 20, 1969, specify that membership shall be terminated without a hearing if there is filed with the Secretary of the Institute a judgment for conviction of a crime defined as a felony under the law of the convicting jurisdiction. The Trial Board of the Institute according to Section 7.4 of the Bylaws may expel a member if he has been convicted of a criminal offense which tends to discredit the profession. More significantly, state boards have the power to revoke a CPA's license to practice. However, it has been held that revocation was too severe a penalty where the improper conduct consisted of preparing and issuing certified statements in which the corporate client's liabilities were deliberately understated when the CPA's professional conduct had previously been unobjectionable and his motivation had been solely to give the corporation a chance to stay in business. *Shander v. Allen,* 28 A.D. 2nd 1150, 284 N.Y.S.2d 142 (1967).

for expansion of the auditors' responsibilities. Two forces may cause this expansion. Section 11 of the 1933 Act[30] has been interpreted to impose a broad responsibility for financial information upon underwriters and signatories of the registration statement. Consequently, they are asking auditors to attest to new financial data. Also, for the first time a court has articulated the responsibilities of independent accountants in S-1 reviews.

The demand for an expansion of the audit function is an outgrowth of the "due diligence" defense in *BarChris*.[31] At issue was that defense as embodied in Section 11 (b). The statute indicates that underwriters and signatories generally must make a reasonable and good faith investigation according to a *prudent man standard;* however, if they make statements in good faith on the authority of an expert, a *lesser standard* is operative with regard to the expertised statements. They must then merely have no reasonable grounds for believing the statements to be incorrect. Applying these standards the Court even held new outside directors to be liable since their investigations consisted only of questions put to officers and tenured directors, individuals who were not experts. Accordingly, directors (on their own initiative and at the request of underwriters) are asking independent accountants (experts within the meaning of Section 11) to expertise a larger portion of the information filed with the SEC, such as sales backlog, plant capacity and floor space.

The Court in *BarChris* also discussed the particular responsibility of the accountants in an S-1 review.[32] The question arose because

---

[30]The most significant prior case discussing Sec. 11 is *Shunts* v. *Hirlman*, 28 F. Supp. 478 (S.D. Cal. 1939). Although the accountants escaped liability in that early decision, it has been roundly criticized by Professor Loss because of "... the surprising low accounting standards which seemed to satisfy the court ..." *L. Loss, Securities Regulation*, 1020 (Supp. 1955).

[31]The so-called "due diligence" defense is embodied in the following provisions of Sec. 11 of the Securities Act of 1933:

Section 11 (b) of the Act provides that "... no person, other than the issuer, shall be liable ... who shall sustain the burden of proof ... (3) that (A) as regards any part of the registration statement not purporting to be made on the authority of any expert ... he had, after reasonable investigation, reasonable ground to believe and did believe, at the time such part of the registration statement became effective, that the statements therein were true and that there was no omission to state a material fact required to be stated therein or necessary to make the statements therein not misleading; ... and (C) as regards any part of the registration statement purporting to be made on the authority of an expert (other than himself) ... he had no reasonable ground to believe and did not believe, at the time such part of the registration statement became effective, that the statements therein were untrue or that there was an omission to state a material fact required to be stated therein or necessary to make the statements therein not misleading. ..."

Sec. 11(c) defines "reasonable investigation" as follows: "In determining, for the purpose of paragraph (3) of subsection (b) of this section, what constitutes reasonable investigation and reasonable ground for belief, the standard of reasonableness shall be that required of a prudent man in the management of his own property."

[32]An accountant carries out an S-1 review to discharge an obligation which arises by implication from the language of Sec. 11. Since the section makes the accountant responsible for his opinion upon the audited financial statements as of the effective date of the registration

the accountants tried to establish the due diligence defense; and, therefore, had to prove that when the registration statement became effective they had, as a result of a reasonable investigation, reason to believe and did believe that the expertised statements, i.e., the audited annual statements, were not misleading. The Court observed that the objective of an S-1 review is "to ascertain whether any material change has occurred in the company's financial position which should be disclosed in order to prevent the balance sheet figures from being misleading."[33] Although the Court ruled that the scope of the S-1 program as written conformed to generally accepted auditing standards, it found that the program was not properly executed.[34] It failed because some of the steps in the program were not taken, because an inadequate amount of time (20½ hours) was spent on the job, and because the in-charge accountant was too satisfied with what the Court styled "glib answers" to his questions.

Part of the program required that the auditors "inquire as to changes in material contracts." Although the in-charge accountant asked the controller about uncompleted contracts and secured a list of them, he did not actually examine each contract. The Court ruled this inquiry to be inadequate since in the Court's opinion the absence of prices from some examined contracts should have prompted further investigation. The Court's ruling illustrates the grave danger to the accounting profession of undefined standards. The Court in *BarChris* has in fact enunciated new and higher procedures for S-1 reviews, than would be considered necessary by many accountants. Although the Court stated that the auditors should not be held to standards higher than those recognized in their profession, the standards were undefined and the Court filled the void.

IMPLICATIONS FOR THE PROFESSION

Let us turn now from the characteristics of the recent cases to a consideration of their implications.

1. Insurance. Accountants have realized for some time that increased legal hazards require greater liability coverage. Through

---

statements, and since the effective date will not occur until sometime after the accountant has completed his audit and issued his opinion, he must satisfy himself as of the effective date, that the audited financial statements still fairly present the financial position and results of operations as of the end of the audited period.

[33] *Escott* v. *BarChris Construction Corp.*, 283 F. Supp., 643, 701 (S.D.N.Y. 1968).

[34] This improper execution denied the accountants the due diligence defense: "[t] here had been a material change for the worse in BarChris's financial position. That change was sufficiently serious so that the failure to disclose it made the 1960 figures misleading. Berardi did not discover it. As far as results were concerned, his S-1 review was useless," *Id.*, p. 702.

the efforts of leaders in the profession higher limits have been obtained, but the uninsured exposure is still staggering. For example, the market value of a major conglomerate's common stock declined more than $250 million in the year from July 1, 1968 to June 30, 1969. The mind boggles at the thought of a class suit by the company's stockholders against its auditors alleging the drop was the consequence of negligent or fradulent auditing. The need for increased liability insurance is obvious.

To the extent that coverage is not available, accountants must either absorb the loss or pass it on as part of their cost of business. The authors believe that miscreants should bear the brunt of loss when liability is the consequence of fraud. However, the recent civil cases fall short of fraud; they do not involve false statements deliberately made with the intent to deceive. The authors are of the opinion that in such cases it is practical and reasonable for accountants to pass on the costs of an evolving and increasingly demanding standard of professional conduct — especially when, as in several current cases, the standard, extant at the time of the engagement, was at best vague. Indeed, as the courts broaden the reach of federal securities laws they are in effect forcing accountants, and others, to assure investors against damage sustained as a result of reliance upon incorrect financial data, a type of information which is inherently imprecise. The authors believe that because of considerations of social advantage, the losses due to the ordinary claims under the securities law should be spread as widely as possible throughout the economy. This spreading of the risk can most conveniently be implemented by accountants' liability insurance, the cost of which ultimately is diffused through the entities of the economy and their participants.[35]

2. Reference of accounting issues to a master. One implication of the phenomenon whereby judges and juries are shaping accounting practice is that defendants may wish to give new consideration to the advisability of urging the Court to refer accounting questions to a special master.[36] It seems reasonable that a master learned in accounting would handle accounting questions more capably than a lay judge or jury.

The Federal Rules of Civil Procedure permit the District Courts

---

[35]A similar argument was made by Judge Traynor of the California Supreme Court in a famous concurring opinion in a case involving product-liability:

"The cost of an injury and the loss of time or health may be an overwhelming misfortune to the person injured, and a needless one, for the risk of injury can be insured by the manufacturer and distributed among the public as a cost of doing business." *Escola* v. *Coca-Cola Bottling Co.*, 24 Cal. 2d 453, 462, 150 P.2d 436, 441 (1944).

[36]*Fed. R. Civ.*, p. 53.

to appoint a special master and to refer matters to him.[37] The judge has considerable discretion over the scope of the reference. For example, the master may be directed to report only on a particular issue, or he may be directed to receive and report on evidence only.

Judicial discretion over the *use* of a master as opposed to the scope of the reference is more limited. In a jury trial a judge is authorized to refer questions to a master only when they are complicated. In a trial without a jury the master may be used only when some exceptional condition requires it. Thus, although a master cannot be used at the whim of the litigants or of the court, the option generally is available since many cases involving accounting issues would qualify as "complicated" or represent "exceptional circumstances."

Reference of accounting issues to a master both solves and creates problems. Difficult questions receive the sophisticated consideration they deserve; but selection of the master becomes a point of contention among plaintiffs, defendants, and judge. In addition, reference to a master generally delays the case and adds to its cost. On balance, the procedure would seem to have particular merit in cases where the accounting questions are either particularly numerous and/or difficult.[38]

3. Probability approach.   Since cases increasingly concern accounting principles as well as auditing procedures, accountants should warn the readers of financial statements regarding the probabilistic nature of their contents. Section 11 of the Securities and Exchange Act refers to "material facts." Unfortunately, accounting statements are still prepared as though their contents were indeed "facts" capable of being measured exactly to the penny. Small wonder the auditors in *BarChris* were sued partly because they failed to require the establishment of a proper allowance for doubtful accounts.

Auditors should not express an opinion on financial statements without qualifications as to the level of confidence for the estimated amounts in those statements. Financial reporting would be greatly improved if a Bayesian probability approach[39] were applied to the

---

[37]Although the Federal Rules of Civil Procedure govern only procedure in federal courts, they are crucial because the diversity of citizenship and size of claims in cases against accountants qualify them for consideration by a federal civil court.

[38]An example of the use of a special master where accounting questions are involved is *601 West 26 Corp.* v. *Solitron Devices Inc.*, CCH Fed. Sec. Law Rep., paragraph 92,611 (S.D.N.Y. Jan. 1970). There the special master supervised the taking of 401 pages of minutes which produced findings on 14 accounting questions. The questions ranged from whether the accountants had subordinated their judgment to that of the client to the determination of whether earnings were artificially inflated or otherwise misrepresented. The District Court disposed of the case — vindicating the accountants — based on the findings and conclusions of law of the special master.

[39]See R. Schlaifer, *Probability and Statistics for Business Decisions.* (1959).

financial statements. Confidence limits should be published for the principal items along with their expected values. For example, earnings per share should be reported as $4.02 with the probability that they are between $3.90 and $4.14 at the 95 percent level of confidence. Many lawsuits would be avoided if auditors would simply indicate that they are not certifying to deterministic facts, but rather are expressing an opinion on estimates from a probability distribution. A caveat should be included in the auditor's opinion putting the reader on notice of the stochastic nature of the quantities covered by the report.

4. Marginal companies. One characteristic common to all of the cases in this article is that they involve businesses which have failed. Clearly, as a matter of self protection, an auditor must perform a more extensive investigation when he suspects financial difficulties. Unfortunately, evidence of business failure may be more apparent in retrospect than at the time of an audit. Nevertheless, the current cases indicate the wisdom of expanding an audit program for a company with declining earnings or weak credit.

The accountant's dilemma in this area has implications for society at large. If it becomes commonplace for stockholders to sue the auditors of every failing company, those firms least able to pay will be hindered by above average audit costs. Additional barriers to competition will be introduced because the cost of raising money and doing business will be higher for marginal companies.

5. Extension of attest function. As a result of *BarChris*, directors, underwriters, and their attorneys recognize that for them to secure maximum protection under the "due diligence" defense of Section 11 (b) as much of the prospectus as possible must be covered by an opinion of independent accountants. This recognition has prompted them to pressure accountants to expand in several ways the scope of their work as it relates to registration statements. Counsel for some underwriters, accepting the accountant's premise that he should only attest to "financial data" have in effect argued that the term "financial" has evolved and today encompasses more data than in the past. For example, in one instance independent accountants were asked to attest to the total floor space in a plant. In another, they were asked to attest to the amount of unfilled orders. Nevertheless, auditors typically have been unwilling to expand their attest function to cover data in the text of the prospectus and new types of data sought to be added to the annual financial statements via footnotes.

In addition, underwriters are asking independent accountants to expand the scope of their investigation of events subsequent to the date of the certified balance sheet. This request is a consequence of the underwriters' increased awareness of the due diligence defense at issue in *BarChris*. It will be recalled that maximum protection under that defense is available to the underwriter if at the time the registration statement becomes effective he had no reasonable ground to believe the expertised portion of the registration statements (audited financial statements, for example) was misleading. In order to satisfy these statutory requirements, the underwriter, aware that accountants conduct S-1 reviews to maximize their own due diligence protection,[40] typically secures from the company's independent auditors, "comfort letters" which contain comments on financial developments during the stub period. These comments are secured either by requesting them from the accountants who provide them as an accommodation, or by requiring in their underwriting agreement that the comments be provided.

In the authors' opinion *BarChris* suggests that standards for S-1 reviews need to be re-examined and made more specific, despite the fact that the Court stated that "[a]ccountants should not be held to a standard higher than that recognized in their profession" and the additional fact that the Court stated that it did not hold them to a higher standard. In the authors' opinion the S-1 review program prepared by the auditors in *BarChris* would have been acceptable to many accountants; and it appears that at least some accountants are out of touch with the standards as perceived by the courts.

Since S-1 reviews and inquiries for comfort letters are generally done at the same time, the authors suggest that the profession re-examine its posture regarding those letters when it reconsiders S-1 reviews. Two basic options are available regarding comfort letters. Accountants can restrict the rendering of them, or they can increase the scope of the work for their preparation. Accountants, generally, have tended to resist an expansion of comfort letters. They prefer that the letters continue to refer only to changes in capitalization and to material adverse changes in financial position which occur subsequent to the latest financial statements in the registration statement. Furthermore, they traditionally state that an examination for the stub period has not been made, and that an opinion is disclaimed. They generally state explicitly that the procedures followed by the accountant would not necessarily disclose adverse changes in either financial position or results of operations and the assurances given are negative, couched in language such as ". . . nothing came to our

---

[40]The reasons for conducting an S-1 review were discussed *supra* at note 32.

attention which caused us to believe that the accounting information requires any material adjustment for a fair presentation. . . ."[41]

Anticipating that some reconsideration of S-1 reviews and comfort letters will be forthcoming, the authors suggest that the profession go far beyond the most pessimistic reading of *BarChris* and consider several radical changes in stub period practice. They believe that the expression of opinions on "adverse changes" should be discontinued since it is impossible for the accountants to determine whether a change was in fact "adverse."[42] They recommend that all unaudited statements be audited and that the auditor attest to such other data contained in the registration statement as is capable of being measured. A complete examination for the stub period, though it would take more time than the present review, could generally be accomplished during the interval between the registration and effective date of the prospectus.[43] The updating of information supplied on initial filing would be accomplished by an amendment. The incremental cost of this work would vary depending upon the length of the stub period; assuming for purposes of illustration that a company went into registration three months after the close of its fiscal period, the authors estimate that in most cases the cost would run between 20 and 40 per cent of the annual examination. If as a practical matter the audit can be carried to within a few days of the effective date of the registration statement, the underwriters will have more due diligence protection, prospectus readers will have more useful information, and the accountants will have avoided the difficult problem of articulating detailed standards for the statutorily implied S-1 review.

6. Accounting principles. The courts, through their judges and juries, are affecting accounting principles as well as auditing standards. For example, the Court enunciated a basis for reporting a sale-leaseback in *BarChris*. These developments challenge the method developed by the AICPA over the years whereby it issues statements on accounting principles only after comprehensive research, publication of exposure drafts, and extended deliberation by the Accounting Principles Board. The courts are in a difficult position and may, inadvertently or otherwise, bypass this careful procedure unless the Institute accelerates its publication schedule.

---

[41]Statements on Auditing Procedure No. 35, p. 23.

[42]For example, an increase in research and development expense with a consequent decrease in income might be beneficial for the company in the long run.

[43]Although Sec. 8(a) of the Securities Act of 1933 provides that the registration statement becomes effective 20 days after filing unless the SEC accelerates the effective date or determines that the statement is incomplete or inaccurate, almost invariably the registrant files a delaying amendment which postpones the effective date substantially. The average time difference between registration and effectiveness was 65 days during 1969.

The authors believe that the development of accounting principles by judges and juries as a by-product of their disposition of a series of cases will not result in the most desirable formulation of guidelines for financial reporting. Present litigation typically involves unusual circumstances, which could prejudice a decision on general principles. For instance, in *Westec* officers of the company have been found guilty on a number of criminal counts, including improper security transactions. The moral taint from these convictions might affect the Court's regard for the defendants and might prejudice its ruling on whether a pooling of interest fairly presented acquisitions by Westec. The authors believe that accounting procedures should be generalized from the experience of going concerns run by ethical managers, not failing companies run by wrongdoers.

The recent cases on accountants' liability highlight the pressing need for a massive expansion in accounting research. The SEC no longer stands alone in pushing the AICPA to narrow the differences in accounting principles. Judges and juries not expert in financial reporting are wrestling with highly complex accounting problems, and there is little reason to hope that they will do any better than the APB in developing viable accounting standards.

The AICPA expended $353,000 on research in 1968,[44] an increase of 64 per cent over 1966; but an amount which constituted less than one-tenth of one per cent of the reputed annual gross billings of the eight largest firms. These figures do not reflect the enormous donation of time and labor to the Board by the individual members and their firms; however, the authors hypothesize that a massive increase in the AICPA research budget with a comparable increase in either donated or paid professional time would be of prime importance in combatting the increasing number of liability cases. In addition, government sponsored research, possibly in the form of support by a National Social Science Foundation, would be helpful.

Some critics of financial reporting take the position that further research and increased output by the APB is less necessary than the creation of an authoritative panel to choose between conflicting accounting procedures. Leonard Spacek's 1958 recommendation for an accounting court was a suggestion in that direction.[45] It will be remembered that Spacek recommended that the AICPA establish a professional tribunal, which was not to be a court of law; hence its

---

[44]American Institute of Certified Public Accountants, *Annual Report, The CPA*, November, 1968, p. 13; *Fortune, supra* note 2, p. 178.
[45]Leonard Spacek, "The Need for an Accounting Court," *Accounting Review*, July, 1958. p. 368.

discussions would not affect the laws nor the administration of the laws by regulatory bodies. One reason why the proposal for an accounting court has languished is that the financial community has never been convinced of the wisdom of putting the supreme rule-making authority on accounting in the hands of three judges, however learned they might be. This skepticism regarding a professional accounting court seems equally applicable to our nation's civil courts.

An interesting parallel exists between formulation of accounting principles and the development of common law. It is desirable that law be equitable, yet it is also essential that particular principles of law be certain and the outcome of litigation involving them predictable. In some situations considerations of equity are inconsequential or competing considerations cancel each other. In such a case it is more important that *some* rule be adopted, rather than that any particular rule be adopted. For example, in contract law it is important that the act for accepting an offer be certain. It makes little difference whether that act be the mailing of a letter by the offeree, or its delivery to the offeror. Some research in accounting might usefully determine the sensitivity of the user to alternative methods of financial reporting. Where it is found that one method of accounting is not better than another, the APB should stipulate the rule in accordance with the principle of certainty discussed above. Eliminating the options available to management for choosing between accounting principles will facilitate intra-industry comparisons. It also will reduce the financial credibility gap that invites litigation under legal doctrines emerging from the cases under review.

The authors believe that by accepting responsibility for the principles underlying financial statements, CPAs will renew the stress on "public" in certified public accountant. The march of recent cases indicates that the courts believe independent accountants should accept a greater responsibility. The profession should respond to the challenge.

SUMMARY

Recent litigation has been characterized by a successful effort on the part of plaintiffs to reach accountants in heretofore untested situations. Occasionally where auditing standards and accounting principles were unclear, the Courts though stating that they adhere to generally accepted accounting principles have selected those which appear to them most reasonable. This expansion of the law and articulation of accounting principles when combined with requests for broader attestation makes it incumbent upon accountants to consider a positive approach to the new problems and opportunities facing the profession. The suggestions presented in this article constitute the thinking of the authors on how this might best be done.

APPENDIX A
BarChris Construction Corp.
(Escott v. BarChris Construction Corp.)[46]

Plaintiffs: Purchasers of 5½% convertible subordinated 15-year debentures.

Defendants: The defendants can be subdivided into three groups: (1) those who signed the registration statement, including officer-directors; the controller, not a director; outside directors, including the company attorney, and another who was a partner of the lead underwriter; (2) the underwriters, consisting of eight investment banking firms led by Drexel & Co.; (3) BarChris' auditors, Peat, Marwick, Mitchell & Co.

Court: U.S. District Court, Southern District of New York (Manhattan). District Judge McLean. By agreement of the parties, Judge McLean, rather than a jury, decided the questions of fact.

Factual Summary: 1. *Re: Certified financial statements as of December 31, 1960.* The Court concluded that earnings had been overstated by 14%, a figure not deemed material given that the securities involved were B rated convertible debentures and that the reported earnings per share on the underlying common would still have nearly doubled compared to the preceding year ($.33 to $.65).

The Court also concluded the current ratio was overstated 16%, a figure deemed material.

The Court gives little insight into why a 16% overstatement of working capital is material whereas a 14% overstatement of EPS is not.[47] Possibly it hinges on the intentional nature of the overstatement. An officer of BarChris persuaded a factor to temporarily release $147,000 of an unconsolidated subsidiary's funds — being held as security —

---

[46]283 F. Supp. 643, (S.D.N.Y. 1968).

[47]A feature of the financial statements not discussed in the opinion tends to rationalize these conclusions. The effect of the balance sheet error was to exacerbate BarChris' violation of the 2:1 test of current ratio used by the financial community. In contrast, as the Court observed, earnings increased dramatically even without this overstatement. The authors conclude that it is worse to minimize violation of a financial standard than it is to overstate the dramatic amount by which a standard has been exceeded.

to the subsidiary; $145,000 of this temporarily available money was then transferred to BarChris and was accounted for by a debit to Cash and credit to the noncurrent asset Investment in Nonconsolidated Subsidiary.

The overstatement of earnings was caused primarily by:

(a) Overstatement of the percentage of completion on some contracts.

(b) The recording of a loan to BarChris as a sale.

(c) The recording of a sale-leaseback to a factor as a sale: a bowling alley sold to Talcott (a factor) who leased it to a consolidated subsidiary of BarChris was treated as a sale by BarChris in its consolidated statements.

(d) The recording of a sale-leaseback to a customer as a sale: a subsidiary leased property to an operator but treated the transaction as a sale.

The overstatement of the current ratio was caused primarily by:

(a) Overstatement of cash by $145,000 transferred from an unconsolidated subsidiary. This cash was received by the subsidiary as a short-term loan from a finance factor. It was not disclosed that the subsidiary, had to repay this money 25 days after acquiring it.

(b) Reserve for bad debts was understated by $50,000.

(c) Accounts receivable contained $150,000 due from a consolidated subsidiary.

(d) All reserves held by a factor were treated as current despite the fact that some of them would in the normal course of events not be released within one year.

(e) Regarding footnotes, contingent liabilities were understated by $375,795 and a direct liability of $325,000 should have been included in the recorded liabilities on the balance sheet.

Plaintiffs unsuccessfully questioned other items. These included:

(a) The theoretical justification for the percentage of completion method of reporting sales.

(b) The absence of a reserve for contingent liabilities.

2. *Re: Unaudited income statement for first quarter 1961.* Sales were overstated by the inclusion of two intercompany transactions.

3. *Re: Unaudited backlog as of March 31, 1961.* Backlog was overstated by $4,490,000 due to the inclusion of transactions for which BarChris had no enforceable contracts.

4. *Re: Unaudited contingent liabilities as of April 30, 1961.* Contingent liabilities were understated by $618,853, and a direct liability of $314,166 was omitted.

5. *Re: Text of prospectus.* Inaccuracies in the prospectus included the following:

(a) It was incorrectly implied that there were no outstanding loans from officers (they amounted to $386,615).

(b) It failed to indicate that substantial sums would be expended to pay prior debts incurred as a result of alley construction already undertaken.

(c) It gave the incorrect impression that BarChris' problems with customers' credit and performance were minimal.

(d) It failed to mention that BarChris was operating alleys as well as constructing them.

Legal doctrines and statutes relied upon by plaintiffs: Section 11, Securities Act of 1933. A registration statement filed with the SEC allegedly contained material false statements and material omissions.

Status: The Court found that the registration statement contained false statements of material facts. It was decided that no defendant established his "due diligence" defense with regard to all the material errors although several established that defense with regard to some of them. The Court reserved decision on such defenses as causation, estoppel, waiver, release, and the statute of limitations. The Court also reserved judgment on the claims of some defendants against other defendants; these included the underwriters' claims against Peat, Marwick based on its comfort letter. The case has since been settled.

CONTINENTAL VENDING MACHINE CORP.
(UNITED STATES v. SIMON)[48]

Plaintiffs: United States through the U.S. Attorney's Office for the Southern Districts of New York.

Defendants: Carl Simon, a senior partner of Lybrand, Ross Bros. & Montgomery, partner in charge of the Continential Vending Machine Corp. audit; Robert Kaiser, partner; Melvin Fishman, audit manager.

Court: U.S. Court of Appeals for the Second Circuit. Circuit Judges Waterman, Friendly and Smith. Opinion by Circuit Judge Friendly.

---

[48]CCA Fed. Sec. L. Rep. 92,511 (2d Cir. Nov. 12, 1969), *cert. denied* (March 30, 1970).

Factual Summary: The appellate court upheld the criminal conviction of defendants for certifying the misleading financial statements of Continental at September 30, 1962. The case turned on the reporting of loans by Continental Vending to its affiliate, Valley Commercial Corp.

Harold Roth, president of Continental, dominated both Continental and Valley. He owned about 25 per cent of Continental which was listed on the American Exchange. He supervised day-to-day operations of Valley, which were conducted from an office on Continental's premises. Roth from 1958-62 borrowed large amounts of money from Continental for his personal stock market dealings, much of which he repaid by the end of each fiscal year. Instead of borrowing directly, he had Continental lend to Valley; Roth then borrowed from Valley.

At September 30, 1962, the receivable from Valley resulting from Roth's borrowing amounted to approximately $3.5 million; and during the 1962 audit Roth informed the auditors that Valley was unable to repay Continental since he was unable to repay Valley. Consequently Roth agreed to post adequate collateral. However 80 per cent of the collateral Roth produced consisted of holdings in Continental; moreover, the total had a value of only $2.9 million on February 15, 1963, the date of the opinion on the 1962 statements. Nevertheless, the auditors attested to a Continental footnote which stated, in effect, that the $3.5 million receivable from Valley, less the balance payable to Valley, was collateralized by marketable securities of an amount greater than the difference between the receivable and payable.

Actually, the reporting of the Valley receivable and its pledged security was complicated by the fact that Valley was used for transactions other than Roth's personal borrowings from Continental. From time to time, Continental secured financing by issuing negotiable notes to Valley which in turn discounted them at banks and transferred the discounted amounts to Continental. At September 30, 1962, these notes amounted to about $1.0 million. The $1.0 million notes payable to Valley could not be offset against the $3.5 million receivable from Valley since the holder of the notes payable (the bank) differed from the debtor on the accounts receivable (Valley and ultimately Roth). Nevertheless, the footnote to the September 30, 1962 statements indicated that the payable was deducted from the receivable in figuring the adequacy of the collateral.

The pertinent sections of the September 30, 1962 Continental balance sheet and related footnotes are as follows:

ASSETS
Current Assets:

. . . .

Accounts and notes receivable:

. . . .

Valley Commercial Corp., affiliate
(Note 2) $2,143,335

. . . .

Noncurrent accounts and notes receivable:
Valley Commercial Corp., affiliate
(Note 2)   1,400,000

. . . .

LIABILITIES
Current liabilities:

. . . .

Long-term debt, portion due within one year

8,203,788

. . . .

Long-term debt (Note 7)

. . . .

Valley Commercial Corp., affiliate (Note 2)

486,130

. . . .

NOTES TO CONSOLIDATED FINANCIAL STATEMENTS

[2]The amount receivable from Valley Commercial Corp. (an affiliated company of which Mr. Harold Roth is an officer, director and stockholder) bears interest at 12 per cent a year. Such amount, less the balance of the notes payable to that company, is secured by the assignment to the Company of Valley's equity in certain marketable securities. As of February 16, 1963, the amount of such equity at current market quotations exceeded the net amount receivable.
[7]. . . . The amounts of long-term debt, including the portion due within one year, on which interest is payable currently or has been discounted in advance, are as follows:

. . . .

Valley Commercial Corp., affiliate $1,029,475

Legal doctrines and statutes relied upon by prosecution: The indictment charged defendants with conspiring and adopting a scheme to violate federal criminal statutes prohibiting one or more of the following: (1) the filing of false statements with a governmental agency (18 U.S.C. Section 1001); (2) the use of the mails to perpetuate a fraud (18 U.S.C. Section 1341); and (3) the filing of false statements with the SEC (Section 32 of the Securities Exchange Act of 1934, 15 U.S.C. Section 78ff.). The appellate court stated that the government's burden "was not to show that defendants were wicked men with designs on anyone's purse, which they obviously were not, but rather that they had certified a statement knowing it to be false."

Status: The three accountants were found guilty by a jury in June 1968 after an earlier trial ended in a hung jury. Simon was fined $7,000. Kaiser and Fishman were fined $5,000 each. The Second Circuit upheld the conviction and the Supreme Court declined to review the case.

In related cases the defendants were Harold Roth, president of Continental; David Roth, his brother; and Clair Gans, his administrative assistant. Harold Roth entered a plea of "guilty," and was put on probation for three years after serving six months of an 18-month term. The case against David Roth and Gans had not gone to trial at December 1, 1969. In November 1967, Lybrand settled a civil suit against it for $1,960,936.

WESTEC CORP.
(CARPENTER V. HALL)[49]

Plaintiff: Trustee of Westec Corporation. The trustee either directly or indirectly represents the interest of (1) Westec Corp., (2) the Fraud Claimants Fund for Creditors Class Six as set forth in the Trustee's Amended Plan of Reorganization, (3) a class of people consisting in part of all persons who sustained a loss as a result of any purchase of or loan against Westec common stock between September 2, 1964 and August 5, 1966.

Defendants: There are 93 defendants. These include: James W. Williams, formerly board chairman of Westec; E. M. Hall, Jr., formerly president of Westec; numerous business associates of Williams and Hall and the companies with which these associates were affiliated; the American Stock Exchange specialists handling Westec trading; a variety of brokerage houses and their employees; and Ernst & Ernst, together with Clarence T. Isensee and Newman T. Halvorson (partners), and John F. Maurer (Audit Manager).

Court: U.S. District Court, Southern District of Texas (Houston).

Factual Summary: The bulk of the 32-page complaint alleges that various defendants joined in or abetted an unlawful conspiracy to misuse the corporate funds of Westec and associated companies; and/or to victimize the company, its shareholders and the investing public through manipulating the company's stock. Several defendants are singled out for different or additional allegations. The complaint directed at Ernst & Ernst alleges:

---

[49]Complaint, C. A. No. 68-H-738 (S.D. Tex., filed August 23, 1968).

1. The auditors made a superficial examination in 1964 which failed to detect (a) that the sale of a plant had not been completed ($90,000 profit), and (b) that the sale of a warehouse ($150,000 profit) made to a company controlled by one of the conspirators was fictitious.

2. The auditors' 1965 examination was inadequate in that it failed to discover (a) that the $1.3 million sale of a production payment by an acquired company was reported as 1965 income although the sale occured prior to the nonpooling acquisition of the company; and (b) a fictitious sale of oil properties was superseded by a non-arm's-length sale of the properties at an inflated price.

3. The pooling of interest approach to the accounting for six acquisitions was improperly applied. The audit report was held open until March 26, 1965, the date when three of the six contested poolings were acquired, so that the prior year's earnings of such acquisitions could be included in the consolidated reports. The plaintiff alleges that earnings of six acquired companies for periods prior to acquisition should not be combined with the parent company. It is also claimed that five of the six acquisitions failed to meet established criteria for pooling.

4. Ernst & Ernst were so involved in the structuring of acquisitions that they lost their status as independent accountants.

5. The auditors deliberately concealed the material impact (23%) of the three pooling acquisitions upon the 1964 earnings. They should have disclosed that the five 1965 poolings produced net earnings of $5 million, whereas reported 1965 earnings were only $4.8 million for the company as a whole.

Legal doctrines and statutes relied upon by plaintiff: The accountants are charged with: (1) common law negligence for breaching contractual and fiduciary duties to Westec requiring professional care; and (2) engaging in fraudulent acts proscribed by the Securities Act of 1933 and the Securities Exchange Act of 1934.

Status: In pretrial stage at May 1, 1970.

YALE EXPRESS
(FISCHER v. KLETZ)[50]

Plaintiffs: Stockholders and debenture holders of Yale Express Systems, Inc. (Yale).

Defendants: Peat, Marwick, Mitchell & Co. (Peat), numerous officers and directors of Yale and underwriters for Yale debentures.

---

[50]266 F. Supp. 180 (S.D.N.Y. 1967).

Court: U.S. District Court, Southern District of New York (Manhattan). Judge Tyler.

Factual Summary: Plaintiffs claim damages from errors and omissions in three sets of financial statements, namely: (1) the unaudited statements appearing in the prospectus for an August 20, 1963 debenture offering; (2) the audited statements for the year ending December 31, 1963; and (3) unaudited interim statements issued during 1964. These statements were distributed to the public and filed with the SEC and stock exchanges. The consolidated earnings for 1963, the interim earnings for 1964 and year-end assets, particularly receivables, appear to have been overstated.

In early 1964, Peat undertook several management service studies for Yale; thus Peat changed its relationship to Yale from that of "independent public accountant" with statutory duties under the 1934 Act to that of management consultant. In this new capacity Peat discovered that figures in the 1963 annual report were substantially false and misleading. The litigants differ on when this discovery was made; Peat contends discovery occurred after the report was filed while plaintiffs contend discovery occurred before the SEC and others received the annual report. Peat did not disclose its finding to the SEC or public until May 1965, when the results of its management studies were released.

Legal doctrines and statutes relied upon by plaintiffs; procedural setting: In what is so far the major opinion in the case, Peat moved to dismiss those parts of the complaint dealing with the 1963 annual report and the 1964 interim reports. This procedural setting required the Court to view the facts in the light most favorable to the plaintiffs and to deny the motion if there was any viable legal theory for sustaining the plaintiffs. Plaintiffs opposed the motion regarding the 1963 reports by arguing that the failure to disclose the inaccuracies as soon as discovered violated common-law deceit doctrines,[51] Sec-

---

[51]The Restatement of Torts identifies the elements of deceit involving business transactions as follows:

    Sec. 525 — Liability for Fraudulent Misrepresentations. One who fraudulently makes a misrepresentation of fact, opinion, intention or law for the purpose of inducing another to act or refrain from acting in reliance thereon on a business transaction is liable to the other for the harm caused to him by his justifiable reliance upon the misrepresentation.

    Sec. 526 — Conditions Under Which Misrepresentation is Fraudulent. A misrepresentation in a business transaction is fradulent if the maker

    (a) knows or believes the matter to be otherwise than as represented or

    (b) knows that he has not the confidence in its existence or nonexistence asserted by his statement of knowledge or belief or

    (c) knows that he has not the basis for his knowledge or belief professed by his assertion.

tion 18(a) of the Securities Exchange Act of 1934 and Rule 10b-5[52] promulgated by the SEC pursuant to Section 10(b) of the Securities Exchange Act of 1934. With regard to the 1964 interim statements, plaintiffs argued that the failure to disclose the findings of its studies constituted a violation of Rule 10b-5. The motion to dismiss was denied.

Status: The case was in the pretrial stages as of May 1, 1970.

---

[52]Rule 10b-5 provides as follows: It shall be unlawful for any person, directly or indirectly, by the use of any means or instrumentality of interstate commerce, or of the mails, or of any facility of any national securities exchange,
  (a) to employ any device, scheme, or artifice to defraud,
  (b) to make any untrue statement of a material fact or to omit to state a material fact necessary in order to make the statements made, in the light of the circumstances under which they were made, not misleading, or
  (c) to engage in any act, practice, or course of business which operates or would operate as a fraud or deceit upon any person,
in connection with the purchase or sale of any security.

12. The Continental Vending Case: Lessons for the Profession*

David B. Isbell†

On November 12, 1969, the United States Court of Appeals for the Second Circuit issued its opinion affirming the convictions of the three accountant-defendants in the *Continental Vending* case, *United States* v. *Simon*, F.2d, CCH Fed. Sec. L. Rep., ¶ 92,511 (2nd Cir. 1969) (see JofA, Feb.70, p.61). Although review by the Supreme Court was sought through the discretionary writ of *certiorari*, on March 31, 1970, that Court denied the writ, thus leaving in effect the decision of the Court of Appeals. 397 U.S. 1006 (1970).

Because of the potential importance of certain aspects of the case to the accounting profession at large, the American Institute of CPAs submitted briefs as *amicus curiae* to the District Court (see JofA, Nov.68, p.54), to the Court of Appeals and to the Supreme Court (see JofA, May70, p.69). Those briefs viewed the case from the standpoint of what its implications might be for the accounting profession, and of what legal rules ought, from the profession's point of view, to apply. Now that the case has come to rest it must be viewed from a different perspective, for the pertinent questions now are not what the implications *might* be, but what they probably are; and not what legal rules *should* apply, but what rules the Court has authoritatively said will apply. This article is an attempt to examine the case from that new perspective.

RESUME OF THE CASE

Because the opinion of the Court of Appeals, which has been printed in the February 1970 *Journal* (p.61), describes fully the history of the case and the facts that were pertinent to the Court's opinion, no elaborate description of the case is necessary here. A brief summary should suffice to set the framework for the discussion that follows.

The defendants, two partners and a manager in Lybrand, Ross Bros. & Montgomery, were charged with fraud in the preparation of

---

*From *The Journal of Accountancy* (August, 1970), pp. 33-40. Copyright (1970) by the American Institute of Certified Public Accountants, Inc. Reprinted by permission of the AICPA.

†David B. Isbell, LL.B., is a Partner in the law firm of Covington & Burling in Washington, D.C.

the 1962 balance sheet of Continental Vending Machine Corporation. Harold Roth was Continental's founder and president and held 25 per cent of its outstanding stock. Roth was also an officer, director and major stockholder of Valley Commercial Corporation, which was thereby an affiliate of Continental. Valley had other auditors. Continental made substantial advances to Valley, resulting in the "Valley receivable"; and Valley, in turn, made substantial advances to Roth, which he used for transactions in the stock market. It was conceded that the defendants knew of these advances to Roth before they issued their opinion on Continental's 1962 financial statements. The defendants also knew that Roth could not repay to Valley the loans then outstanding, and that Valley could not repay Continental. In order to insure collectibility of the Valley receivable, collateralization was undertaken by hypothecation of securities held by Roth and his family. Eighty per cent of the securities pledged were the common stock and convertible debentures of Continental itself.

The defendants issued an opinion on the 1962 financial statements of Continental, which represented that the financials "present fairly the consolidated financial position of Continental . . . in conformity with generally accepted accounting principles." The financial statements disclosed, *inter alia*, the loans to Valley, the fact that Roth was an officer, director and stockholder of Valley, and that the loans were secured by Valley's equity in "certain marketable securities." The financial statements showed a large net loss, and trading in Continental stock was suspended shortly after the annual report containing the financial statements was insured.

Roth and the defendant accountants were indicted for fraud and conspiracy to commit fraud. Roth pleaded guilty to one count and testified against the accountants (hereinafter "the defendants") at their trial.

The charges with which the trial was concerned were these:

1. The principal charge was that the balance sheet was fraudulent in failing to disclose that Roth had received from Valley sums which Valley had received from Continental.
2. Footnote 2 to the financial statements was charged to be false and misleading generally in representing that the Valley receivable was adequately secured, and specifically

    a. In representing that the Valley receivable and Valley payable could be netted.
    b. In failing to disclose that a substantial part of the collateral consisted of securities of Continental itself.

c. In failing to disclose a post year-end increase from $3.4 to $3.9 million in the amount of the Valley receivable.

All but one of these charges raised sharp issues regarding proper accounting practice. The exception was the netting of the Valley payable and receivable, which the defendants conceded could not be netted because the payable was represented by notes which Valley had discounted with banks. The defendants also conceded that footnote 2 erroneously implied that the payable and receivable might be netted but asserted that this was an innocent error.

Eight defense experts testified that none of the disclosures was required by generally accepted accounting principles and that the statements taken as a whole did present the financial position and results of operation fairly in accordance with generally accepted accounting principles. Two prosecution experts testified to the contrary. After two trials (the first having ended in a hung jury) the defendants were convicted. No jail sentences were imposed; the defendants were fined $5,000 to $7,000 each.

Post-trial motions for acquittal and new trial, on which the Institute made its first *amicus curiae* submission, were denied, and as has been mentioned, the United States Court of Appeals affirmed and the Supreme Court denied *certiorari*.

GENERAL SIGNIFICANCE OF CASE

The decision of the Court of Appeals is an important one for the accounting profession. It is significant in two prime respects: first, for what it says about the weight the law will attach to the standards of the accounting profession; second, for what it says about obligations, over and above those imposed by the standards of the profession itself, which the law will impose upon accountants in the course of their professional work.

The case is also instructive. The decision of the Court of Appeals tells much of a practical nature about how accountants can get into legal trouble and by the same token suggests ways in which at least some risks may be avoided.

In the perspective in which the case must now be viewed, an aspect that rendered it particularly shocking when it was brought — and while it was pending — becomes virtually without significance. That is the fact that it was a criminal case rather than a civil case. None of the major lessons of the case turns on the fact that it was a criminal rather than a civil proceeding. The major implications of the case to be discussed below apply as fully to the risk of civil as to criminal liability.

The fact that the case was a criminal matter did, of course, give particular poignancy to the fate of the individual defendants. It also serves as an important warning of the gravity of the hazards with which professional life is fraught. There are also some peculiar twists related to the criminal nature of the proceeding which deserve a preliminary word or two.

One such twist lies in the fact that the criminal prosecution certainly served as leverage to force the settlement of the companion civil suit, in the amount of $2.1 million. Another is the peculiar irony that the specific charges in this particular case would not have supported a civil damage action even though they did support a criminal action. The reason for this is that no one was damaged by the failures of disclosure in Continental's 1962 balance sheet for which the defendants were held responsible. To be sure, the market for Continental stock collapsed as soon as the financials appeared, and people were hurt by its collapse, but this was because of what the financial statements showed and not because of what the jury found they had wrongfully concealed.[1]

IMPLICATIONS OF THE CASE FOR THE ACCOUNTING PROFESSION

As has been mentioned, the case appears to have general significance to the accounting profession in three areas: (1) the weight to be given professional standards, (2) the standards of inquiry and disclosure proclaimed by the Court and (3) the practical lessons taught by the case.

WEIGHT OF PROFESSIONAL STANDARDS

The case is significant in what it says about the weight that the courts will give, where liability is concerned, to the standards of the accounting profession. The defendants offered eight expert witnesses, all eminent in the profession, to testify that Continental's balance sheet, which was charged to be fraudulent, fairly presented the financial

---

[1]Lybrand's opinion was withdrawn within a week after it was published and the SEC contacted because the collateral supporting the loans in question had fallen in value.

position of Continental in conformity with generally accepted accounting principles. Two prosecution witnesses testified to the contrary, but the Court of Appeals observed that:

> With due respect to [the latter] . . . , they hardly compared with defendants' witnesses in aggregate auditing experience or professional eminence.

There were thus critical factual issues for the jury, as to which of the expert witnesses should be believed (on which issues the Institute took no position); and, underlying these, there was a critical legal issue, on which the Institute moved to participate at all three levels of the proceeding, as to the weight to be given to the standards of the profession. That issue was framed in terms of the instructions to the jury.

The defendants had asked the trial court for instructions that would have required the jury to acquit if it found that the balance sheet was in conformity with generally accepted accounting principles. The trial court instead gave instructions which said that the "critical test" was whether the balance sheet fairly presented the financial position without reference to generally accepted accounting principles.

The trial court also said in its instructions that evidence of compliance with generally accepted accounting principles would be very persuasive, but not conclusive. It also gave other instructions which the jury might have taken as an invitation to test the fairness of presentation, not against generally accepted accounting principles, but against their idea of what an investor or other layman might want to know.

It was this seeming invitation to apply a lay standard rather than to look at the balance sheet as an accountant does — and as the defendants by their opinion on the Continental financials had represented that they had — that prompted the Institute's concern.

The position of the Institute in its submissions was not quite the same as that which had been proposed by the defendants' instructions. If the Institute had proposed instructions embodying its position, they would have required the jury to test the balance sheet against generally accepted accounting principles and to acquit if they found it in conformity with generally accepted accounting principles, *unless* the jury found from evidence beyond the financials themselves that the defendants had an intent to defraud. The Institute's position thus recognized the possibility of formal compliance with all professional standards which is a mere sham or subterfuge. As the Institute's brief in the Supreme Court specifically recognized, the jury might have convicted the defendants in this case even under such instructions because of the evidence (to be discussed below) which the jury could have taken as showing wrongful intent. The problem was that the instructions actually given by the trial court allowed, if they did not invite, the jury to take what the Institute considered to be an improper route (of appraising the financials in purely lay terms) in reaching that result.

The Court of Appeals, however, substantially narrowed the possibility which the trial court had left open, of a jury's being allowed to take a purely layman's view and to disregard the standards of the profession in a future case, whether civil or criminal.

The Court of Appeals emphasized that fair presentation was the "critical test"; indeed, it equated the trial court's emphasis on fair presentation with that of the defendants themselves. The Court of Appeals gave no emphasis to — in fact, did not refer to — the lay investor's standard which had been mentioned in the instructions of the trial court:

> We do not think the jury was . . . required to accept the accountants' evaluation whether a given fact was material to overall fair presentation, at least not when the accountants' testimony was not based on specific rules or prohibitions to which they could point, but only on the need for the auditor to make an honest judgment and their conclusion that nothing in the financial statements themselves negated the conclusion that an honest judgment had been made. Such evidence may be highly persuasive, but it is not conclusive, and so the trial judge correctly charged.

Thus, the Court of Appeals seems to cast the difference between the accountants' view and the view permitted the jury in terms of materiality — i.e., in terms of the relative weight to be given to different factors — rather than in terms of potentially wholly differing standards of accountants and laymen.

Moreover, the Court of Appeals in the passage quoted is limiting its holding that less than conclusive weight may be given to professional standards to cases where such standards involve no specific rules on prohibitions but leave the matter to the judgment of the individual auditor. The Court's "at least" implies that in cases where there are specific rules or prohibitions they may be conclusive. This also is what the *BarChris* case suggests: "Accountants should not be held to a standard higher than that recognized in their profession." (*Escott* v. *BarChris Construction Corp.*, 283 F. Supp. 643, 703 (S.D.N.Y. 1968)).

The Institute would, of course, have preferred a rule requiring more conclusively that a jury weigh matters from the perspective of the accountant. Moreover, the areas where judgment alone applies — so that evidence as to professional standards is, under the Court of Appeals' formulation, only "persuasive" and not "conclusive" — will remain large. Nonetheless, the rule enunciated by the Court of Appeals does not appear to be one that the profession cannot live with.

Two practical lessons can be drawn from this point: one for the profession as a whole, and the other for individual practitioners. For the profession the case points out once more the very real advantage, at least from the point of view of legal responsibility, in having professional standards spelled out. Had there been specific rules or prohibitions governing the matters about which there was dispute among the expert witnesses in this case, to which the defendants could refer, it is quite probable the result would have been different. There would very possibly have been different instructions; very likely a different verdict; and altogether likely, if neither of those had occurred, a different decision by the Court of Appeals.

For the practitioner, the opinion of the Court of Appeals suggests the desirability of adopting a procedure whereby, at least in cases where pure judgment does govern, a special review is made to determine whether disclosures are adequate and understandable from a layman's point of view. The Lybrand firm has adopted a procedure requiring in every case, prior to release of a published report, a "cold look" by a partner unassociated with the engagement with a view to whether the disclosures made are understandable to laymen. This is certainly a sensible course, although it is not one that is required by the Court of Appeals' decision.

INQUIRY AND DISCLOSURE

The case has further significance in the rules of inquiry and disclosure laid down by the Court of Appeals. There were four issues of this nature on which the expert testimony was divided:

1. Whether disclosure had to be made of the fact that sums advanced by Continental to Valley had in turn been lent to Continental's president, Roth.
2. Whether there was a duty on the defendants to make inquiry into the affairs of Valley, Continental's affiliate, which had its own auditors.
3. Whether disclosure was required to be made of the composition of the collateral which was pledged to secure the Valley receivable,

which collateral consisted largely of stock and debentures of Continental which was owned by and pledged by Roth.

4. Whether disclosure should have been made of the post-fiscal year-end increase in the Valley receivable from $3.4 million to $3.9 million.

Loans by Valley to Roth. It is the first of these issues, i.e., whether disclosure had to be made of the fact that money advanced by Continental to Valley had been lent to Roth, about which the Court had most to say, and on which its holding is, for precedential purposes, most important.   Unfortunately, its language on this point is not altogether clear:

> We join defendants' counsel in assuming that the mere fact that a company had made advances to an affiliate does not ordinarily impose a duty on an accountant to investigate what the affiliate has done with them or even to disclose that the affiliate has made a loan to a common officer if this has come to his attention. But it simply cannot be true that an accountant is under no duty to disclose what he knows when he has reason to believe that, to a material extent, a corporation is being operated not to carry out its business in the interest of all the stockholders but for the private benefit of its president. For a court to say that all this is immaterial as a matter of law if only such loans are thought to be collectible would be to say that independent accountants have no responsibility to reveal known dishonesty by a high corporate officer. If certification does not at least imply that the corporation has not been looted by insiders so far as the accountants know, or if it has been, that the diversion has been made good beyond peradventure (or adequately reserved against) and effective steps taken to prevent a recurrence, it would mean nothing, and the reliance placed on it by the public would be a snare and a delusion. Generally accepted accounting principles instruct an accountant what to do in the usual case where he has no reason to doubt that the affairs of the corporation are being honestly conducted. Once he has reason to believe that this basic assumption is false, an entirely different situation confronts him. Then, as the Lybrand firm stated in its letter accepting the Continental engagement, he must "extend his procedures to determine whether or not such suspicions are justified." If, as a result of such extension or, as here, without it, he finds his suspicions to be confirmed, full disclosure must be the rule unless he has made sure the wrong has been righted and procedures to avoid a repetition have been established. At least this must be true when the dishonesty he has discovered is not some minor peccadillo, but a diversion so large as to imperil if not destroy the very solvency of the enterprise.

The Court says too much here, and in language too pungent, to leave the meaning of this crucial passage as clear as its importance warrants. Careful analysis, however, suggests its proper interpretation.

First of all, it seems clear enough that the Court is saying that there is *not ordinarily* a duty on an auditor to disclose the disposition of funds advanced by its client to an affiliate. It is only in certain circumstances where the Court says such a duty of disclosure arises. Unfortunately, the uncertainty arises when the Court comes to identifying those circumstances.

The Court's language in the passage quoted suggests four possible definitions of the circumstances giving rise to the duty of disclosure. First, the Court refers to "looting" — and elsewhere in its opinion repeatedly uses that term. Second, the Court refers to dishonesty — "known dishonesty by a high corporate officer." Third, the Court refers to a corporation being operated to a material extent for the private benefit of its president. Finally, the Court refers to diversion of funds.

Which of these, in the Court's view, gave rise to the additional duty of disclosure here involved? I suggest that it is only the last — that is, diversion of funds — which gives rise to such a duty of disclosure.

"Looting" is no more a term of art or certain meaning in the law than it is in accountancy. It is not clear in this case when, in the Court's view, Roth's borrowings became looting. Looting, presumably, does not mean illegality, since the trial court instructed the jury, in this case, that Roth's borrowings were not illegal. It thus appears that the word "looting" is merely a literary touch rather than an operative analytical element of the Court's opinion.

The Court's second possible test for bringing into play the duty of disclosure is operation of a corporation, to a material extent, for the private benefit of the president. This is even less helpful than the "looting" test for analytical purposes, at least as a formulation divorced from the facts of this particular case.

Virtually every corporation is operated, to some extent, for the benefit of its officers and other insiders. Indeed, it is quite proper and usual for a corporation to attempt to link the self-interest of the principal officers and employees to the corporation: that, of course, is the governing principle of stock options. Moreover, especially in smaller corporations and those which have recently gone public, the officers are likely to be the principal stockholders themselves. (In the case of Continental, the president owned about 25 per cent of the outstanding stock.) And in corporations of all sizes the insiders, rather than the stockholders as a group, typically control the corporation. To require the accountant to make judgments as to the extent to which the decisions of the principal corporate officers are governed by self-interest rather than stockholder interest, and to draw lines short of specifically prohibited conduct, would indeed be to launch accountants on an uncharted and perhaps unchartable sea.

The third phrase, "known dishonesty by a high corporate officer," in itself is surely not the key, either. The accountant may know that his client's president has cheated the Internal Revenue Service, or fellow investors in a different enterprise, or has been convicted of a crime, but the Court was surely not saying that the accountant has a duty to pass along such information to his client's stockholders.

The key factor bringing into play the special duty of disclosure, it seems to me, is the diversion of funds. The Court defines what sort of diversion of funds it is talking about: a *dishonest* (though not necessarily illegal) diversion, and one "so large as to imperil if not destroy the very solvency of the enterprise." By these terms the Court describes the situation in which a special rule of disclosure applies sufficiently precisely so that there should not be inordinate difficulty in following the rule.

Where disclosure is so required, what should its content be? The Court of Appeals' opinion indicates that "full disclosure" must be the rule — but what does this mean? The Court does not say in general terms, but it does in specific terms: it sets out a version of footnote 2 which, it says, presents the disclosure which the government claims should have been made, and which the Court by implication indicates would have been sufficient in this case. Comparison of that footnote with the footnotes and pertinent excerpts of the Continental balance sheet quoted in the Court of Appeals' opinion offer, I suggest, a clear enough idea as a practical matter of what the Court means by full disclosure. It does not mean that there should be a characterization made of the transactions being disclosed, or an opinion expressed upon them; the Court does not suggest that the labels "diversion," or "dishonest" or "looting" should be used. But the disclosure made includes all the facts, quite neutrally stated, which a reader of the note would have to be apprised of in order to make his own evaluation of the "diversion of funds" in question.

Two further, and important, points should be made about this aspect of the Court's opinion: about a contingency that could possibly render disclosure unnecessary, and about the timing of disclosure.

In the passage of the opinion quoted above, the Court twice makes reference to a situation where the diversion has been made good or adequately secured against and procedures have been established to prevent a repetition. In such a situation, the Court quite clearly says, the special rule of disclosure does *not* apply. With respect to this exception to the general rule of disclosure, the Court indicates that more is required than a reasonable assurance of collectibility. The defense experts said, in effect, that collectibility made disclosure in this case unnecessary, and the Court specifically rejected this contention. Of course, an accountant may not always be able easily to determine what steps should be taken to prevent the recurrence of a dishonest diversion, or whether steps taken are sufficiently effective to meet the Court's test so that disclosure is no longer necessary. The Court offers no guidance on this problem. This may, perhaps, be a subject deserving study by an appropriate body of the Institute.

The other point to be noted about this part of the Court's opinion is the clear implication that an accountant's duty of disclosure applies only at the time that his opinion is issued. This is an important point, because it has been suggested that the *Continental Vending* case implies a general duty on the part of accountants to disclose improprieties on the part of their clients or their clients' officers, no matter when they learn of them and no matter when they occur. I believe the case carries no such implication.

In this case, the Court of Appeals accepted the prosecution's evidence (which the defendants denied) that all three defendants knew at least as early as December, 1962 that the funds advanced to Valley had wound up with Roth. Although the Lybrand opinion was not issued until more than two months later, the Court does not suggest that disclosure should have been made prior to the issuance of the opinion. Moreover, when the Court talks about disclosure it is clearly talking about disclosures as of the time when the opinion was issued. Still further, the Court is clearly saying that if as of that time the diversion had been made good and steps taken to prevent a repetition, then it need not be disclosed. Thus, there are no grounds in the opinion for asserting that accountants have a duty of disclosure with respect to the activities of their clients apart from the issuance of their opinion on the client's financial statements.

In a recent case, a federal district court and court of appeals held that an insurance company which had knowledge of fraudulent conduct by a broker making a market in the company's stock was liable to investors under Section 10 of the Securities and Exchange Act of 1934 and the SEC Rule 10b-5 thereunder, in part by reason of its failure to report the broker's activities to the State Securities Commission (*Brennan* v. *Midwestern United Life Ins. Co.*, 286 F. Supp. 702 (N.D. Ind. 1968, *aff'd*, 417 F.2d 147 (7th Cir. 1969), *cert. denied*, 397 U.S. 989 (1970).). It might be suggested that the *Brennan* case implies a similar duty of accountants to report to public authority all improper activities of their clients, quite apart from the accountants' responsibility with respect to their opinion. This, however, would be reading the *Brennan* case too broadly. For one thing, the Court of Appeals there found active participation by the insurance company in the broker's fraud. More importantly, the relationship of the insurance company to the broker there was quite different from that of an accountant to his client. The accountant has a professional obligation of confidence with respect to his client, wholly absent in the relationship of corporate issuer to its market maker. Moreover, the issuer in that case stood to benefit by the broker's improper activities.

Thus, it seems clear that an accountant's obligation with respect to disclosure or reporting of improper activities by the client or the client's officers is limited to matters affecting the accountant's opinion on the client's financial statements (or, if no opinion is issued, his association therewith: see AICPA Committee on Professional Ethics, Opinion No. 8, "Denial of Opinion Does Not Discharge Responsibility in All Cases"; and AICPA Committee on Auditing Procedure, Statement on Auditing Procedure No. 38, "Unaudited Financial Statements"). Such an obligation may, of course, arise not only with respect to an opinion being issued, which is what the *Continental Vending* case was concerned with, but also with respect to an opinion previously issued, which was the problem raised in the *Yale Express* case (*Fischer* v. *Kletz*, 266 F. Supp. 180 (S.D.N.Y, 1967)), and which is more fully dealt with in SAP No. 41, "Subsequent Discovery of Fact Existing at the Date of the Auditor's Report."

Inquiry into affairs of Valley. The second issue on which the expert witnesses disagreed was whether accountants are under a duty of inquiry into the affairs of affiliates to which advances are made.

The passage from the opinion quoted above suggests that where there is reason to believe that a material dishonest diversion of funds has occurred, an auditor may well have an obligation to investigate the affiliate through which the suspected diversion was made to see if his suspicions are well founded. The Court clearly indicates, however, that this duty of investigation arises only in such exceptional circumstances. There is no implication in this decision that in ordinary circumstances an auditor has an obligation to inquire into the affairs of an affiliate which is audited by other auditors. It may be noted, however, that the Committee on Auditing Procedure has under study the question of an auditor's obligation with respect to such transactions with affiliated companies.

It is also of interest in this connection that the Lybrand firm has now adopted the policy of requiring, as a condition of engagement, that it be engaged to audit not only the principal company but also that company's affiliates.

Composition of collateral. The third question of a technical nature as to which the expert witnesses disagreed involved disclosure of the composition of the collateral pledged against the loans to Valley. The ruling of the Court on this point is quite narrow. It did not hold that collateral must always be described, or even that collateral must always be described where it consists in large part of securities of the creditor entity. Rather, the Court held that failure to describe the collateral in this case must "be judged in light of [the defendants'] failure to reveal the looting by Roth"; and that the jury might infer that this failure to disclose "was part of a deliberate effort to conceal what defendants knew of the diversion of corporate funds that Roth had perpetrated."

An accountant, however, would be well advised to disclose the make-up of the collateral securing a loan in a case such as *Continental Vending*, i.e., where the collectibility of the loan is essential to avoiding an excess of current liabilities over current assets (particularly where there is a serious operating loss), and where the collateral consists in substantial part of the stock of the lending company, whose value is necessarily dependent on the perceived financial condition of the company itself. As the Court observed, the securities of the company whose solvency is at issue are "the one kind of property ideally unsuitable" to collateralize a receivable such as the Valley receivable.

Increase in Valley receivable. The final technical question as to which the expert witnesses disagreed concerned the nondisclosure of the increase in the Valley receivable from $3.4 million to $3.9 million between the fiscal year-end and the date of the auditors' opinion.

The Court treated this question in the same fashion as the question of disclosure of the composition of collateral: that is, not in terms of any general principle of disclosure, but in terms of the light which the jury might think that the nondisclosure cast upon the defendants' purposes, given the central fact that the known diversion of the funds was not disclosed.

Thus, so far as standards of professional conduct are concerned, the Court of Appeals' opinion enunciates only one general rule that is, to any significant degree, a new one. The rule is that where the auditor knows of or suspects a dishonest diversion of funds sufficiently large to imperil his client's solvency, there must either be exceptional disclosure or exceptional measures to make it good and to prevent a recurrence.

PRACTICAL IMPLICATIONS

The third major group of lessons to be learned from the case are practical, rather than legal, in nature.

First, the case suggests two general rules of a practical character whose implications may be seen throughout the Court's opinion. One is that where an accountant discovers such a diversion as was involved in this case (and, I would suggest, whether or not the diversion is made good), he would do well to consider every action that he takes thereafter, every disclosure or nondisclosure, and every contact with the client, in the light of how it may subsequently appear in a court of law. The other is that the accountant in such circumstances, in order to protect himself, should as a practical matter exercise an extraordinary degree of caution: a much higher degree of caution than, to their misfortune, was exercised by the defendants in this case.

The case illustrates why such extra care and circumspection are called for: conduct that could well have been less than negligent was, in the light of hindsight, made to appear to be deliberately fraudulent and, indeed, criminal. Thus, for example, the Court of Appeals makes specific reference to

- The fact that, as the defendants conceded, footnote 2 to the Continental Vending financials erroneously implied that the Valley payable and Valley receivable could be netted.

- The fact that the defendants apparently did not consult with a partner in their firm with whom problems in audits were supposed to be discussed.

- The fact that two of the defendants failed to tell the assistant who confirmed the collateral about liens on the collateral at certain banks.

- The fact that the defendants failed to require effectuation of Roth's promised pledge of his house and furnishings.

- The fact that although the defendants asked to have Continental's board approve the transactions involved in securing the Valley receivable, they did not, before issuing their opinion, see to it that this had been done.[2]

The case also suggests some more specific practical rules, applicable where a problem of potentially serious nature is discovered:

1. The accountant should not be rushed by supposedly urgent deadlines. The client can stand a little delay in issuing its annual report, or in filing its 10-K, much better than the accountant can bear the blame for the economic misfortunes of the client or its stockholders.

2. The accountant should not rely on promises of the client's officers as to important matters; he should see to it that they are carried out.

3. The accountant should not rely on representations made by the client with regard to such important matters if they are matters which the accountant can check for himself.

4. The accountant should consult with a partner or a colleague who can bring objectivity to bear on the matter before he issues his opinion.

5. Finally, it may be useful for the accountant to consult his attorney, if he has one. Such consultation should not take place merely after the accountant has issued his opinion or after trouble has developed, but while trouble — or at least legal involvement of the accountant in such trouble — may still be avoided. The attorney may not be able to bring great expertise to bear. Unfortunately, expertise in accounting matters is not widely spread in the legal fraternity, in part because accountants have not until recently consulted attorneys much. But the attorney, even if he does not possess accounting expertise, should be able at least to bring judgment to bear as to how the accountant's opinion and his conduct will look to a lay jury, a judge and a prospective plaintiff's attorney in the event that trouble develops.

---

[2] At both trials, the defendant who had been in charge of the audit testified without contradiction that Roth had told him of the board's "reluctant" approval at a meeting two days before certification. The draft of the minutes of that meeting, indicating disapproval, was not received until after the collapse of the company and notification to the SEC.

13. Accountants' Responsibility for Unaudited Financial Statements*

Emanuel Saxe†

During the 1960s, the accounting profession witnessed a substantial outbreak of litigation directed principally against the larger firms. The cases arose, for the most part, in the federal courts under the Securities Act of 1933 and the Securities Exchange Act of 1934, as a result of the expression, by independent public accountants, of their professional opinions on clients' *audited* financial statements. The resulting court decisions enlarged the ambit of professional responsibility in these circumstances by recognizing new categories of claimants and by imposing new, higher standards of professional conduct upon the defendants.

On the other hand, a case of first impression, involving the responsibility of a firm of certified public accountants for services of a "write-up" nature resulting in the preparation of an *unaudited* financial statement, was recently decided against them by Justice Riccobono,[1] following a trial without a jury in the New York Supreme Court.

An appeal from this decision was promptly undertaken by the defendant-accountants in the Appellate Division (First Department) of the New York Supreme Court. Since the lower court's opinion seemingly imposed upon certified public accountants responsibilities with respect to *unaudited* financial statements which appeared to be directly contrary to standards established and recognized by their profession, both nationally and in New York State, the American Institute of CPAs and the New York State Society of CPAs, by permission, filed a joint brief, *amici curiae*, requesting modification of the lower court's opinion and judgment to bring it into accord with the accepted standards of the accounting profession. The judgment appealed from was just affirmed by a divided court.[2]

*From *The New York Certified Public Accountant* (June, 1971), pp. 419–423. Reprinted by permission of the New York State Society of Certified Public Accountants.

†Emanuel Saxe, CPA, is Distinguished Professor of Accounting and Dean, *Emeritus*, Bernard M. Baruch College, City University of New York.

[1]*1136 Tenants' Corp.* v. *Max Rothenberg & Co.*, Index #10575/1965, New York County, Trial Term, Part VII, opinion dated June 16, 1970.

[2]*1136 Tenants' Corp., Plaintiff-respondent,* v. *Max Rothenberg & Co., defendant-appellant* (#3305), *New York Law Journal*, April 9, 1971; all concurred except Justice Steuer, who dissented in a separate memorandum.

BACKGROUND OF THE CASE

The subject action was brought by plaintiff (a cooperative apartment corporation) against defendant (a firm of certified public accountants) or recover for defendant's failure to uncover certain alleged
defalcations of plaintiff's funds by Riker & Co., Inc., (plaintiff's former
managing agent) and by I. Jerome Riker, individually (formerly president and director of plaintiff as well as president of Riker & Co., Inc.).

The underlying facts are as follows:

Sometime in 1958, Riker and others purchased the premises 1136
Fifth Avenue, in New York City, and then incorporated the plaintiff
which became the owner thereof and proceeded to sell the apartments
therein. Riker & Co., Inc., acted as managing agent of plaintiff's property under a contract to that effect.

Late in August, 1963, plaintiff, via I. Jerome Riker, engaged the
defendant, as successor accountants, to perform certain accounting
services (the scope and nature of which comprise a principal issue
in this case) under an oral retainer agreement providing for payment
therefor in the amount of $600 per annum.

Early in March, 1965, it was discovered that Riker & Co., Inc.,
was in financial difficulties and that certain of plaintiff's obligations
that had been reported as paid on the managing agent's monthly
statements to plaintiff were, in fact, not paid. Plaintiff thereupon
commenced this action, based on two alternate theories: breach of
contract or negligence.

DEFENDANT'S POSITION AS TO ENGAGEMENT AND SERVICES

The defendant's position as to the import of the oral agreement
was that it had been engaged to perform bookkeeping services, or
"write-up" work, and to draw up unaudited financial statements,
without verification, solely from information furnished by the managing agent on the client's behalf; in other words, defendant denied
any obligation to go behind these reports and audit the books and
records of plaintiff and Riker & Co., Inc. Defendant was also to prepare a letter setting forth the tax deductions for mortgage interest
and real estate taxes to which the tenant-cooperators would be entitled, as well as prepare the plaintiff's Federal and New York State
income tax returns.

Accordingly, defendant "wrote-up" the plaintiff's books of account
relying on the data set forth in the monthly management statements

of Riker & Co., Inc., which purported to report all monies received and disbursed by the managing agent. On the basis of the data contained in plaintiff's "written-up" books and records, which were founded on the information supplied by Riker & Co., Inc., defendant-accountants prepared and submitted unaudited financial statements to plaintiffs.

All the financial statements so submitted were accompanied by letters of transmittal which began as follows:

> "Pursuant to our engagement, we have reviewed and summarized the statements of your managing agent and other data submitted to us by Riker & Co., Inc., pertaining to 1136 Tenants' Corporation. . . ."

and concluded thus:

> "The following statements (i.e., the financial statements and appended schedules) were prepared from the books and records of the Corporation. No independent verifications were undertaken thereon. . . ."

The financial statements themselves contained an inscription on each page which stated:

> "Subject to comments in letter of transmittal."

However, either through thoughtlessness or loose wording the defendant used the term "audit" in the financial statements.

PLAINTIFF'S CONTENTION

Plaintiff's contention was that it had engaged defendant as an auditor, not as a bookkeeper, to check the accountants of Riker & Co., Inc., by performing an audit thereof ("to perform all necessary accounting and auditing services for it"); that defendant in complete disregard of its duty to plaintiff under its retainer agreement failed "to examine and audit the books, records, invoices, bank statement and cancelled check vouchers of plaintiff and Riker & Co., the Managing Agent," and that it failed to demand of Riker & Co. cancelled check vouchers and other evidence of payment of bills; further, that as a result of the defendant-accountants' breach of contract and their failure to exercise their duty of due care by adhering to generally accepted professional standards, they failed to uncover the defalcations being committed by the plaintiff's managing agent; and that had the plaintiff-corporation been properly advised by defendant of the existing financial conditions, the defalcations committed by the managing agent would have been thwarted.

THE TRIAL COURT'S DECISION

The two principal issues[3] presented for trial and decision were therefore:

1. What was the nature and scope of the defendant's engagement?
2. Did defendant perform its duties pursuant to such retainer agreement?

On the first issue the trial court held, on the basis of the testimony adduced at the trial, that defendant-accountants undertook to perform an audit, "as an independent voice to verify and confirm the books and records of its managing agent and to establish the authenticity thereof." The court further held that the proof supported a finding of negligence in the performance of its duties on defendant's part by reason of carelessness and "its deviation from accepted professional standards"; also, that defendant's contention that plaintiff was guilty of contributory negligence was without merit.

In his decision following the trial, Justice Riccobono (a) denied defendant's motion made at trial to dismiss the complaint; (b) awarded plaintiff $174,066.93 on its cause of action, together with interest, costs and disbursements, for a total of $237,278.83; and (c) awarded defendant $1,000 on its counterclaim for additional accounting services rendered, together with interest, costs and disbursements, for a total of $1,349.51. Defendant appealed the decision awarding plaintiff the sum of $237,278.83.

THE DANGER TO THE PROFESSION

Since one interpretation which might be placed on the trial court's decision in this case — virtually one of first impression — was that it ignored the substantial and important differences between audited[4] and unaudited[5] financial statements in respect of the procedures followed and the responsibilities assumed by certified public accountants, the Institute and the Society felt constrained to participate in

---

[3]Defendant's pre-trial motion on the pleadings for summary judgment dismissing the complaint was denied at Special Term, and that decision was affirmed by the Appellate Division (27 A.D. 2d 830; 1st Dept., 1967) and by the Court of Appeals (21 N.Y. 2d 995; 1968). The denial was predicated upon the reason that the record raised these two triable issues.

[4]Financial statements which are examined with a view to rendering an opinion on their fairness of presentation in conformity with generally accepted accounting principles are known as audited financial statements, and this type of examination is described as an auditing service commonly known as an audit.

[5]The non-auditing, or accounting, services may be of a "write-up" nature (i.e., limited to assistance in maintaining or preparing a client's books and records) or may extend to the preparation of unaudited financial statements which are not aimed toward, and do not permit the expression of an opinion thereon.

the appeal to overcome any undeservedly wide precedential impact that might result if the decision were left undisturbed.

As previously noted, two issues of fundamental importance to the accounting profession at large were presented in this case, namely,

1. The professional obligations of certified public accountants in preparing unaudited financial statements and the reasonable expectations of users of such statements as to the work performed by certified public accountants with respect thereto.

2. The scope of the defendant's oral undertaking.

The first issue.   The trial court, sitting without a jury, made certain findings with respect to these issues which seem to run counter to the professional standards by which all certified public accountants perform their professional duties.   For example, with respect to the first issue, the court said:

". . . the need for a certain amount of auditing procedures is required even in a 'write-up.' This is especially true where an accountant is called upon to perform accounting services for a cooperative apartment venture. It is in this type of situation, where even a minimal amount of internal auditing procedures would have revealed whether major expenditures and liabilities of the plaintiff corporation had been met and paid and therefore this type of procedure is mandated as a necessary prerequisite, albeit to an adequate 'write-up.' "

Also,

". . . whether the scope of the defendant's retainer agreement with the plaintiff was to perform a 'write-up' or an 'audit,' certain definitive auditing procedures were necessitated and mandated under this oral retainer. . . ."

Further,

". . . regardless of whether defendant received the invoices for purposes of audit or otherwise, it had a duty to detect defalcations and on the basis of the evidence adduced could have and should have, noted these defalcations. This it did not do."

The second issue.   With respect to the second issue, that of the scope of the defendant's oral undertaking, despite the fact that defendant's financial statements clearly reflected that it had not performed an audit and contained no expression of its professional opinion with respect to the statements submitted, the trial court's holding that an audit was called for appears to have been predicted on its above-noted conclusion that certified public accountants must always perform auditing procedures, even in cases involving unaudited financial statements.   That the trial court apparently did not comprehend the distinction between audited and unaudited financial statements may be sensed from its statement that

> "Plaintiff does not claim that defendant was retained to make an 'independent verification' of the accountants.   It rather contends, as was sufficiently established during the trial, that a certified public accountant can make an examination which constitutes an audit without making independent verifications."

THE APPELLATE DIVISION'S DECISION

The Appellate Division's affirmance was based on its conclusion that the record amply supported the trial court's findings (1) that defendant was engaged to audit and not "write-up" plaintiff's books and records and (2) that the procedures performed by this defendant in this respect were "incomplete, inadequate and improperly employed."

In support of this position, the majority opinion further stated that one of the defendant-accountants' senior partners admitted that his firm had performed services which went beyond the scope of a "write-up," and that it had actually performed some auditing procedures for plaintiff. Also, that defendant's worksheets indicated that it did examine plaintiff's bank statement, invoices and bills; that one of the worksheets entitled "Missing Invoices 1/1/63 - 12/31/63" disclosed invoices missing from the records of Riker & Co. totalling more than $44,000; and that utilization of the simplest audit procedures would have revealed Riker's defalcations. It went on further to say:

> "Moreover, *even if* defendant were hired to perform only 'write-up' services, it is clear, beyond dispute, that it did become aware that material invoices purportedly paid by Riker were missing, and, accordingly, had a duty to at least inform plaintiff of this. But even this it failed to do. Defendant was not free to consider these and other suspicious circumstances as being of no significance and prepare its financial reports as if same did not exist."

In this respect, it reiterated the previously indicated position of the trial court.

Dissenting opinion. In his strong dissent, Justice Steuer concluded that the proof was overwhelming that the defendant-accountants were engaged to do a "write-up" only, especially since it unequivocally demonstrated that the statements issued by all the accountants hired by Riker (including both the defendants and their predecessors on the job) "bore legends to the effect that they were unverified and no independent examination had been made." He also stated that Riker's testimony to the effect that he engaged them to perform an audit conflicted with evidence previously given by him in an earlier trial and in a deposition; and that it was "hardly credible that an embezzler would engage an accountant to make an audit which would immediately reveal his own peculations"; further, that the paltry fee for the engagement ($600) could not be reconciled with the responsibility involved if, in fact, an audit had been contracted for.

With respect to the plaintiff's contention that even if an audit had not been contracted for, the defendants performed negligently in that they should have learned that there was something questionable about Riker's management, Justice Steuer contended:

> "This was argued primarily from observations that could have been made had an audit been made. The only specific factor coming to defendant's attention was that Riker's statement showed defendant's own bills to have been paid when in fact they had not been, and that certain tax bills were not in defendant's files. Neither of these facts involved a breach of defendant's obligation. They might, conceivably, cause a fiduciary to report to his principal. But to require one in the relationship of defendants to take action would expand the obligation from bookkeeping to criminal detection."

He concluded his dissent by stating that the verdict was against the weight of evidence, and that since this was a non-jury trial, the Appellate Division should have made new findings and rendered a verdict for the defendants.

Further appeal may be taken. It is anticipated that a further appeal will be undertaken to the Court of Appeals, to settle the issues in this important case with finality. In any event, practitioners would do well to make sure that all engagements undertaken by them are evidenced by specifically descriptive, written retainer agreements, and that in the case of the preparation and issuance of unaudited statements, the requirements of Statement on Auditing Procedure #38 are duly carried out.

PART THREE

The Examination

The examination as performed by auditors today is drastically different from that performed by colleagues at the turn of the century. Changes in basic audit objectives coupled with the increased size and complexity of business organizations have required new approaches to auditing which have led to the adoption of new auditing techniques. Some of the tools currently used by the auditor were unheard of or in their embryonic stage in the early 1900's.

Auditing standards emphasize the importance of the auditor's evaluation of internal control. Current advances in the knowledge of the operation of the firm suggest that the auditor must gain new insights into human behavior characteristics to effectively evaluate the client's operational controls. A fuller understanding of the nature of operations of the firm may result in the auditor's placing less reliance on the traditional concept of a client's internal control system.

The auditor has been applying statistical sampling techniques in recent years to permit him to draw inferences from a mass of data more efficiently and effectively. Further development of sampling techniques and more widespread understanding and use by the auditor seem clearly desirable.

During the last decade, the advent of the computer has had the greatest single impact upon the auditor's approach to and technique of examination. This phenomenon will undoubtedly provide continued and increased challenge in future years.

Approach

The manner in which the auditor approaches his examination of a client's financial statements should receive very careful consideration. Indeed, the effectiveness of the audit is closely related to the way the auditor conceives of and undertakes his task.

In the first article, A. Carl Tietjen challenges auditors to consider a fundamental change in procedure relative to the annual recurring audit examination. Mr. Tietjen believes that the auditor should consider his engagement as a continuing examination, essentially uninterrupted in character, but with an expression of opinion as to the fairness of the statements submitted annually.

An auditor must at all times keep in mind the necessity for securing sufficient and competent evidential matter in planning and carrying out his audit program. In the second selection, R. K. Mautz compares evidence from both judicial and auditing viewpoints. The direct relationship of audit evidence and basic audit techniques is explained and attention is directed to standards for judging the reliability and adequacy of audit evidence.

Ivor B. Wright, in the final article, stresses the unique problems involved in initial audit engagements. Special emphasis is placed on the planning, timing, and implementation of auditing procedures peculiar to such initial audits.

14. A Suggested Change in Examination Approach*

A. Carl Tietjen†

Business management is perhaps more cost-conscious and efficiency-minded today than at any time in history. Automation in the plant and in the office is well under way, and will undoubtedly move forward rapidly. Businessmen are constantly re-examining their methods of manufacturing and ways of doing business, with a view to achieving the maximum volume at the minimum cost.

Does this trend have a bearing on the accounting profession?

The answer would appear to be a definite yes. The profession must make certain that it continues to keep in step with industry by continually re-examining its own concepts and techniques, with the objective of rendering maximum service to clients at a cost that is within sound economic limits.

While tax work, system studies, and other special phases of accounting practice are of great importance, it is quite likely that more than 50 per cent of the profession's fees arise from recurring examinations. Many of these engagements have been performed by the same accounting firms for a number of years. As a result of their work over an extended period, these firms are generally satisfied with the internal accounting controls, records, personnel, and the basic integrity of the managements. It seems logical that this type of engagement offers the best opportunities for reduction of time expended by junior accountants in checking the ordinary day-to-day accounting routines, and the substitution therefor of time of more experienced accountants.

It would appear that the profession makes no basic differentiation in approach between an initial examination and a recurring examination, aside from obvious differences involving work on prior year property, surplus, minutes, etc. At present, each year of a recurring engagement is treated as a separate examination. The working papers of each year are expected to be complete in themselves, and are so handled physically for binding, filing, and the like. Thus, the fundamental audit steps (cash reconciliations, checking of accounts receivable, vouching of property ad-

---

*From *The Journal of Accountancy* (April, 1956), pp. 47–49. Copyright (1956) by the American Institute of Certified Public Accountants, Inc. Reprinted by permission of the AICPA.

†A. Carl Tietjen, CPA, is a partner of Price Waterhouse & Co., New York.

ditions, and so on) are carried out in substance each year. Of course, tests
are often reduced as the accountants become more familiar with a client's
accounts, emphasis is shifted from year to year, and other refinements are
employed. But in broad terms it seems fair to state that fundamental procedures are performed each year, and that each annual examination is
made to stand on its own.

Could this concept that recurring examinations are separate annual
events and that it is necessary to perform all procedures every year be one
of the traditional practices that needs to be re-examined? I think it is. A
more up-to-date approach to a continuing engagement is, in my opinion,
the viewing of it as *essentially uninterrupted in character, with an expression
of opinion submitted annually.*

How can the foregoing concept be applied? In my judgment the most
practical answer lies in the use of the established technique known as
rotation on a much broader scale than has been done up to this time. What
work could be placed on a rotating basis? Almost every phase of an examination could be so handled, but the sections which consume the most
time, cash, accounts receivable, inventories, property, and the like, are
most susceptible to the rotation technique.

THE CONTINUING CONCEPT IN PRACTICE

An example is a substantial company — not one of the giants — with
a number of divisions and accounting locations having many bank accounts. While there is a minimum of internal auditing, over a period of
some thirty years the independent accountants have developed considerable
confidence in the internal accounting controls, records, personnel, and in
the integrity of management. On this engagement, despite streamlining
the program over the years, routine cash work continues to require several
hundred hours every year, which is high in relation to total time on the
examination.

What is proposed in the situation outlined above is to carry out the full
cash program only every second or third year, with the work on cash during
the off years being in the nature of a review of client records and interrogation of employees by the senior accountant or an experienced assistant,
to determine that the company's usual methods have been followed.

If this seems to be a bold proposal, let it be remembered that less than
twenty-five years ago the entire idea of interim work — that is, auditing at
a date other than the end of the period under examination — was considered radical by many experienced members of the profession. Changing
circumstances, particularly the wartime shortage of personnel, had the effect of forcing the profession to spread the work over a greater period of

time, using fewer men. Today the profession is faced with another serious situation in that qualified men are not only scarce but very expensive. At the same time client companies have improved their accounting routines and internal controls to a point where costly junior time expended in routine checking seems to be diminishing in economic value.

It is my view that rotation is a logical next step to the concept of performing work at a date other than the year end, and within a few years would become a routine practice, just as has interim work.

What would be the accountants' position if something went wrong on a company's accounts being examined on a rotating basis? As I see it, their position would be little — if at all — different from what it is now when an irregularity occurs, provided they could show that their work was properly planned and systematically carried out, and not performed in a sporadic fashion. In this regard it should be borne in mind that under present methods there is ordinarily a twelve-month interval between the accountants' tests, and the extension of this interval to a period greater than twelve months on a recurring engagement would not appear to change their fundamental position to any great extent.

There seems to be unanimous agreement that junior time should be reduced. Many seem to favor trimming annual tests to a bare minimum in order to accomplish this objective. In the event of trouble leading to a court case, might not the accountants' position be better had they done a rather thorough job less frequently than had they performed minimum annual procedures?

All sections of the work should not, of course, be curtailed in the same year. Examinations would have to be planned for several years in advance in such a way that the work and time spent would be balanced, with certain segments of the work performed in the usual manner and others on a review basis in each year. Sound professional judgment would, as always, be required in the application of this technique.

In line with the afore-mentioned concept of the continuing examination, perhaps working papers could be prepared to cover several years rather than one, thus reducing paper volume.

The continuing concept, if wholeheartedly accepted and applied, would enable the profession to spread its work throughout the year to a much greater extent than is done now. This might well accomplish more toward alleviating the peak season problem than any switch to the natural business year that could be hoped for.

APPLICATION OF TIME SAVED

Let us assume that the concept outlined herein is to be applied to an engagement, with a substantial saving in junior time anticipated. What disposition is to be made of this saving? I would suggest that it be applied in the following manner:

1. Devote at least one fifth of the time saved to work at the semi-senior and higher levels, designed to give the accountants a more intimate knowledge of internal controls, the business, its problems and peculiarities, the company's operations, and the industry.

2. Obtain income for services commensurate with a salary scale high enough to attract and hold staff assistants of top professional caliber.

It will be noted that additional work by experienced personnel is proposed. This dovetails with a long held conviction that there should be greater numbers of experienced assistants in the profession and fewer but better qualified juniors. Some might say that under present conditions the more experienced personnel would find it difficult to perform additional work. In answer to this it might be pointed out that the type of work indicated could be performed at almost any time of year, thus making for more efficient utilization of the time of experienced staff. Furthermore, it seems clear that widespread application of the rotation approach would enable the profession to practice with substantially fewer juniors, a highly desirable objective in these times. Also, with fewer juniors and less detail work, there would obviously be less supervision and review time required of seniors, managers and partners. The suggested approach would give younger assistants experience in review and interrogation techniques at an earlier stage in their careers, which might logically be expected to accelerate their development as professional men and women.

ORIENTATION TO THE NEW PROCEDURE

As clients have come to expect accountants to follow certain procedures, some educational work would be required, but this could hardly be any more difficult than was the change to the interim approach some years ago. In fact, there are indications that clients generally would welcome a reduction in detail work, with greater emphasis being placed on high-level services instead.

It seems unnecessary to request the AIA committee on auditing procedure to give formal sanction to the rotation technique. The wording of the present standard short-form opinion and AIA pronouncements on auditing standards would appear to give plenty of latitude for its use. In this regard the committee on auditing procedure might wish to consider the advisability of incorporating recognition of a difference between an initial and a recurring examination in its pronouncements.

Passing the twenty-year mark as a public accountant recently perhaps entitles one to a little reminiscing and an attempt at forecasting future developments.

SOME CLOSING OBSERVATIONS

Twenty years ago the profession still employed many temporary men for busy seasons only. Frequently large staffs of assistants, often inexperienced, performed examinations in relatively short periods of time. There was little interim work. Many noncollege men were established in the profession and others were still entering it. From this it is obvious that much progress has been made, including the quality of personnel and the manner in which they are used. The improvement in personnel might well have been even greater had it not been for the war and the difficult employment conditions which have been prevalent in recent years.

Yet much remains to be done. Too great a proportion of the profession's work is still performed by relatively inexperienced staff; too much time is spent in merely assembling working paper information for the review of more experienced assistants. Further progress will require continued improvement in the quality of personnel and the methods they use, together with continued improvement in client personnel and records.

Without stating when it will come to pass, the prediction is ventured that, in the examination of the future, assistants of supervisor caliber will carry out a substantial part of the field work; that the accountants' work will be mainly a study and substantiation of client's data and interrogation of officials and employees; and that client information will be so comprehensive, and the accountant's personnel so experienced, that the working papers will be confined largely to summaries of what was done and the conclusions that were reached.

15. The Nature and Reliability of Audit Evidence*

R. K. Mautz†

The importance of evidence in auditing is expressed clearly and forcefully in *Generally Accepted Auditing Standards*, in which the third standard of field work states:

> Sufficient competent evidential matter is to be obtained through inspection, observation, inquiries and confirmations to afford a reasonable basis for an opinion regarding the financial statements under examination.[1]

In its emphasis on audit evidence, this standard of field work raises some very interesting questions. How does an auditor know when he has acquired "sufficient" evidential matter? How does one judge the "competence" of evidential matter? For that matter, what is "evidential matter" as used here? Do the various methods of acquiring evidence suggested in the standard all provide evidence of equal validity, or is the evidence provided through the application of different techniques of varying usefulness?

Questions of this nature serve to emphasize the fact that we do not as yet have available in auditing literature a complete exposition of the nature, types, uses, and limitations of audit evidence. Of course, public accounting is still a youthful profession, and we cannot expect a complete theory on such a complex subject to appear overnight. Yet lack of a comprehensive theory of audit evidence is a real handicap to educators, a limitation in the attainment of professional standards, and may be something other than impressive to practitioners of other professions. Development of a comprehensive theory of evidence is a sizable undertaking and will call for serious effort over a considerable period. The purpose of this article is merely to suggest some problems and conclusions pertinent to the general subject.

A first thought in attempting to answer these questions might be to turn to the field of law, in which evidence is also of crucial importance.

*From *The Journal of Accountancy*, Vol. 105 (May, 1958), pp. 40–47. Copyright (1958) by the American Institute of Certified Public Accountants, Inc. Reprinted by permission of the AICPA.

†R. K. Mautz, Ph.D., CPA, is a partner of Ernst & Ernst in Cleveland, Ohio.

[1] *Generally Accepted Auditing Standards* (New York: American Institute of Certified Public Accountants, 1954), p. 14.

Much experience must have been accumulated by the courts and practicing attorneys which may be of help to auditors in defining and evaluating evidence. Even a brief acquaintance with the theory of judicial proof impresses one with the importance of evidence and the care with which classes of evidence have been developed and analyzed. But a little additional study uncovers some differences between law and auditing which imply rather strongly that the legal experience with evidence will have but limited applicability in auditing.

EVIDENCE IN LAW AND AUDITING

The jury system, first of all, causes the law to view evidence differently than auditors might and to develop rules which we find unnecessary. Jurors are laymen, not experts either in law or in evidence. They are unskilled in reasoning from that which is presented to them as evidentiary facts to appropriate conclusions; they are likely to be ruled by emotions rather than by reason; and without protection, they may be led to improper conclusions by a skillful courtroom lawyer using evidence not pertinent to the issue or colored somewhat for his purposes. To protect jurors from the influence of inappropriate evidence and to guide them in arriving at a reasoned rather than an emotional conclusion, rules of admissibility have been developed and are rigorously applied. These rules have to do with what evidence may and what may not be introduced. The courts, in developing the basic rules of admissibility and in applying them in specific cases, thus screen the evidence so that only what is considered appropriate and pertinent is permitted to influence the jury and its verdict.

There is no parallel in auditing. Instead of a jury of laymen, the auditor himself, an expert in accounting and in audit evidence, evaluates the evidence and reaches a decision. The auditor decides what evidence to consider and what to ignore. In effect, there are no rules of admissibility; any and all evidence is permitted to reach the auditor. He must decide what evidence he will "admit" in reaching his decision. Legal rules as to the admissibility of evidence are of little aid to us either directly or as a pattern because we have nothing even remotely similar to the jury system.

The second difference lies in the fact that in a legal case the opposing attorneys serve as officers of the court; each is charged with the responsibility of doing everything he can within the bounds of ethics and legal practice to present his side of the case thoroughly and effectively. This provides assurance that all pertinent, admissible evidence will be presented. Our judicial system is based on the assumption that if experts on each of the two opposing sides of an issue present the facts of their respective positions in a fair contest, the truth will be revealed and justice will prevail.

Again, we have no similar practice or assumption in auditing. There is nothing in an audit situation comparable to the activity, the attitude, or the approach of opposing attorneys. The company under examination does not try to "make a case" for its financial statements; neither does the auditor try to disprove them. In most examinations both the company under audit and the auditor are interested in the same result — a fair presentation of the company's financial position and results of operations. When differences of opinion do arise, they are settled, not by formal argument before a tribunal, but in almost every case through a simple discussion on an "out-of-court" basis.

These two differences between auditing and courtroom procedures — no rules of admissibility to protect a jury and no opposing attorneys — are so substantial as to make legal developments and experience in matters of evidence of relatively little aid to us in auditing. We may learn a good deal from the definitions and basic classifications used by our legal friends and perhaps from concepts with respect to the general validity of different types of proof, but in the main it appears that auditing must draw upon its own resources and experience for a theory of audit evidence.

Before leaving the matter of differences between auditing and law, it might be well to point out that these differences place important burdens on auditors, burdens which we probably recognize but which because of their importance are worthy of emphasis.

The absence of rules of admissibility for evidential matter in auditing leaves an auditor with no guides for screening evidence other than his own judgment and training. He has before him a great quantity of information in the company's records and supporting documents, and, beyond that, additional information available through inquiry, confirmation, and other audit techniques. To each type of evidence he must give appropriate weight and no more. Evidence that is not pertinent, that is not reliable, that is inconclusive, that can be misunderstood, he must recognize and use with caution, if at all. He must know not only how to obtain evidence but also its usefulness and limitations once obtained.

THE AUDITOR'S RESPONSIBILITIES

Because an auditor works alone without the spur and competition of an opposing point of view, he has two additional responsibilities. First, he must, in effect, serve on both sides of the case simultaneously; he must be equally alert to evidence for or against any assertion in the client's financial statements. Second, he must make a diligent effort to be as exhaustive as possible in his examination, knowing that if he does not dig out all pertinent evidence available it will most likely never receive consideration. This calls for thoroughness and painstaking effort to be impartial and independent.

NATURE AND CLASSIFICATION OF EVIDENCE IN AUDITING

Evidence has been defined as "the facts presented to the mind of a person for the purpose of enabling him to decide a disputed question."[2] In the case of an examination by an independent accountant, every assertion in the financial statements, although not a matter of dispute, must be considered subject to question, and any factual information brought to the mind of the auditor to enable him to decide the truth or falsity of financial statement assertions is evidential matter. Thus, financial statements may be viewed as a whole series of propositions to be proved, and audit evidence includes all facts which the auditor uses in proving or disproving these propositions.

Wigmore, the outstanding legal authority on evidence, writes:

Evidence is always a relative term. It signifies a relation between two facts, the factum probandum, or proposition to be proved, and the factum probans, or material evidencing the proposition. The former is necessarily hypothetical; the latter is brought forward as a reality for the purpose of convincing the tribunal that the former is also a reality.[3]

To further explain the nature of the evidence, Wigmore states:

There are two possible modes of proceeding for the purpose of producing persuasion on the part of the tribunal as to the probandum. The first is by the presentation of the *thing itself* as to which persuasion is desired. The second is the presentation of some independent fact, by *inference* from which the persuasion is to be produced. Instances of the first are the production of a blood-stained knife; the exhibition of an injured limb; the viewing of premises by the jury; the production of a document. The second falls further into two classes, according as the basis of inference is (a) the assertion of a human being as to the existence of the thing in issue, or (b) any other fact; the one may be termed testimonial or direct evidence, the other circumstantial or indirect evidence.[4]

It is interesting to note that this three-way classification is directly

---

[2]*The Encyclopedia Britannica*, 1957 Edition, Vol. 8, p. 905. Wigmore defines evidence more formally as: "Any knowable fact or group of facts, not a legal or a logical principle, considered with a view toward its being offered before a legal tribunal for the purpose of producing a conviction, positive or negative, on the part of the tribunal, as to the truth of a proposition, not of law or of logic, on which the determination of the tribunal is to be asked." Wigmore, J. H., *Wigmore on Evidence*, Vol. I (Boston: Little, Brown and Company, 1904), p. 3.

[3]Wigmore, J. H., *The Science of Judicial Proof* (3rd ed.; Boston: Little, Brown and Company, 1937), p. 8.

[4]*Ibid.*, p. 11.

applicable in auditing. Just as a blood-stained knife may be presented in court, so the actual cash, inventory, or securities may be exhibited to an auditor. Assertions of human beings are obtained to support a company's claims against customers, to gain an understanding of internal control, to indicate the extent of contingent liabilities, and for a wide variety of other purposes through confirmations, representations, and replies to oral questions. The "all other" category in auditing would include such evidential matter as various types of documents, actions by the company officers and employees, and the existence of records or related facts

Wigmore proceeds to a discussion of suitable titles for these three classes of evidence and to the inferences to be drawn from each. For our purposes, the terms "real evidence," for examination of the thing itself; "testimonial evidence," for assertions of human beings; and "indirect evidence," for all other facts, will be satisfactory. Although these are not the terms which Wigmore finds most useful for his purposes, they are suitable for ours.

AUDIT EVIDENCE AND AUDIT TECHNIQUES

A direct relationship exists between these classes of evidence on the one hand and basic audit techniques on the other. Various lists of basic audit techniques have been suggested, but here I shall use the one with which I am most familiar.[5] It includes:

1. Physical examination and count
2. Confirmation
3. Examination of authoritative documents and comparison with the record
4. Recomputation
5. Retracing bookkeeping procedures
6. Scanning
7. Inquiry
8. Examination of subsidiary records
9. Correlation with related information

Each of these techniques is a device for obtaining audit evidence. They provide the means by which an auditor gets the facts, the evidential matter, which convince him directly or permit him to infer that the proposition to be proved is correct. The relationship may be indicated as follows:

Real evidence is provided by:
    Physical examination and count
    Recomputation
    Retracing bookkeeping procedures

---

[5] Mautz, R. K., *Fundamentals of Auditing* (New York: John Wiley & Sons, 1954), p. 49.

Testimonial evidence is provided by:
    Confirmation
    Inquiry
Indirect evidence is provided by:
    Examination of authoritative documents
    Scanning
    Examination of subsidiary records
    Correlation with related information

Real evidence is material which convinces one of the truth of the proposition to be proved without the necessity of an inference. Thus, if one sees inventory he knows it exists; if he handles and counts a petty cash fund he has proof of its existence. Likewise, if he foots a trial balance or proves a bonus calculation or traces postings he is convinced without the necessity for any inferences that the footing shown is or is not correct for the figures listed, the bonus is or is not calculated correctly from the amounts given as components in the calculation, that the posting was or was not carried in the right amount to the appropriate side of the account indicated.

Testimonial evidence is obtained through statements from others and requires an inference by the auditor. On an audit, testimonial evidence comes in reply to requests by the auditor. He sends written requests to customers of the client company asking them to confirm certain facts. He inquires of officers, employees, and professional people such as the company's counsel for information to support the financial statements. Sometimes the answers to these questions are in writing, sometimes an oral answer is deemed sufficient. All have an important characteristic in common: they are statements of human beings from which the auditor infers the correctness or incorrectness of the financial statements — the propositions to be proved.

Indirect evidence is the "all other" category, composed of a great variety of information. A considerable portion of audit work consists of reviewing business papers, various documents from which the authenticity of recorded facts is inferred by the auditor. Subsidiary records are referred to as well, and their existence and nature are taken into account by the auditor in coming to conclusions about the statements. Throughout the examination he scans the accounting records for unusual or apparently inappropriate entries that might require additional investigation by means of one of the other techniques. If no unusual or inappropriate entries are discovered, he tends to infer that the records are in order. Correlation with related information includes such diverse facts as the reconciliation of nominal accounts, such as insurance expense, with related balance sheet accounts, such as prepaid or unexpired insurance, the subsequent payment of debts in the amounts shown in the financial statements under audit, and the compatibility of the inventory amount with purchases and sales demonstrated through application of the gross profits test.

BASES FOR JUDGING RELIABILITY

Division of the entire area of evidence into these three classes is helpful in evaluating the reliability of audit evidence, although it may at first be misleading. A first conclusion as to the reliability of audit evidence might be that "real evidence" is the most reliable, "testimonial evidence" is next, and "indirect evidence" is the weakest. In general, there is some truth in this conclusion, but it also is subject to such important exceptions as to make reliance on it downright dangerous. Actually, the range of relative reliability within each category of evidence is so great that the best indirect evidence available may be as reliable as much of the real evidence submitted to an auditor. Perhaps some analysis of the bases for judging reliability may be helpful in explaining this statement.

DANGERS OF AUDIT EVIDENCE

What are the dangers in using audit evidence? What questions of reliability may be raised? To a considerable extent this varies with each class of evidence, but there are certain questions which may be raised about facts in all three classes. These are: (1) pertinence to the question at issue, (2) possibility of misinterpretation, and (3) conclusiveness.

UNWARRANTED INFERENCES

Unless evidence is pertinent to the proposition under consideration, it is not valid for purposes of proof. But, as Wigmore points out, there is often a considerable risk of unconscious inference that may lead one to accept evidence that is not at all pertinent. To illustrate, if an experienced person takes a trial balance of the customer's ledger, foots it, and finds that it agrees with the control account balance, he may be impressed with the reliability of the subsidiary ledger. Actually, all that has been proved is a mathematical agreement; the individual accounts may or may not be real, collectible, or properly classified. As another example, sighting an inventory is evidence only that it exists, not that it is owned, that it is currently useful, or that it is described or priced appropriately. A bank reconciliation may establish that there are funds in the bank to support the balance claimed in the cash account and balance sheet; it cannot prove that this is the total cash which should be on hand, an inference readily drawn by an inexperienced auditor. A reply to a confirmation request may establish that a receivable exists; it rarely if ever proves collectibility. So it is throughout the area of audit evidence. At every point the auditor must be wary in his use of evidential material. Unless it is pertinent to the precise point at issue, it cannot be considered competent for his purposes.

Part of the problem here lies in the difficulty of separating the several propositions to be proved with respect to a given item in the financial statements and questioning each of these propositions separately. The balance sheet item "Marketable Securities......$20,000" contains at least four propositions requiring competent evidential matter for their disposition:

1. That the company owns the investments
2. That the amount shown is reasonable and determined in accordance with generally accepted principles of accounting
3. That the investments are actually marketable
4. That they are classified appropriately in the financial statements

Evidential matter offered in support of any one of these propositions may or may not be pertinent to the others. An examination of the security certificates may convince the auditor that the company owns a given number of shares; it is not sufficient in itself to convince him that the valuation is satisfactory. An auditor must make an effort to identify each proposition at issue and avoid inferences not supported by evidence.

MISINTERPRETATION

The possibility of misinterpretation is so obviously a problem in every instance as to appear not to warrant mention. Yet we cannot afford to overlook the obvious any more than we can neglect the less apparent. Frequently, evidence does not mean what it appears to an untrained auditor to mean. The terms of a contract are an obvious illustration. An auditor, even a trained one, may be led astray by the wording of a particularly technical agreement. To cite a more simple illustration, account titles may fail to describe the contents of an account; journal entry explanations may not be clear; apparent approvals on documents may mean something quite different; internal control procedures may be less effective than they appear to be at first consideration. With respect to evidence obtained from other people, the danger of misinterpretation is twofold: the question itself may be misunderstood by the person asked, and the reply may be misunderstood by the auditor. Every auditor of any experience has received replies to confirmation requests which indicate that the recipient did not understand the request. Not only does this illustrate the point at issue, it also, it seems to me, raises some grave questions as to the real reliability of evidence obtained through the application of this technique, which many of us feel is one of our most reliable.

Conclusiveness

Relatively little audit evidence is fully and finally conclusive. Our work on cash may convince us that the balance stated is absolutely correct. Very likely, however, there will be a few outstanding checks that failed to clear by the time the cut-off statement was obtained. More important will be the doubts we may have as to inventory quality, the extent of contingent liabilities, adequacy of depreciation rates, and similar matters. Auditors do not guarantee any precise accuracy, of course; they merely give an opinion that the statements "present fairly." But this is more than a matter of accuracy. The illustration mentioned in the preceding paragraph suggests that in some cases evidence obtained through confirmation, which we consider to be one of our most reliable techniques, may be worth very little. If we are to avoid error in relying too heavily on unreliable evidence, we must constantly be concerned with the conclusiveness of the evidence accumulated in support of a given proposition. If it falls short of being conclusive, we must at least give consideration to the desirability of acquiring more.

Reliability of Evidence

In many cases, really conclusive evidence is not available. How can we know, for example, whether a given litigation will be settled adversely or favorably to the company under examination? The answer must be that we cannot know, and that we must make clear to those who rely on our work that there are matters on which no one can obtain conclusive evidence.

Additional Problems of Real Evidence

In addition to the problems of reliability already noted, pertinence, possibility of misinterpretation, and conclusiveness, special questions of reliability apply to each of the individual classes of evidence. In addition to the problem of unwarranted inferences, which is probably the most serious possibility in the use of real evidence, the question of timing is also of importance. Is the time at which the auditor physically examined securities such that he can be confident the company owned them as of the audit date? Has he counted three separate petty cash funds or did he count some of the same cash two or three times? Was the inventory taken close enough to the balance sheet date to be reliable in arriving at the balance sheet amount? Were account footings proved at a time when they could not be altered before the trial balance was taken by the auditor?

Certainly real evidence, because it is direct proof, is reliable, but the auditor must be especially cautious of making unwarranted inferences on propositions not proved by the physical evidence. He must also assure himself that the timing of the evidence does not render it inappropriate for his purposes.

RELIABILITY OF TESTIMONIAL EVIDENCE

Testimonial evidence (statements of human beings) opens up a whole new series of questions about reliability. It is difficult to say that one of these outweighs the others in importance; any one of them could render a person's statement useless as evidence. The reliability of testimonial evidence may vary with: (1) the knowledge of the one testifying, (2) the responsibility and integrity of the one testifying, and (3) the extent of bias or self-interest on the part of the one testifying.

Certainly the character and qualifications of the testifier are of the very essence of testimonial evidence. Unless he is knowledgeable on the point in question, responsible, honest, and free from deliberate or unintentional bias, his statements are of little value as evidence.

Of course, the auditor is not always in a position to know whether or not the person of whom he inquires has knowledge, is responsible, honest, and free of bias and self-interest. If an auditor has information leading him to the belief that certain respondents are not qualified, he must look for evidence elsewhere; their replies cannot be considered "competent evidential matter." He should not ask the chairman of the board if the inventory was taken by actual count, weight, and measure unless the chairman has knowledge of this. The reply of a happy-go-lucky store-room clerk on such matters as obsolescence of inventory is scarcely satisfactory evidence by itself. The statement of a petty cash custodian as to the authenticity of an alleged cashed check in his fund is of little validity unless supported by other facts. In many cases, however, an auditor has no knowledge one way or the other as to the character and qualifications of people offering testimonial evidence. In effect, this takes us back to the question of conclusiveness. If other pertinent evidence is available, an effort should be made to secure something more conclusive. If questionable testimonial evidence is the most conclusive that can be had, then it must be accepted, but at the same time the auditor should recognize the risk involved and take steps to make this known to those who rely on his opinion.

RELIABILITY OF INDIRECT EVIDENCE

Indirect evidence adds at least one new possibility of unreliability to those discussed so far; this is the possibility of manipulation or falsification. This unpleasant possibility applies particularly to documentary evidence of all kinds. An invoice, a sales slip, a reconciliation, approvals on a journal voucher, any and all of these may be fictitious. The existence of a satisfactory system of internal control may give the auditor some assurance that documents and approvals on them are authentic. The possibility of manipulation must not be overlooked, however, and until the auditor has reason to trust the indirect evidence submitted to him, he must be wary of inferring the truthfulness of the propositions they support.

One of the least tangible forms of evidence is one that is not satisfactory in and of itself but is often sufficient to make competent other evidential matter which by itself would not be satisfactory. This is the existence of an enterprise actively acquiring goods and services, manufacturing or processing, satisfying customers, paying and receiving cash, and dealing with employees, taxing bodies, and shareholders. The very atmosphere in which an auditor works is such that from it he can and should draw certain inferences as to the truthfulness of the several propositions in the financial statements. He may not be able to tell from the size of the plant the dollar amount of the inventory, but from his observations of the business he should be able to infer the general order of magnitude of the inventory, whether substantial portions are likely to be obsolete, whether consignments in or out are an important problem, whether amounts are stored in public warehouses as claimed, and other pertinent conclusions to support evidence gained in other ways.

Of course, there is a danger here also. An inexperienced man may be so impressed by activity that his judgment is faulty. Even a skillful and experienced auditor should be careful to specify to himself those facts of existence and activity that influence him. His problem is to relate conclusions to the facts on which they are based in order to avoid unwarranted inferences and conclusions unsupported by evidence which others would accept as competent. Appearances can indeed be deceiving. An auditor must not overlook this most indirect of evidence, but neither can he permit it to influence his judgment unduly.

ATTITUDE TOWARD EVIDENCE

Rightly or wrongly, some auditors gather evidential matter not so much to provide themselves with facts on which to judge the assertions made in the financial statements as to satisfy what they consider to be the requirements for issuance of a certificate. Their attitude is negative rather than positive. Rather than requiring sufficient evidence to establish the financial statement assertions as true or in error, they act on the assumption that if they gather a reasonable amount of evidence and find nothing wrong, then all must be well.

The danger in such an approach is real. To find nothing wrong is not to establish the fairness of the financial statements. Especially is this true in view of the fact that we work with tests and samples. The attitude that such an approach is likely to develop in those who follow it is not one that an auditor should have. Rather than an honest questioning of every assertion, it is more likely to be one of "let's get the work done and go on." An auditor does not look for errors; neither does he search for sufficient evidence to support the claims of the client. His task is to obtain and evaluate such evidence as is available and from it to infer the truthfulness of the financial statements in question.

The auditor who sees an examination as the performance of enough work so that, should he become involved in litigation, expert witnesses can testify that he has satisfied professional standards, has not really met those standards at all. Indeed, it is questionable whether he even understands them.

NATURE OF EVIDENTIAL MATTER

CONCLUSIONS

Although much attention has been given to the importance of audit evidence and to the basic techniques for obtaining it, relatively little attention has been directed to the nature of evidential matter in auditing or to guides or standards for judging its competence and adequacy. If the ideas expressed in the preceding paragraphs have validity, the following conclusions appear to be appropriate:

1. Audit evidence includes any factual matter available to an auditor from which he may know or infer the relative truth or falsity of the assertions in financial statements.

2. "Competent evidential matter" includes:
   a. Real evidence — actual examination by the auditor of the thing in question.
   b. Testimonial evidence — oral or written statements by people.
   c. Indirect evidence — documents, books and records, actions and events, and any other fact that the auditor uses in forming an opinion on financial statements.

3. The principal problems in dealing with audit evidence include:
   a. Obtaining "sufficient competent evidential matter" to afford a reasonable basis for an opinion.
   b. Screening and evaluating evidence. This includes the question of pertinence to the issue at hand, possibility of misinterpretation, and degree of conclusiveness for all types of audit evidence and certain other questions of reliability relating to subclasses of audit evidence.
   c. Reasoning from available evidence on the questions at issue. This is a simple matter if evidence on the issue is conclusive but a more

difficult matter if the available evidence is inconclusive or judged unreliable.

4. The danger of unwarranted inferences from audit evidence is such that an auditor must be extremely careful in his use of any and all evidence; his conclusions on every financial statement assertion should be related directly to the specific evidence on which it rests.

5. Audit evidence varies considerably in reliability among the major classes of evidence and also within each class.

6. In the absence of conclusive evidence on any given issue, an auditor must rely on the most conclusive evidence available. When evidence sufficiently conclusive to support a judgment is not available, the auditor should refrain from making a judgment.

7. The existence and activity of the enterprise under examination constitute evidence from which reasonable inferences are justified, but, as with other types of evidence, care is required in its use.

8. Because he alone collects, screens, evaluates, and uses evidential matter to determine the validity of assertions in the financial statements, the auditor must exercise special diligence in discharging his responsibility under Standard of Fieldwork Number 3.

16. Guidelines for First-Time Audits*

Ivor B. Wright†

A first-time annual audit is a challenge to the accountant who will undertake its direction, lay out the audit program and revise it as developing conditions dictate.

Since an initial audit may be more time-consuming than a recurring one, the auditor confronts the problem of lateness in completion of the audit and in furnishing the financial statements. To reduce the extra time to a minimum, he must do everything possible at the earliest opportunity. Once he is certain that the understanding with the client is definite, he should devise a time-table whereby large, time consuming matters and anticipated "bottle-neck" items are started as early as possible. Reviews of documents (corporate charter or partnership agreement, by-laws, meeting minutes, important contracts and agreements, and other instruments), for example, should be made as quickly as possible. The examination must be seen as having managerial aspects and sound and timely planning will make for efficiency and better results.

In planning one, it is essential that the auditor continually keep in mind the scope of his engagement and that he thoroughly understand exactly what he is to produce. Advisedly, the scope should be detailed in an engagement letter, approved by the client. It will serve both as a reference point for the accountant and as a written confirmation of the arrangement in the event a procedural question arises.

In the event that the engagement involves a parent company and one or more subsidiaries the accountant should know whether or not his attestation will cover a consolidated report only, or consolidating reports and possibly separate company reports. He should also understand whether it includes the preparation of federal tax returns as well as state and city tax returns. If the securities of the company are traded on a securities exchange or over-the-counter, the accountant should understand what reports will be required under the various Securities and Exchange Commission rules and who will be responsible for other segments of the reports.

If the company is one regulated by a federal or state agency, the auditor should determine what agency reports may be required of him.

---

*From *The CPA Journal* (March, 1972), pp. 197-202. Reprinted by permission of the New York State Society of Certified Public Accountants.

†Ivor B. Wright, CPA, is a partner of Smith & Harder in New York.

He should also know whether or not he is to submit both a short form and long form audit report and any special purpose reports.

This article deals essentially with the *initial probings* of a first-time audit of a going concern, with particular emphasis on substantiation of unobserved inventories and excludes, with occasional exceptions, measures that are common to later audits. The company here considered is a medium sized one and some of the procedures therefore may not be applicable to much larger or much smaller companies. However, many of the procedures will be applicable regardless of the size of the entity.

The procedures here described relate primarily to a situation where a company, in existence for some period of time has, for one reason or another, changed its auditors. Where the predecessor accountant, in such instances, is well known and has supplied unqualified opinions, the task may be eased considerably, particularly if consultation between the retiring and succeeding accountants can be had and if prior workpapers can be reviewed. Where a company is new or has not previously been audited, the accountant obviously must rely solely upon the company's own records.

ETHICAL PROBLEMS

More often than not the company will have had a prior auditor. In some instances the company will already have informed the former auditor that his services have been terminated. If not, the new auditor should urge them to do so and have them request that workpapers required by the new auditor be made available for his inspection. If the company has not notified the former auditor, then the new auditor should do so pursuant to his Rules of Professional Conduct.

In any event, the request for making available the former auditor's workpapers must come from the company. While the former auditor is not required to permit inspection and possible copying of some of his workpapers under these circumstances, it is usually done as a matter of professional courtesy. The new auditor will do well to wait until he is well along in his own planning before arranging to review the former auditor's workpapers, in order that he may have greater knowledge of what to review and what questions to ask. In addition to the embarrassment involved in making a second request for the papers, the new auditor also risks the possibility of a refusal to grant a second review of the workpapers.

KNOWLEDGE OF THE COMPANY

The size of the company, the complexity of its operations, the condition of the records, the caliber of the bookkeeping and supervisory personnel, the caliber of the owners and key officials, the company's status as a public or non-public company, its financial condition, and other factors, all bear on the planning and direction of the audit.

The auditor should acquire information of a general nature about the company at an early stage of his planning. The following are illustrative examples:

- History of the company, including reorganizations. A credit agency report may be very informative on company and management.

- Nature of the business (i.e. Manufacturing, Wholesale, Retail, Service, etc.), credit policies, financing methods, sales methods and terms, and the impact of any seasonal fluctuations.

- Description of the company's product or products or the services it renders.

- Type of organization (corporation, partnership, sole proprietorship, etc.).

- The auditor should secure a list of the locations of the company's plants and offices as well as a list of states in which the company is qualified to do business.

- The auditor should also secure copies of prior years' financial statements including audit reports to stockholders and to the Securities and Exchange Commission, registration statements, listing applications, etc.

- Copies should also be secured of written company procedures and policies covering all areas of operation, to the extent available, together with information relating to internal controls.

- The accounting principles and policies followed by the company, particularly with respect to such items as inventories, fixed assets and depreciation, prepaid expenses and deferred charges.

- Copies of reports of examinations of prior years' tax returns by the Internal Revenue Service, the status of examinations in process and the years for which federal income tax returns are still subject to examination.

TOUR OF FACILITIES

An inspection of major facilities (factories, warehouses, branches and offices), at the earliest possible date, is very desirable. The auditor (generic term for those who will play an important role in the examination) should visit factories to visualize and understand what is manufactured and how, raw materials used, and, to an extent, might incidentally make some internal control observations. Receiving and shipping department should be toured; factory offices and other segments could be inspected.

Important branch offices, and distribution and warehouse branches deserve a visit. Finally, the main office should be toured, key officials met and, not the least, working space for the audit staff arranged. Office rules — working hours, overtime arrangements, smoking rules and other relevant details — can be ascertained at the same time.

Any important facilities not preliminarily inspected could be covered during the course of the audit.

PRELIMINARY REVIEW OF THE RECORDS

A memorandum on the accounting system should be prepared, including, amongst other details, the following:

- Books and other records maintained, location, and personnel in charge;

- Internal reports prepared and distribution;

- Internal auditing, if any, reports prepared and distribution, personnel involved;

- Use of EDP facilities, if any — in house or service bureau;

- Personnel to whom inquiries should be addressed;

- General condition of records, subsidiary ledgers, agreement with controls, etc.;

- Other aspects as warranted in the individual case.

It should be obvious that these early observations will permit the examination to get off to a good start with minimum irritation and interruption of company personnel, an important consideration.

Copies of records to be obtained for review. The auditor should request access to or copies of basic company records, for review and permanent file purposes. They include:

- Closing trial balances for the fiscal period immediately preceding the subject year and for the subject year;

- A copy of the chart of accounts and the manual, if any, explaining the details to be recorded in them.

In addition, the auditor should request the company to furnish him with copies of various corporate documents and agreements not previously received which will require examination by him and which will form a part of his permanent file to which reference will be made at various times during the course of the audit. While the type of items to be requested will vary to some extent dependent upon the circumstances, and the reader may undoubtedly think of additional items to be requested at this time, the following are representative:

1. Certificate of Incorporation, Partnership Agreement, or similar basic type of organization agreements, together with any amendments thereto.

2. Minutes of Directors and Stockholders meeting. Initially, perhaps a three year period would be sufficient with a later review of the minute books themselves with respect to important resolutions in prior years.

3. Leases covering both real and personal property and deeds to real property.

4. Current union contracts, employment agreements, stock option agreements and plans, employee pension and other welfare plans, and similar items.

5. If closely held, a list of stockholders and shares owned together with copy of stock repurchase agreements, if any. If not, a list of all stockholders owning 10% or more of the company's stock.

6. Marketing agreements together with any descriptions of the company's marketing policies including the use of employee salesmen or sales representatives.

7. A list of patents, patent applications, trademarks and trade names together with the amounts, if any, at which they are carried in the accounts.

8. Loan agreements.

9. Catalogs and price lists.

10. Comments written by former auditors.

11. Opinions from attorneys on pending litigation, both for and against the company.

In requesting copies of the foregoing items or similar other items that may be required in a particular engagement, judgment must be exercised so as not to request copies of documents unless essential to the auditor's examination. Where a number of contracts are made with identical terms and provisions and only the names and possibly dates and amounts are different, it is obvious that all the auditor needs is a sample copy of one such contract together with a list of the names of the parties and dates and amounts of the contracts.

PRELIMINARY AUDIT PROGRAM AND PLANNING

After having secured the foregoing information and having summarized his notes of meetings with company personnel and of observations during tours of company plants and offices, the auditor is in a position to draft most of the preliminary audit program. Of necessity, the program at this point must be prepared in somewhat less detail than would ordinarily be done where the auditor is more familiar with detailed records and procedures. As the field work progresses, the audit program can be elaborated and, as is common, revised as more knowledge is acquired with respect to the company's records and procedures as well as the adequacy of internal controls.

The preliminary audit program should provide for the following, as a minimum:

- A careful review of internal controls and company procedures as to their adequacy.

- Tentative methods for testing whether the stated internal controls and procedures are in fact functioning sufficiently to permit the auditor to rely upon them.

- A comparison of the accounting principles as applied in the current period with those applied in the prior period to provide a means of determining the consistency of application of generally accepted accounting principles.

- Running accounts of the capital stock and surplus accounts.

- Representation letter with particular emphasis on the consistent application of generally accepted accounting principles.

In his initial planning the auditor must develop a time table discussed earlier providing for the audit functions such as circularization of receivables, inventory observation, and the maximum assistance from company personnel. It is essential that any problems that may develop during the course of the audit be discussed with management at the earliest possible time to minimize the risk of delaying the completion of the audit unduly.

SUBSTANTIATION OF INVENTORIES

Where significant, the examination of the inventory amount is usually the most difficult and time-consuming phase of an audit. This requires no explanation to accounting practitioners. The difficulties become more acute where, in a new engagement, the auditor has not observed the opening inventory and, in some cases, to exacerbate the situation, he may even have been engaged after the closing inventory was taken.

Unless this condition can be satisfactorily resolved, the auditor will have no choice but to disclaim an opinion, an eventuality that will probably chagrin the client.

If only the opening inventory cannot be verified, even by satisfactory alternative methods, the disclaimer would apply to the income and retained earnings statement and an unqualified opinion expressed as to the balance sheet.

Employment of satisfactory alternatives. In some cases a *satisfactory* alternative method may be available. If so, obviously, it would eliminate the disclaimer. In fact, if an alternative has been employed it no longer need be disclosed in the scope section of the auditor's report (see paragraphs 19 and 20, SAP No. 43.) but he may do so, and describe them, if he prefers.

The use of an alternative method must be approached with care and caution. One should carefully review SAP No. 43 (Confirmation of Receivables and Observation of Inventories) to assure adequate compliance.

Other available auditing procedures are here described based on the writer's own experiences in various first-time audits. The selection of procedures and the extent of their application are matters to be governed by the conditions encountered and the auditor's judgment. During the course of the substantiation of inventories, the auditor must be sure to have sufficient knowledge of the accounting principles employed by the company in order that these may be compared with those applied at the end of the year to determine their consistency. The consistency of both inventories with the prior year's closing inventory is also necessary. Where alternative procedures are applied to the opening and closing inventories, their consistency to each other and to the prior year's closing inventory are equally needed.

Inventory valuation basis. By inquiry and by reference to prior year financial reports, the auditor should ascertain the basis upon which the company values its inventories; such as cost, lower of cost or market, or market, and whether cost is determined on an average, first-in, first-out, or last-in, first-out basis. By inquiry, he should also ascertain the items normally included in inventories. For example, are supplies, containers, packaging materials, etc. included in inventory or are they expensed? Determination should also be made as to the method and calculation of overhead for inclusion in the inventory valuation of finished goods and work-in-process.

Examples of alternative procedures. Some of the procedures which the auditor should consider using, if the available records permit, are outlined below.

If a complete physical inventory was taken at or near the end of the previous year:

1. Secure a copy of the priced inventory listing.

2. If the previous auditor has made his workpapers available for review, determine the basis and extent of the testing done by him by reviewing his copy of the inventory listing and related workpapers. This review should include the following wherever possible:

- Comments in the auditor's workpapers as to the adequacy and effectiveness of the inventory planning and taking.

- Extent of test counts made by former auditor and traced to final inventory listing.

- Extent to which prices were verified, and evidence of testing mathematical accuracy of extensions and footings.

- Procedure followed by former auditor to determine the extent of obsolete, slow-moving or unsalable items and the indicated total and disposition of such items.

- Procedures followed with respect to verification of appropriate cut-offs of sales and purchases at the inventory date and of transactions between the physical inventory date and the audit date.

- Comments as to the causes or reasons for any significant difference between book inventory and the priced physical as of the inventory date.

The auditor must exercise judgment at this point to determine the extent to which he need perform some independent testing of the company's records to satisfy himself as to the appropriateness of the amount of the opening inventory.

3. If there was no previous auditor or if his workpapers are unavailable, then the auditor must satisfy himself with respect to the items under Step 2 by independent examination and testing of the records. Obviously, he cannot satisfy himself as to quantities by any current test counts. However, if the company maintains well kept and reliable perpetual records a comparison of the inventory listing with such records on a test basis should enable the auditor to conclude whether or not he is satisfied with the quantities disclosed by the inventory listing.

In the absence of reliable perpetual records, the auditor may be able to satisfy himself as to quantities by an examination of the original inventory tags and their comparison with the listing on a test basis. Particular attention should be given to the initialing by counters and checkers, and to instances where quantities have been changed. The inventory tag control sheet should also be examined as should voided tags.

In other words, the auditor should review all the available evidence, including the physical inventory instructions, to determine whether or not it appears that the inventory was well planned and carefully taken. It is this accumulation of evidence upon which the auditor will form his judgment as to the reliability of quantities, rather than upon one or two isolated pieces of evidence.

If inventories are taken periodically during the year:

1. Under these conditions, the auditor has probably already observed some of the current year's periodic physical inventories and has, therefore, become informed as to the basis for determining frequency of counts and the items or groups of items counted each time. If statistical sampling is used, the auditor must be satisfied that the plan has statistical validity, has been properly applied, and that the results are reasonable. (See paragraph 11 of SAP No. 43). Based upon his observations and comparisons of results of periodic inventories with book records, the auditor should have formed some opinion as to the effectiveness of the company's inventory procedures and controls as well as the reliability of the physical counts.

2. If the workpapers of the previous auditor have been reviewed, the auditor should note any comments of the previous auditor relating to the periodic counts observed by him and to the comparison of results with the accounting records.

3. All significant differences between physical counts and book records should be carefully investigated by the company and the results reviewed by the auditor. Through inquiry and by reference to the accounting records the auditor must satisfy himself that differences between physical and book quantities do not represent weaknesses in, or lack of, adequate controls in the system of procedures applied by the company in determining book inventories. Otherwise, the auditor cannot express an opinion on the book inventories at the end of the current period, and he may not be able to satisfy himself as to the inventory at the end of the preceding year.

4. Tests for appropriate pricing of the inventories and for appropriate adjustments for slow-moving, obsolete or otherwise unsalable items usually will be made in the same manner as if complete physical inventories were made at or near the year-end, although the mechanics of accumulating the information may vary.

Other alternatives. There are other procedures and analyses which the auditor can use to help fortify his satisfaction or dissatisfaction with the inventory. A comparison of gross profit percentages over several years is sometimes helpful, but it is the writer's conclusion that it must be used with extreme care. If a company has several product lines, calculations of gross profit percentages should be by product line to the maximum extent possible as an aid in disclosing the possibility of an unhealthy inventory situation that might not be indicated by an overall gross profit percentage. Also, an analysis of sales and closing inventories by product lines may disclose an extremely slow-moving line of products.

In conclusion, the auditor must still use his own inquisitiveness and imagination to ferret out the information he must have in order to satisfy himself not only as to opening inventories in first-time audits, but also with respect to closing inventories in the usual year-end audits.

Internal Control

The second standard of field work requires a study and evaluation of the existing internal controls so as to determine the extent of the examination. The profession stresses the auditor's responsibility for "accounting" controls and places secondary emphasis on "administrative" controls.

The lead article by Kenneth W. Stringer elaborates on the definition of accounting controls and the need for clarification of these controls. Emphasis is placed on the basic concept of financial controls established by the client and the relationship of the auditor's review of the client's control system with other auditing procedures.

In the second article R. K. Mautz and Donald L. Mini outline a proposed body of theory to aid the auditor in internal control evaluation and audit program modification. Within this body of theory the auditor would find guides tending to stimulate the exercise of judgment rather than use of mechanical aids. The auditors underline the need for an awareness of the interrelationship of internal control, irregularities, and audit procedures.

In the last article in this section, Larry F. Konrath argues that auditors should concentrate more attention upon the collection of evidence in support of transactions and less on internal controls. Auditors are primarily concerned with financial controls rather than with the total control system and do not adequately consider the unpredictability of a control system so highly dependent on human behavior. The auditor, therefore, assumes considerable risk (stemming from his evaluation approach) by relying upon internal control to the extent implied in current auditing standards and procedures.

17. Conceptual Aspects of Internal Control Evaluation*

Kenneth W. Stringer†

Presented before the Annual Meeting of American Institute of Certified Public Accountants, New York — September, 1970

In planning this program we were somewhat concerned that making a presentation on internal control to an audience of practicing CPAs might seem like "carrying coals to Newcastle." A similar concern was felt initially by the Committee on Auditing Procedure when this subject was placed on its agenda.

Our committee soon became convinced, however, that there are sufficient unresolved questions and problems in this area to justify reconsideration and issuance of a pronouncement. We hope that those in the audience today will feel the same way about this program.

Reconsideration of internal control by the committee was motivated largely by two reasons:

First, the length of time elapsed since the last pronouncement on this subject, coupled with several developments in business and in the profession in the meantime; second, some indication of a need to amplify and clarify concepts in the light of experience with the existing pronouncements.

Nevertheless, experience has demonstrated that the rationale and basic concepts comprehended in those pronouncements are fundamentally sound, and consequently no radical departures will be proposed on this program, despite the reference to "new directions" in the program brochure.

Some of the developments in business and in the profession in the last several years and their relation to internal control will be mentioned briefly.

The increasing trend for CPAs to provide management advisory or consulting services involving the review, evaluation, and improvement of management information systems increases the need for clearly distinguishing between these extended services and those required for compliance with the auditing standard relating to internal control.

The rapidly increasing use of computers for processing accounting and other business information has introduced additional problems

*From *Selected Papers* (1970), pp. 177-190. Reprinted by permission of Haskins & Sells.
†Kenneth W. Stringer, CPA, is a partner in the executive office of Haskins & Sells, New York.

in reviewing and evaluating internal control for audit purposes, as well as in making the distinction between audit services and extended services.

Closely related to the increasing use of computers is the trend toward integration of accounting information required for financial and other operating purposes into coordinated management information systems. This development increases the need to identify clearly the elements of the total system that are comprehended in the standard concerning internal control.

These developments and distinctions are important not only for the purpose of defining the nature and scope of the auditor's review and evaluation of internal control but also in clarifying his reports thereon. This need is accentuated by the increasing requests for such reports for use by management or by regulatory agencies and sometimes for inclusion in published reports.

The need for clarification of certain aspects of the existing pronouncement will be presented following a brief discussion of the purposes of the auditor's study and evaluation of internal control and of the present definition and classification.

PURPOSES

The primary purpose of the auditor's study and evaluation of internal control, as expressed in the auditing standard previously referred to, is to establish a basis for reliance thereon in determining the extent of audit tests to be applied in his examination of the financial statements.

A secondary, but nevertheless important, purpose is to provide constructive suggestions to clients. This purpose is recognized in the following excerpt from the comments in Statement No. 33 with respect to the auditing standard concerning internal control:

> As a by-product of this study and evaluation, the independent auditor is frequently able to offer constructive suggestions to his client on ways in which internal control may be improved.

Although auditors are interested in both of the foregoing purposes, it is important to recognize an essential difference between them. The study and evaluation for audit purposes is a professional requirement, while constructive suggestions to clients are desirable but nevertheless discretionary. Consequently, the study and evaluation for audit purposes should be adequate for each year, while the attention given to constructive suggestions may properly vary from client to client or from year to year for a particular client.

PRESENT DEFINITION AND CLASSIFICATION

The essence of the present definition of internal control is included in the following excerpts from Statement No. 33:

> 5. In the broad sense, internal control includes . . . controls which may be characterized as either accounting or administrative, as follows:
> a. Accounting controls comprise the plan of organization and all methods and procedures that are concerned mainly with, and relate directly to, safeguarding of assets and the reliability of the financial records.
> b. Administrative controls comprise the plan of organization and all methods and procedures that are concerned mainly with operational efficiency and adherence to managerial policies and usually relate only indirectly to the financial records.

The foregoing subdivision of internal control into accounting controls and administrative controls was made in Statement No. 29 primarily for the purpose of clarifying the scope of the study required under generally accepted auditing standards, in order to facilitate the distinction between these requirements and other purposes. The committee's conclusions in that respect, as codified in Statement 33, were as follows:

> 21. The independent auditor is primarily concerned with the accounting controls. . . . If the independent auditor believes, however, that certain administrative controls may have an important bearing on the reliability of the financial records, he should consider the need for evaluating such controls.

NEED FOR CLARIFICATION

The present committee believes that clarification of the existing definition of accounting controls is desirable because of possible differences in interpretation with respect to the two key elements comprehended in it: the safeguarding of assets and the reliability of financial records.

SAFEGUARDING OF ASSETS

The definition of "safeguard" that appears relevant in the context of the present definition is "a means of protection against something undesirable." Use of this definition conceivably could lead to a broad interpretation that the protection of existing assets and the acquisition of additional assets is the primary function of management, and therefore that any procedures or records entering into management's decision-making processes are comprehended in this element of the definition of accounting controls. Under this concept, for example, a management decision to sell a product at a price which proves to be unprofitable might be regarded as a failure to protect existing assets, and therefore as evidence of inadequate accounting control. The same interpretation might be applied to a decision to incur expenditures for equipment which proves to be unnecessary or inefficient, for materials which prove to be unsatisfactory in production, for merchandise which proves to be unsalable, for research which proves to be unproductive, for advertising which proves to be ineffective, and to similar management decisions.

A second possible interpretation is that safeguarding of assets refers only to protection against loss arising from intentional or unintentional errors in processing transactions and handling the related assets. Errors of the latter type include understatement of sales through failure to prepare invoices, or through errors in pricing or computation; overpayments to vendors or employees arising from errors involving quantities of materials or services, prices or rates, or computations; and physical loss of assets such as cash, securities, or inventory. In some situations errors of this type might also include improper allocations of certain costs, which would result in failure to recover these costs from customers.

A third possible interpretation is that safeguarding of assets refers only to protection against loss arising from intentional errors. This type of error includes defalcations and similar irregularities, the latter including falsification of records for the purpose of causing erroneous payments of commissions, profit-sharing bonuses, royalties, and similar payments based on the recording of other transactions.

RELIABILITY OF FINANCIAL RECORDS

Possible differences in interpretation concerning the "reliability of financial records" arise from the different purposes for which the financial records may be used. The two broad uses are for internal management purposes and external reporting purposes. One interpretation would extend the scope of accounting control to include reliability of the financial records for both of these purposes, while another would restrict it to external reporting purposes only.

To illustrate the foregoing distinction, the degree and accuracy of classifications, details, and allocations required to provide reliability of records for such management purposes as establishing sales policies and prices, estimating future costs, and measuring performance by divisions, products, or other lines of responsibility, ordinarily exceeds that required to provide reliability for external reporting purposes.

REVISED DEFINITION

The committee believes the present definition of accounting control extends only to the safeguarding of assets against loss from unintentional or intentional errors or irregularities, and to the reliability of financial records for external reporting purposes. It believes also that a revised definition expressed in relation to the functions involved in the flow of transactions is desirable to clarify the understanding and application of the second standard of field work.

Transactions are the basic components of business operations, and therefore are the primary subject matter of business control. The primary functions involved in the flow of transactions and related assets include: the authorization, execution, and recording of transactions, and the accountability for resulting assets.

As indicated earlier, the committee believes the present definitions of administrative and accounting controls can be clarified by redefining them in relation to these functions as follows:

Administrative controls include but are not limited to the plan of organization and the procedures and records that are concerned with the decision processes leading to management's authorization of transactions. Such authorization is a management function directly associated with the responsibility for achieving the objectives of the organization, and is the starting point for establishing accounting control of transactions.

Accounting controls comprise the plan of organization and the procedures and records designed to provide reasonable assurance that:

1. Transactions are executed only in accordance with management's authorization.
2. Transactions are recorded as necessary (a) to permit preparation of financial statements in conformity with generally accepted accounting principles or any other criteria applicable to such statements, and (b) to recognize and maintain accountability for assets.

3. The recorded accountability for assets is compared with the existing assets at reasonable intervals.

The foregoing definitions are not necessarily mutually exclusive, because some of the procedures and records comprehended in accounting controls may also be involved in management's decision processes. This possible overlapping area, however, is not critical for the purpose of the proposed statement since it is concerned more with clarifying the outer boundary of accounting control than the inner boundary of administrative control.

In comparing the definition of accounting control in Statement 33 with the proposed revised definition, the committee believes that "safe-guarding of assets" referred to the execution of transactions in accordance with management's authorization and the accountability for assets acquired, while the "reliability of the financial records" referred to their reliability for the purposes of maintaining accountability for assets and preparing financial statements in conformity with generally accepted accounting principles or other applicable criteria.

BASIC CONCEPTS

Certain basic concepts are implicit in the proposed definition of accounting control, which are applicable generally, but the organizational and procedural requirements for applying them may differ considerably from case to case because of the variety of circumstances involved. Therefore, it is not feasible to discuss these requirements in detail on this program.

REASONABLE ASSURANCE

The definition requires reasonable, but not absolute, assurance that the objectives comprehended in it will be accomplished. This recognizes that the cost of accounting control should be justified by the benefits derived. The benefits consist of reductions in the risk of loss from errors or irregularities involving the financial statements or the accountability for assets. Although the benefits are difficult to measure, the cost-benefit relationship is the conceptual criterion that should be applied in designing and evaluating a system of internal accounting control.

INCOMPATIBLE FUNCTIONS

Incompatible functions for accounting control purposes are those that place any person in a position both to perpetrate and to conceal errors or irregularities in the normal course of his duties. Generally, anyone who prepares records or has custody of assets is in a position to perpetrate errors or irregularities. Accordingly, accounting control necessarily depends largely on the elimination of opportunities for concealment. This, in turn, requires that procedures designed to detect errors and irregularities be performed by persons other than those who are in a position to perpetrate them — i.e., by persons having no incompatible functions.

EXECUTION OF TRANSACTIONS

Obtaining assurance that transactions are executed as authorized requires that authorizations be examined and compared independently with the documents evidencing the transactions. The purpose of the examination of authorizations is to obtain evidence that they were issued by persons acting within the scope of their authority. The purpose of the comparison is to obtain evidence that the transactions conform with the terms of the authorization.

RECORDING OF TRANSACTIONS

The objective of accounting control with respect to the recording of transactions requires that they be recorded at the amounts and in the accounting periods in which they were executed, and be classified in appropriate accounts.

Obtaining assurance that these objectives are achieved depends partially on the competence and integrity of personnel, the independence of the assigned functions, and the completeness and understanding of the prescribed procedures. Although these factors are important, their contribution to accounting control nevertheless is to provide an environment conducive to proper recording, rather than to provide assurance that it has occurred.

The possibilities for obtaining assurance that transactions have been recorded depend largely on the availability of some independent source of information that will provide an indication that the transactions have occurred. These possibilities vary widely with the nature of the transactions, and time does not permit presentation of examples illustrating this concept.

COMPARISON OF RECORDED ACCOUNTABILITY WITH ASSETS

The purpose of the comparison of recorded accountability for assets is to determine whether the actual assets agree with the recorded accountability, and consequently it is closely related to the foregoing discussion concerning the recording of transactions. Typical examples of this comparison include cash and securities counts, bank reconciliations, and physical inventories.

If the comparison reveals that the assets do not agree with the recorded accountability this is evidence of unrecorded transactions. The converse, however, does not necessarily follow. For example, agreement of a cash count with the recorded balance is not evidence that all cash received has been recorded. This illustrates an unavoidable distinction between fiduciary and recorded accountability: The former arises immediately upon acquisition of an asset, while the latter cannot be recognized until the initial record of the transactions is prepared.

The frequency with which such comparison should be made depends on the nature and amount of the assets involved and the cost of making the comparison. For example, it may be reasonable to count cash daily but not reasonable to take a physical inventory at that interval. However, a daily inventory of products in the custody of route salesmen, for example, may be practicable as a means of determining their accountability for sale. Similarly, the value and vulnerability of some products may make frequent complete inventories worth while.

LIMITATIONS

There are certain limitations on the potential effectiveness of accounting control that should be recognized in any consideration of the subject. In the performance of most control procedures there are possibilities for errors arising from such causes as misunderstanding of instructions, mistakes of judgment, and personal carelessness, distraction, or fatigue. Furthermore, procedures whose effectiveness depends on segregation of duties obviously can be circumvented by collusion. Similarly, procedures designed to assure the execution and recording of transactions in accordance with management's authorizations may be ineffective against either errors or irregularities perpetrated by management with respect to transactions or to the estimates and judgments required in the preparation of financial statements.

STUDY OF SYSTEM

SCOPE OF STUDY

As redefined in the proposed statement, accounting controls are within the scope of the study and evaluation of internal control required by generally accepted auditing standards, while administrative controls are not.

The study to be made as the basis for the evaluation of internal control includes two phases as indicated in the following excerpt from Statement No. 33:

> Adequate evaluation of a system of internal control requires (1) knowledge and understanding of the procedures and methods prescribed and (2) a reasonable degree of assurance that they are in use and are operating as planned. (Numerals added)

These two phases of the study are referred to hereinafter as the review of the system and tests of compliance, respectively.

Review of system. The review of the system is primarily a process of obtaining and recording information about the organization and procedures prescribed to serve as the basis for the tests of compliance and for the evaluation. The information required for this purpose ordinarily is obtained through discussion with supervisory client personnel and reference to documentation such as procedure manuals, job descriptions, flow charts, and decision tables.

The information obtained from the review of the system may be recorded by the auditor in the form of answers to a questionnaire, narrative memoranda, flow charts, decision tables, or any other form that suits the auditor's needs or personal preferences.

In order to clarify their understanding of information obtained from such sources, some auditors follow the practice of tracing one or a few of the different types of transactions involved through the related documents and records maintained. While this practice may be useful for the purpose indicated, it should *not* be confused with tests of compliance.

Tests of compliance. The nature of internal control procedures and of the available evidence of compliance necessarily determines the nature of the tests of compliance and also influences the extent of such tests.

NATURE OF TESTS

Adequate accounting control requires not only that certain procedures be performed, but that they be performed independently. Tests of compliance, therefore, are concerned primarily with two questions: whether the necessary procedures were performed and, if so, by whom.

Some aspects of accounting control require the performance of certain control procedures that are not necessarily required for the execution of transactions. This class of procedures includes the approval of documents evidencing external transactions and the preparation, checking, or approval of internal documents such as accounting records, reconciliations, and reports. Tests as to whether, and by whom, such procedures are performed require observation of the related documents to obtain evidence of compliance in the form of signatures, initials, and audit stamps, and the like.

A second aspect of accounting control requires a segregation of duties so that certain incompatible procedures are not performed by the same persons. The performance of some of these procedures is largely self-evident from the operation of the business or the existence of its essential records; consequently, tests of compliance with such procedures are primarily for the purpose of determining whether they were performed by persons having no incompatible duties. Examples of this class of procedures may include the receiving, depositing, and disbursing of cash, the recording of transactions, and the posting of customers' accounts. Since such procedures frequently leave no audit trial of documentary evidence as to who performed them, tests of compliance in these situations necessarily are limited to corroborative inquires of different personnel and observation of office routines to supplement the information obtained during the initial review of the system. While reconciliations, confirmations, or other audit tests performed in accordance with the auditing standard relating to evidential matter may substantiate the accuracy of the underlying records, these tests frequently provide no affirmative evidence of the necessary segregation of duties since the records may be accurate even though maintained by someone having incompatible duties.

The foregoing distinction as to the nature of control procedures and available evidence of compliance also influences the extent of tests of compliance.

EXTENT OF TESTS

As indicated earlier, the purpose of tests of compliance with accounting control procedures is to provide "a reasonable degree of assurance that they are in use and are operating as planned." What constitutes a "reasonable" degree of assurance is a matter of auditing judgment. The "degree of assurance," however, is necessarily a function of the nature and extent of the tests and of the results obtained.

As to accounting control procedures that leave an audit trail of documentary evidence of compliance, the committee believes that tests of compliance should be spread throughout the year or other audit period. For this type of test, statistical sampling is a practicable means for expressing in quantitative terms the auditor's judgment as to reasonableness, and for determining the extent of tests and evaluating the results on that basis. As indicated by earlier pronouncements of the committee, the use of statistical sampling is compatible with, but not required by, generally accepted auditing standards. This topic will be discussed further by the next speaker.

As to accounting control procedures that depend primarily on segregation of duties and leave no audit trail, the committee believes that tests of compliance may appropriately be confined to the periods during which the auditor is present on the client's premises in conducting other phases of his audit.

EVALUATION OF SYSTEM

The auditor's evaluation of the system of accounting control and his tests of compliance should, of course, be related to the purposes of his evaluation.

From the viewpoint of management, the purposes of accounting control are stated in the definitions given previously. These purposes apply equally, of course, to the independent auditor, but they have been stated somewhat differently and more directly as follows:

A function of internal control, from the viewpoint of the independent auditor, is to provide assurance that errors and irregularities may be discovered with reasonable promptness, thus assuring the reliability and integrity of the financial records. The independent auditor's review of the system of internal control assists him in determining other auditing procedures appropriate to the formulation of an opinion on the fairness of the financial statements.

A suggested general approach to the auditor's evaluation of accounting control, which focuses directly on the purpose of preventing or detecting errors and irregularities, involves the following steps:

1. Analyze the types of errors and irregularities that could occur in processing the various kinds of transactions and handling the related assets.

2. Determine the accounting control procedures that should prevent or detect such errors and irregularities.

3. Determine whether the necessary procedures are prescribed and being followed satisfactorily.

4. Evaluate any weaknesses — i.e., types of errors and irregularities not covered by existing controls — to determine their effect on (a) the nature, timing, or extent of auditing procedures to be applied, and (b) suggestions to be made to the client.

This suggested approach emphasizes the possibilities for, and controls against, particular types of errors and irregularities concerning particular classes of transactions and related assets. Controls and weaknesses affecting different classes of transactions are not offsetting in their effect. For example, weaknesses in cash receipts procedures are not mitigated by controls in cash disbursement procedures; similarly, weaknesses in billing procedures are not mitigated by controls in collection procedures. For this reason, evaluation of accounting control should be made with reference to the procedures pertaining to particular classes of transactions or related assets; unless equally applicable to all procedures being evaluated, generalized or over-all evaluations are not likely to be useful for auditors or others.

The auditor's final evaluation of internal control for his primary purpose should be in the form of conclusions as to (a) whether the prescribed procedures are adequate, subject to the inherent limitations discussed earlier, to prevent or detect with reasonable promptness material errors and irregularities and (b) whether compliance with such procedures is satisfactory.

CORRELATION WITH OTHER AUDITING PROCEDURES

Since the purpose of the evaluation required by the second auditing standard of field work is to provide a basis "for the determination of the resultant extent of the tests to which auditing procedures are to be restricted," it is clear that its ultimate purpose is to contribute to the "reasonable basis for an opinion" comprehended in the third standard, which is quoted below:

> Sufficient competent evidential matter is to be obtained through inspection, observation, inquiries and confirmations to afford a reasonable basis for an opinion regarding the financial statements under examination.

The evidential matter required by the third standard is obtained generally through the auditor's (a) substantive tests of details of transactions and balances, and (b) analytic review of significant ratios and trends and resulting investigation of unusual fluctuations and questionable items.

The committee believes it is desirable to make clear that the second standard does not contemplate that the auditor should place complete reliance on internal control to the exclusion of other auditing procedures with respect to material accounts in the financial statements.

In considering the more difficult question as to the extent of restriction contemplated in the second and third standards, the committee believes the following excerpts from a Special Report issued by the AICPA Committee on Statistical Sampling in 1964 provides a useful conceptual analysis of the intricate relationship between these standards:

> . . . the ultimate risk against which the auditor and those who rely on his opinion require reasonable protection is a combination of two separate risks. The first of these is that material errors will occur in the accounting process by which the financial statements are developed. The second is that any material errors that occur will not be detected in the auditor's examination.
>
> The auditor relies on internal control to reduce the first risk, and on his tests of details and his other auditing procedures to reduce the second. The relative weight to be given to the respective sources of reliance . . . are matters for the auditor's judgment in the circumstances.
>
> The second standard of field work recognizes that the extent of tests required to constitute sufficient evidential matters under the third stan-

dard should vary inversely with the auditor's reliance on internal control. These standards taken together imply that the combination of the auditor's reliance on internal control and on his auditing procedures should provide a reasonable basis for his opinion in all cases, although the portion of reliance derived from the respective sources may properly vary between cases.

Statistical sampling provides a means for expressing in quantitative terms the auditor's judgment as to the reliance to be placed on his substantive tests of details of transaction and balances, and for determining the extent of such tests and evaluating the results on that basis. As mentioned earlier, however, the use of statistical sampling is compatible with, but not required by, generally accepted auditing standards.

The committee will be giving further consideration to the difficult but important question as to the degree of reliance that may be placed on internal control in determining the extent of other audit tests. Whether any consensus can be reached on useful guidelines expressed in terms of statistical sampling or on any other basis remains to be determined.

Any constructive suggestions on this question or on other aspects of the proposed statement on internal control will be welcomed by the committee.

18. Internal Control Evaluation and Audit Program Modification*

R. K. Mautz†
Donald L. Mini

The relationship of internal control effectiveness to audit program planning has been acknowledged repeatedly by representatives of the auditing profession. The second standard of field work included in the ten generally accepted auditing standards emphasizes this relationship in these terms:

> There is to be a proper study and evaluation of the existing internal control as a basis for reliance thereon and for the determination of the resultant extent of the tests to which auditing procedures are to be restricted.[1]

Apart from the general statement of interdependence expressed in this standard, however, little more has been presented concerning audit program modification and internal control. Statements are found to the effect that this is an area requiring the highest degree of judgment and professional experience, but very little aid is given to the practitioner to help him in making specific adjustments on the basis of internal control.

To be sure, the role of judgment and professional experience in internal control evaluation and program modification cannot, and should not, be minimized. Judgment is inevitably an essential part of any professional activity, and any attempt to reduce or eliminate this professional function would rightly be resisted by the vast majority of practitioners. On the other hand, judgment is not exercised in a vacuum; direction and support must come from some body of theory, even though the dimensions of this body may not be clearly established and its components may be difficult to define.

It is the purpose of this paper to suggest an outline for such a body of theory, within which the auditor would find guides which stimulate

*From *The Accounting Review* (April, 1966), pp. 283-291. Reprinted by permission of the American Accounting Association. This article is based largely on a doctoral dissertation by Donald L. Mini under the direction of Professor Mautz at the University of Illinois. It incorporates certain concepts developed from Professor Mautz's participation in research studies being conducted by Haskins & Sells. Since these studies have not been completed, Haskins & Sells have not reached final conclusions as to certain positions taken in this paper.

†R. K. Mautz is a partner, Ernst & Ernst, Cleveland, Ohio. Donald L. Mini is an accountant, Haskins & Sells.

[1]American Institute of Certified Public Accountants, Committee on Auditing Procedure, "Auditing Standards and Procedures," *Statement on Auditing Procedure No. 33* (1963), p. 16.

the exercise of judgment in program planning, rather than mechanical aids which suppress this judgment. Fundamental to the formulation of such guides is an understanding of the concept of a "minimum" audit program, which the auditor adjusts to meet the weaknesses of a specific internal control situation.

The Minimum Audit Program

Modification of a "minimum" audit program on the basis of weakness in a system of internal control might seem to imply the existence of a "standard" audit program. Actually, this is not the case at all. In fact, the very idea of "modification" should emphasize the dynamics of program planning and dispel the false assumption of a standard program. The minimum audit program represents only a point of departure for required modifications; as such, it represents the nature and extent of audit work which would be necessary under conditions of excellent internal control.

This minimum program might vary among client companies or among industries, but the underlying reasons which create the need for a minimum amount of testing remain the same regardless of the company or industry involved. These reasons relate to (1) the general fallibility of control devices in preventing errors and (2) the fact that certain types of actions affecting the reliability of reported data are not subject to the enterprise control process.

The Probabilistic Nature of Enterprise Controls

Controls in an enterprise are designed to eliminate the harm that might occur to a company due to the misuse of assets, inaccurate and unreliable accounting data, operational inefficiency, and deviation from prescribed managerial policies.[2] Stated more concisely, controls are designed to eliminate inefficient and irregular actions. If control mechanisms could attain these objectives invariably, the presence of wholly satisfactory controls in an enterprise would present the auditor with compelling evidence of the absence of irregularities, or deviations from fact, in the firm's financial data. But the enterprise control system is not subject to perfectly predictable behavior of this type. It is probabilistic[3] and, therefore:

---

[2]Ibid., p. 27.
[3]In a computer system, the computer itself is a "deterministic" system. The computer *system*, however, with its surrounding human elements, is probabilistic.

... is one about which no precisely detailed prediction can be given. The system may be studied intently, and it may become more and more possible to say what it is likely to do in any given circumstances. But the system simply is not predetermined, and a prediction affecting it can never escape from the logical limitations of the probabilities in which terms alone its behavior can be described.[4]

The probabilistic nature of enterprise controls has important implications for the concept of the minimum audit program, since it indicates the quality of evidence which can be obtained through the study and evaluation of a system of internal control. While the existence of a satisfactory system eliminates the probability[5] of irregularities, it cannot eliminate the possibility of irregularities.

Even the best of control systems cannot eliminate, or even reduce, the possibility of unintentional irregularities resulting from temporary system breakdowns.[6] A number of conditions can arise to motivate the people working in a system of internal control to act in other than an expected fashion. For instance, a perfunctory performance of duties, whether a matter of habit or a momentary result of an interruption, can allow an unintentional irregularity to slip by unnoticed; a change in personnel or thinking at the bookkeeper level may result in a lack of uniformity in an apparently effective control procedure; or negligence or unawareness of the necessity for care in handling year-end transactions may result in unintentional cut-off irregularities. In short, whenever human judgment and volition are involved, the possibility of a breakdown in an essential control process is present. For this reason, the auditor's minimum program must be sufficient to test for the occurrence of unintentional irregularities.

One might assume that the same analysis would hold true for non-collusive employee frauds. Control failures which permit such irregularities to be concealed would always seem possible, even under conditions of excellent internal control. We suggest, however, that this is not the case. Whereas in all but rare instances, the possibility of unintentional irregularities cannot be reduced when internal control is excellent, a substantial reduction in the possibility of employee frauds can be achieved under conditions of excellent internal control. This difference between fraudulent acts and unintentional acts arises from the nature of the control failure which must occur to permit each type of irregularity.

---

[4]Stafford Beer, *Cybernetics and Management* (John Wiley & Sons, Inc., 1959), p. 12.
[5]"Probability" is here used in its non-mathematical sense of being more likely than unlikely.
[6]As an exception to this statement, the possibility of certain types of unintentional irregularities may be reduced in the electronic computer control system.

In the case of unintentional acts, the failure is generally one of judgment or mechanics — inadvertent errors in the mechanics of dealing with large quantities of figures or errors of principle in making accounting judgments. On the other hand, for a non-collusive employee defalcation to occur and remain undetected under conditions of excellent internal control, the control failure would have to be one of two types:

1. A physical safeguard, such as the division of duties among employees, must break down. For example, someone who is not supposed to have access to cash in his normal course of duties would suddenly have to gain such access — a failure so improbable that the possibility of resultant errors could be considered remote.

2. A review procedure must break down with the would-be defaulter foreseeing this breakdown. To conceal an abstraction of recorded cash receipts through clerical errors in the bank reconciliation procedure, for example, the defaulter must anticipate when such a clerical error would be made. Notice that the defaulter is anticipating a rare clerical error, a temporary breakdown, not a recurring lapse in the reconciliation procedure. If a recurring failure existed, this would be considered a weakness in internal control and the auditor would judge the system something less than excellent. In addition, the defaulter would be anticipating an error by someone else. If the guilty employee had the ability to manipulate the reconciliation himself, internal control would again be judged weak in this respect.

The necessity of foreseeing a breakdown in apparently excellent controls, with the related uncertainty that such a breakdown will even occur, reduces substantially the possibility of a would-be defaulter committing an abstraction. As one author has recently pointed out, employees are discouraged from defalcation when they believe that close control is being exercised over their actions, whether this close control exists or not.[7] This type of "perceived control," in fact, seems to be more effective than actual control in suppressing embezzlement.[8]

Since the possibility of non-collusive employee frauds can be reduced substantially under conditions of wholly satisfactory internal control, we suggest that the minimum audit program need not be designed to test for the occurrence of such irregularities. This conclusion seems consistent with various statements by representatives of the auditing profession which stress the importance of "suspicion"

---

[7]Russell Taussig, "Internal Control: The New Look," *Municipal Finance*, February, 1963, p. 149.
[8]Ibid.

in describing the auditor's responsibility for testing for the presence of fraud in the accounts. Only where specific circumstances, such as weaknesses in internal control, lead the auditor to suspect the existence of fraud, should the auditor make the investigation necessary to determine whether fraud has in fact occurred.[9]

ACTIONS NOT SUBJECT TO CONTROL IN AN ENTERPRISE

Besides the fallibility of control mechanisms in preventing unintentional irregularities, the second reason that creates a need for minimum testing is the fact that certain types of actions affecting the reliability of reported data are not subject to control.

It is fundamental that a given control mechanism can reduce irregularities and inefficiencies only in those actions which lend themselves to the control process or in those actions which are provided for by the system design. In the case of actions that occur outside the system, or that occur in a manner not contemplated by that system, internal controls are inoperative.

As an example of actions occurring outside the control system, one may cite the case of deliberate management irregularities. Since internal control is a management tool, the administrators of this tool could hardly be under its influence. Being above the system of internal control, management officials are in a position to perpetrate irregularities in spite of the existence of controls that would prevent similar irregularities by minor employees who are a part of the system. Therefore, it is clear that the auditor's minimum audit program must be sufficient to test for the occurrence of deliberate management irregularities.[10]

Internal control is also ineffective in preventing policy errors by management. Even the most well-conceived controls will not guarantee sound accounting principles and policies to be reflected in the accounts when these goals are opposed or ignored by an unsound management. Consequently, the auditor must provide for the possibility of policy errors in his minimum program regardless of the strength of the system of internal control.

Finally, internal controls cannot be effective against actions which occur in a manner not contemplated by the control process. Typical of this type of action are irregularities involving collusion among

---

[9]Compare with *Statement on Auditing Procedure No. 33*, pp. 11-12.
[10]Under certain conditions, the existence of an "independent" internal audit staff may reduce the possibility of deliberate management fraud.

two or more employees of a firm. However, since the probability
of collusive errors is substantially less than for other types, tests
for the occurrence of such errors properly may be reduced substantially
or possibly eliminated in the minimum audit program.

In summary, then, the scope of the auditor's work under conditions of excellent internal control should be sufficient to provide
reasonable assurance that they (the internal control procedures) are
in use and are operating as planned[11] and to provide reasonable
assurance of detection of material errors of types not susceptible to
effective internal control.

MODIFYING THE MINIMUM PROGRAM

The minimum audit program so conceived would, in all likelihood,
meet the needs of few, if any, specific audit engagements. Rarely do
conditions of excellent internal control exist throughout a company,
and the auditor is generally faced with the problem of modifying
this minimum program in the light of particular weaknesses in internal
control which permit non-collusive employee frauds or which increase
the probability of unintentional irregularities. This modification may
come in the form of:

1. Variation in the nature of audit techniques and procedures
selected for use;

2. Extension in the application of audit procedures;

3. Modification of the time at which techniques are applied;

4. Modification in selecting the documents examined in the application of certain techniques;

5. Variation in the direction in which transactions are verified; or

6. Variation in the emphasis of "what to look for" when applying
audit techniques.

A moment's consideration of this list suggests the complexity
of audit program planning and modification. As mentioned previously,
this is an area requiring a high degree of judgment, but one that,
unfortunately, has been somewhat neglected in the literature of auditing. Avoidance of any extensive discussion of program modification
perhaps stems from the belief that this discussion would only lead to
attempts at reducing audit program planning to a formula or standard
plan. We are in full agreement that it would be detrimental to the
profession in the long run if the practitioner felt free to follow some

[11] *Statements on Auditing Procedure No. 33*, p. 32.

authoritative pattern rather than plan each audit program on the basis of the particular engagement involved. In fact, there is considerable doubt that such a complex problem as program planning could ever be the subject of standardization. We do suggest, however, that guides can be developed which should encourage, rather than shackle, judgment formation in program planning, and that these guides are available in the effective evaluation of internal control, *the essence of which is the translation of the internal control situation under review into the specific irregularities made probable thereby.*

INTERNAL CONTROL, IRREGULARITIES, AND PROGRAM MODIFICATION

This belief that a knowledge of probable irregularities is of the utmost importance to audit program modification gains support from the relationship among internal control, irregularities, and the audit objective.

Few will deny that auditing concerns itself with the faithfulness with which reported data portray realities — the desired relationship between the two being expressed in terms of "fairness." In the process of the audit, however, the degree to which the auditor can ascertain the validity of reported financial data is tempered by considerations of time and cost, as well as by the extent of evidence available. Program planning, then, is essentially a problem of allocating audit resources as effectively and economically as possible in an effort to achieve the audit objective. As a basis upon which to allocate these audit resources, the auditor must concern himself with the relative probabilities that an array of possible irregularities, or deviations from fact, will be present in the financial data under review; that is, the extent and nature of his audit procedures must be directed primarily at those irregularities that are most probable in his particular client's organization.

The latter idea leads to an understanding of the precise relationship that internal control has with the audit objective. Since the existence of a satisfactory system of internal control eliminates the probability of irregularities, it follows that the system of internal control provides the basis for modifying the minimum program, and the existence of specific strengths and weaknesses in the system of internal control should be reflected in the audit program.

This analysis is actually little more than a basic reaffirmation of the interrelationship of internal control and the audit program, but it also serves to point out two correlative ideas. On the one hand, we have reasoned that the audit program must take into account the relative probability of various types of irregularities occurring in the reported data under review. On the other hand, we have reasoned that the program must reflect the strengths and weaknesses in the existing system of internal control. These statements are correlative in the sense that neither can exist independently of the other. If no irregularities are made probable under a given system of internal control, no weakness in that system should be apparent to the auditor. Consequently, from the standpoint of the audit objective, weaknesses in internal control should be said to exist only in relation to the irregularities that are permitted thereby.

This correlation of weaknesses in internal control with probable irregularities underlies our belief that the essence of effective internal control evaluation is the translation of the internal control situation under review into the specific irregularities which are made probable thereby. In response, the auditor can then modify his program so as to test most effectively for the presence of such irregularities.

To illustrate the vital role of error conditions in audit program modification, let us return to the six forms of program modification mentioned previously and direct our attention to some specific examples.

1. Variation in the nature of audit techniques and procedures selected for use. The increased probability of errors of omission in recording fixed asset transactions might lead the auditor to decide that more decisive evidence is needed than would be provided by vouching procedures included in his minimum program. In that event, a physical inventory of plant assets might be required.

2. Extension in the application of audit procedures. Error conditions revealed by the review of internal control would also be important in deciding upon the extent to which audit procedures should be applied. Where the occurrence of errors of principle in recording purchases, such as charges to wrong accounts, becomes something more than possible because of weakened internal controls, the auditor would likely extend his tests of purchase transactions. On the other hand, even though weakened internal controls permitted abstractions of cash receipts to be concealed through the overstatement of cash discounts, it is doubtful that the practitioner would extend his tests of discounts beyond that required by his minimum program. Due to the very nature of discount irregularities, individual manipulations necessarily would be for small amounts, and in order for a material misstatement to result, they would have to be frequent in occurrence. Consequently, a random test of a small sample size would be very likely to disclose the fraud.

3. Modification of the time at which techniques are applied. Although audit limitations concerning man-hour scheduling must always enter timing decisions, the practitioner would still undoubtedly insist on a physical inventory of merchandise at, or very near, year-end if he was aware that the system of internal control permitted abstractions of merchandise inventory to be concealed through manipulations of the perpetual records.

4. Modification in selection of the documents examined in the application of certain techniques. An awareness of the concealment possibilities open to those who are in a position to perpetrate an irregularity might lead the auditor to substitute receiving documents for the credit authorizations or customer correspondence normally examined when vouching returned sales transactions. This could be the case, for example, where the arrangement of duties in the internal control system under review permitted an unrecorded abstraction of a customer's remittance to be concealed by an employee having the ability to authorize credits for sales returns but not having the ability to introduce fictitious receiving reports.

5. Variation in the direction in which transactions are verified. If understatements of sales were permitted by the internal control situation, the auditor would emphasize vouching sales transactions from underlying documents forward to books of original entry. On the other hand, if overstatements rather than understatements were probable, he would reverse the direction of this emphasis.

6. Variation in the emphasis of "what to look for" when applying audit techniques. Finally, a knowledge of the particular type of irregularity most likely in a specific area of internal control might lead the auditor to place more emphasis on particular aspects of the evidence he is examining than he would otherwise. For example, the possibility of certain types of irregularities would require that the auditor's attention be directed to bank payment dates or the validity of payees on checks to a greater extent than would be the case where weaknesses in internal control permitting such irregularities were absent.

EFFECTIVE INTERNAL
CONTROL EVALUATION

This demonstrated relationship between irregularities and program modification has important implications for the proper study and evaluation of internal control.

THE NEED FOR POSITIONAL ANALYSIS

Since irregularities are brought about, intentionally or unintentionally, by individuals working within the limitations of given organizational positions, the auditor's primary concern in studying a client's system of internal control must be with the duties attached to positions and the irregularities these duties permit. Unless extreme care is taken in the application of various internal control survey methods, such as the questionnaire, this important aspect of the study of internal control will be overlooked. An example will help to clarify this idea.

Assume that an internal control questionnaire contains the following questions and replies thereto:

	Yes	No
1. Is the handling of customer remittances separated from the recording of such remittances in the cash receipts journal and accounts receivable subsidiary ledger?		X
2. Is a pre-listing of mail receipts prepared?	X	
Is this list compared with cash book entries?	X	

Although, at first, the information contained in this partial questionnaire appears highly useful, a moment's consideration suggests that the auditor's study has been relatively unproductive. From this information it is impossible to determine whether the conditions described in the survey actually constitute a weakness in internal control — that is, permit an irregularity. If, for example, the person handling and recording customer remittances was the same person working with the pre-list of mail receipts or had access to this pre-list, control would be quite weak. On the other hand, if an independent party prepared and used the pre-list, control could be quite good.

This is not to say, of course, that the questionnaire cannot be so constructed as to facilitate a positional analysis of internal control. This could be achieved readily by careful wording and selection of inquiries.

SEQUENTIAL NATURE OF JUDGMENT FORMATION

A second important element of effective internal control evaluation is found in the sequential nature of the judgment process by which internal control is related to the audit program. As suggested previously, this process of judgment formation takes the form of a line of reasoning illustrated by the following questions:

1. What features of internal control are missing?
2. What irregularities are thereby permitted?
3. What modifications to our minimum audit program will be of most help in testing for the occurrence of such irregularities?

The sequence of this judgment progression indicates that the practitioner does not approach the review of internal control from the standpoint of looking for probable irregularities. He looks for an absence or an undesirable combination of certain internal control procedures, which he terms "weaknesses" in internal control. But the sequential nature of this judgment process also illustrates that the evaluation of internal control cannot be a process of merely checking for the existence of certain required procedures, and where these procedures are lacking, applying certain audit steps. On the contrary, until the omission of certain internal control procedures results in a situation whereby an irregularity is made probable, no conclusion as to the presence of weaknesses in internal control can be made; and, hence, no program modification is called for. This means that although an important element of internal control may be lacking (separation of handling of customer remittances from accounts receivable bookkeeping), this may not represent a weakness because a combination of other circumstances makes an irregularity unlikely.

Failure to consider the interdependence of all three steps of the judgment process might also result in faulty program planning despite a correct identification of internal control deficiencies. This would be the case whenever there is a lack of common understanding concerning the type of irregularity permitted by a given weakness in internal control. For example, where a failure to separate the duties of handling customer remittances and accounts receivable bookkeeping is considered an internal control deficiency, care must be taken in assessing the effect of this weakness on the audit program. If lapping is thereby permitted, confirmation of accounts receivable may be extended. On the other hand, where other circumstances make lapping improbable, the failure to separate these particular duties may lead to a condition under which an abstraction of customer remittances can be concealed by credits inconsistently distributed between the control and subsidiary ledger. In this event, confirmation of accounts would not be effective in testing for this irregularity; some measure to test for a lack of agreement between the controlling account and subsidiary ledger is necessary.

Conclusion

These comments concerning the necessary judgment process by which internal control is evaluated effectively suggest that over-all appraisal of internal control must be replaced with precise analysis. In analyzing internal control, the auditor must deal with specifics, not with generalities. The auditor must determine whether specific weaknesses exist, the irregularities thereby permitted, and the specific modifications of his program called for by these conditions. In this way many of the problems associated with the over-all, more subjective approach to internal control evaluation would be eliminated. For instance, if the situations by which irregularities are permitted are analyzed in a logical manner, the circumstances under which two auditors would disagree as to the presence or absence of weaknesses in a given system of internal control should be rare. Personal standards could undoubtedly affect an auditor's assessment of the seriousness of a given weakness (probable irregularity), but not his conclusion as to the presence of that weakness.

The reasoning ability necessary for internal control evaluation and audit program modification is not easily developed. Yet, it is so important to the economic and effective use of audit resources that educational efforts at both the college and professional staff levels should be directed to this task. A training approach which emphasizes that judgment is best developed and most effectively utilized when supported by an awareness of the interrelationship of internal control, irregularities, and audit procedures can justly be described as professional in approach and concept.

19. The CPA's Risk in Evaluating Internal Control*

Larry F. Konrath†

Given the premise that the volume of transactions consummated by most entities precludes a detailed audit, the question arises as to the degree to which the auditor should be permitted to rely on the system of internal control as an alternative. The second standard of audit field work states that the independent auditor is to study and evaluate his client's system of internal control "as a basis for reliance thereon" and for determining the extent of testing to be done under the circumstances.[1] The purpose of this article is to consider the question of permissible reliance by carefully evaluating the auditor's present concept of what internal control is and what it is supposed to do.

Specifically, the study addresses itself to the following questions:

1. Is the auditor correct in assuming that the "system" of internal control is a self-contained system? Or is internal control really part of a broader system of control? If the answer is the latter, can internal controls be installed and evaluated without considering the overall control system?

2. Can the auditor really determine the functioning (or malfunctioning) of internal control by utilizing the conventional methods of inquiring and observing? Or does the auditor's evaluation actually relate to only one of many possible states which internal control may have assumed during the period under review?

THE QUESTION OF SYSTEM

Let us look at two concepts of control — one as viewed by the managerial accountant and the other as viewed by the independent auditor. Welsch defines control as "the action necessary to assure that objectives, plans, policies and standards are being achieved."[2] The Committee on Auditing Procedure defines internal control as "the plan

*From *The Journal of Accountancy* (October, 1971), pp. 53-56. Copyright (1971) by the American Institute of Certified Public Accountants, Inc. Reprinted by permission of the AICPA.

†Larry F. Konrath, Ph.D., CPA, is Associate Professor of Accounting, University of Toledo in Ohio.

[1]Committee on Auditing Procedure of the AICPA, Statement on Auditing Procedure No. 33, "Auditing Standards and Procedures" (New York City: American Institute of Certified Public Accountants, 1963), p. 27.

[2]Glenn A. Welsch, *Budgeting, Profit Planning and Control*, 2nd Edition (Englewood Cliffs, New Jersey: Prentice-Hall, Inc., 1964), p. 13.

of organization and all of the co-ordinate methods and measures adopted within a business to safeguard its assets, check the accuracy and reliability of its accounting data, promote operational efficiency and encourage adherence to prescribed managerial policies."[3]   These definitions of control are quite similar; but they are not concerned with the same variables to be controlled.   The first deals with cost and budgetary control, while the latter is more directly related to asset control and the accuracy of recorded information.

If one were to classify control within the economic entity according to the things to be controlled, the list would be long indeed.   Included in the classification might be asset control, personnel control, cost control, equity control, production control, divisional control, market control, economic control, supplier control, etc.   The question which arises here is whether any of these controls can be dealt with in isolation.   That is, can costs be controlled without considering asset controls?   Can irregularities be prevented without considering the behavioral characteristics of the people performing clerical functions?   If we can answer these questions affirmatively, then each of the above forms of control is self-contained and can be evaluated as such.   To the extent the above areas of control interact, however, they cannot be considered in isolation.

Beer maintains there is but one system to be controlled and that separate parts cannot be sealed off for exclusive consideration.

> What we see in industry is a collection of separate and specialist functions. . . . Ludicrously, each of these activities may be caught laying claim to being the key mechanism of managerial control.   In fact, as the senior management knows and the careful observer can detect, the success of the enterprise depends on the ability of the senior management to coalesce these many activities into some central theme. . . . Hence all the modes of control that are visible are not more than outward signs of control-like activities which have no ultimate connection.[4]

Ashby defines a system as "any set of variables that he (the observer) selects from those available in the real world."[5]   Although it follows from this definition that any tangible or intangible set of variables may be viewed as a system, Ashby further states that, "Given an organism, its environment is defined as those variables whose changes

---

[3]Committee on Auditing Procedure, Statement on Auditing Procedure No. 33, p. 27.

[4]Stafford Beer, *Decision and Control, the Meaning of Operational Research and Management Cybernetics* (New York City: John Wiley & Sons, Inc., 1966), p. 245.

[5]William Ross Ashby, *Design for a Brain*, 2nd Edition (New York City: John Wiley & Sons, Inc., 1960), p. 16.

affect the organism, and those variables which are changed by the organism's behaviour."[6]

Ashby and Beer would agree, therefore, that whether or not one defines internal control (or any other set of controls) as a system is really unimportant. Of much greater concern is the degree to which the various systems interact — that is, the extent to which the variables of one set of controls affect the state of another set. As Ashby further observes, "The stability of a dynamic system depends on the parts and their interrelations as a *whole*."[7] (Emphasis supplied.)

The overriding objective of control, whether it be asset control, cost control or whatever, must be to promote the survival of the firm.[8] Accountants and managers should not delude themselves into thinking that the primary objectives of control are to safeguard assets, maximize profits, maintain high morale among employees or keep costs at a minimum. These are simply methods of promoting the survival of the entity. Once this fact is recognized, one can understand the importance of viewing control in its broadest context.

In order to satisfactorily achieve the survival objective, exceedingly complex systems should be self-regulating. Dechert defines homeostasis as the "process whereby an organism acts so as to restore its internal equilibrium."[9] A thermostat, for example, is a homeostat. Thus, the homeostat provides the control loop necessary for the system to modify its behavior on the basis of information inputs regarding the environment. That is, the homeostat causes the system to be self-regulating.

Two kinds of elements are necessary for homeostasis to be complete. Sensor elements perceive environmental changes which affect the system. Effector elements receive the information from sensor elements and act upon it so as to restore the system to its desired state.[10] From this, one may observe that a most important characteristic of control is that it involves the communication of information. If, however, the various subsystems of control are treated in isolation, the control loop may be incomplete. That is, sensor elements may perceive only a portion of the environmental disturbances affecting the system. And the effector elements accordingly may not act in the best interests of the firm.

To illustrate, several empirical studies have been made concerning

[6]*Ibid.*, p. 36.
[7]*Ibid.*, p. 57.
[8]Stafford Beer, *Cybernetics and Management* (New York City: John Wiley & Sons, Inc., 1959), p. 133.
[9]Charles R. Dechert, Editor, *The Social Impact of Cybernetics* (Notre Dame, Indiana: University of Notre Dame Press, 1966), p. 12.
[10]*Ibid., p. 15.*

the reactions of employees to various types of pressure placed upon them. Stedry, for example, studied the effects of different types of budgets on a single department. He concluded that "management cannot choose a rate of budget reduction independent of considerations of the motivation structure of the department's head."[11] Churchill and Cooper observed employees' reactions to the internal auditing function and found that most of them considered the internal auditor to be more of a policeman than an agent for work improvement.[12]

These studies imply that personnel control, asset control and cost control do interact, and that they must be considered together within a broad context of control. Consider that part of internal control dealing with the review of transactions for genuineness and propriety. Without proper motivation of employees charged with this function, the review process might be performed in a perfunctory manner, thus greatly weakening the sensor elements and destroying the control loop.

Physical controls over assets and separation of functional responsibilities are important asset controls but must also be balanced against the cost of establishing controls (cost control) and the degree of specialization needed to maximize efficiency (personnel control).

The system of internal control with which the independent auditor deals, and which is the concern of this article, is thus part of a broader and exceedingly complex system. Perhaps the only way of effectively harnessing this system is through the science of cybernetics, which deals with communication and control within such very complex systems.[13] Students of cybernetics, however, have yet to devise an effective homeostat for the business firm — one which can generate enough variety to cope with the high variety contained in the control area.[14] Until they do, the auditor should be careful to avoid an undue degree of reliance upon a system which is not adequately defined.

THE QUESTION OF STATE

As noted above, internal control (as presently conceived) is only part of a broader system of control and cannot safely be considered

---

[11]Andrew C. Stedry, *Budget Control and Cost Behavior* (Englewood Cliffs, New Jersey: Prentice-Hall, Inc., 1960), p. 40.

[12]Neil C. Churchill and William W. Cooper, "A Field Study of Internal Auditing," *The Accounting Review*, Vol. XL, No. 4 (October, 1965), pp. 767-781.

[13]John F. Young, *Cybernetics* (New York City: American Elsevier Publishing Co., Inc., 1969), p. 1.

[14]According to Beer, "control must be capable of generating as much variety as the situation to be controlled." Stafford Beer, *Management Science* (Garden City, N.Y.: Doubleday & Company, Inc., 1968), p. 37.

independent of the overall control situation. Moreover, given the conventional approach to control evaluation, the auditor assumes a serious risk of faulty statistical inference. He is, after all, evaluating the system on the basis of his personal observation; but that which he observes is only one of many possible states of the system. Due to illness, duties may not have been adequately separated throughout the period covered by the audit. Because of temporary lapses, transactions may have been perfunctorily reviewed during part of the period. As Beer states:

> All too often gross mistakes are made in setting up control systems by accepting a situation as it is at the moment. The result is that by next week, or next month, or next year some of the factors have changed and the situation is not the situation that it was.[15]

Carmichael likewise implies the existence of several possible states of the control system when he contrasts the formal organization with the informal organization.[16] Although the author is primarily concerned with the reasonableness of the assumptions underlying internal control, one can easily observe that the auditor's concept of the formal organization is a static one, while Carmichael's informal organization is in a state of continual change.

Mautz and Sharaf make essentially this same observation with regard to the dynamic nature of internal control:

> A system of internal control is made up of people and procedures, procedures in which people are expected to perform and report in a normal fashion. But unknown to the reviewer, the pressures which motivate the people in the "system" may change sufficiently that they cease to act in an expected fashion, whereupon the internal control procedure loses its effectiveness.[17]

The authors, therefore, believe that it is hazardous, at best, for the independent auditor to assume responsibility for evaluating internal control.

In short, for the auditor to arrive at an evaluation of internal control on the basis of completing a questionnaire and observing a few transactions is tantamount to the statistician's describing a population on the basis of a sample of one. This is a risk which the auditor should

---

[15]*Ibid.*, p. 37.

[16]D. R. Carmichael, "Behavioral Hypotheses of Internal Control," *The Accounting Review*, Vol. XLV, No. 2 (April, 1970), pp. 235-245.

[17]R. K. Mautz and Hussein Sharaf, *The Philosophy of Auditing* (Iowa City, Iowa: American Accounting Association, 1961), p. 145.

not be forced to assume. At the same time, a return to the detailed audit is out of the question. What, then, is the answer?

Swieringa and Carmichael suggest a "positional" analysis of internal control, whereby the auditor concentrates on people rather than tasks.[18] The approach takes account of the dynamic nature of the internal control situation inasmuch as people are asked questions concerning their continuing relationships with other people in the organization.

Another possible approach might be for the auditor to make more than one observation of internal control during the period under review. The cost constraint would probably be a limiting factor here, however.

Serious control weaknesses might be discovered were the auditor to introduce intentionally irregular documents into the system for the purpose of detecting perfunctory approvals and reviews. Undue disruptions of work flow, however, could result from this practice and therefore pose a strong argument against the approach.

Turning once more to cybernetics, the ultimate answer to the above problem would be to install a homeostat, or self-regulating device, which would cause the system "to regain its equilibrium after it has been disturbed from any cause, even a cause not hitherto experienced at all."[19] Here again, however, cyberneticians have not been able to suggest ways of implementing cybernetic concepts in the area of internal control. A step in the direction of self-regulation might be to set standards relating to the time required to perform various approval and review functions. The standards could be expressed in terms of the time required to handle a particular document. Initials and dates would indicate who reviewed what and when. Periodically, actual times could be compared with the standard, and follow-up action taken upon finding significant deviations. An excess of documents handled by a single individual in a single day, in other words, may indicate that the individual is not carefully scrutinizing those documents passing through his hands.

Many kinds of control exist within an economic entity, of which internal control is only one. These various control areas interact with one another, the output of one often constituting the input of another. This phenomenon argues against the installing and evaluating of internal control without careful consideration being given to the other areas

---

[18]Robert J. Swieringa and D. R. Carmichael, "A Positional Analysis of Internal Control," JofA, Feb.71, pp. 34-43.

[19]Beer, *Management Science*, pp. 154-155.

of control. In other words, control must be concerned with the state of the overall system interacting with its environment via sensor and effector elements, and should *not* attempt to seal off the parts and deal with them in isolation.

In reviewing internal control, by utilizing conventional procedures, the independent auditor fails to take account of the multitude of states which internal control may have assumed during the period under review. These states are undergoing continual change due to the influence of people within the organization.

The auditor, therefore, assumes a serious risk by relying upon internal control in the conduct of his audit. This risk stems from his evaluation approach. First, he attempts to seal off a single area of control and deal with it in isolation. Second, he fails to take into account the dynamic nature of internal control.

Until a way is found to install a homeostat which would make internal control — as well as other areas of control — self-regulating, the auditor should not place an undue degree of reliance on his client's system of internal control. At the same time, a return to the detailed audit is certainly not feasible. This article does suggest, however, that the auditor concentrate more of his attention upon collecting evidence in support of transactions and account balances, and less on the system of internal control.

SECTION C

Statistical Sampling

While the auditing profession has officially sanctioned statistical sampling for some time and encourages the use thereof, reliance on this technique by practitioners is not uniform. Many auditors still feel that substantive obstacles exist to prevent universal adoption of statistical techniques.

T. W. McRae focuses on practical problems which an auditor may encounter in applying statistical techniques to supplement his more traditional verification procedures. The auditor is warned of several pitfalls which are to be avoided in using statistical sampling.

Yuji Ijiri and Robert S. Kaplan, in the second article, provide a four-way classification of the auditor's objectives in sampling. Further development of the application of statistical sampling to accounting and auditing problems may provide a single sampling plan which will integrate the four varied objectives of the auditor.

In the last article, John A. Tracy compares the Bayesian approach with the "classical" approach for the interpretation of sample results. The Bayesian method can yield significantly different interpretations, that in many cases would allow optimal allocations of audit time and resources.

20. Applying Statistical Sampling in Auditing: Some Practical Problems*

T. W. McRae†

DRAWING THE SAMPLE

If statistical methods are to be used to make inferences about a population from a sample drawn from that population, then the sample *must* be a random sample. By a random sample we mean that every unit of the population must have an equal chance of selection on each draw. This sampling procedure has been criticized by many auditors.

W. H. Whitney writes: —

> "An experienced auditor knows where he is most likely to find error or fraud, just as an experienced detective knows where he is most likely to find a wanted criminal. Neither makes a random search and neither should do so. Geologists are employed by oil companies, and wells are drilled at the spots they designate because intelligent selection of these spots is believed to be better than random selection."[1]

The argument is well put and sounds convincing, but it reveals a basic misunderstanding of the statisticians' argument. If one part of a population to be audited is thought to be more likely to contain errors than another part, *then the population is not homogeneous.* Where this is so, the statistician will *stratify* his population into several parts, so that, *as far as he knows*, each part *is* homogeneous. He then selects a different confidence level for each part, requiring a higher confidence level in those parts where he believes error to be more likely. If an auditor has prior knowledge about a population which leads him to believe that error and fraud are more likely to be found in a unit with a given attribute, he will use this attribute to stratify the population into sub-populations which are believed to be homogeneous. That is, no unit of these sub-populations is believed to have a higher probability of being in error than any other unit in its sub-population.

*From *The Accountant's Magazine* (July, 1971), pp. 369-377. Reprinted by permission of the Institute of Chartered Accountants of Scotland.
†T. W. McRae is Professor of Management Accounting, Graduate School of Business Administration, University of the Witwatersrand, South Africa.
[1]"Letters to the Editor," *Journal of Accountancy* (July, 1968), p. 23.

If an auditor decides to use statistical sampling methods and therefore to draw a random sample of a given size, he will almost certainly use random-number tables for selecting his random sample. It is not easy to generate a truly random set of numbers. I would recommend therefore that auditors use tested random-number tables rather than attempt to generate their own random numbers by using a random number device like a roulette wheel or an electronic computer. *Untested* computer-generated random numbers are notoriously unreliable.

Assuming that the auditor uses a table of random numbers which has been rigorously tested for randomness — the Rand Corporation's 1,000,000 random digits is a good example — he should decide on the rules of selection in advance. The initial digits should be selected using a random procedure, *i.e.,* by asking a colleague for a page, column and row number. The remaining digits should be selected according to a prearranged formula, *i.e.,* "every four digits moving left to right, incomplete end of row digits running through the next page."

Since auditors normally use sampling without replacement, duplicate numbers should be ignored and a few additional numbers selected at the end to replace duplicates. Numbers not falling within the required range will, of course, be ignored. When selecting, say, 1,000 random numbers, 000 should be treated as 1,000. Since European languages read from left to right I see no advantage in selecting numbers otherwise than in this direction. Students of Arabic will presumably select numbers from right to left. Chinese from top to bottom and Carthaginians diagonally.

One obvious advantage of using random numbers is that no-one, not even the auditor himself, can predict in advance what units from the population he will choose. Smurthwaite has shown that conventional audit selection methods are by no means random. They could, therefore, be predicted by a potential misfeant.

When *pure* random sampling is expensive in audit time, alternative methods of random sampling may be more appropriate.

Systematic random sampling selects every nth unit of the population where $n = p/s$, p being the number of units in the population, and s being the required sample size. The author has found that it is quicker to select a systematic random sample than a pure random sample, especially where the population to be audited is not numbered in sequence. However, the auditor must beware lest the interval n correspond closely to some pre-existing cyclical sequence in the population. An extreme example would be where $n = 100$ and there are exactly 100 employees who are paid weekly.

Whatever employee we select in the first batch of 100 will be audited 52 times in the year! Such an extreme situation is highly improbable, but if n corresponds closely to a group sequence the auditor might find himself drawing most of the sample from the same group of units which are not truly representative of the population as a whole.

I have never come across this situation in practice and I do not consider it to be a serious obstacle to the use of systematic random sampling, but an auditor should always test for the non-existence of this improbable condition, when using systematic random sampling.

Another alternative to pure random sampling is called *cluster* sampling. If a sample, say, of 300 units is required, rather than selecting 300 random numbers and 300 independent units from the population, the sampler selects, say, 30 clusters of 10 units each. Obviously this method speeds sample selection and it is particularly helpful in speeding up sample *replacement*, a topic seldom considered by statisticians. Since conventional audit procedures use cluster sampling, the cluster being one month, one week, one department, etc., it might be thought that cluster sampling provides a vehicle for drawing traditional and statistical audit procedures closer together. This is not so. The statistician is always careful to qualify his advocacy of cluster sampling with the remark that the minimum number of clusters must be of the order of 20. The number of clusters used in auditing is almost invariably very much less than this, usually less than half a dozen, and often a single cluster.

The trouble with cluster sampling is that the variability of the characteristics within a cluster is likely to be less than the variability between clusters. This is another way of saying that the sample drawn from a cluster will not provide a true reflection of the whole population. A group of units form a cluster because they have something in common, the same date, customer, product, etc. This common factor *may* invalidate an inference about a population made from a sample drawn from a cluster. On the other hand it need not do so. This is a question of fact. If cluster sampling is particularly appropriate to a given audit situation, the auditor would be well advised in the first year of the audit to select several clusters and test the variability of the condition, *i.e.* error value, he is attempting to assess by comparing them with a random sample of equal size. If the variability within clusters is not significantly different from the variability between them or the pure random sample, he can with reasonable confidence use cluster sampling in future years.

A common complaint against statistical sampling is the time required to draw the random sample, particularly where the population is very large, say a million units

A sampler can often speed up random sampling with a little ingenuity. In one case known to the author a random sample of 3,000 units was required from a population of approximately 500,000 vouchers. The vouchers were batched in groups of approximately 1,000 and stored in the company vault. If laid out end to end the vouchers would have covered, say, a distance of 6,000 inches. The sampler selected his samples by using an inch-tape. He selected a voucher every 2″ along each batch. In another case a population of invoices was stored on microfilm. The sampler stopped the microfilm every *n* seconds to select his random sample. When the population is not numbered in sequence, these latter methods can save a great deal of audit time.

Another problem in sampling is the question of what to do when a voucher selected by the random sample is missing? If, say, three vouchers are missing in a random sample of 100, this suggests that around 3% of the vouchers are missing, a cause for concern which must be investigated by the auditor. However, this is a separate investigation. I suggest that, if a voucher etc. is found to be missing, the sampler replace this with an alternative random voucher and complete the sampling investigation. Later he will tackle this missing voucher problem and in the light of this latter investigation he may have to modify his conclusion on the former investigation.

Finally we should note that, if an auditor is checking several attributes on a voucher, say authorization signature, extension, and pricing, each of these attributes makes up a *separate population*. However, since the sample is a random sample, the same vouchers can be used for testing each population. If each of these populations does not require the same level of confidence, precision limit, etc., the sample size for each population will not be identical. The auditor should therefore draw a sample equal to the *largest* sample required and use a fraction of this for testing the other populations.

Note, however, that this economical procedure applies only when the attributes are *independent* of one another. If several of these attributes were filled in by the same person, so that, say, an error in extending a price might increase the probability of an error in summation on the same invoice, then the attributes are not independent of one another, and using the same random sample for both populations is an invalid procedure. Since empirical evidence suggests that errors tend to cluster, the qualification is not as academic as it may sound. The auditors should test for interdependence, if several errors cluster on the same document.

Finally we should note that there is no reason why a population which is geographically separated into several sub-populations should not be treated as a single population so long as, to the auditor's knowledge, the population is homogeneous. Suppose, for example, that an auditor is testing the inventory held by 15 branches of a given retail store, each selling 5,000 identical stock lines. He can treat the 15 x 5,000 = 75,000 lines as a single population, which will massively reduce the required sample size from what it would be if he tested each store's inventory as a separate population. If, for example, the ratio of acceptable sampling error to standard deviation remained constant at 0.10 for each population and for the total population, the sample size for *each* population would be 257, *i.e.,* 15 x 257 = 3,855, but the sample size for 75,000 population, treated as a single unit would be only 270! We repeat that the size of this procedure is valid only if the total population is relatively homogeneous.

POPULATION SIZE

The key point in the economics of sampling is that the accuracy of prediction from a sample depends upon the *absolute* size of the sample. The size of the population from which the sample is drawn does not affect the accuracy of the prediction very much. For example, to test the likelihood of an error rate in a population being 2% at a 90% level of confidence and using a confidence limit of ± 2%, the sample sizes for various populations are: —

Population *Size*	Sample *Size*
1,000	118
10,000	131
100,000	133
500,000	133

A sampling method which determines sample size as a fixed proportion of a population is clearly a most inefficient sampling method. This fact is, or ought to be, well known among auditors; yet many professional auditors continue to fix sample size as a proportion of the total population by, say, auditing one month's vouchers in the year. Airlines, for example, sample their inter-airline debt flight coupons by sampling all coupons with a given random digit in the junior position of the coupon number. This results in the sample's always being approximately 10% of the population, an uneconomic procedure, unless the population is stable and a 10% sample, by coincidence, provides the required sample size.

At the other extreme we have "depth vouching," where a single voucher, or very few vouchers, are checked against the companies' accounting procedure manual. The problem here is that the sample is much too small. The auditor is presumably attempting to verify the population of clerical operations performed during a given period. Even at a 90% level of confidence with a wide confidence limit of, say, ±2%, the required sample size must surely run into three figures. Yet most depth vouching tests I have come across employ a sample size much smaller than this.

I am often asked the question "What must the *minimum* population size of an audit be before statistical sampling becomes economic?" There is no simple answer to this question: it all depends on how long it takes to sample a single unit of the population. There is quite a high "set up cost" involved in statistical sampling and this might discourage us from tackling populations of less than, say, 10,000 units. Yet if it takes, say, 30 minutes to audit a single unit of a population, it may be worth while using statistical sampling on populations as small as 1,000 units. However, there is no denying the fact that statistical sampling is of most value to those firms who audit the larger companies and institutions.

Sometimes an auditor will find that he does not know the exact number of units in a population, if, for example, the population is large and not numbered, or if the population is scattered through a ledger or group of vouchers. Must an auditor who is using statistical sampling methods know the *exact* size of the population he is auditing?

In the case of attribute (error) sampling, the answer is definitely "no." A rough idea of population size is sufficient to provide an estimate of the requisite sample size to measure the *proportion* of error. This applies to estimation sampling of attributes, acceptance and discovery sampling. In the case of estimation sampling of variables the situation is somewhat different. Here the auditor is attempting to estimate a *value*. To do this he will estimate the mean value of a unit of the population and multiply this by the total number of units in the population to arrive at an estimated total value. An error in estimating population size will generate a proportionate error in the estimate of total value. This requires the auditor to make a rather precise estimate of population size in the case of estimation sampling of variables. The population is almost certain to be "batched" in some way, *i.e.* so many lines per voucher, so many vouchers per batch, so many lines per page. If this is so, the auditor must estimate the mean and standard deviation of the units per batch and use this *with a narrow precision limit* to estimate the number of units in the population from the *known* number of batches. Note the effect of this additional estimate on the final statement of level of confidence.

THE NEEDLE IN THE HAYSTACK PROBLEM

Statistical sampling is a powerful tool which has proved helpful over a wide range of auditing and accounting problems. It is not, however, of much use for finding needles in haystacks.

Take, for example, the situation where an auditor is testing a population of 10,000 vouchers. The probability of picking up one defective unit, if one unit from the 10,000 is defective, is as follows: —

Size of Random Sample	Probability of finding one error in sample
100	1%
1,000	10%
5,000	50%
9,000	90%

Even when the number of errors increases to 10, the sample size has to be very large to give the auditor a reasonable probability of picking up a *single example* of the error, *i.e.*

Size of Random Sample	Probability of finding one error in sample
100	9.6%
500	40.1%
1,000	65.1%
2,000	89.3%
3,000	97.2%

If we accept the conventional minimum confidence level of 90%, the auditor would have to check a random sample of 2,000 units to have a 90% chance of picking up *one* error. If 10 defective units occur in various population sizes, the sample size needed to achieve a confidence level of 90% in finding one defective is as follows: —

Population Size	Sample Size needed
2,000	400
5,000	1,000
10,000	2,000
100,000	20,000

The sample size is a constant 20% of the population size.

Statistical sampling, then, is not of much use for finding errors which constitute a very small proportion of the population, say less than 0.5%. The auditor must rely on his experience and intuition to select likely erroneous units using a judgment sample, *i.e.* he stratifies the population, as we mentioned earlier.

Statistical sampling is useful for measuring error proportions in populations in which error is endemic and of significant relative proportion. Examples are sales slips, invoice extensions, perpetual inventory error checks and so on.

Once the proportion of error is established, estimation sampling of variables can be used to estimate the value of error.

GRAPHS V. TABLES

Some professional auditing firms use graphs rather than tables for determining sample size. This fact has given rise to a legend that graphs provide a more sophisticated approach to statistical sampling than tables. This is not so. One can determine sample size rather faster using graphs, and perhaps the auditor can get a more complete picture allowing him to balance precision against cost, but these advantages are not very significant. Since Arkin,[2] Brown and Vance[3] and the U.S. Air Force[4] have provided useful sets of tables, I can see no reason why we should not use them.

SAMPLE SIZE, CONFIDENCE LEVELS AND PRECISION LIMITS

When statistical sampling is used the sample size depends upon —

1. the required level of confidence in the inference about the population;

---

[2]H. Arkin, *Handbook of Sampling for Auditing and Accounting* (New York: McGraw Hill Inc., 1963).

[3]R. G. Brown and L. L. Vance, "Sampling Tables for Estimating Error Rates in Other Proportions" (Berkeley: University of California, 1961).

[4]Tables of Probabilities for use in Stop or Go Sampling" (U. S. Air Force, 1964).

2. the width of the precision (confidence) limit;
3. the standard deviation, *i.e.* variability, of the population; and
4. the size of the population.

We have already noted that, once the population exceeds a few thousand units, the size of the population has little influence on the size of the sample. Also, an auditor cannot alter, except perhaps by stratification, the variability of a population: this is given. The determinants of sample size which are under the auditor's control are therefore the confidence level and the precision limit. If the confidence level is set high and/or the precision limit made very narrow, the sample size will be relatively large. What confidence levels and precision limits should the auditor use?

Let us tackle precision limits first. I believe that it is of the nature of accounting and auditing that precision limits should be narrow, either ± 1% or ± 2%. Most of the auditors I have discussed this point with use narrow precision limits. I suggest that a professional auditing firm should take a once-and-for-all decision to use a given precision limit of, say, ± 2% for estimation sampling of variables. Where the inference is very important, the auditor can move, without permission, to ± 1%, but if he wishes to use a precision limit wider than ± 2% he must request specific permission and give convincing reasons. For example, in the case of an estimate of a bad debts provision, a precision limit of ± 5% seems reasonable.

Note that widening the precision limit has a pretty dramatic effect on sample size, *i.e.*

Population	10,000
Estimated error rate	3%

Sample size required to check error rate with various precision limits: —

Precision limit	Sample size at x% level of confidence		
	99%	95%	90%
±1%	1,617	1,005	730
2%	460	272	193
3%	210	123	87
4%	119	69	49
5%	77	45	32

Table 1: **Sample sizes at various levels of confidence and various precision limits — estimation sampling of attributes**

A similar situation arises with estimation sampling of variables. For example: —

Population size	10,000
Estimated value	£100,000
Standard deviation	£2

Sample size required to check valuation with various precision limits: —

Precision limit	Sample size at x% level of confidence		
	99%	95%	90%
£1,000	2,103	1,332	997
2,000	624	370	263
3,000	287	168	119
4,000	164	96	68
5,000	106	62	44

Table 2: Sample sizes at various confidence levels and various precision limits — estimation sampling of variables

It seems that a precision limit of ±2% is the *minimum* economically feasible with estimation sampling of variables, if confidence levels are to be kept above 90%. Narrower precision limits would generate uneconomically large sample sizes.

Having fixed our precision limit at ±2% we are left with only one controllable variable, the level of confidence. The auditor can manipulate this variable to suit the importance of the inference from the sample. If the inference is most important, he can use a confidence level of 99% or even 99.9%. If it is not so important, he can use a confidence level of 90%. Under normal circumstances I suggest he should use a confidence level of 95%. It is unlikely that an *auditor* would wish to use a level of confidence lower than 90%, although certain *accounting* applications might allow him to use a lower confidence level. See, for example, an earlier article of mine.[5]

A careful examination of Tables 1 and 2 will show that at a given level of confidence widening of the precision limit had the following effect on sample size: —

Precision limit	Approximate % reduction in previous sample size
±1%	—
2%	73%
3%	55%
4%	43%
5%	36%

---

[5]T. W. McRae, "Statistical Cost Allocation," *Accountancy* (February, 1970), p. 101.

Notice the massive reduction in sample size as we move from a precision limit of $\pm 1\%$ to $\pm 2\%$.

When the *precision limit* was fixed, a reduction in confidence level had the following effect on sample size: —

Confidence level	*Approximate % reduction in previous sample size*
99%	—
95%	40%
90%	30%

If the precision limit is fixed at $\pm 2\%$, the auditor must select a given confidence level by trading off the cost of checking a given sample size against the corresponding confidence in the inference. To do this an auditor must calculate the cost of sampling, *i.e.* the clerical cost to his firm of drawing, testing and replacing a random sample of a given size. This cost can, of course, vary from job to job, but a three point cost estimate of cost per unit for easy, average and difficult jobs should be sufficient to provide an adequate measure for "trading off" purposes.

The objective in sampling is to calculate the *minimum* sample size which provides the auditor with an adequate confidence in his test. But suppose the proportion of the audit fee for this job cannot cover the cost of this size of sample. What should the auditor do?

I suggest that such a situation provides strong support for increasing the audit fee. The auditor *could* calculate the economically viable sample size and work back from this to a lower confidence level or wider precision limit, but I would not support this approach. The required confidence level and precision limits ought to be fixed *in advance* of calculating the sample size.

It sometimes happens that, to whip up support for statistical sampling methods, an auditor attempts to calculate the level of confidence which can be placed in the audit conclusions of previous years when statistical sampling was not applied. The previous years' sample sizes are probably too large, but the fact that they are almost certainly cluster samples may reduce their accuracy as a guide to the population characteristics.

In the usual sampling situation, population size, confidence level, precision limit and standard deviation are known. From these parameters we calculate sample size. In looking at past years' audits, sample size is known, population size and standard deviation can be estimated from the current year, and the precision limit can be fixed at, say, ±2%. The unknown variable is now the level of confidence. To find the level of confidence we search the relevant sampling tables to find a given sample size which corresponds to the given population size, etc. Having found this sample size we look up to the head of this column to find the requisite level of confidence.

For example: —

Population size   10,000
Unit precision limit/standard deviation 0.11
Sample size in previous year's audit   834 items

We look up the estimation sampling of variables tables and find that under these conditions a sample of 826 units gives a confidence level of 99.9%. This suggests that our sample size in the past was much too large. But this level of confidence depends upon the sample's being a pure random sample, while in fact the sample was a cluster sample. How does this affect the issue? Cluster sampling usually, but not necessarily, reduces the confidence level, but since this is a *single* cluster we cannot calculate by how much. It depends upon the variability within the cluster relative to the variability between the cluster and other possible clusters in the population. We can, however, say that the sample is much too large if a 95% level of confidence is required and pure or systematic sampling is to be used. A sample of 300 units would be sufficient to satisfy the required level of confidence in the inference. We have already stated above that it may be worth while comparing the mean, standard deviation and, perhaps, skewness of the cluster sample against a pure random sample of equal size drawn from the same population. We can then test if the differences are significant at, say, a 95% level of confidence. If the differences are *not* significant, we conclude that clustering has no effect on the viability of a sample drawn from a population ordered in this sequence.

Before we leave confidence levels we should, perhaps, say a cautionary word about the technique of increasing the confidence level at a fixed sample size by abolishing one or other of the precision limits.

Figure 1.1 shows the frequency distribution of a population of debts which are normally distributed, that is the debts are symmetrically distributed about the mean debt in a known fashion.

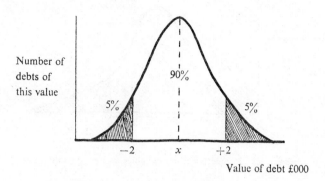

Number of
debts of
this value

90%

5%   5%

−2   *x*   +2

Value of debt £000

Figure 1.1: **Population of debts — normally distributed**

The facts in this problem are: —

Population	5,000 units
Confidence level	90%
Precision limit	±£2,000
Standard deviation	£4

The required sample is therefore 257 units. But suppose the auditor is not interested in the *upper* precision limit. Suppose he is only interested in checking that the debts *exceed* an amount of £2,000 less than the estimate but is not worried if they are more than £2,000 above the estimate. He can then abolish the upper precision limit and increase his confidence level to 95% *with the same sample size*. This is so because, as Figure 1.1 illustrates, if 90% of the area falls between the precision limits, *and if the distribution is symmetrical about the mean*, then 5% falls below the lower precision limit and 5% above the upper precision limit. By abolishing the upper precision limit the auditor can state that, if the statistical estimate comes out at £*x*, he can be 95% confident that the *actual* value of the debt exceeds £(*x* − 2,200).

However, this useful economy applies only if the distribution is symmetrical around the mean. Figure 1.2 shows the frequency distribution of a population of error values.

The distribution is skewed to the right, and a few errors account for a high proportion of the total value of error.[6] In this case the

---

[6]Fortunately, even if the population is highly skewed, the population of sample means drawn from this population is reasonably normal.

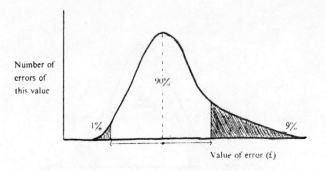

Number of
errors of
this value

90%

1%   9%

Value of error (£)

Figure 1.2: Population of error values — skewed to the right

auditor may decide that he is not interested in the *lower* precision limit: he is unlikely to be troubled by the prospect of the value of error being too small! He therefore abolishes the lower precision limit. Does this increase his level of confidence from 90% to 95%? It certainly does not, because, as Figure 1.2 shows, the proportion of the total area under the curve and to the left of the lower precision limit is only 1%. This arises when the distribution is skewed and the precision limits are fixed at the same distance above and below the mean as measured in standard deviations. Therefore, by abolishing the lower precision limit, the auditor only increases his level of confidence from 90% to 91%. This caution applies particularly to estimation sampling of attributes where the attribute is an error. Error rates in accounting populations are almost invariably very low; therefore the population of sample means is highly skewed to the right; therefore by abolishing the lower precision limit we obtain a very small increase in confidence. Conversely, since asset populations like debtors and inventory are skewed to the right, by abolishing the *upper* precision limit we obtain an increase in confidence which is *greater* than half the difference between the initial confidence level and 100%.

THE ACCURACY OF THE ESTIMATED STANDARD DEVIATION

When the auditor uses estimation sampling of variables he must estimate the standard deviation of the population he is auditing.

He can make the estimate in three ways. First, he can make a very precise estimate of standard deviation in the first year of the audit and use this estimate in future years or at least for four or five years thereafter. Accounting populations tend to have stable parameters, so that this method is viable. Second, he can classify the population into, say, 20 classes and calculate the standard deviation each year, using the conventional method which is set out in all the standard textbooks. Chapter 4, for example. However, if the population is very large, it is just not economically feasible to use the conventional method. Several "short-cut" methods are available for *estimating* the standard deviation of a large population. The most suitable would seem to be the method described by Grubbs and Weaver[7] called the *average range method.* A preliminary random sample of about 50 units is chosen from the population, and from these an *initial* estimate of standard deviation of the population is made.[8]

The idea behind the method is to estimate the number of standard deviations which lie between the means of one distribution describing the estimates of the lower limit of the average range and one distribution describing the upper limit of the average range.

Figure 2 illustrates these two shaded distributions lying within the larger distribution.

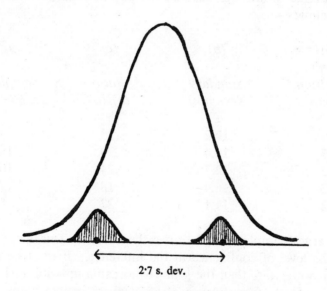

2·7 s. dev.

Figure 2: Estimating the standard deviation

Note that the means of the two shaded distributions, which consist of the upper and lower value units in several small groups of seven drawn from the population, are 2.7 standard deviations apart. A

---

[7]F. E. Grubbs and C. L. Weaver, "The Best Unbiased Estimate of the Population Standard Deviation Based on Group Ranges," *Journal of the American Statistical Association,* Vol. XLII (1947), p. 224.

[8]For a simplified explanation of the method see Arkin, *Handbook of Sampling,* p. 108.

precise estimate of the average range divided by 2.7 will, therefore, give us the standard deviation. But how accurate is the initial estimate of the average range? It is most important for the auditor to realize that the initial estimate from the preliminary sample of 50 is only a rough guide and must be checked later.

Five groups were set by the author to estimate the standard deviation from the following populations: —

No. of units	500
Total value	£78,000
Level of confidence required	99%

Using a random sample of 49 units divided into seven groups of seven, the five groups answered as follows: —

£12.2, 15.4, 12.7, 16.4, 11.1, showing a variance of 32% between the highest and the lowest estimate!

'What effect would this have on the population size? The effect is shown below: —

(a) Unit precision limit £	(b) Standard deviation £	(c) Ratio (a)/(b)	(d) Sample Size at 99% C.L.
3	12.2	.25	96
3	15.4	.20	143
3	12.7	.24	105
3	16.4	.18	171
3	11.1	.27	81

The largest sample size is 2.1 times the smallest. This fact, of course, affects the level of confidence in the inference. If the true standard deviation were 16·4, then the group who came up with 11·1 believed they had a level of confidence of 99% when, in fact, if we examine the tables, we find they had a level of confidence of only 90%. It is therefore important for the auditor to ensure that he does not *underestimate* the standard deviation. This means that he must recheck his estimate of the standard deviation from the full sample.

Grubbs and Weaver describe how a sampler can place precision limits on his estimate of the standard deviation. However, a much simpler and quicker method is to check the initial estimate from the full sample. Suppose the initial sample of 49 random units generates a standard deviation of 12·7. This suggests a sample size of 105. The auditor now has 15 groups of 7 and, keeping them in the same order in which they are drawn, he can calculate the average range from these 15 ranges and divide by 2·7 to calculate a more precise standard deviation. Alternatively he can regroup the initial sample of 50 drawn, if the sample size is $\leqslant 50$. If the first grouping was 7 x 7 and is divided by 2·70, the second grouping could be 8 x 6 and be divided by 2·53. The auditor will then use the *larger* of the two standard deviations derived in this way to calculate the required sample size.

USING THE COMPUTER

Many companies today store their records on magnetic tape ready for processing on a digital computer. When the population of records to be audited, or a copy of them, is available on magnetic tape or disc, the auditor can use this fact to speed up certain statistical sampling procedures.

The computer can be programmed to calculate, or at least estimate, the mean, standard deviation, and skewness of the population. "Off the peg" utility programs are almost certain to be available for this purpose. The computer can also draw the random sample of required size and it can be programmed to calculate the sample mean and standard deviation. So far as generating random numbers is concerned it is better to feed a tested table of random numbers into the computer rather than to rely on the computer's generating its own set of random numbers. The latter procedure would be untested and therefore suspect.

The computer can also assist in *stratifying* a population: the measures of standard deviation and skewness may suggest that this procedure would be advantageous. The computer can also draw a judgment sample from the population, the attributes determining the sample being decided by the auditor. Notice that the computer can be programmed to carry out random and judgment sampling on the same run.

The analytical power of the computer is sometimes useful for carrying out certain tests on the population. For example, a sample of unit values can be converted to their logarithms to test whether they form a log-normal distribution.

Finally, let us note the statistical sampling procedures which *cannot* be performed by the computer. The computer cannot decide the confidence level or precision limits suited to a given case: these depend on the auditor's judgment. Neither can the computer perform the actual verification of the voucher, etc., chosen for audit, nor can it decide what to do next if the inference from the sample is unsatisfactory.

THE RELATIONSHIPS BETWEEN SAMPLING METHODS

Four sampling methods have been used by auditors to test accounting populations: these are estimation sampling of attributes, acceptance sampling, discovery (exploratory) sampling, and estimation sampling of variables.

Figure 3 illustrates the relationships between these four sampling techniques.

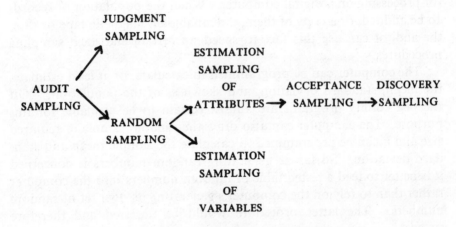

Figure 3: A tree diagram of sampling methods

The basic division is between attributes and variables sampling. Acceptance sampling is a simplified form of estimation sampling of attributes, and discovery sampling is a simplified form of acceptance sampling where the acceptable number of defectives is zero.

Estimation sampling of attributes and its two simplified forms are used to estimate the proportion of a population having a given attribute, while estimation sampling of variables is used to measure the total value of some variable of a population.

Each of the three attribute sampling methods requires successively smaller sample sizes and consequently provides successively less information, although the less informative method may supply *sufficient* information: The objective in sampling, as we noted above, is to achieve a given objective with a minimum sample size. Take the following example: —

Population	10.000
Minimum unacceptable error rate	2%
Expected error rate	1%
Confidence level	95%

The required sample sizes are: —

	Sample Size
(1) Estimation sampling of attributes	850
(2) Acceptance sampling	300 (2)
(3) Discovery sampling	150

(1) gives us a 95% probability of the error rate lying between 0.5% and 1.9%, a rather precise estimate. (2) tells us that, if a 300 random sample contains more than two errors, there is a 95% probability of the population's containing 2% of errors or more. This provides rather less information than (1). It does not, for example, attempt to measure the actual error rate, but it may provide sufficient information for the auditor who is prepared to accept a batch with less than 2% of errors.

Discovery sampling provides even less information than acceptance sampling. If we draw a random sample of 150 units from the population and find *no* errors we can conclude that there is a 95% probability that the error rate is *less than* 2%. We have no idea what the actual error rate is — and what is more to the point we shall frequently *reject* batches with an error rate less than 2%, *i.e.* we shall find one error or more in these populations. This point is not sufficiently emphasized by the advocates of discovery sampling.

For example, in the problem under discussion, if no errors are found in a random sample of 150, we are 95% sure that the error rate in the population is less than 2%, but we shall be rejecting batches with error rates as low as 1% roughly 80% of the time! However, if the objective of the test is to find batches deserving a closer scrutiny or to control the quality of batches, discovery sampling will provide us with *sufficient* information at an economical cost in sampling.

Estimation sampling of variables is the most useful sampling technique in both auditing and accounting, but it is often necessary to combine this method with estimation sampling of attributes. The latter estimates the proportion of a population with a given attribute, *i.e.* debts three months overdue; the former then estimates the *value* of these units. Note that under these conditions, if we require a 90% level of confidence in the final estimate, both parts of the estimate, the proportion and the mean value, must be calculated at a 95% level of confidence, *i.e.* 95% x 95% = 90%.

Summary

The auditor who attempts to apply statistical sampling methods to test accounting populations runs into several practical problems which have received scant attention in the literature.

I have pointed to some of these problems and suggested possible solutions.

Perhaps the more important of the suggestions are: —

1. A systematic measure method of sampling from bulky unnumbered populations.

2. The use of fixed, narrow precision limits of, say, ±2% in scientific auditing, making the level of confidence the only "judgment" variable.

3. The introduction of a double check on the average range calculation of standard deviation where sample size is ⩽ 50.

I have also warned against several pitfalls in applying statistical sampling to auditing.

The more important of these warnings are: —

1. Guard against a regular cycle in the population coinciding with the interval in a systematic sample.

2. A single random sample can only be used to test several populations on a single set of documents if the populations are independent of one another.

3. Statistical sampling is of little value when confronted with the "finding a needle in a haystack" type of problem.

4. Increasing the confidence level by eliminating one of the tails of the distribution is a viable method, but the auditor must know the distribution of the area *outside* the given confidence limits to calculate the increase in confidence.

5. Discovery sampling will reject a large number of batches containing acceptable error rates.

6. If a sampling estimate is generated from two operations, each of which provides a 95% level of confidence in the inference, the final inference has a level of confidence of only 90%.

21. The Four Objectives of Sampling in Auditing: Representative, Corrective, Protective, and Preventive*

Yuji Ijiri
Robert S. Kaplan†

In this article, we review the role of sampling in auditing and introduce new objectives for the sampling process. In addition to the traditional objectives of estimation and acceptance sampling which we label *representative sampling*, we suggest the following objectives: to maximize the number of errors found in the sample so that these may be corrected *(corrective sampling)*, to maximize the dollar value of the items included in the sample *(protective sampling)*, and to minimize frauds by taking random samples in all possible control areas *(preventive sampling)*. A simple example illustrates each of the sampling objectives.

THE AUDITOR'S OBJECTIVES

In classifying the auditor's objectives in sampling, it is often revealing to ask him to describe an ideal sample for a given population. Suppose that an inventory consists of 10,000 items with an average dollar value of $1,000 per item and that 200 items are recorded in error. What is an ideal sample in estimation sampling? Clearly, if the auditor is interested in estimating the average or total inventory dollar value, the ideal sample is one whose average value is exactly equal to $1,000 per item, while if the auditor is interested in estimating the proportion of error items, the ideal sample is one in which exactly 2 percent of the sampled items are in error. The same is true with acceptance (and discovery) sampling. An ideal sample here is one in which exactly the same proportion of items are in error as actually exist in the population. The auditor could then take an appropriate action as if he had observed the entire population rather than just a portion of it.

We may call such sampling, whose objective is to obtain a sample which *represents* the population as accurately as possible, *representative sampling*. It is clear that traditional statistical sampling theory falls

*From *Management Accounting* (December, 1970), pp. 42-44. Reprinted by permission of the National Association of Accountants.
†Yuji Ijiri, Ph.D., is professor of Industrial Administration, Carnegie-Mellon University, Pittsburgh, Pennsylvania. Robert S. Kaplan, Ph.D., is an Associate Professor of Industrial Administration, Carnegie-Mellon University, Pittsburgh, Pennsylvania.

into this category. However, representative sampling is a broader concept in the sense that it also includes judgment sampling in which the auditor uses his experience to improve the chances of getting a fair representation of the population in the sample.

CURRENT PRACTICE — REPRESENTATIVE SAMPLING

In 1960, Professor Lawrence L. Vance reviewed the numerous articles on sampling for accountants and auditors written up to that time.[1] In this article, he classified various applications of sampling techniques to accounting into three categories: estimation sampling, acceptance sampling and discovery sampling (a special case of acceptance sampling in which the population is accepted only if a sample contains no defective items).

Although a number of interesting articles have been written on this subject since 1960, each can still be classified into one of the three above categories. In other words, the development of sampling theory, as far as accounting and auditing is concerned, has been basically confined to classical statistical inference; focusing on estimation and hypothesis testing.

More recently, some articles have appeared[2] in which the use of Bayesian analysis is suggested. Bayesian analysis is a promising approach since it enables the auditor to qualify his prior experience and judgment, and incorporate them into the formal analysis. This results in smaller sample sizes being required for an estimate to have a pre-specified precision and confidence level than if classical analysis, in which no prior knowledge on the part of the auditor, is used. Note, however, that the objective of the Bayesian analysis is still assumed to be for estimation and acceptance sampling.

The fact that the development of sampling theory in accounting has been confined to estimation and acceptance sampling (discovery sampling being a special case of the latter) is quite remarkable because the auditor's objectives in sampling are much broader than those aimed at in estimation and acceptance sampling.

It is our position that auditors have at least three other objectives when they sample a population. For convenience, we shall name them *corrective sampling, protective sampling* and *preventive sampling*.

---

[1]L. L. Vance, "A Review of Developments in Statistical Sampling for Accountants," *The Accounting Review*, Vol. XXXV, No. 1 (January, 1960), pp. 19-28.

[2]W. H. Kraft, "Statistical Sampling for Auditors: A New Look," *Journal of Accountancy* (August, 1968), pp. 49-56; J. A. Tracey, "Bayesian Statistical Methods in Auditing," *The Accounting Review* (January, 1969), pp. 90-98; J. E. Soreson, "Bayesian Analysis in Auditing," *The Accounting Review* (July, 1969), pp. 555-561.

CORRECTIVE SAMPLING

When an auditor takes a sample, often his objective is not just to estimate how many items are in error but rather to find items in error and correct them. From this viewpoint, an ideal sample is one which contains as many error items as possible.

Evidence in support of the corrective sampling objective comes from the observation that good auditors always try to take samples from those areas where errors are more likely to occur. They do this not because they believe that they can obtain a fairer representation by doing so, but rather because they are interested in correcting as many errors as they can.

Checking items which are not in error is a waste of time for corrective sampling. Thus, if the population has 2 percent of its items in error, a sample of 100 which contains 2 error items is a poor sample from the viewpoint of correction since one without any auditing skills can, on the average, draw such a sample. (Remember, however, that this is an ideal sample from the viewpoint of representative sampling.)

A good auditor, by using his judgment and experience, should be able to draw a sample which contains significantly more error items than a sample drawn randomly from the entire population. An auditor stratifies the population by the estimated proportion of error items, and starts sampling from the stratum which is likely to contain the highest proportion of error items. As a matter of fact, it is quite common in the procedures of good auditors to check heavily the transactions in the end or the beginning of a month or a year, the items that have been newly added or dropped, the accounts with unusually high or low values, or those with negative balances. These actions cannot be justified from the representative sampling viewpoint. They are aimed at correcting the maximum number of error items.

PROTECTIVE SAMPLING

Protective sampling is aimed at maximizing the dollar value of the items included in the sample. When a good auditor is asked to take a sample from inventory or receivables records, he invariably includes a disproportionately large number of high-value items. This action can be explained in part from the representative sampling viewpoint if the variance of high-value items is greater than low-value items. One could then improve his estimate by allocating disproportionately more items to the high-value category. It can also be explained in part from the corrective sampling viewpoint if the chance of an item being in error is greater for high-value items than for low-value items or if the dollar value of errors divided by the number of all items in the category is greater in the high-value category than in the low-value category. However, there seems to be an intrinsic attraction to high-value items since the auditor tends to sample high-value items even if those high-value items are less likely to be in error because of the added internal checks on them.

Protective sampling explicitly recognizes that the auditor's tendency toward checking high-value items is one of the objectives of the sampling plan. If an auditor is allowed to take a sample of 100 inventory items out of 10,000, he feels more secure if he has checked 50 percent of the total value of inventories than if he has checked only 1 percent.

Contrary to corrective sampling which is, in a sense, an offensive approach against errors and frauds, protective sampling is a defensive approach. The auditor recognizes the difficulty of detecting errors and frauds which may occur in only a small fraction of the population and tries to protect himself from a disaster by verifying that at least a relatively significant portion of the population is free from errors and frauds.

PREVENTIVE SAMPLING

The last type of sampling discussed here, preventive sampling, is aimed at creating the maximum degree of uncertainty in the mind of auditees as to which items are likely to be audited in the future. An auditor may take a sample from an area not because he wants to do something with the sample, such as in representative, corrective and protective sampling, but rather because he wants to create the impression in the auditees' mind that the area is not audit-free, in order to prevent the occurrence of frauds in this or related areas in the future. Thus, for this purpose, an auditor tries not to show any patterns in the items he samples. Random sampling is therefore used quite often for this purpose.

Note however, that the purpose of random sampling here is quite different from that used in representative sampling. In representative sampling, random sampling is used so that one can make mathematically supportable statements about the precision and reliability of the estimate. In preventive sampling, random sampling is used to produce a sample without any explicit pattern, so that the auditees can not predict which areas are likely to be sampled in the future.[3]

IDEAL RESULTS

We may summarize the basic features of the four types of sampling by specifying an *ideal sample result* for each sampling objective:

1. Representative — sample characteristic equals population characteristic.

2. Corrective — sample contains the maximum number or dollar value of error items.

3. Protective — sample includes the maximum total dollar value.

4. Preventive — sample creates the maximum degree of uncertainty about the scope of future audits.

AN ILLUSTRATION

To show the differences in the approach among the four types of sampling, consider a population of 10,000 accounts receivables which are classified in two dimensions into 5,000 high-value items and 5,000 low-value items as well as 5,000 high-error items and 5,000 low-error items. Assume that the error rate is generally smaller but is expected to be four times as high in the high-error items as in the low-error items. Assume also that the standard deviation of the high-value items is the same as the standard deviation of the low-value items. Finally, assume that there are 2,500 items in each combination. The population of 10,000 can thus be stratified as:

Dollar Value	Error rate.	
	High	Low
High	2,500	2,500
Low	2,500	2,500

How should one allocate a sample of 300 items to each of the four categories under each one of the four objectives?

---

[3]For evidence on the psychological function of audits, see N. C. Churchill, and W. W. Cooper, "Effects of Auditing Records: Individual Task Accomplishment and Organization Objectives," Chapter XIV in W. W. Cooper, H. J. Leavitt and M. W. Shelly II, eds., *New Perspectives in Organizational Research*, John Wiley and Sons, Inc. (New York, 1964).

For representative sampling,[4] if one is interested in estimating the average or total dollar value of accounts receivables, 150 samples should be allocated to both high-value items and low-value items. If one is interested in estimating the proportion of number of items in error in the total population of 10,000 items, 200 samples should be allocated to high-error items and 100 to low-error items, since the standard deviation of error rate is approximately twice as large in the high-error items as in the low-error items. Of course, in estimating the population proportion of error, the number of error items from the high-error category should be divided by 200 while the number of errors from the low-error category should be divided by 100, before adding the two error rates together and averaging.

For corrective sampling, all 300 samples should be allocated to high-error items if the correction of the maximum *number* of items in error is the objective. If it is desired to correct the maximum *dollar value* of items in error, all 300 samples should be allocated to high-error, high-value items.

For protective sampling, all 300 samples should be allocated to high-value items.

Finally, for preventive sampling the 300 samples should be allocated randomly to each of the four categories. In this case, there may be classifications along further dimensions than the dollar value and error rate used here and the auditor may wish to verify that his preventive sample includes at least a few items in each of these sub-classifications.

CONCLUSION

In selecting a sample in actual audits, auditors appear to have all four objectives in mind: (1) to estimate the population characteristics, (2) to correct errors, (3) to increase the dollar value of items that are verified correct, and (4) to increase the uncertainty as to the pattern of future audits. How auditors weigh or should weigh these four objectives is an area that needs to be explored.[5] Just because the accounting literature on sampling has concentrated almost exclusively on representative sampling does not mean that it is the most important objective.

---

[4]See W. Cochran, *Sampling Techniques*, 2nd edition, Wiley (New York, 1963), for a discussion of sample allocation in stratified populations.

[5]See Ijiri and Kaplan, "A Model for Integrating Sampling Objectives in Auditing," Management Science Research Report No. 167, Carnegie-Mellon University, for a mathematical formulation of these multiple objectives.

In fact, the experience of the Lower Manhatten Branch of the Internal Revenue Service which "has abandoned random sampling of accounts because there were too many unproductive returns being audited; instead, examiners scan every return and audit only those that prove the most promising based on predetermined criteria and the overall impression the return makes on the reviewer,"[6] is not uncommon in CPA audits.   Such a phenomenon indicates that corrective and protective sampling may perhaps be more important to the auditor than representative sampling.

In sampling for accounting and auditing purposes, we should certainly take into account the special nature of the field.   For this reason, we need further developments in sampling . . . theory as to its application in accounting and auditing.   Such developments would enable us to design sampling procedures which integrate the various objectives of an audit.

[6] R. C. Mogis, and D. Rogoff, "Statistics Offers a Solution to Tomorrow's Auditing Complexities," *The Accounting Review* (October, 1960), p. 705.

22. Bayesian Statistical Confidence Intervals for Auditors*

John A. Tracy†

The auditor is faced with a decision situation common to most economic problems — allocation of scarce resources to produce optimal results. The auditor must allocate available man hours to each segment of the overall audit program to gather "sufficient evidential matter" upon which to base his opinion. This problem is especially difficult in those areas of the audit where test samples are used instead of a complete review. How large a sample is adequate? Exactly what conclusions can be reached from the sample results? How much confidence can be placed in the conclusion? Are too many man hours being allocated to the sample? Would a smaller sample be adequate?

Several recent articles have stressed the advantages of using random selection for sample items and statistical interpretation of sample results.[1] This article continues along this line, with one important modification. The previous articles have presented the so-called "classical" approach for the interpretation of sample results. The classical approach looks at the sample results — and only the sample results — to draw an inference about the population test area. Any other audit evidence that may have a bearing on the test area is ignored.

In many cases the auditor may have already gathered evidence by other audit procedures that is relevant to the test area. The Bayesian method incorporates such "collateral" evidence into the statistical interpretation of the sample results. Compared to the classical method, the Bayesian method can yield significantly different interpretations that in many cases would allow optimal allocation of audit effort. The auditor could have the same degree of confidence with a smaller sample size, or a greater degree of confidence with the same sample size.

*From *The Journal of Accountancy* (July, 1969), pp. 41-47. Copyright (1969) by the American Institute of Certified Public Accountants, Inc. Reprinted by permission of the AICPA.
†John A. Tracy, Ph.D., CPA, is Professor of Accounting, University of Colorado, Boulder, Colorado.
[1] Perhaps the best point of departure for review of such articles is the special report by the AICPA committee on statistical sampling, "Statistical Sampling and the Independent Auditor," *Journal of Accountancy* (February, 1962) pp. 60-62, and the special report by the same committee, "Relationship of Statistical Sampling to Generally Accepted Auditing Standards," *Journal of Accountancy* (July, 1964), pp. 56-58. This second report has a good bibliography of publications on statistical sampling for auditors. Also, see Morris Hamburg, "Bayesian Decision Theory and Statistical Quality Control," *Industrial Quality Control* (December, 1962), pp. 10-14; Paul E. Green, "Bayesian Classification Procedures in Analyzing Customer Characteristics," *Journal of Marketing Research* (May, 1964), pp. 44-50; R.E. Schafer, "Bayesian Operating Characteristic Curves for Reliability and Quality Sampling Plans," *Industrial Quality Control* (September, 1964), pp. 118-122; and Robert D. Smith, "Quality Assurance in Government and Industry: A Bayesian Approach," *The Journal of Industrial Engineering* (May, 1966), pp. 254-259.

The purpose of this article is to illustrate the Bayesian approach with a payroll test example. The payroll example is a likely area where the auditor would have collateral audit evidence in addition to the sample evidence.

HYPOTHESIS TESTING

A randomly selected sample is on average the most representative sample that can be selected from the whole population. Although any one sample is not the exact duplicate of the whole population, sample results tend to cluster about the population characteristic being sampled for. Otherwise there would be little reason to sample. For example, assume that as part of the audit program for the client's system of processing payroll checks the auditor decides to test a sample of payroll checks. Assume that 1,000 payroll checks were issued during the year. Of course the auditor does not know how many of these checks may contain errors. However, to illustrate the clustering tendency of sample results, assume that 40 checks are in error, a 4 percent error rate for the population.

Next assume that a sample of 64 checks was selected at random. How many of these 64 checks should we expect to find with errors?

Number of Checks With Errors In Sample of 64 Items	Probability of Occurrence Given a Population of 1,000 Checks Having 40 Checks With Errors
0	.0672
1	.1917
2	.2623
3	.2291
4	.1436
5	.0689
6	.0263
7	.0082
8	.0021
9	.0005
10 or more	.0001
	1.0000

For checks 5 through 10 or more, the bracketed total = .1061

Figure 1

Obviously we cannot get exactly 4 percent of the sample items to be in error; i.e., 2.56 checks. We would expect to get 2 or 3 errors most of the time, but occasionally we may get only 1 error or maybe 4 errors. We may even get no errors, or 5 or more errors. This situation lends itself to a mathematical formula for the exact probabilities as shown in Figure 1 above.

These probabilities were computed by writing a FORTRAN computer program for the appropriate mathematical function.[2]   The probabilities could have been approximated by other methods, but the increasing accessibility of the computer is gradually displacing the necessity of using "second best" approximation methods.

If the auditor were testing the hypothesis that the error rate for processing payroll checks was 4 percent (if this were the predicted error rate), the probability schedule presented in Figure 1 provides the information for establishing a decision rule. We see from the schedule that the probability of getting 4 or less errors is 89.39 percent. Thus, we could establish the rule that if the sample contains 4 or less checks with errors we would accept the hypothesis. However, occasionally our sample would contain 5 or more errors even though the hypothesis is true. This is the risk involved in using samples.

Samples cost less than a complete review, but there is the risk of making a wrong conclusion from the sample evidence. From Figure 1 the auditor knows the probability of getting 5 or more errors. In this way he knows the chance of making a wrong decision. The probability of getting 5 or more errors (when in fact the whole population has 40 errors) is 10.61 percent. Thus, the chance of rejecting a true hypothesis is 10.61 percent. On the other hand, the probability of making a correct conclusion is 89.39 percent. The auditor must exercise professional judgment to decide if this balance of odds between a right and wrong decision is sufficient for the purposes of the audit.

STATISTICAL INFERENCE

Of course, in most situations the auditor does not know exactly what error rate to expect; his purpose of sampling is to discover the rate. In this situation we have just the reverse of hypothesis testing. Above we recognized that several different sample results could be drawn from one population; we decided which sample results would

---

[2]The probabilities were computed using the hypergeometric probability function.   For instance, see George Hadley, *Introduction to Probability and Statistical Decision Theory* (San Francisco: Holden-Day, 1967), p. 262. The author programed this problem in the FORTRAN IV language and ran it on the University of Colorado's Control Data Corporation 6400 computer.

be accepted as being consistent with the hypothesis. In discovery sampling we must turn our analysis around and recognize that one sample result could come from several different populations. We must decide which populations are consistent with the sample result we got.

For example, assume that our sample of 64 payroll checks contained 2 checks with errors. This is an error rate of 2/64, or 3.125 percent. Does this mean that 3.125 percent of the checks in the population are in error? Not necessarily; in fact, probably not. There could be 31 errors in the whole population. Or, there could be 20, or 40. Our problem is to decide which kinds of populations could have produced the sample result. For each feasible population condition (number of errors) we can compute the probability of getting 2 errors in a sample of 64 items. To illustrate, for several different population conditions probabilities are shown in Figure 2, below.

Condition of the Population	Probability of Getting 2 Errors In Sample of 64 Items
10 errors	.1085
15 errors	.1831
20 errors	.2393
25 errors	.2723
30 errors	.2841
31 errors	.2842
32 errors	.2838
35 errors	.2791
40 errors	.2623
45 errors	.2382
50 errors	.2106
55 errors	.1820
60 errors	.1544
65 errors	.1289
70 errors	.1061
75 errors	.0863
80 errors	.0694
90 errors	.0436

Figure 2

We can see from the probability schedule presented in Figure 2 that the sample result is not unique to any one possible condition of the population; it could have "come from" quite a range of possible conditions of the population. We cannot pinpoint the estimate with

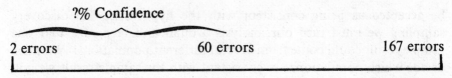

Figure 3

any degree of confidence. For instance, from our sample result we could infer that the number of checks with errors in the population is 60 or less. But what is the chance that the actual number of errors in the population is more than 60? Without knowing this probability the auditor does not know the probability of being correct in this conclusion. The auditor needs a degree of confidence measure; he needs to know the balance of odds between being wrong and being right in this conclusion.

The basic idea of a statistical "confidence interval" is to specify a range of possible conditions of the population from which our sample result could have been drawn so that the probability of being correct in this conclusion can be determined. In our example we found 2 errors and 62 nonerrors in our sample of 64 items randomly selected from the population of 1,000 payroll checks. Thus, we could draw the conclusion: "The number of errors in the population is between 2 and 938." We would be 100 percent confident in this conclusion. That is, we have accounted for all possible conditions of the population. Of course, this confidence interval is too wide to be of any use.

Let us change the conclusion to: "The number of errors in the population is between 2 and 937." Wouldn't we be virtually as certain in this conclusion? But why? The answer is that the probability of getting the sample result we did from a population having a total of 938 errors (the one condition excluded from our conclusion range) is zero. We give up virtually no confidence by reducing the conclusion range by one. As a matter of fact we can proceed in this manner to reduce the range of possible conditions of the population to between 2 errors and 167 errors. In other words, the probability of getting only 2 errors in 64 sample items from a population having 168 (or more) errors is zero for all practical purposes.[3] Thus, we can "chop off" quite a bit of the range if we simply know the probabilities.

However, we are still left with a rather wide conclusion range of between 2 errors and 167 errors. Let us subdivide the range as shown in Figure 3, above.

---

[3]The probability for a population condition of 168 errors is equal to .000481, and decreases as we increase the errors in the population. For sake of convenience the list of feasible conditions of the population was truncated at 167 errors. The eventual effect on the confidence interval is immaterial.

In words, if we are 100 percent confident for the range of 2 to 167 errors, how confident can we be in the range of 2 to 60 errors? This depends on the probability that the sample result was "contributed by" a population having 61 errors, or 62 errors, or 63 errors, . . . up to 167 errors. The reduction in the conclusion range reduces the degree of confidence we can place in the conclusion by the probability that the conditions of the population being excluded from the range could have contributed the sample result.

The auditor need not necessarily get involved in the mathematical procedures or the computer programing to determine the probabilities. However, the auditor must supply certain information to the statistician. Otherwise the statistician may make an assumption which is not correct, and which may cost the auditor more man hours than he would have to allocate to the payroll test.

A Priori Probabilities

The so-called "classical" statistical approach assumes that all the possible conditions of the population, or "states of nature" as they are called, are equally likely to be true. In our example this is equivalent to saying that each state of nature (condition of the population) has a 1/166 probability of being the actual condition of the population this audit period. These probabilities are called a priori probabilities. They are our prior estimates of the likelihood of each condition of the population. In essence, the classical assumption is that we have no reason to think that one state of nature is more likely to be the case than any other. On the other hand, the Bayesian method assumes that some of the states of nature are more likely to be true than others. Unequal probabilities are assigned to the possible states of nature.

Obviously one and only one state of nature is the actual condition of the population this audit period; we don't know which one. Presumably there is a "chance factor" at work in the payroll system that causes the condition of the population to vary. This chance factor could be carelessness on the part of the employees, a poorly designed payroll processing computer program, incorrect deductions information, and so on. This combination of factors causes an unknown number of payroll checks to have errors.

As we saw above, our audit sample result is not unique to any one of the possible states of nature. There are 166 possible conditions of the population which could have contributed the sample result, from which the sample result could have been drawn. Given the condition of the population we can compute the probability of getting the sample result we did (see Figure 2). These are called conditional probabilities. These probabilities were computed for each of the 166 possible conditions of the population by writing a FORTRAN computer program for the appropriate mathematical function.[4]

Thus, from either end of the problem we cannot be certain of the condition of the population. The chance factor could generate a range of possible conditions of the population, and the sample result could have come from a range of possible conditions of the population. Our problem can be illustrated as shown in Figure 4, on the next page.

The distribution of the a priori probabilities among the 166 possible states of nature directly determines the degree of confidence we can have in our conclusion. The a priori probability weights we attach to each feasible condition of the population represent the chance that the population condition could be true. To illustrate this point assume that the auditor is convinced from other audit evidence that there is no chance that there could be more than 100 errors in the population. Thus, even though the sample result could have been drawn from a population with 100 or more errors, as can be seen from the conditional probabilities in Figure 4, we would have to disregard the states of nature beyond 100 errors. In other words, we would attach .0000 probabilities to all the a priori lines above 100 errors in Figure 4 since such population conditions could never occur. We would be saying in essence that the sample must have come from a population condition between 2 and 100 errors.

The auditor must assign a priori probabilities to the feasible conditions of the population. One choice is to adopt the classical method and assign equal a priori probabilities to all the feasible conditions of the population. Of course, this is an easy way out. But the auditor may be wasting other relevant audit evidence. Let us continue with our example to make this point clear.

First, let us determine the degree of confidence in our conclusion by using the classical method. Each of the 166 possible conditions of the population would be assigned an equal probability of occurrence, 1/166 in this case. These a priori probabilities would be multiplied by the conditional probabilities for each of the 166 possible states of nature. The result is called a joint probability and represents the probability of being in that state of nature *and* getting 2 errors in 64 items. In other words, two things must occur jointly — the condition of the population and the sample result.

---

[4]These conditional probabilities were computed using hypergeometric probability function since it is assumed that each payroll check is not replaced before the next one is selected.

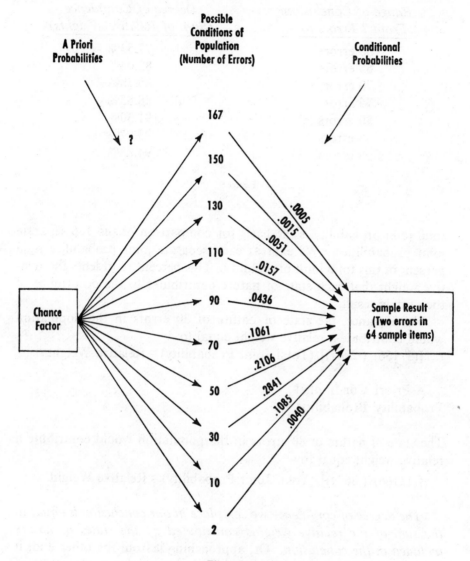

Figure 4

All of the 166 joint probabilities are added to give the total joint probability. This represents the probability of getting 2 errors in 64 items, given that all feasible conditions of the population (from 2 errors to 167 errors) have an equal chance of being the population from which our sample was drawn. This total joint probability is far less than 1.0000 since we are dealing with only one sample result of the many sample results that could be drawn from the various states of nature. But, since we have only one sample result to work with, this

Range of Conclusion: From 2 Errors to —	Degree of Confidence (Sum of Relative Weights)
60 errors	77.53%
65 errors	82.04%
70 errors	85.78%
75 errors	88.83%
80 errors	91.30%
85 errors	93.27%
90 errors	94.83%

Figure 5

total joint probability is the basis for comparison of the 166 separate joint probabilities. We express each separate joint probability as a percent of this total joint probability. This percent represents the relative weight that each state of nature contributes to the occurrence of the sample result.

For instance, the state of nature of 30 errors in the population would contribute a relative weight equal to:

$$[(1/166)\ (.2841)]/(\text{Total Joint Probability}) = \text{Relative Weight}$$

A Priori   Conditional
Probability   Probability

The state of nature of 80 errors in the population would contribute a relative weight equal to:

$$[(1/166)\ (.0694)]/(\text{Total Joint Probability}) = \text{Relative Weight}$$

The degree of confidence we can place in our conclusion is equal to the sum of the relative weights contributed by the states of nature included in the conclusion. Or, approaching it from the other end, it is equal to 1.0000 less the sum of the relative weights of the states of nature excluded from the conclusion, which is 61 errors to 167 errors in our example. The sum of the relative weights contributed by the states of nature included in the conclusion equals 77.53 percent; this is the degree of confidence we can place in our conclusion. Of course, the broader the range of conclusion, the higher the degree of confidence. Thus, the computer was programed to print out the schedule shown in Figure 5.

To get exactly 90 percent confidence our conclusion would be that the population has between 2 errors and 77 errors.

AN ANALOGY

Perhaps an analogy or model of our problem would help to explain and summarize what we have done so far. Assume that we have 166 urns placed in front of us. Each urn contains 1,000 balls. The first urn has 2 black balls and 998 white balls. The second urn has 3 black balls and 997 white balls; the third urn has 4 black balls and 996 white balls, and so on. Each urn represents one of the possible states of nature. A black ball represents a payroll check with an error; a white ball is a payroll check with no errors.

Suppose we then select one of the urns at random. The urns are opaque and not marked in any way. Thus, we do not know which urn we have selected. Since we selected an urn at random, each urn has a 1/166 chance of being selected. This represents the auditor assigning equal a priori probabilities to each possible condition of the population.

Next we draw a random sample of 64 balls from the urn we have selected. Our sample result is two black balls and 62 white balls. Which urn did we select? Or put another way, how many black balls are there in the urn we selected? Of course we cannot say which one urn we have selected. Our sample result is not unique to any one of the urns. Any of the 166 urns could have yielded the sample result we got. The probability of getting the sample result from each urn can be calculated. These are the conditional probabilities; given the condition of the urn we can compute the probability of getting 2 black balls and 62 white balls. Some of these probabilities are listed in Figure 2, page 293.

We next multiply the conditional probability for each urn by the probability of selecting the urn. This is called the joint probability and represents the probability of getting the sample result from a particular urn. All 166 joint probabilities are added to give the total joint probability. This represents the probability of getting the sample result we did given that each urn has an equal chance of being selected.

Each separate joint probability is expressed as a percent of the total joint probability. These relative weights represent the contribution of each urn (state of nature) to the occurrence of the sample result. Thus, we can ask: "What is the probability that the sample result came from one of the urns that have between 2 black balls and 60 black balls?" The answer would be the sum of the relative weights for these 59 urns, which is .7753. Put another way, if we draw the conclusion that the number of black balls in the urn is between 2 and 60, then we can be 77.53 percent confident in this conclusion.

Assume we are not told that all the urns having more than 100 black balls were withdrawn before we selected the urn. Furthermore, assume we were also told that some of the remaining urns were more likely to be selected than others. This change of circumstances corresponds to audit evidence from other sources that is relative to the payroll test area. To make use of this additional information is the essence of the Bayesian method.

THE BAYESIAN DIFFERENCE

The above analysis may appear quite scientific and precise, but the final answers are no better than the assumption we made regarding what a priori probabilities to assign to the possible states of nature. Was it proper to assign equal a priori probabilities? This implies that the auditor has no reason or evidence to believe that one condition of the population is more likely to be the case than any other, that a population condition of 30 errors is just as likely to be true as 160 errors. But, as suggested above, this would not seem to be the situation in most audits.

In many cases the auditor may have collateral or indirect evidence that is relevant to the payroll processing system. The auditor may have good reason to think that the error rate for processing payroll checks probably could not be much over, say, 5 percent, or a total of 50 checks with errors in the population. This opinion could be based on several factors. One might be that the auditor found few instances of payroll check adjustments, or no evidence of employee complaints in other parts of his audit program. Another factor might be a good plan of internal control for processing payroll checks. Perhaps another factor would be an excellent computer program for processing payroll checks, with several checks and tests built into the program. And of course management's policy would be to have "zero defects" in an employee area as sensitive as payroll checks. Thus the auditor may have a good deal of such collateral evidence.

To use the Bayesian method the auditor would have to quantify his collateral evidence into a set of a priori probabilities. For example, the auditor may think the allocation (see Figure 6, on the next page) of a priori probabilities among the 166 feasible states of nature is reasonable.

This may be a very conservative weighting. The auditor is assigning a 20 percent chance to population conditions of more than 51

	Condition of Population:				A Priori Probabilities
From	2 errors to	11 errors			.05
"	12 "	" 21	"		.15
"	22 "	" 31	"		.25
"	32 "	" 41	"		.20
"	42 "	" 51	"		.15
"	52 "	" 61	"		.08
"	62 "	" 71	"		.06
"	72 "	" 81	"		.03
"	82 "	" 91	"		.02
"	92 "	" 101	"		.01
Over 101 errors					.00
					1.00

Figure 6

errors, which he may think would not have gone unnoticed in other audit procedures.

In any case, the crux of the Bayesian approach is to assign a priori probability weights to the possible states of nature based on whatever evidence is available. These a priori probabilities are substituted in place of the equal probabilities we used above. Otherwise the procedures are the same. The result of the Bayesian method is a rather significant change in the degree of confidence, as shown in Figure 7, below.

CONCLUSION— Condition of Population Is From 2 Errors to—	DEGREE OF CONFIDENCE	
	Classical Method	Bayesian Method
50 errors	65.88%	86.96%
55 errors	72.16%	91.21%
60 errors	77.53%	94.28%
65 errors	82.04%	96.35%
70 errors	85.78%	97.95%
75 errors	88.83%	98.75%
80 errors	91.30%	99.28%
85 errors	93.27%	99.59%
90 errors	94.83%	99.81%

Figure 7

The auditor is more than 90 percent confident that the condition of the population is 55 errors or less by using the Bayesian method. By using the classical method the auditor would have to extend his conclusion to 77 errors to achieve the same degree of confidence. This difference in the range of conclusion necessary to achieve 90 percent confidence may be the difference in whether or not to extend audit procedures.

SUMMARY

This article has explored one facet of the Bayesian statistical method in auditing. The Bayesian method can significantly change the range of the confidence interval as compared to the classical method. The auditor can take advantage of whatever historical and current collateral evidence is available that is relative to the expected conditions of the audit test area. The Bayesian method recognizes such evidence in the form of a priori probabilities, which represent the auditor's best informed expectations about the possible conditions of the population that the sample is drawn from. These a priori probabilities are decided upon prior to and should be independent of the sample result.

The sample result represents additional evidence in the form of conditional probabilities. These two sources of evidence are blended together in the form of joint probabilities; each joint probability contributes a percent or relative weight to the total joint probabilities. The sum of these relative weights for the conditions of the population included in the conclusion range (the confidence interval) is the percent of confidence that can be placed in the conclusion.

The alternative to the Bayesian method is to assign, either intentionally or by default, equal a priori probabilities to all the possible states of nature. This is the classical method. The result frequently would be a much wider conclusion range, which may extend beyond a tolerable audit limit. The auditor may have to sample for additional items to resolve the question. The Bayesian method would prevent such an extension of audit procedures in many cases, since the conclusion range would be more narrow.

Tolerable audit limits are a matter of judgment and depend on the degree of confidence demanded by the auditor. The auditor may allow for collateral or indirect evidence in setting the tolerable limits for sampling results under the classical method, and of course the Bayesian method should not prevent an extension of audit procedures where judgment indicates the need for further testing. The main distinction of the Bayesian method is the requirement that the auditor *quantify* his collateral knowledge in the form of a priori probabilities. The general result should be a more optimal allocation of audit effort.

In conclusion, it should be pointed out that we have only scratched the surface of the Bayesian method. The Bayesian approach would be very useful in deciding upon initial sizes for samples,[5] and in deciding whether to extend audit procedures. Also, there are many other applications that seem very promising.[6]

Auditors frequently blend several sources of evidence to reach a conclusion in many test areas. In this sense, auditors are probably more Bayesian than they realize.

---

[5]William H. Kraft, "Statistical Sampling for Auditors: A New Look," *Journal of Accountancy* (August, 1968), pp. 49-56.

[6]See for example, Robert Schlaifer, *Probability and Statistics for Business Decisions* (New York: McGraw-Hill, 1959), and Kyohei Sasaki, *Statistics for Modern Business Decision-Making* (Belmont, California: Wadsworth, 1968).

SECTION D

The Computer and Auditing

Auditing of clients using computers in their accounting operations is a fact of life for medium sized and large CPA firms today. The following three selections are presented to illustrate and to clarify some of the many problems confronting the auditor in such examinations and to indicate the possible uses of the computer in the conduct of an audit.

Use of a generalized computer-audit program is described by W. Thomas Porter in the first article. Porter utilized the Auditape system developed by Haskins & Sells as a basis for his discussion.

Richard C. John and Thomas J. Nissen review some of the problems involved in evaluating internal controls in an EDP environment. Accompanying this article is a letter from Howard F. Stettler regarding the alternative uses of "test decks" and "packaged audit programs." The rejoinder from John and Nissen observes that the two approaches are not interchangeable.

In the final article in this section, Jerome Lobel discusses the problems to be encountered in auditing the fourth generation computer systems. With many auditors facing a dilemma in auditing third generation computer systems, Mr. Lobel calls for drastic action on the part of the auditing profession to prepare for the auditing of on-line systems which will face the profession in the very near future.

23. Generalized Computer-Audit Programs*

W. Thomas Porter†

Much has been written about auditing electronic systems in the past few years. Most of the techniques recommended for the auditor who uses the computer require some specialized knowledge about computers and programing.[1]

The purpose of this article is to discuss the use of generalized computer-audit programs in evaluating and testing records produced by the client's system. In my discussion, some analysis will be made of the Auditape system, developed by Haskins & Sells, since this system is an important example of generalized computer-audit programs.

USES OF COMPUTER PROGRAMS IN AUDITING

A computer program can be used for any computational or comparison task for which quantitative criteria can be established. Examples of these types of tasks in auditing are:

1. Testing extensions and footings
2. Summarizing data and performing analyses useful to the auditor
3. Examining records for quality — completeness, consistency, invalid conditions, etc.
4. Selecting and printing confirmations
5. Selecting and printing audit samples
6. Comparing the same data maintained in separate files for correctness and consistency
7. Comparing audit data with company records.

A common characteristic of these applications is the fact that the auditor can define clearly and precisely what is to be computed, compared, summarized, printed, etc.

Testing extensions and footings. The computer can be used to perform the simple summations and other computations in order to

*From *The Journal of Accountancy* (January, 1969), pp. 54-62. Copyright (1969) by the American Institute of Certified Public Accountants, Inc. Reprinted by permission of the AICPA.

†W. Thomas Porter, Ph.D., CPA, is Professor of Accounting, University of Washington, Seattle, Washington.

[1]Many authors have advocated the use of test decks and specialized computer-audit programs by the auditor. Both these techniques require extensive knowledge about the computer and the programing process for the design and implementation to be effective.

test the correctness of extensions and footings. The speed and low cost per computation of the computer means that it takes only a small amount of extra time and expense to perform the test in all records rather than a sample.

Summarizing data and performing analyses useful to the auditor. The auditor frequently needs to have the client's data summarized in different ways for analysis. Examples are aging of accounts receivable, preparation of annual usage, requirements of parts and inventory, listing all credit balances in accounts receivable and all debit balances in accounts payable, etc.

Examining records for quality. The quality in visible records is readily apparent as the auditor makes use of them in his examination. Sloppy record-keeping, lack of completeness, and other conditions affecting the quality of the records are observed by the auditor in the normal course of the audit. If the auditor obtains a complete printout for use in manual evaluation methods, the records can be tested for evidence of unsatisfactory record-keeping. If the records are in machine-readable form, the auditor has the option of using the computer for testing the records. In using the computer, a program is written to examine the records for completeness. For example, the customer file records might be examined to determine the number of records in which there is no credit limit specified. The records can also be tested for consistency between different items in valid conditions; e.g., account balances exceeding credit limit in unreasonable amounts (more than ten dependents for payroll deduction purposes on a man's payroll record).

Selecting and printing confirmations. Based on quantifiable selection criteria, the computer can select and print out the confirmation requests. As an example, one auditing firm has designed a multipart form which is prepared on a computer. A single printing prepares a first request, a mailing envelope, a return envelope, a control copy and a second request should it be needed. The form is designed so that the first request is stuffed in the mailing envelope which contains the return envelope. The savings in audit time when preparing large numbers of confirmations is substantial. A computer program can be written to select the accounts according to any criteria desired and using any sampling plan.

Selecting and printing audit samples. A computer can be programed to select audit samples either through the use of random numbers or systematic selection techniques. The sample selection may be programed to use multiple criteria, such as random samples of items under a certain dollar amount plus all items having certain characteristics such as high dollar values. The samples selected in this way can be used for audit tests such as confirmation, price tests of inventory items, etc.

Comparing the same data maintained in separate files for correctness and consistency. Where there are two or more separate records having data fields which should be the same, the computer can be used for testing for consistency. For example, the pay rates on the payroll master tape may be compared with the pay rates used in computing the payroll as shown on a transaction tape.

Comparing audit data with company records. Audit data such as inventory test counts can be compared to the inventory records by using computer programs. This requires that the audit data be converted to machine-readable records. Other examples of this use are tracing cash receipts to accounts receivable records or comparison of inventory costs with the master file cost data.

OBTAINING AN AUDIT PROGRAM

Three approaches have been used in obtaining suitable computer programs for use in the evaluation and testing of records: (1) programs written by the client, (2) programs written by or under supervision of the auditor and (3) generalized audit programs.

Programs written by client. Much analysis desired by the auditor is sometimes useful to the client. Therefore, the client will frequently write computer programs for his own use or will prepare the program for the installation if the auditor requests the analysis and there is also internal use for it. Examples are programs to age accounts receivable, analyze inventory turnover and obsolescence, review open order files, etc. Obviously, to use such programs the auditor will need to test the client's program. The extent of testing would depend, of course, on the reliance the auditor can place on the installation's control over programs and operations. As a general rule, the auditor should, at the minimum, obtain a copy of the run book for the application, review the documentation for the run and be present when the program is run.[2]

Writing an audit program. Since a computer-audit program is written in the same way as any other computer program and since the programing process is explained very well in other literature,[3] I will

---

[2]For a discussion of programing documentation, see the author's "A Control Framework for Electronic Systems," *Journal of Accountancy* (October, 1965), p. 56.

[3]There are several excellent references available if one is interested in understanding the programing process. For example, Gordon B. Davis, *An Introduction to Electronic Computers* (New York: McGraw-Hill Book Company, 1965); Robert H. Gregory and R. L. Van Horn, *Automatic Data-Processing Systems* (Belmont, California: Wadsworth Publishing Company, Inc., 1965); Frederick G. Withington, *The Use of Computers in Business Organizations* (Reading, Massachusetts: Addison-Wesley Publishing Company, 1966).

not discuss, in any detail, the steps involved in preparing a computer program to perform audit activities. Basically, there are four aspects of developing computer-audit programs: (1) determining audit objectives and procedures, (2) developing systems flowcharts, (3) developing program flowcharts and (4) coding, assembling and testing programs. The extent to which the auditor can or should perform each of these tasks depends upon many factors, such as the auditor's knowledge of data processing and competence in developing computer programs, the complexity of the programs being developed, the source language being used and the availability of client programing assistance.[4]

Generalized audit programs. It has become apparent to auditors involved in computerized systems that there are many audit functions which change very little from client to client. This is not really a very novel observation. Indeed, public accounting firms have guides to the preparation of audit programs which are issued to all audit personnel. The guides suggest an outline of procedures to be employed in audit examinations and to be included in the individual audit programs prepared for each client.

The idea of generalized computer programs is also not a novel one. Equipment manufacturers and other organizations involved in supplying computer programs to clients have been involved in developing generalized programs or software for a number of years. These programs perform activities related both to the operation of the computer system (systems programs) and to the manipulation and processing of data used in the management of the business (applications programs). Generalized programs, such as assembly routines, utility routines and compilers, and application programs, such as payroll, inventory control and demand deposit accounting, find widespread use in many computer installations today. The availability of such programs is a great aid to personnel trying to use the computer in that these programs preclude the development of systems flowcharts, programing flowcharts, source language instruction and the assembling and testing of programs. Generalized programs, if developed, designed and tested properly, are available for use in performing functions designed to be performed by the computer with a minimum of preparation on the part of the user.

Until recently, generalized computer-audit programs have been used to a limited extent. One approach has been the use of an industry program which is applicable to all clients in an industry. The best

---

[4]For a detailed discussion of the development and use of computeraudit programs, see the author's book, *Auditing Electronic Systems* (Belmont, California: Wadsworth Publishing Company, Inc., 1966), pp. 76-101.

example is the brokerage audit where generalized audit programs have been used to perform standard audit procedures having to do with confirmation, margin computations, etc. The client's files are transferred to a standard format on magnetic tape. The conversion program is unique for each client having a different computer; the data file in standard form is processed by an audit program used for all clients. The client's computer is used only if it fits the model and configuration specifications for which the audit processing program was written. It should be noted that even though two computer systems are not program compatible, they are probably data compatible if the data are put on magnetic tape.

THE AUDITAPE SYSTEM

The second approach is a generalized set of audit routines which can be useful for a variety of audit and management purposes and used on a restricted set of compatible computers meeting specified configuration requirements. Currently the best and most promising example of this approach is the Haskins & Sells Auditape system, designed to be used:

> By persons having no specialized knowledge of computers or programing languages, and having only a nominal amount of simple instruction.
>
> On a wide variety of records interchangeably, without any need for preparation of special programs for each type of application to be processed.[5]

The primary component of the system is Auditape itself, a series of audit routines written in machine language which are executed by virtue of specification cards developed by the auditor. In addition, the system includes an instruction sheet for computer operators, specification sheets and an operating manual. The operating manual includes a general discussion of the Auditape system, excerpts of which follow:

> The Auditape is in machine language, ready for immediate use, and includes several programs or what might be better referred to as routines to perform specific operations and a monitor routine to control the selection of these several operating routines.
>
> The instruction sheet for the computer operator includes all explanations necessary for operation of the equipment. The person using the

---

[5]*Haskins & Sells Auditape System Manual*, Section 1, page 1.

Auditape system need not be concerned with any actions taken by the computer operator unless the application is being made for an audit purpose that requires control against possible manipulation of data by intervention of the operator.**

The specification sheets are the means by which the person using the Auditape system adapts it to his purpose and to the input records available for each application. The specification sheets are used as a source document from which specification cards are key punched and read into the computer memory and combined with instructions read from the Auditape to complete the program for the particular routine being processed.

The routines, other than the monitor routine, comprising the Auditape are:

1. Edit routine, including the subtotal subroutine and an include-exclude subroutine
2. Print/punch routine
3. Summarize routine
4. Mathematical routine
5. Audit sample routine

Edit Routine

The principal problem in developing the Auditape system, or any set of generalized programs, arises from the wide variety in the format of the computer records to be processed. This variety occurs not only in the records used by different companies for similar applications, but also for different applications by any one company. . . . In the absence of a generalized program, a separate program is required for each specific record format to be processed, even though the basic operation to be performed by each of the specific programs might be the same.

The problem is solved in the Auditape system by the use of the Edit Routine, which causes selected data to be read from any specified position in the input record regardless of its format and written in any specified field on an output tape in the Auditape record format. This output tape then becomes the input for any of the other routines in the system.

The Subtotal or Include/Exclude Subroutine can be processed simultaneously with the Edit Routine at the option of the person using the Auditape system. These subroutines can be used for special analyses and other purposes by providing subtotals of input data in certain specified classifications and by including or excluding input data based on certain specified criteria.

**AUTHOR'S NOTE: Haskins & Sells has recommended that the auditor using the system observe all processing with the system since it is possible for the operator to alter the contents of the computer core memory during processing by switches on the console of the central processing unit. The system as designed does not require any such manipulation during the auditor's processing of any routine. Accordingly, physical observation of the processing should be sufficient to maintain control.

Print/Punch Routine

Aside from control totals and processing messages, the results from each of the other routines are written on an output tape in the Auditape record format. With any of these tapes as input, the Print/Punch Routine can be used to provide printed or punched card output or both. This routine also includes options to permit the fields in the Auditape record to be printed out in any desired order, and to print appropriate descriptive headings over each column of data.

Summarize Routine

The Summarize Routine can be used to summarize details of records by some identifying characteristic such as customer number or inventory part number.

Mathematical Routine

The Mathematical Routine performs addition, subtraction, multiplication, or division of amounts in any two quantitative fields in the Auditape record, or of amounts in one of such fields and a specified constant amount.

Audit Sample Routine

The Audit Sample Routine computes the approximate optimum sample size required to obtain the statistical precision and reliability specified for a particular sample and selects the items to be included in the sample.[6]

USE OF AUDITAPE SYSTEM

There is evidence that the Auditape system has been used very successfully by Haskins & Sells in performing audit tasks and by their clients in analyzing files for management purposes. My objective in using the system was to confirm my understanding of the system and to compare it with the approach of using programs written by or under the supervision of the auditor. The situation I used was an accounts receivable application for which special computer-audit programs had previously been written to perform certain audit procedures. The audit procedures included in these specialized audit programs were accounts receivable year-end procedures in a medium-sized manufacturing company. The auditor's objectives were (1) to determine the validity

---

[6]*Ibid.*, Section 3, pages 1 and 2.

of the client's year-end accounts receivable amount and (2) to evaluate
the collectibility of the accounts.

Data Field	Number of Characters	Data Field	Number of Characters
Customer number	7	Last month delinquent	4
Current A/R balance	9	Highest delinquency	
Amount on order		Number of items	3
Steel	9	Amount	9
Tungsten	9	Date	4
Sundry	9	Date last sale	6
Credit limit		Sales history (material amount	
Amount	7	only) (By-product line — steel,	
Date limit established	6	tungsten, sundry)	
Credit history		3rd prior year	9
Date account opened	6	2d prior year	9
Highest credit extended	9	1st prior year	9
Date highest credit extended	6	This year to date	9
Original credit limit	9	This month	9
Date original credit limit		Potential	9
established	6	Profit at standard — year to date	9
Previous credit limit	9	Payment history	
Date previous credit limit		Payment ratings (company es-	
established	4	tablishes payment ratings 0–9	
Number of months of previous		based on payments for each	
credit limit	2	quarter):	
Number of items currently		3rd prior year — by quarter	4
delinquent	3	2d prior year — by quarter	4
Amount currently delinquent	9	1st prior year — by quarter	4
Delinquency history		This year — by quarter	4
Months reporting	2	Dollars paid this quarter:	
Months delinquent	2	By discount date	9
Consecutive months delinquent	2	By due date	9
		Customer name and address	136

Accounts Receivable Basic Record
Figure 1

The company processed accounting and operational data on an
IBM 1401 data processing system. This system included a teletype-
writer order entry network, 1011 paper tape reader, 7330 magnetic
tape units, a 1402 card-read punch and a 1403 printer. The central
processing unit had a storage capacity of 16,000 characters.

Trade accounts receivable, in the aggregate, averaged approximately $2,500,000 and consisted of over 6,000 accounts, approxi-
mately 5 percent of which represented about 80 percent of the total
dollar value. The accounts receivable were on two magnetic tape files,
one being the basic record file that contained data records for each
customer as shown in Figure 1, this page; the other tape file was the
item record file that contained the details — i.e., invoices, unidentified
cash payments — which supported the basic record account balance
(see Figure 2, page 313, for item record of unpaid invoices).

| | *Number of* |
Data Field	*Characters*
Item record code	1
Customer number	7
Date	5
Invoice number	12
Gross amount of invoice	9
Net amount of invoice	9
Cash discount	7

A/R Item Record for Unpaid Invoices
Figure 2

Audit procedures. In performing the year-end audit procedures for the accounts receivable files, the auditor developed certain computer programs using the client's accounts receivable basic record file and the item record file. These files were then processed with the computer-audit programs as shown in Figure 3, page 314. The procedures performed by the three programs were:

1. Select for positive confirmation and print, on the circularization report, accounts with:
   a. Balance ≥ $5,000 (type Code 1).
   b. Balance ≥ $1,000 but ≤ $5,000 and with any portion of the account 30 or more days delinquent (type Code 2).
   c. Balance ≥ $1,000 and with sales this year 500 percent ≥ last year's sales or ≤ 20 percent of last year's sales (type Code 3).

2. Randomly select for negative confirmation and print, on the circularization report, 10 percent of the remaining accounts (type Code 0).

3. Age all accounts.

4. Select and print on the exception report all accounts:
   a. Over credit limit (type Code 4).
   b. Whose basic record balance is not in agreement with the total amount of all items in its item record (type Code 5).
   c. With credit balance ≥ $500 (type Code 6).

5. Accumulate and print, on the circularization report:
   a. Number of accounts in basic record file.
   b. Aged totals of all accounts in basic record file.
   c. Number of items in item record file.
   d. Total balance of all items in item record file.
   e. Total balance of all accounts with credit balances.

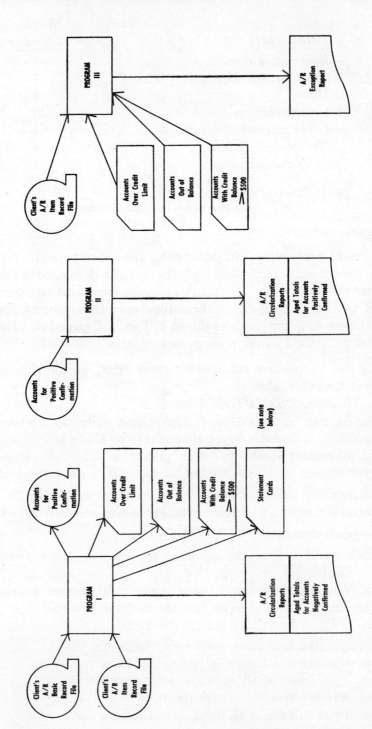

FIGURE 3

System Flow Chart-Computer Audit Programs

Note: Statement cards are processed with the client's statement preparation program to produce customer statements for mailing with confirmation requests.

f. Number of accounts selected for negative confirmation and aged totals for these accounts.

g. Number of accounts selected for positive confirmation and aged totals for these accounts.

Developing computer-audit programs. After formulating the audit procedures for the accounts receivable work and the systems flowcharts, the auditor prepared program flowcharts and designed output records to include the required audit information.

Of the three programs shown on the system flow-charts, Program I includes most of the processing logic and decision criteria. Programs II

Number	Name and Address	T	S	Balances	Difference	No Reply	Explanation and Disposition
0333500	ACE INC. 2105 WINSPEAR AVE. MADISON, ILL.	1	0	7,280.31 937.41	BALANCE 30 DAYS 60 DAYS 90 DAYS		
0350000	ACME COMPANY 7055 BEST RD. LANSING 4, MICH.	1	0	12,408.47 2,463.94	BALANCE 30 DAYS 60 DAYS 90 DAYS		
0514000	ADDER CO. YAKIMA, WASH.	1	0	33,347.91 23,180.43	BALANCE 30 DAYS 60 DAYS 90 DAYS		
1161000	BOOM TOOLS 12360 ASPEN LANE BOULDER, COLO.	1	0	6,037.19 3,022.76	BALANCE 30 DAYS 60 DAYS 90 DAYS		
1466000	CRISP FORGING MFG. LOWELL, MASS.	1	0	34,246.84 23,082.57	BALANCE 30 DAYS 60 DAYS 90 DAYS		
2511000	DUNHILL SUPPLY 4890 SOUTH CANTON ST. CANTON, OHIO	1	0	5,772.28 2,236.99	BALANCE 30 DAYS 60 DAYS 90 DAYS		
2620075	EARTH-MOVERS INC. PUYALLUP, WASH.	1	0	11,784.47 7,121.74	BALANCE 30 DAYS 60 DAYS 90 DAYS		
2646000	ESTHER TOOLS COLLEGE LANE WILLIAMS, PA.	1	0	7,234.73 255.96	BALANCE 30 DAYS 60 DAYS 90 DAYS		
3170000	FIRST SUPPLY 6360 DIVISION RD. BATTLE CREEK, MICH.	1	0	8,098.33 75.20	BALANCE 30 DAYS 60 DAYS 90 DAYS		
3262310	GUNN FORGING BARNESVILLE, IND.	1	0	6,738.26 3,212.17	BALANCE 30 DAYS 60 DAYS 90 DAYS		

PAGE TOTAL 10 ACCOUNTS BALANCE 132,948.79 30 DAYS 65,589.17 60 DAYS 90 DAYS

Accounts Receivable Circularization Sept. 30, 19XX

Figure 4

and III merely print machine-readable output resulting from Program I.

The primary output from the computer processing is the accounts receivable circulation report (see Figure 4, page 315). The report was set up in working paper form ready for the auditor's analysis. The digit under the "T" column in the report corresponds to the type of confirmation request — that is, 1 represents a positive confirmation request. File totals are printed at the end of the report for comparison with file totals shown on the client's aged trial balance.

The Auditape system applied. In using the Auditape system to perform the audit procedures enumerated above, I completed the relevant specification sheets required to use the system. There were 38 separate computer runs required to perform the necessary audit procedures. Many of these runs were necessary to get the data into the Auditape record format for performing the audit procedures. The scope of this article does not permit any discussion of the technical aspects related to the completion of the specification sheets and details of operating the system.[7]

Based on my analysis, I concluded that the Auditape system can perform all of the significant procedures included in the specialized programs. It does not provide the same flexibility in report format — i.e., aged information on the circularization report, type code — but this seems to be a rather insignificant item.

As to a comparison of time requirements of both approaches, my analysis indicates:

	Specialized Programs	Auditape	
Analysis of problem (including flowcharting, input-output design)	150.0	30-50	(estimated)
Programing (including coding, key-punching, assembly and testing)	70.0		
Completion and key-punching of specification sheets		12	(estimated 2 hours for key-punching)
Run time	.5	2.5	
	220.5	44.5 — 64.5	

---

[7]For those who wish such details, they may contact the AICPA's professional development division about courses on the H & S Auditape system, Haskins & Sells, or me on the specifics of this research.

One footnote to the above time analysis should be added. The actual time for the analysis of the problem originally was 230 hours; this reflected some developmental and learning time. Discounting this time, it is more realistic to think in terms of 150 hours, which I have shown above, for the analysis of the problem. Approximately 100-120 of the 150 hours would be required for flowcharting and input-output design and would be unnecessary when using the Auditape system; hence the 30-50 hours for analysis under Auditape.

Conclusions About Auditape

Based on my knowledge of and experimentation with the Auditape system, my major conclusions are:

1. The Auditape system, by virtue of the Edit Routine, can be applied to a variety of EDP installations involving a variety of record and file formats "without any need for preparation of special programs for each type of application to be processed."

2. The system, by virtue of the Include/Exclude Subroutine of the Edit Routine, can be a very powerful auditing tool in a variety of auditing situations that require examination of records for qualitative characteristics and conditions. In relation to the auditing uses of computer programs discussed earlier in this article, my analysis indicates that the Auditape system can be used to:

a. Test extensions and footings through its Edit Routine and Mathematical Routine.

b. Summarize data and perform analyses according to specified criteria by virtue of the Include/Exclude or Subtotal Subroutines of the Edit Routine and the Summarize Routine.

c. Examine records for quality through the use of the Include/ Exclude Subroutine.

d. Select and print audit samples through the use of the Audit Sample Routine and Print/Punch Routine.

At the present time, the Auditape system cannot print confirmation requests, and it cannot very easily compare data maintained in separate files. However, Haskins & Sells plans to develop routines in the near future which will print confirmation requests and which will handle multiple input files and permit comparisons of data in separate files.

3. The system has been developed for use with the following equipment:

a. Processing units — IBM 1400 series tape systems or system 360 with 1401 emulators, with memory capacity of at least 8,000 characters. Honeywell Series 200 tape systems, with memory capacity of at least 8,000 characters. IBM System 360 tape or disk systems, with memory capacity of at least 32,000. Certain other equipment for which 1401 simulators are provided by the manufacturers.

b. Card read-punch.

c. Printer or a console typewriter.

d. Input/output units — at least three units for applications requiring an output tape or disk; at least two units for other applications.

However, the nonavailability of the above equipment at a particular location may not be a limitation if the input data are available on tapes or disks that can be transcribed into punched card or IBM tape format and the required equipment is available at another location (such as a service bureau). For example, in using the system for internal audit purposes at the University of Washington, we analyzed, on the university's IBM 1401 computer system, files previously generated on the university's Burroughs B5500 computer system.

4. The system significantly reduces the time required by the auditor in using the computer in auditing as compared to the alternative approach of developing specialized computer programs for individual client situations without any significant decrease in effectiveness in performing audit procedures with a computer.

5. The system, although requiring no programing on the part of the auditor, does require some knowledge of the computer and programing to allow *efficient* completion of the specification sheets. For example, terms and activities such as low-order positions, data fields, record formats, control cards and character manipulation all require more than a basic knowledge of the computer and programing on the part of the user of the Auditape system to effectively and efficiently use the system. Haskins & Sells, in recognition of this problem, has designed and conducted an Auditape System Seminar sponsored by the AICPA's professional development division. This program provides instruction for practicing CPAs in the use of the system. This program coupled with a few on-the-job experiences in using the system should be sufficient to allow efficient use of Auditape.

6. The system requires that even auditors experienced in the use of the computer have a nominal amount of instructions about the system in addition to knowledge gained by reading the operating manual. This is

extremely evident when trying to use the Include/Exclude Subroutine. This was borne out in a recent classroom experiment with M.B.A. candidates most of whom had previous knowledge of computers and actual programing experience. All of the students had difficulty in applying the Include/Exclude Subroutine to an auditing application. Comments on problems they encountered in using the system included:

> I was not able to determine from the information provided in the operating manual how one indicates the information pertinent to the Include/Exclude operations on the specification sheets.
>
> In relationship to the Include/Exclude Subroutine, it would appear advisable to include in the operating manual an appendix which demonstrates how a simple representative problem is worked out.

7. The system as currently designed is somewhat cumbersome to use and would be greatly improved if certain functions could be combined so as to minimize the number of runs. The current version of the Auditape system was designed for the IBM 1400 series with a minimum of 8,000 characters of memory. It is obvious to users of EDP equipment that such a small memory capacity places constraints on the design and running of computer programs, particularly generalized computer programs. Haskins & Sells is working on a new version of the system which will combine certain routines so as to minimize the number of runs required for some audit applications.

SUMMARY

This article has examined the development and use of generalized computer-audit programs with particular emphasis on the Haskins & Sells Auditape system. The idea of generalized audit programs is a good one. H & S has taken one approach; other but not mutually exclusive possibilities include:

1. Generalized industry programs to perform audit steps common to an industry.

2. Generalized programs to perform common tasks such as confirmation, aging, testing for obsolete items, examination of file quality, etc.

3. Standard COBOL subroutines which the auditor combines to develop an individualized program for a particular client.

4. An audit language, based perhaps on a special version of the RPG (Report Program Generator) language.

I believe that there will be considerable activity in the area of generalized audit programs by different CPA firms and perhaps by software companies. In view of the high costs involved in developing such programs, the duplication of effort that may result from individual firms' developmental activities and the relevance of such programs for the entire profession, it is comforting to know that the AICPA has appointed a computer users committee which, among other things, is looking into this entire problem area.

24. Evaluating Internal Control in EDP Audits*

Richard C. John and
Thomas J. Nissen†

"I could steal a company blind in three months and leave its books looking balanced" boasts a data processing specialist. His method would be electronic embezzlement using the company's own computer. A manager of a brokerage firm did use his company's computer to siphon off $250,000 during an eight-year period. He programed the computer to transfer money from a company account to two customers' accounts — his own and his wife's. The computer was further programed to show that the money had been used to purchase stock for the two accounts. He then sold the stock and pocketed the cash.[1]

An enterprising employee at another firm instructed its computer to write checks to fictitious persons over a four-year period and send them to his home address. His scheme was uncovered only when the post office accidentally returned one of the checks to the firm and the clerk who received it became suspicious!

These examples of defalcations dramatize the need for adequate internal controls and continual monitoring of EDP systems.

> Internal control comprises the plan of organization and all of the co-ordinate methods and measures adopted within a business to safeguard its assets, check the accuracy and reliability of its accounting data, promote operational efficiency, and encourage adherence to prescribed managerial policies. This definition . . . recognizes that a "system" of internal control extends beyond those matters which relate directly to the functions of the accounting and financial departments.[2]

Weaknesses in internal control provide opportunities for defalcations to go undetected. Although an audit usually is not designed to detect fraud, every auditor is charged with reviewing internal control. To evaluate internal control in the EDP area, the auditor must have some skilled understanding of EDP.

*From *The Journal of Accountancy* (February, 1970), pp. 31-38. Copyright (1970) by the American Institute of Certified Public Accountants, Inc. Reprinted by permission of the AICPA.

†Richard C. John, CPA, is Associate Professor of Accounting, University of Wisconsin Extension in Milwaukee. Thomas J. Nissen, CPA, is Controller, Container Division, Jos. Schlitz Brewing Company.

[1]Alan Adelson, "Crooked Operators Use Computers to Embezzle Money From Companies," *The Wall Street Journal* (April 5, 1968), p. 1.

[2]*Auditing Standards and Procedures*. Statement on Auditing Procedure No. 33, Committee on Auditing Procedure of the American Institute of Certified Public Accountants, New York, 1963, p. 27.

The importance of internal control in auditing is stated in the second standard of field work:

There is to be a proper study and evaluation of the existing internal control as a basis for reliance thereon and for the determination of the resultant extent of the tests to which auditing procedures are to be restricted.[3]

Since this standard demands that *all* internal control be evaluated, review of internal control must include a review of internal control in the EDP function.

This article is concerned with the specifics of an auditor's competence as he complies with the second standard of field work in an EDP situation.

EVALUATING INTERNAL CONTROL IN THE EDP FUNCTION

Whether the audit is of a computer system or of a manual system, internal control is evaluated in terms of the same criteria — i.e., the controls must provide reasonable assurance that information is correctly processed and complete. To assure himself concerning the EDP function, the auditor should evaluate three major areas of internal control: (1) organizational, (2) administrative and (3) procedural.

ORGANIZATIONAL CONTROLS

Organization has always been important in the structure of internal controls. Because of the greater concentration of data processing duties in the EDP system, organization becomes even more important. Although the attest function does not require it, most clients expect their auditors to recognize opportunities for improving utilization of the computer and to make constructive suggestions as a by-product of their audit. Organizational controls fall into two areas: the placement of the EDP function within the organization and the division of duties within the EDP group.

Within the organization, the EDP group should be functionally independent in its relationship to other operating departments. To be effective from a control standpoint, this independence should include a separation of responsibilities which results in a system of checks and controls throughout the organization. However, controls must be flexible enough so that the EDP group retains its service nature to all

---

[3]*Ibid.*, p. 16.

other functions within the organization. Where possible, data processing should be a separate functional area. Such an organizational setup enhances control by preventing domination of the equipment by one user such as accounting or manufacturing.

The other major group of organizational controls concerns division of duties within the data processing group. Frequently the functions of systems design and programing are combined in one subgroup. This group generally is responsible for systems design, systems development, and programing. To avoid undue concentration in one person or group, design and development should be separated from programing if at all possible.

For the same reason, the group responsible for operation of the equipment should be separated from the functions of programing and systems design and development. In smaller applications, this operating group may also have control over data files and records in process, as well as control over data flowing into and out of the data processing area. In larger applications a librarian, who acts as a storekeeper, should have physical control over all data files and records not actually being used.

Organizational controls are the basic framework of a successfully functioning information system. Proper division of duties within the EDP department means dividing duties among the available personnel to minimize opportunities for manipulation. These controls are part of a sound organizational structure in which administrative and procedural controls can function effectively.

ADMINISTRATIVE CONTROLS

After reviewing the placement of EDP within the organization and the division of duties within the data processing department, the auditor should review administrative and procedural controls. The administrative areas of major interest to the auditor are program documentation and program testing.

Program documentation. Documentation is an important aspect of internal control; it helps assure consistency in operations, particularly during personnel changes. Ideally, the company should be using its own manual of programing standards which details documentation requirements.

Documentation of programs should follow a summary-to-detail pattern somewhat as follows:

Program specification summary.
General system flowcharts.
Supplemental narratives, and decision tables (as required).
Block diagrams of computer logic.
Record descriptions: input, output, storage areas.
Program listings of coding, and program decks.
Detailed operating instructions.[4]

Proper documentation primarily serves the purposes of management, but from an audit standpoint, it is an invaluable part of the review of internal control. Details of record formats, layouts, code structures, system flowcharts, etc., assist the auditor in developing meaningful tests of the system — especially if he intends to audit through the computer.

During his review of the documentation, the auditor must recognize those program features which perform data editing functions. Editing functions test the data for reasonableness against known possible error conditions. The computer can be a tremendous aid to management (and a strong point in internal control) by quickly and accurately performing routine edit functions. Wherever possible, such checks should be built into the program by the system designer. Edit checks are discussed with other processing controls in a later section.

Program testing. The second aspect of administrative control is the program testing procedures applied to new programs by the client. The auditor should determine that such procedures are indeed performed and, if so, review the procedures in use.

Some of the essential characteristics of thorough testing procedures are as follows:

Mock data designed to violate the edits and other controls of the system.

A large dose of "live" transaction data as an assurance check on the comprehensiveness of the mock data.

"Controlled answer" violations of the system, with proper follow-up of variations from the controlled answer.

Tests of more than one cycle of the same program to verify its updating capability.

"String tests" of the entire system to verify program compatibility from input, through processing programs to reporting.[5]

---

[4]Michael R. Moore, "EDP Audits; A Systems Approach," *The Arthur Young Journal* (Winter, 1968), p. 10.
[5]*Ibid.*, p. 11.

Program modification procedure is an important aspect of program testing. In theory, the procedure should be the same as for new programs — i.e., documentation and testing. However, in practice, program revision suffers from a lack of enthusiasm among personnel as to application of sound modification procedures. Good modification procedures are well worth the effort involved; the auditor should direct management's attention to their absence.

PROCEDURAL CONTROLS

The third area of internal control to be investigated in the EDP function is procedural controls. These controls include source data or input controls, processing controls, and output controls.

Input is the weakest link in the chain of processing events. Controls can be designed into computer programs to check for various errors. Routines can be established between and within the various departments to detect errors. However, if at the point of origin of the transaction an error is made in recording the data, it may easily pass undetected through the system. In EDP systems, the conventional control techniques to reduce the possibility of error in the initial recording of the data are extremely important.

Once data have been recorded by an initiating department, they will be transferred through other departments for processing. To ensure that all the data leaving Department A arrive in Department B, there must be control over the movement of data. One widely used control is a batch control.

A batch may include all the transactions for some period of time or it may be a fixed number of items. In using the technique a total of the critical data in the batch is obtained, usually by the use of an adding machine, prior to its submission to the data processing department. The originating department and the receiving department each keep an independent log of the totals. The auditor can make a comparison of those logs for specific time periods.

As mentioned in the discussion of program documentation, the auditor must be concerned with data editing functions designed into the EDP programs. Because of the speed and consistency of the computer, well-designed programmed edits can perform a continuous internal audit of all data entering the computer. Edit checks are used to detect data which are inaccurate, unreasonable or incomplete. They include checks for reasonableness of data, e.g., a check to assure that a disbursement does not exceed some specified limit. Common edit routines include: limit checks, validity checks, sign checks, field checks, historical comparisons and logical relationships.

Michael R. Moore points out that "comprehensive edits are of great value to a batch processing system. They are absolutely essential in a real-time environment, in which records are updated immediately upon input from remote locations and are available for information inquiry after updating."[6] Well-designed edits filter out "garbage" and only valid data flow through to the reports.

In addition to these procedural controls, which are of especial importance in EDP situations, other necessary controls include such things as transaction counts and visual checking. Since auditors are familiar with these and they are not peculiar to computer installations, these methods are not discussed in this article.

Another area of procedural control is control over operations in the data-processing department. Good internal control reduces the possibility of unauthorized manipulation of data. Access to the computer must be limited. An organization with good controls limits access to the computer room to only those employees concerned with operation of the equipment. Another area of strict control is programs. Once written, object programs should be accessible only to equipment operators; source programs should not be accessible to them. This control makes very difficult the unauthorized modification of programs by the equipment operator.

These procedures and controls are designed to reduce the possibility of operator intervention in the day-to-day processing. Manipulation of records requires a working knowledge of the programs, sufficient time at the console, and motivation. Important elements of this kind of control, for which the auditor should be looking, include:

1. Organizational division of functions as outlined earlier.
2. Effective scheduling techniques and standards for operations such as halt logs and controlled console printouts.
3. Written instructions covering each job.
4. A log of computer running time with appropriate control.
5. Control over movement of data — especially of rejection and return of bad batches of data.

These elements of control should be included in any well-designed set of EDP procedures.

Output controls are established as final checks on the accuracy and propriety of the information processed. Output control methods include control totals, sampling and prenumbering.

---

[6]*Ibid.*, p. 10.

Control totals of processed information are compared to input control totals. These can be batch totals of the number of records processed or totals of some other significant figures in the batch. This comparison of totals is the fundamental control feature in a batch processing system.

The use of prenumbered forms is helpful in maintaining output control. Prenumbered output documents can be accounted for in the same manner as input documents. The number of payroll check forms, for example, can easily be checked against the number of input records. Through the use of sampling, auditors can check output by tracing randomly selected transactions from source documents through the processing system to the output destination.

SUMMARY OF EDP CONTROLS

A well-designed EDP system should incorporate all of the controls mentioned earlier. It should have firm organizational controls with appropriate division of duties within the EDP function. The EDP group should be located within the organization in a way which balances independence, control and service. The programs should be documented, tested and retested upon modification. Procedural controls should exist which edit the data entering the system and assure that they are correctly processed. A well-controlled computer installation will help management attain its objectives. In addition, management should be able to rely on it as an essential element in the company's overall system of controls.

AUDITOR'S NEEDED SKILLS

The auditor must have enough expertise in EDP to review, understand and evaluate the three broad areas of organizational, administrative and procedural controls. He needs this expertise to enable him to prepare meaningful tests of the controls in the system. To perform such an evaluation, the auditor must have some fairly technical knowledge of EDP including some understanding of equipment, programs, operations and the types of controls needed in each. Unfortunately, a 1965 survey showed that 39 percent of staff auditors had neither a general understanding of how computers function, nor the ability to read and interpret flowcharts and block diagrams.[7]

---

[7]Wayne S. Boutell, *Auditing with the Computer* (Los Angeles: University of California Press, 1965), pp. 164-169.

AUDIT TESTS OF INTERNAL CONTROL AND EDP AUDIT TRAILS

After the auditor has studied the system and determined what controls the client purportedly has in effect, he must design tests of transactions to determine if these controls are in operation and if they are providing the checks that they were intended to provide.

Of primary concern in the design of tests is the changing nature of the audit trail. In an EDP system, source documents and visible historical records can more easily be altered or eliminated. In a non-EDP data system the audit trail consists of the journals, ledgers, workpapers and other documents which permit the auditor to trace transactions backward or forward through the system. In an EDP system the form, content and accessibility of records frequently is such that the auditor is unable to follow a single transaction completely through the system.

Typical changes in the EDP audit trail are cited by Gordon B. Davis:[8]

1. Source documents, once transcribed onto a machine-readable input medium, are no longer used in the processing cycle. They may be filed in a manner which makes subsequent access difficult.

2. In some systems, traditional source documents may be eliminated by use of direct input devices.

3. Ledger summaries may be replaced by master files which do not show the amounts leading up to the summarized values.

4. The data processing cycle does not necessarily provide a transaction listing or journal. To provide such a listing may require a special action, with significant additional cost.

5. It is sometimes unnecessary to prepare frequent printed output of historical records. Files can be maintained on computer media and reports prepared only for exceptions.

6. Files maintained on a magnetic medium cannot be read except by use of the computer and a computer program.

7. The sequence of records and processing activities is difficult to observe because much of the data and many of the activities are contained within the computer system.

---

[8]Gordon B. Davis, *Auditing and EDP* (New York: American Institute of Certified Public Accountants, 1968).

This changing audit trail is a growing challenge to the auditor. Records once easy to read are becoming visible only to the computer. Source documents are being eliminated. Printed listings are being replaced by totals; to do otherwise unnecessarily slows the equipment. As managements develop EDP systems to their fullest potentials, auditors will be less and less able to rely on traditional audit trails.

AUDITING THE COMPUTER

There has been a good deal of discussion of the relative merits of auditing around the computer vs. auditing through the computer, without defining either phrase. "Auditing around the computer" usually has meant little, if any, evaluation of internal controls in computer operations and programs. Instead, emphasis has been placed on tracing selected input to output and vice versa. On the other hand, "auditing through the computer" has involved analysis of internal controls within the EDP function and has utilized the computer to test the programs.

In his book, *Auditing and EDP*, Professor Davis emphasizes that when auditing *around* the computer, the auditor should evaluate and test internal control within the EDP function. He suggests interviews with data processing personnel, use of an EDP questionnaire and thorough review of the general system and controls. Presumably, such an audit would include a flowchart analysis of the system.

AUDITING AROUND THE COMPUTER

Auditing around the computer assumes that a test comparing selected audited input with output will prove the reliability of the internal controls in effect within the system. Auditing around the computer has the advantage of minimizing the interference with the client's day-to-day processing operations and presents no risk of tampering with "live data." The around-the-computer approach works well if the system is on a batch processing basis, if transactions are initially recorded manually and if the audit trail is characterized by extensive printouts. However, as the EDP system becomes more advanced, this auditing method becomes more cumbersome and costly.

If the client's EDP system is to develop to its fullest potential, auditors and management must be able to accept the reliability of the computer. Extensive printouts slow the system to the pace of its slowest component — the printer. In a study cosponsored by the American Institute of CPAs, the authors noted ". . . the CPA must realize that he cannot expect computerized systems to be modified to provide output that only he needs in order that he may perform his audit in the traditional way. . . ."[9] An auditor who insists on following a paper trail must justify the cost of the additional time and effort required to prepare a report for his use alone.

In auditing around the computer, the auditor cannot ignore the computer. He must make a thorough evaluation of the organizational, administrative and procedural controls in the EDP department even though he tests around the computer. Thus, evaluation requires a knowledge of EDP on the part of the auditor, if he is to comply with the second standard of field work.

AUDITING THROUGH THE COMPUTER

The alternative to auditing around the computer is to audit through it. In auditing through the computer, the computer is used to obtain information about the operation of the programs and about controls built into the machine itself. There are three audit approaches: using test decks, using "packaged" programs or using unique programs for each client.

Test-deck audit approach. The most used and currently the most economical method of auditing through the computer is the test deck. In this approach, simulated problems or data using the client's programs and equipment are processed under the auditor's control. Test data are introduced in whatever form is appropriate for the particular system. The term "test deck" implies the use of punched cards. However, other media may be used, such as magnetic tape, magnetic ink, or optical characters.

The auditor must design his test in a manner that will assure him that the system of controls is functioning properly. Both valid and invalid conditions are included in the test deck. The auditor "should concentrate on developing invalid data and control violations. The error input should relate directly to the specific system controls which are critical to his objective of being assured that he can rely on the

---

[9]Robert H. Roy, and James H. MacNeill, *Horizons for a Profession* (New York: American Institute of Certified Public Accountants, 1967).

system as an information source. He will probably want to attempt to violate all the designed quality checks in the edit program."[10]

The test conditions might include:

1. Out-of-balance batches of input
2. Normal transactions
3. Invalid data such as (a) alpha data where numeric should be, (b) invalid dates or account numbers, (c) incomplete data or (d) data larger than the field size
4. Edit routine violations
5. Out-of-sequence processing
6. Processing with the wrong file.

To develop an adequate test deck, the auditor must completely understand the system and its control features. His understanding should include knowledge of the controls discussed earlier in the sections on organizational, administrative and procedural controls. Of course, knowledge of these controls is also necessary to audit effectively around the computer.

Auditing through the computer has other problems not encountered in auditing around the computer. Frequently, a through-the-computer approach means that the auditor will be merging his test data in with the client's processing of "live" data. If so, the auditor must identify his test data so that they may later be "reversed out" of the live data. For example, if the auditor tests a program which updates master records, he might use:

1. Current master records or
2. Special audit records maintained in the current master file or
3. Obsolete master records or copies of current master records or
4. Simulated master records in a separate test file.[11]

In the first two methods, the auditor's test data are merged into the client's live data on the master records; in the last two, the master records used are dead. If the auditor chooses one of the first two, he must be careful not to distort or destroy real data. However, these methods don't require a special computer run for the audit and are therefore less expensive. Under methods 3 and 4, no data are live, but

---

[10]Moore, *op. cit.*, p. 13.
[11]Davis, *op. cit.*, p. 164.

a separate computer run is required. To use either method, the auditor must justify either the live data risks or the costs of an additional run.

A big advantage of the test-deck approach is that program changes are of little concern to the auditor, if the revised programs continue to produce acceptable output from the test data. Once a test deck is developed, it can be run and evaluated frequently. On the other hand, a test deck is costly to develop and can be used on only one client's system.

The successful run of test data through an existing program assures the auditor that the tested controls exist in the program. That is all it will do. The question of whether the tested program was in use during the entire period is a separate question, one not unique to EDP systems. This question is answered through analysis of organizational, administrative and procedural controls.

"Packaged" audit programs. To date, the use of packaged computer audit programs has been very limited. These programs are standardized programs developed to audit one segment of the client's records, such as the securities account; or, they are generalized sets of audit routines, such as Haskins and Sells' Auditape system. The Securities Account Program is intended for use in auditing securities of every client having an EDP system; the program should not have to be rewritten for each client. Similarly, Auditape is presumed to be applicable to all clients having EDP systems. These packaged computer programs assume that audit procedures in computerized systems change very little from client to client. They assume transferability of audit program among various EDP installations.

As a practical matter today, differences in equipment and software sometimes make extensive use of packaged audit programs impractical. Equipment differences may prevent the immediate applicability of a packaged program to an individual client's system. A test deck or an approach using the client's programs is usually less costly. However, the trend in equipment manufacture is toward more uniformity in design. Packaged programs, therefore, will likely be much more attractive in the future.

Using computer programs in conducting the audit. Using computer programs in conducting his audit requires the auditor to have a higher level of EDP knowledge than either auditing around the computer or the test-deck approach through the computer. This is probably why auditors seldom use them. However, the auditor could work with a programmer to write his audit programs. He might use client personnel to write programs, or use his firm's management services personnel. Some would suggest that the auditor should write the program himself. But there are very few auditors who can also program.

Using the client's personnel to write the program is the most economical, from the client's viewpoint. Some of the programs required for the audit may be already prepared by the client — such as programs for inventory turnover and obsolescence. To use the client's programs, the auditor must be capable of technically evaluating the programs to determine that they meet his requirements.

Using management services personnel to develop audit programs has the advantage of independence, but is more costly than using the client's personnel. If the auditing firm has a programmer available, he must learn the client's programing conventions and become familiar with the equipment and system involved — all at a cost to the client. Often, a practical alternative is to use MS people to review programs prepared by the client's personnel.

AUDIT CHALLENGES IN ON-LINE AND REAL-TIME SYSTEMS

As managements become increasingly reliant on the computer, computer systems are becoming more and more complex. Today's most advanced systems, of which there are relatively few, are known as "on-line," "real-time" and "integrated."

On-line refers to peripheral equipment connected directly to the central processing unit. Data are recorded at remote input terminals and are processed immediately by the computer. Transactions are processed when recorded instead of accumulated in batches. On-line processing generally requires a random access file storage unit.

Likewise, real-time systems usually require random access storage. Real-time refers to the time required for the system to respond to an inquirer. If the response is soon enough to affect current decision-making, the system is said to be real-time. A fine example of an on-line and real-time system is the computerized ticket reservation system used by some airlines.

All seats for upcoming flights constitute an inventory in random access computer storage. At any given moment, each seat is either sold, unsold or reserved pending sale. Every ticket selling point has an on-line connection to the computer inventory. The selling points make inquiries to the computer concerning unsold space available for sale. They also generate input data, which is immediately recorded, concerning sales, cancellations and reservations. This on-line input is processed immediately, making the inventory completely up to date at all times. The real-time updating is necessary to provide adequate answers to inquiries about seat availability.

In most systems, records are maintained functionally, such as purchasing records, accounts payable records and sales records. An integrated system recognizes that these various sets of records are interrelated. In an integrated system, one comprehensive set of records replaces the various functional sets. In an integrated system, the recording of a single transaction usually initiates several actions. For example, the recording of a sales order which has items identified by quantity and stock number might automatically result in: (1) reducing finished goods inventory, (2) pricing the order, (3) preparing the billing, (4) updating receivables, (5) updating sales analysis, (6) costing the order and (7) updating cost of sales.

This example suggests future data processing systems. Single inputs will initiate a number of data processing activities. Such systems will be considerably more difficult to understand and test from an audit standpoint. To understand such systems, the auditor must acquire a sound conceptual knowledge of computer capabilities. As these advanced systems come into general use, he must possess sufficient technical competence to perform a satisfactory audit.

CONCLUSION

The central problem faced by auditors of EDP installations is the greater or lesser omission of the traditional audit trail. Insistence upon maintaining conventional audit trails would only inhibit the development of EDP. Therefore, the professional must develop procedures and techniques by which his audit can be satisfactorily performed. "The auditor must recognize the full impact of the computer revolution. He must view the computer as a centralized tool of control previously not available to accomplish his objectives. A 'through the computer' (audit) approach must be adopted . . . to insure that factors of reliability, timeliness, and control inherent in computer systems are realized."[12]

If the auditor has enough expertise to audit through the computer, he can use the machine to assist him in performing the audit. An advantage of auditing with the computer is that the auditor is able to review the complete universe of the client's records. And, by delegating routine tasks to the computer, the auditor can devote more time to areas requiring his professional judgment. He thereby secures better evidence to support his opinion.

---

[12]Max S. Simpson, "How Do Electronic Computers Affect Accounting and Auditing Techniques?" *Financial Executive*, Volume XXIV (February 1966).

Professor Davis points out that all auditors should have at least a general understanding of the following topics and an in-depth understanding of them if they are responsible for computer audits:

1. EDP equipment and its capabilities
2. Characteristics of computer-based systems
3. Fundamentals of computer programing
4. Computer center operations
5. Organization and management of the data processing function
6. EDP documentation
7. Controls in EDP systems
8. Auditing techniques not using the computer
9. Auditing techniques using the computer.[13]

The problem facing the auditing profession is not whether the CPA is capable of auditing a system with a computer; given adequate training he could most certainly handle it. With the constant expansion of the use of computer systems, public accounting firms will have to make some important decisions regarding their audit approach. In complex EDP systems, where the traditional audit trail has virtually disappeared, it is most economical to audit through the computer. An on-line real-time integrated system is extremely complex and a through-the-computer audit approach is essential. As the degree of complexity of the EDP system increases, so does the level of competence required by the auditor.

To meet the problem of competence, each firm performing EDP audits should have a few computer audit specialists. They should have a level of understanding of EDP which will enable them to manage the audit of an EDP system. To become specialists, they should be given the necessary training in data processing through university instruction, vendors' courses in systems and programing, firm or professional seminars, AICPA professional development courses, or on-the-job experience in an EDP installation for several months. A CPA with this training is capable of performing an audit which completely meets the second standard of field work.

Over the years accounting firms of all sizes have developed various specialists in their organization — inventory specialists, industry specialists, SEC specialists, etc. The specialist approach reduces the need for detailed technical knowledge on the part of every auditor. While every staff auditor should be able to evaluate and flowchart an EDP system, he needs, on the job, only enough EDP knowledge to

---

[13]Davis, *op. cit.*

follow instructions and to earn the client's respect. Therefore, EDP specialists are a logical development in the profession.

CPAs must meet the challenge of the computer with people adequately trained in EDP. A high level of technical knowledge is required to evaluate and test internal control in an EDP system. Evaluation of program controls and equipment controls are especially technical; organization and procedural controls are less technical but do require a general understanding of EDP. To obtain information on the system, the auditor must be able to discuss the system intelligently with the client. Once the auditor understands the system, he must be qualified to develop meaningful test data. Again, a high level of technical knowledge is required. Designing and using test decks, converting clients' programs to audit use, and the use of generalized audit programs require a technical knowledge of EDP. As EDP systems become more advanced, the level of competence required to evaluate and test them will likewise increase.

Because EDP auditing is a highly specialized subject, a public accounting firm cannot afford to develop a high level of competence in *every* staff person. Therefore, as with taxes, EDP audit specialists are a logical development. The firm which expects to comply with the second standard of field work in performing EDP audits must have auditors technically competent to evaluate and thoroughly test these systems.

LETTER FROM HOWARD F. STETTLER*†

"Rather than test decks and packaged programs being alternative means of auditing through the computer, as the authors have suggested, they are intended to accomplish fundamentally different objectives."

In an otherwise accurate and comprehensive treatment of the matter of evaluating internal control in audits of computer-based systems (*JofA*, Feb. 70, p. 31), Richard C. John and Thomas J. Nissen may have generated a misunderstanding that could be troublesome to an accountant preparing for an initial encounter with a computerized data processing system. Under the heading " 'Packaged' Audit Programs," the authors suggest that problems associated with applying a packaged

---

*From *The Journal of Accountancy* (July, 1970), pp. 30-31. Copyright (1970) by the American Institute of Certified Public Accountants, Inc. Reprinted by permission of the AICPA.
†Howard F. Stettler, is Professor of Business Administration, The University of Kansas, Lawrence, Kansas.

program to an individual client's system may be avoided and cost savings may be realized by using a test deck instead of the packaged program.

The authors make this assertion in the context of auditing "through the computer," a term that is being superseded by the more comprehensive and more accurate term of auditing "with the computer." Rather than test decks and packaged programs being alternative means of auditing through the computer, as the authors have suggested, they are intended to accomplish fundamentally different objectives. As the authors have stated, the test deck approach is used primarily to test programs for the presence of desired edit checks and program controls. A packaged program, however, is relatively useless for such tests, which may be referred to under the broad classification "test of transactions" or "system tests."

Instead, the packaged program is designed to execute for the auditor the type of tests that may be referred to as "tests of balances." Thus, with the packaged program the auditor may gain access to machine-language files to carry out such auditing procedures as summing detail accounts to balance with a control account, selecting accounts for confirmation on the basis of a variety of criteria, or aging all or certain selected accounts.

Another aspect of the authors' treatment of packaged programs is that not only are the programs not interchangeable with test decks in the area of systems tests, but they were actually designed to be a cost-saving alternative to writing individual programs. Yet, under the heading "Using Computer Programs in Conducting the Audit," the authors fail to mention packaged programs as an alternative to the many problems associated with any attempt to write individual programs for use in a specific situation.

The authors do suggest, however, the possibility of using the client's own programs in some instances, although I see little chance that such an opportunity would be likely to exist. Should the opportunity present itself, I would question the necessity for the auditor to be ". . . capable of technically evaluating the programs to determine that they meet his requirements." It is extremely difficult and time-consuming to attempt to read through a program to determine exactly what the program accomplishes, even if the program is reviewed in source-language form. Furthermore, should the auditor have managed to accomplish that step, the auditor would still have to ascertain that the object program in company use contains the same steps identified in the source program. The most efficient way to answer this question is the previously referred to test deck, but given the use of a properly developed test deck, there would be no need to make a technical evaluation of the source program. The test deck would provide all the answers that the auditor would need.

REJOINDER FROM JOHN & NISSEN

"We do not infer that packaged programs could be interchangeable with the test deck. . . . The auditor can more economically attain his overall objectives by performing on the computer tests which are best accomplished by a test deck approach."

Apparently, Professor Stettler's experiences with packaged audit programs have been more productive than our own. As we recognized in the article, "packaged programs (for many reasons) will likely be much more attractive in the future." However, in an article which focuses on evaluation of internal control and on the "state of the art," the two paragraphs devoted to packaged programs seem to us to provide sufficient explanation, while concisely meeting the overall objectives of the article.

We do not infer that packaged programs could be interchangeable with the test deck. What we do say is that, in the kinds of situations encountered today, the auditor can more economically attain his overall audit objectives by performing on the computer tests which are best accomplished by a test deck approach. The economic promise of packaged programs is only beginning to become a reality. To date, these audit tests have been generally performed manually. Our point in the article, therefore, was that the auditor, intending to audit through the computer to any extent, might be wise to use an expanded test deck approach, rather than packaged programs.

As Professor Stettler acknowledges, the auditor will likely have a test deck prepared for his internal control evaluations. In such circumstances, he may devise further audit tests which utilize the clients' programs: Among other things, these procedures may be used to accumulate audit data which would otherwise be sought through use of a packaged program.

Although "with the computer" may be more correct jargon, we feel that "through the computer" more graphically describes the approach of a competent EDP auditor. A technically qualified auditor includes testing procedures to aid him in evaluating his client's programs. Guided by his evaluation of internal control, he uses his technical competence to develop effective and efficient methods to carry out the body of the audit. And, these procedures often include use of the client's own programs.

25. Auditing in the New Systems Environment*

Jerome Lobel†

To hit a moving target, you have to aim ahead of it. And if the target is accelerating, you must aim much farther ahead.

In essence, this portrays the dilemma the professional auditor faces today, as a result of the increasing use of electronic computers. Three major questions surround this moving-target problem:

First, what particular aspects of the new data processing systems environment should concern an auditor?

Second, how successfully has the profession demonstrated its ability to audit the present computer systems?

Third, what types of plans and actions are necessary to assure that the profession can carry forward its responsibilities in the new systems environment of the 1970's?

NEW SYSTEMS ENVIRONMENT

The new systems environment has grown out of four generations of computer technology:

1. The first generation of computer systems spanned the years 1946 to 1957 and was characterized by use of the vacuum tube, which represented the first application of electronic components of this type for a computational device.

First-generation computers introduced the concept of the "stored program." They placed emphasis on computing ability rather than upon input-output capabilities.

Input first consisted of punched cards and punched paper tape. Magnetic tape was introduced as an important medium of external storage in 1953.

Storage units employed "electrostatic tubes," "mercury acoustic delay lines," "magnetic drums" and "magnetic core storage."

2. The second generation of computer systems was introduced approximately in 1958, when transistors first were used in commercial computers.

*From *The Journal of Accountancy* (September, 1971), pp. 63-67. Copyright (1971) by the American Institute of Certified Public Accountants, Inc. Reprinted by permission of the AICPA.

†Jerome Lobel, M.B.A., is a consultant with the law firm of Laventhol Krekstein Horwath & Horwath.

Transistorized — or solid-state — circuitry resulted in improved speed, reliability and lower cost.

Internal storage was characterized by magnetic core elements in most computer systems, magnetic drum storage in some small-scale systems and the introduction of thin-film memory in 1960.

An increased range of input and output capabilities also became available, including magnetic and optical character readers, high-speed magnetic tape units and data transmission devices and communications equipment.

3. The third, or present, generation of computer systems is character-ized by integrated circuitry, which makes use of extremely small silicon chips. These chips serve basically the same function as vacuum tubes and transistors in previous generations. Integrated circuitry has in-creased substantially internal processing speeds and reduced power requirements.

Third-generation computers are also characterized by a consider-able change in computer design and system philosophy. These sys-tems combine the capabilities of a scientific computer and a business computer within a single machine. They are modular in design; they provide a broad variety of input-output capabilities — including such features as audio-response units and graphic display and plotters — and they place increased emphasis on communications and the need for data transmission over communication lines.

Systems capabilities include *multiprograming*, which is the pro-cessing of several different jobs at the same time within a single ma-chine; *real-time* operation, or the ability to respond immediately to incoming data; *continuous processing* of a job stream; *interrupt capabilities;* and the ability to serve numerous remote terminals which may be transmitting data simultaneously.

We are now supposed to be on the verge of entering the fourth generation, or what might be called the new systems environment.

In concentrating on this new systems environment, the impression may be given that little can be done to improve appreciably the pres-ent, or third-generation, systems audits.

Much can be done to improve current computer systems' auditing practices. The problem, however, is that we are presently aiming so far behind the moving target that to change our overall approach it is necessary to advance our sights by a considerable margin.

This means that auditors must now line up their sights on the training that will be needed, and the techniques that will have to be developed, if the same auditing dilemmas of the 1960's and early 1970's are not to be repeated.

FOURTH GENERATION

There is presently a general disagreement in the computer industry about exactly what this new fourth-generation environment is going to look like. There is general unanimity, however, that the new systems will be delivered and implemented long before the present decade is over.

That this is a reasonable prediction may be demonstrated by the fact that IBM, the industry leader, already has announced its IBM 370 product line.

Experts think the fourth-generation hardware/software environment, technically, will look this way:

1. Graceful degradation. This means computers will never shut down from a problem such as power failure to the extent of losing the data being processed at a given time.

2. Advanced memory systems. The new memories will be able to store much more information in a smaller space at a significantly lower cost.

3. Information utilities. Data processing and communication systems are being integrated to improve total information systems, and to provide what is being referred to as "three-dimensional" information systems. These systems permit computing in three modes concurrently: Local and remote batch processing; time-sharing; and remote access to a central data storage facility.

Just as we presently license telephone and electric companies, we may have to license computer communications utilities.

4. Common or shared data banks and networks. These will be implemented to permit extensive sharing of information by users who have common information needs. The data banks will be an outgrowth of technical advances in computer memories, communications equipment and related software.

What all of this progress means is this:

1. More information than ever before is going to be stored in smaller and smaller "black boxes."

2. Information will be more quickly and concurrently accessible to users — at their desks, offices and homes — or wherever they may happen to be.

3. Information will be shared to a greater degree than ever thought possible before, by the middle of the 1970's. This means that the shared data bank is essentially on top of us.

Successful technical accomplishment in the areas listed above has been astounding. For instance, a recent laboratory experiment demonstrated a device that is able to store several hundred thousands of computer words on an area as small as the cross-section of a human hair. This device could store on a memory device the size of a human hand a trillion words and figures. This is somewhere near the present storage capacity of all of the world's present computers.

In another case, the ILLIAC IV, presently being built by Dr. Daniel L. Slotnick in Paoli, Pennsylvania, is estimated to have the processing capacity of all of the other computers in the world combined. According to the November 1970 *National Geographic Magazine*, it is estimated that this computer would contain 256 processing elements and should be able to perform a billion calculations every second.

THE AUDITOR

And what effect will these many technical advances have on the auditor?

First, the tremendous additional quantity of information that is going to be held in the new memories and mass storage devices will make the systems more valuable for accounting business data processing purposes. On the other hand, they also will become more susceptible to manipulation and accidental or intentional destruction. Internal control problems become much more critical. Problems involving human error in present systems can become transformed into even more serious problems, if they are allowed to, in the fourth-generation systems environment.

Second, the accessibility of information with the new communication terminals can be considered both a blessing and a catastrophe. For example, we will encounter the potentially serious problem of the disappearing audit trail. Unless planning for this is intentional, it is easy to see how tempting it will be to avoid completely the creation of a source document — or even some form of transaction log — when almost all of the original data comes in through a machine-readable keyboard or other type of input device.

Third, the shared data bank can become a system nightmare in the event of unauthorized or accidental data access.

The whole subject of computer data bank and communications security, all of a sudden, appears as something that should be thoroughly understood by every responsible systems auditor.

Present EDP Audit Success

The second major question surrounding the moving-target problem was, how successful are the audits of our present computer systems?

Auditors have long held themselves responsible for reviewing and appraising the soundness of operating controls; for ascertaining the extent of compliance with established policies, plans and procedures; and for ascertaining the extent to which company assets are accounted for and safeguarded from losses of all kinds.

With the advent of EDP, many auditors have been somewhat shocked to find so many new business information systems being implemented with what often appears to be serious disregard for basic internal control principles. This dismay is usually justified. Audits normally reveal weak internal controls and raise serious questions about the competence of key data processing personnel.

Although not consistently so, the auditor discovers that the data processing organization simply cannot be relied on to provide adequate controls within the computer systems that they themselves design and implement.

Some of the underlying reasons that tend to support this situation are:

1. EDP personnel often do not have enough detailed familiarity with all of the control requirements directly and indirectly related to the applications that they are responsible for automating.

2. The orientation of most EDP personnel is related more to technical design and accomplishment than operating effectiveness. They think that they are primarily responsible for getting the system designed, debugged and "on the air." In addition, they tend to believe that this is the basis on which they will be evaluated or measured, come salary review time.

3. Important policy and procedural decisions are being made by relatively low levels of staff in the company's EDP operation. Many of these decisions involve controls, but too often the people making the

decisions do not have sufficient background or authority to make them. They do make these decisions, however, in the absence of other management direction.

4. Controls once included in the initial design or even implemented are occasionally ignored or deleted from the system without the approval or knowledge of responsible individuals.

5. EDP staffs attempt to design systems that will operate at lowest cost and greatest speed. The inclusion of internal control devices works against this objective.

For these reasons, auditors are finally getting involved. They are assigned broader responsibilities and are being directed to participate in EDP systems design, at least to the degree that they outline the controls that need to be incorporated in the new system.

Considerable improvement in data processing systems design and integrity is expected to result from these actions. For example, auditors:

1. Are beginning to have an opportunity to contribute their own strong backgrounds to the design of necessary controls included in the EDP system.

2. Are in a much better position to review the testing, operation and continuance of EDP controls.

3. Can assist in the discovery of EDP control violations.

4. Can assist the EDP operation by adding materially to the overall quality assurance of the computer system. The auditor can design and use his own EDP internal control questionnaire or checklist to assist him when conducting his EDP audits.

In addition, many auditors have become familiar with and are capable of using all of the current or state-of-the-art system auditing techniques, including auditing around the computer, auditing with the computer and auditing through the computer.

Unfortunately, the press of meeting daily schedules has prevented many auditors from taking enough time out from their daily work to acquire the right training and to develop enough confidence in the more advanced techniques. Yet this is exactly the reason for much of the auditing profession's dilemma in dealing with third-generation systems.

With the fourth generation poking its challenging head just around the corner, it would seem that there is a call for some drastic action.

ANTICIPATING FOURTH-GENERATION AUDIT REQUIREMENTS

The solution to the fourth-generation or new systems environment audit problems requires prompt attack in four major areas.

First, there is a language barrier. Like many other professions, including auditing, the data processing industry is full of buzzwords, like multiprograming, time-sharing, real-time, on-line, multiprocessing and many others. However, none of the basic concepts of business data processing are beyond the capacity of the average auditor. Equally important, there are many data processing professionals who might have more than just a slight problem understanding auditing.

This communications gap between auditing and data processing can easily be cleared up with a concerted training or retraining effort on the part of both professions. And this is not a one-time proposition; it must go on continuously if anyone is going to be able to hit the moving target discussed earlier.

From a training viewpoint, what should an auditor know?

1. He should know and understand what he sees when he enters the computer systems environment. That is, he must recognize how and why the data are manipulated by the system, how the system is organized and how effective are its internal controls.

2. He should be able to identify visually all of the major system components and be able to discuss the functions of these components in a fairly lucid manner with the people who design, program or operate the system.

3. He should be able to recognize the important weaknesses and strengths that affect the internal control of the particular systems he is responsible for auditing.

4. He should be able to recommend changes in the design or operation of the system that may be needed to resolve potential control problems.

Obviously, training cannot make a computer expert in a matter of days and weeks. The value of the training can only enhance the already proven expertise of an auditor.

Second, there is a need to concentrate more on principles. For the most part, there is very little difference between the principles of auditing in an EDP environment and the principles of auditing in a manual systems environment.

For example, EDP does not lessen in any way the need for evaluating and testing the internal control system. The differences that do exist are:

1. The fact that computer hardware is involved.

2. The fact that the auditor may have to acquire new techniques or tools in order to continue to do his job effectively.

3. The fact that the auditor has a greater opportunity than ever before to contribute his special knowledge to the design of the systems that will eventually be so important to his job.

The basic internal control principles do not change merely because the data are being processed or stored in a computer.

Third, there is a need for auditors to accept more responsibility. Auditors should:

1. Be consulted about the development of new applications.

2. Recommend control features for proposed applications.

3. Introduce any needed control changes to existing applications.

4. Review documentation practices and changes to programs.

5. Review deviations from the planned operations schedule.

Of course, evaluation of the system of internal control, and evaluation of the records produced by the system must be maintained as basic objectives. Also, the classic areas of concern with regard to internal control, including organization, input, processing and output, must remain the same.

The answer to successful computer auditing is learning how to recognize these basic functions wherever they exist in the computer-oriented system.

Incidentally, it would be very helpful if more auditors were familiar enough with the computer to use its own power to make the audit easier, since EDP systems often are much more complex than manual systems.

Fourth, there is the opportunity to implement what is called "on-line auditing." The future will show that after-the-fact auditing will become increasingly more difficult, and that drastic innovation is going to be required if audits in the new system environment are going to have as much meaning as, or even more meaning than, they do today.

On-line auditing involves the implementation of special programed controls recommended by the auditor. The controls are those which, if always operable, will assure the auditor that the system is continuously guarding against the processing of illegal transactions or of incomplete or inaccurate data.

Periodic audits of a computer-oriented system will be made much easier by use of the on-line auditing concept. This is also a concept which should be considered in all systems which, themselves, are basically on-line or communications-oriented.

Communications-oriented data processing systems often process transactions at very high speeds and in such ways that it is impossible for periodic audits to test adequately the integrity of the system or even the validity of all the records being processed.

Where master records, for instance, are being constantly updated by on-line or real-time processing, there is almost no other way but through on-line auditing to assure that the system is under control at all times. Even where each transaction is recorded or saved for later evaluation, the large number of subsequent transactions may make auditing and recovery extremely difficult.

On-line systems permit the logical extension of traditional audit concepts to a point at which, for the first time, an auditor is able to devote himself *totally* to the concept of "audit by insight."

What makes this possible are the following system features described by Downs, Harlow and Hudson in their article "On-Line Bank Auditing."[1]

1. All the actual record compilation is done remotely [i.e., on magnetic media].
2. The basic elements of audit control (repetitive tasks such as condition verification, totaling, validating and balancing) are separated from the auditor's primary task of investigation.

The result, according to the authors, should be operational program confidence. It is upon the acceptance of this concept that all normal on-line auditing depends.

The authors also contend that the best way to achieve "audit by insight" is for the auditor to demand "program confidence." That is, programs must demonstrate that they:

1. Are designed to maintain the controls desired.
2. Are operating correctly 100 percent of the time.
3. Are not being tampered with.

---

[1]Melvin T. Downs, Walter A. Harlow, and Charles W. Hudson, "On-Line Bank Auditing," *NAA Bulletin* (January, 1965), p. 57.

The result of this confidence will be the ability to eliminate all the daily or periodic controls necessary in a manual system. The reason for this is that once a computer has been introduced to do something and it is established that the computer is doing it, the computer will continue to do it until instructed to do something else.

Further, the authors contend that the information is completely up to date, that criteria are applied instantly during processing and that criteria are applied to every account, not just a sample.

To date, there has not been an adequate amount of research performed or literature published on on-line auditing. This is rather unfortunate, since it is the understanding and rapid implementation of these techniques that will produce the most encouraging results in audits in the new systems environment.

There is still time to take deliberate aim at this advancing new systems environment. But like any accelerating target, it can move by extremely fast if the planning and the aiming are not far enough ahead of it.

PART FOUR

Selected Reporting Problems

The audit report is the final product of the audit examination. Through the report the auditor communicates his findings and conclusions to outside parties. The report thus plays a key role in setting a basis for and delimiting the auditor's responsibility to third-party users.

Selected reporting problems are treated in this section and are classified as to their fundamental orientation.

The nature of the organization which the auditor is reporting upon calls for concern by the auditor in the format and wording of his report. Various adaptations in the audit report may arise due to the auditor's relationship to the client or events surrounding the examination. Reporting problems may, of course, arise in any auditing situation and the auditor must be alert to professional standards and guidelines to arrive at an appropriate solution.

SECTION A

Organization Oriented

Two types of organization-oriented reporting problems have received considerable attention by the profession. The following articles are designed to treat the more troublesome aspects of the reporting problems of the development-stage and not-for-profit firms.

In the lead article, Don Wharton presents the intriguing question of "How can the public make sound investments in development-stage companies when accounting, reporting and format problems are unresolved?" Current alternative accounting treatments resulting in greatly diverse financial statements are responsible for the dilemma. Recommendations are made which would eliminate or minimize the alternative treatments resulting in more uniform statements containing considerably more information for investor analysis.

Emerson O. Henke, in the second article, suggests that readers of audit reports and the related financial statements of not-for-profit organizations may well be misled by the terminology and representations made in the report and statements. The primary problem relates to the extent of use of the accrual basis by the reporting organization. Suggestions are made to eliminate alternatives and to clarify the auditor's report.

26. Accounting and Reporting for Companies in the Development Stage*

Don Wharton†

Most business enterprises, like human beings, pass through certain clearly discernible stages in their life cycle. For a business enterprise, the earliest of these is the development stage, or, as it is sometimes called, the preoperating stage — the period from the date on which it is organized to the date on which operations begin. During this period a company is getting ready to operate, and, depending on the nature of its business, it might be engaged in recruiting and training personnel; acquiring property, plant, and equipment; conducting research and development; lining up sources of supply; and/or developing production and marketing capabilities. Virtually every enterprise passes through such a development stage, including companies which are not "developing" a product or service. The essential and distinguishing characteristic of the development stage is that the company is getting ready to conduct operations but has not yet begun them.

Figure 1, page 352, shows, in condensed form, the hypothetical (but not unrealistic) results of transactions which might be reported by a company while in the development stage and for the first year thereafter. The figures in column A are so different from those in column B that, at first glance, one might suppose that the two columns represent two different companies. Both columns, however, are based on the same set of data for the same hypothetical company. Column A shows the figures that would have resulted if the company had elected to use the full write-off method to account for preoperating costs, while column B shows the figures that would have resulted under the full deferral method. Actually the company could have elected still a third alternative — the partial write-off method — and reported "net losses" in amounts somewhere between those shown in columns A and B.

The existence of alternative accounting methods is not the only serious weakness affecting the accounting and reporting for companies in the development stage. In many cases financial statements and the reports of independent auditors do not adequately disclose the nature of the information which the statements present, the basis on which

*From *The Journal of Accountancy* (July, 1970), pp. 39-52. Copyright (1970) by the American Institute of Certified Public Accountants, Inc. Reprinted by permission of the AICPA.
†Don Wharton, CPA, is a principal of Arthur Young & Company in Los Angeles.

the information is presented, or whether deferred costs are expected to be recoverable from future revenues. These weaknesses assume unusual importance because of the high degree of risk that is typically involved — a large number of these companies have an idea for a product or service and little else — and because of the large number of development-stage companies which have filed registration statements with the Securities and Exchange Commission in the past few years.

The purpose of this article is to analyze current practices in accounting and reporting for companies in the development stage and to recommend improvements. Accordingly, the article is divided into two main parts: (1) a description of present practices and the apparent

	Development stage		First year of operations	
	(Thousands of dollars)			
Results of transactions during the period	A	B	A	B
Revenues	—	—	$100	$100
Costs and expenses:				
Product development	$300	—	—	60
Selling	—	—	50	50
General	200	—	100	100
Amortization of preoperating costs	—	—	—	100
Net loss	$500	$—	$ 50	$210
Financial condition at end of period				
Assets:				
Deferred costs:				
Product development	—	$300	—	$300
Other preoperating	—	200	—	200
Less: Amortization	—	—	—	(160)
Other	$100	100	$100	100
	$100	$600	$100	$440
Liabilities and stockholders' equity:				
Accounts payable	$150	$150	$200	$200
Paid-in capital	450	450	450	450
Deficit	(500)	—	(550)	(210)
Net stockholders' equity	(50)	450	(100)	(240)
	$100	$600	$100	$440

Two Sets of Figures
One Set of Facts
Figure 1

rationale behind them, and (2) a discussion of the evident weaknesses in present practice and the author's recommendations for eliminating or overcoming these weaknesses.

PRESENT PRACTICE

The following comments on present practice are based on the author's study of approximately a hundred prospectuses issued by companies in the development stage during 1968 and 1969. After describing the accounting and reporting practices used, and exploring some of the reasons for their use, we will consider briefly certain problems which companies typically encounter as they pass from the development stage to the operating stage.

STATEMENT FORMAT

The two formats. Development-stage companies use one of two reporting formats:

1. *The balance sheet format*, which usually consists of a balance sheet and a statement of cash receipts and disbursements.

2. *The "5A format,"* so called because it is prescribed by Article 5A of Regulation S-X of the Securities and Exchange Commission (SEC). The 5A format usually consists of four statements, covering (a) assets and unrecovered deferred charges, (b) liabilities, (c) capital shares, and (d) cash receipts and disbursements. In some cases assets and unrecovered deferred charges are dealt with in two separate statements.

If costs have been charged off, a company using either format may also present a statement of operations. Some companies, however, disclose the write-off in a note or in the statement of cash receipts and disbursements, while others do not disclose it in any manner. Also, some companies using the 5A format present a statement of stockholders' equity instead of a statement of capital shares when costs have been written off, apparently to disclose the accumulated deficit.

Conditions under which the formats are used. The balance sheet format is used only when all capital shares have been issued under conditions which permit the company to determine objectively the fair value of the shares issued or of the consideration received — or, in certain cases, the cost of the consideration to the promoter. If such values cannot be determined, current practice (as well as Regulation S-X) requires that the 5A format be used and that the shares and the consideration received be expressed in number of shares instead of dollars.

The 5A format was developed by the SEC in 1948 to avoid problems relating to the valuation of undeveloped mining properties acquired for capital stock, but it is now used whenever an objective valuation cannot be made, regardless of the nature of the consideration involved. In fact, the 5A format is sometimes used when all capital shares have been, or can be, objectively valued. Although the staff of the SEC has indicated in informal discussions that it prefers the balance sheet format when all shares can be objectively valued, it has not yet made the use of that format mandatory under those conditions.

The choice of accounting practices from among the alternatives described below does not seem to affect the choice of format. For reasons which will be discussed later, however, there seems to be a tendency to use the 5A format when there is uncertainty as to the recoverability of deferred costs.

Information presented and basis of preparation. Audit reports of independent public accountants indicate the nature of the information which the financial statements present and the basis on which the information is presented. The balance sheet is, in almost all cases, described as presenting financial position in conformity with generally accepted accounting principles.[1] Conversely, 5A statements are rarely described as presenting financial position, but in about one-third of the reports studied they were said to be based on generally accepted accounting principles. They are usually described as presenting one of the following sets of information:

1. Assets and deferred costs, liabilities, and capital, in conformity with generally accepted accounting principles.
2. Assets and deferred costs (at cost), liabilities, and capital
3. Assets and deferred costs (no basis given), liabilities, and capital
4. Information required to be stated therein (no basis given).

Financial position and generally accepted accounting principles are mentioned *together* only when all capital shares issued have been valued. In many of the reports studied, however, generally accepted accounting principles were not mentioned, even though all capital

---

[1] "'Generally accepted accounting principles' are those principles which have substantial authoritative support." Action of Council of the American Institute of CPAs, as reported in Special Bulletin, "Disclosure of Departures From Opinions of the Accounting Principles Board," October 1964.

shares issued had been valued. In both formats, the statement of cash receipts and disbursements is described as presenting either the cash receipts and disbursements or the cash transactions; and, in some cases, the statement is said to be in conformity with generally accepted accounting principles.

GENERALLY ACCEPTED ACCOUNTING PRINCIPLES

Description of present practice. The principal differences in accounting practices among development-stage companies and between some such companies and operating companies have to do with the treatment of preoperating costs. For the purposes of this discussion the term "preoperating costs" is used narrowly, to refer to the costs of research and development of products or services, marketing research costs, start-up costs, general and administrative costs, and interest costs. It does not include organization or financing costs or the costs of property, plant, and equipment or of other assets, capital or intangible. The following comments deal only with the accounting for such preoperating costs and not with the broader question of accounting for research and development costs by operating companies.

Development-stage companies follow one of three alternative methods in accounting for preoperating costs:

1. *Full deferral.* Defer all preoperating costs which can reasonably be expected to be recoverable from future revenues. Amortize them against revenues after operations begin. Write off costs which cannot reasonably be expected to be recoverable. (Some accountants believe that development-stage companies should defer *all* costs, even those which may be, or are believed to be, unrecoverable. However, it is not clear from the prospectuses studied whether any of the companies involved actually followed this practice.)

2. *Partial write-off.* Defer only research and development costs, as in the full deferral method. Charge off other preoperating costs as incurred.

3. *Full write-off.* Charge off all preoperating costs as incurred.

Revenues, if any, are deducted from related preoperating costs. Thus, revenues are deferred under the first method but are offset against costs under the other methods. The full deferral method is used by the great majority of companies in the development stage, but the other two methods are used widely enough to constitute substantial authoritative support and thus to be in conformity with generally accepted accounting principles. Each of the three methods is used in both statement formats.

Research and development costs which have been deferred are usually amortized over the period in which the related product or service is expected to be sold — by some companies under the straight-line method, by others under the units-sold method, and by still others under whichever of the two methods results in the greater annual charge-off. In some cases, such costs are amortized over a very short period — e.g., the first year of operations. Deferred pre-operating costs other than research and development costs are usually amortized on a straight-line basis over two or three years, but periods as short as one year and as long as five have been used. Companies do not ordinarily disclose the factors considered in selecting an amortization policy. In any event, what is suitable for one company is not necessarily suitable for another.

Rationale for the alternative methods. No authoritative body has determined whether there are special or different generally accepted accounting principles for companies in the development stage; indeed, accounting literature has very little to say on this subject. The following are suggested as the theoretical justifications for the various accounting practices currently in use:

FULL DEFERRAL METHOD. The write-off of costs is *not* appropriate for a company in the development stage unless the costs cannot reasonably be expected to be recoverable. This position is supported by two principal arguments:

- *The matching concept.* The matching concept[2] which underlies generally accepted accounting principles, as described by the Accounting Principles Board, requires that costs which are identifiable with future revenues or future periods and which can reasonably be expected to be recoverable from future revenues be deferred and charged against such revenues or periods. Since a development-stage company has

---

[2]"Matching is one of the basic processes of income determination; essentially it is a process of determining relationships between costs (including reductions of costs) and (1) specific revenues or (2) specific accounting periods. Expenses of the current period consist of those costs which are identified with the revenues of the current period and those costs which are identified with the revenues of the current period and those costs which are identified with the current period on some basis other than revenue. Costs identifiable with future revenues or otherwise identifiable with future periods should be deferred to those future periods. When a cost cannot be related to future revenues or to future periods on some basis other than revenues, or it cannot reasonably be expected to be recovered from future revenues, it becomes, by necessity, an expense of the current period (or of a prior period)." APB Opinion No. 11, paragraph 14d. Although this definition is contained in the Opinion on income tax allocation, it is described as a "general concept or assumption."

no current revenues (or only insignificant revenues), all of its costs, if prudently incurred and reasonably expected to be recoverable, are necessarily identified with future revenues or future periods. As to recoverability, costs may reasonably be regarded as recoverable until the weight of evidence indicates that they are not. The fact that an independent auditor qualifies his opinion or disclaims an opinion because of uncertainty as to the recoverability of costs does not mean he believes that the costs are unrecoverable and therefore should be written off. Quite the opposite. If he really believes that the costs should be written off, he is required to give another kind of opinion altogether — a qualified or adverse opinion, on the grounds of a departure from generally accepted accounting principles. An opinion qualified or disclaimed because of uncertainty means that the auditor is not reasonably assured that the costs will be recovered but also is not reasonably assured that they will not be recovered. Costs should not be written off until the evidence indicates that management no longer can reasonably expect them to be recoverable. With respect to disposing of deferred preoperating costs, it is true that no amortization policy can produce a perfect matching. However, a better matching is achieved if costs which are reasonably expected to be recoverable are deferred and amortized than if such costs are charged off as incurred. Deferral achieves some degree of matching, whereas immediate write-off produces a total mismatch, the result of which is to report losses from so-called operations in a preoperating period and to correspondingly overstate net income in future operating periods.

• *Stage of development.* By definition, a company that is in the development stage has not begun operations, and thus cannot have either net income or net loss from operations. In the usual case, preoperating costs can be written off either to reflect operating income or loss or because they are unrecoverable. Since a development-stage company, by definition, cannot have either operating income or loss, costs should be written off only if they are believed to be unrecoverable. In the typical situation, deferral of costs is the only proper practice.

PARTIAL AND FULL WRITE-OFF METHODS. Supporters of these methods believe that development-stage companies should follow generally accepted accounting principles for operating companies. Accordingly, development-stage companies should in most cases write off marketing costs, start-up costs, interest, and general and administrative costs as incurred and may either defer research and development costs or write them off as incurred. Two main arguments are used to support these methods.

• *No accounting rules for so-called development-stage companies.* Some argue that there is no such thing as a "development stage" in the sense of a preoperating stage because there is no logical reason for distinguishing between the operating and preoperating stages. Operations begin as soon as a company incurs costs, because that is when it first conducts business with outsiders — not later, when the company first has substantial sales. Therefore, a so-called "development-stage company" is really an operating company and should comply with generally accepted accounting principles for operating companies.

• *The matching concept.* The matching concept permits the writing off of preoperating costs. It permits deferral of such costs only when they are identifiable with future revenues or future periods and can reasonably be expected to be recoverable from future revenues (see footnote 2). In most cases, general and administrative costs are not identifiable with the future. (If they are, why don't all companies have to defer them?) As to recoverability, experience shows that a high percentage of development projects, even those of seasoned companies, are unsuccessful, so that deferral of costs incurred on the typical, highly speculative projects of development-stage companies would violate the doctrine of conservatism.[3] Even if preoperating costs can be identified with the future and are considered to be recoverable, the amortization policy adopted is bound to be arbitrary to some extent because it is impossible to identify preoperating costs precisely with the future revenues or future periods to which they should be charged. As a result, proper matching can rarely be achieved. Thus, in almost all cases, lack of identification with the future, uncertainty as to recoverability and the futility of trying to achieve a proper matching indicate that preoperating costs should (or at least may) be written off as incurred.

Rationale behind amortization policies. In selecting an amortization policy, most companies seem to be influenced by one or more of several factors or attitudes, including the following:

1. The policy is bound to be arbitrary to some extent.

2. In most cases the deferred costs are of uncertain recoverability; therefore, the greater the uncertainty, the faster the write-off.

---

[3]"From the viewpoint of generally accepted accounting principles, the concept of conservatism comprehends the (idea) that: . . . All known liabilities or losses should be recorded regardless of whether the definite amounts are determinable." Paul Grady, *Inventory of Generally Accepted Accounting Principles for Business Enterprises*, Accounting Research Study No. 7 (New York: American Institute of CPAs, 1965), p. 36.

3. Rapid amortization results in higher net income later on; people expect losses in the early years.

4. Companies which elect to defer preoperating costs while in the development stage do so in order to achieve a proper matching. Some such companies believe that the amortization policy selected should be the one which comes closest to achieving this objective.

Companies that select a relatively short amortization period apparently are influenced by one or more of the first three considerations. Those that select a longer period seem to be guided more by the last consideration.

REPORTING BY INDEPENDENT AUDITORS

Figure 2, page 360, contains six examples of audit reports. The author's analysis follows. The reports are representative of those appearing in recent prospectuses and cover the usual situations encountered by auditors of companies in the development stage. The first three reports are on statements in the balance sheet format; the last three are on statements in the 5A format.

Description of current practice. An unqualified audit report on statements in the balance sheet format is shown in Example A. Such a report is relatively rare because there is usually some uncertainty as to the recoverability of deferred costs. When the recoverability of material deferred costs is uncertain, the auditor's opinion is qualified or disclaimed as in Examples B and C, respectively.

A typical audit report on 5A statements when, in the rare case, there is no material uncertainty as to the recoverability of assets and all capital shares issued have been valued is presented in Example D. When the recoverability of deferred costs is uncertain, which is usually the case, this fact may be mentioned in the audit report or in a note to 5A statements, but even when it is, it is extremely rare for the auditor to qualify his opinion or disclaim an opinion. A typical example is shown in Example E. When 5A statements include capital shares which have not been expressed in dollars, the audit report may disclose this fact, as in Example F.

Analysis. A study of these six audit reports discloses several interesting points, especially the way that auditors handle the following matters in reports on statements in the balance sheet format, as contrasted with reports on 5A statements:

Examples of Reports
on Statements in the Balance Sheet Format

Example A: Unqualified opinion

"We have examined the accompanying balance sheet of ABC Co. at December 31, 19—, and the related statement of cash receipts and disbursements for the period from _____ (date of inception) to December 31, 19—. Our examination was made in accordance with generally accepted auditing standards, and accordingly included such tests of the accounting records and such other auditing procedures as we considered necessary in the circumstances.

"In our opinion, the financial statements mentioned above present fairly the financial position of ABC Co. at December 31, 19—, in conformity with generally accepted accounting principles applied on a basis consistent with that of the preceding year, and the results of its cash transactions for the period from _____ to December 31, 19—."[1]

Example B: Qualified opinion
(Uncertain recoverability of deferred costs)

Scope paragraph as in Example A.
"As explained in Note X, the Company is in the development stage, and accordingly all of its costs are being deferred. Recovery of the deferred costs of $_____ is dependent upon achievement of a level of operations which would permit such recovery. The eventual outcome cannot be determined at this time.

"In our opinion, subject to such adjustment, if any, as may result from the outcome of the matter described in the preceding paragraph, the statements mentioned above present fairly. . . ."

Example C: Disclaimer of opinion
(Uncertain recoverability of deferred costs)[2]

Scope paragraph as in Example A.
"As explained in Note X, the Company is in the development stage, and accordingly all of its costs are being deferred. Recovery of the deferred costs of $_____ is dependent upon achievement of a level of operations which would permit such recovery. The eventual outcome cannot be determined at this time and we are accordingly unable to express an opinion on the financial position of ABC Co. at _____ .
It is our opinion, however, that the statement of cash

receipts and disbursements presents fairly the results of the cash transactions of ABC Co. for the period from _____ to December 31, 19—."

Examples of Reports
on Statements in the 5A Format

Example D: No uncertainty as to recoverability of deferred costs (All capital shares valued)

"We have examined the accompanying statements of assets and deferred preoperating costs, of liabilities and of capital of the XYZ Co. at December 31, 19—, and the related statement of cash receipts and disbursements for the period from _____ (date of inception) to December 31, 19—. Our examination. . . .

"In our opinion, the statements mentioned above present fairly the cost of assets and deferred costs,[3] the liabilities and capital of XYZ Co. at December 31, 19— (in conformity with generally accepted accounting principles)[4] and the results of its cash transactions[5] for the period from _____ to December 31, 19— (all on a basis consistent with that of the preceding year)."[4]

Example E: Uncertainty as to recoverability of deferred costs (All capital shares valued)

Scope paragraph as in Example D.
"(As explained in Note X, the Company is in the development stage, and accordingly all of its costs are being deferred. Recovery of deferred costs of $_____ is dependent upon achievement of a level of operations which would permit such recovery. The eventual outcome cannot be determined at this time.)[4]
Opinion paragraph as in Example D.

Example F: No uncertainty as to recoverability of deferred costs (Some capital shares not expressed in dollars)

Scope paragraph as in Example D.
"In the accompanying statements, assets acquired for capital shares and capital shares issued for services and property have been stated in number of shares rather than in dollars. This, in our opinion, represents an acceptable method of presenting the accounts of the Company at this time."
Opinion paragraph as in Example D, except that the word "capital" is replaced by "capital shares."

---

[1] In some reports the reference to consistency is omitted and in others it is applied to both statements. In some reports, the statement of cash receipts and disbursements is said to be in conformity with GAAP.
[2] It should be mentioned that a disclaimer of opinion is not acceptable to the SEC in a filing under the Securities Act of 1933.

[3] See discussion of "Statement format," pp. 40-41, regarding other information which the statement of assets and deferred preoperating costs is said to present.
[4] Parenthetical information is not always included.
[5] In some cases the statement of cash receipts and disbursements is said to be presented in conformity with generally accepted accounting principles.

Figure 2

1. Information which the statements present.
2. Basis on which the information was prepared.
3. Uncertainty as to the recoverability of deferred costs.

The apparent rationale behind these differences is discussed below.

Audit reports on statements in the balance sheet format contained expressions of opinion as to whether the balance sheet presented fairly the company's financial position in conformity with generally accepted accounting principles. In contrast, only one of the reports on 5A statements mentioned financial position and only about one-third mentioned generally accepted accounting principles. From this it seems clear that the great majority of auditors take the position that 5A statements do not purport to present financial position even when all shares issued are valued; and that 5A statements, therefore, do not have to be evaluated in terms of generally accepted accounting principles, but may be so evaluated. (Since the statements do not "purport to present financial position," the auditor does not have to comply with the first reporting standard, which would otherwise require him to state whether the statements are presented in conformity with generally accepted accounting principles.)[4] Stated another way, omission of an opinion as to conformity with generally accepted accounting principles is proper, they seem to say, because 5A statements do not purport to present financial position.

In reporting on statements in the balance sheet format, all of the independent auditors qualified or disclaimed their opinions when the recoverability of material amounts of deferred preoperating costs was uncertain. Conversely, in reporting on 5A statements, they rarely qualified or disclaimed, even when the recoverability of material amounts of deferred preoperating costs was clearly uncertain. Also, in many of these cases the apparent uncertainty was not disclosed in the audit report or the statements. What is the rationale behind this divergence in position? Generally accepted accounting principles (see footnote 2) require that a cost which cannot reasonably be expected to be recoverable from future revenues be treated as an expense of the current period (or of a prior period). Since a balance sheet is prepared on the basis of generally accepted accounting principles, and since generally accepted accounting principles imply recoverability, a material uncertainty as to recoverability requires that the auditor qualify his opinion or disclaim an opinion on a balance sheet.[5] On the other hand, some auditors appear to take the position that 5A statements need not be based on generally accepted accounting principles, and therefore the auditor does not have to qualify or disclaim because of such an uncertainty. He may remain silent as to generally accepted accounting principles and report that the statements present fairly the cost of assets and deferred costs or the other information discussed

---

[4]The first standard of reporting reads: "The report shall state whether the financial statements are presented in accordance with generally accepted principles of accounting." Statement on Auditing Procedure No. 33, page 40, paragraph, 1. However, page 88, paragraph 4, of this Statement provides: "The first standard of reporting does not apply to statements which do not purport to present financial position. . . ."

[5]Statement on Auditing Procedure No. 33, page 73, paragraphs 46 and 47.

above. Conversely, if there is no such uncertainty, the auditor can take the position that 5A statements are presented in conformity with generally accepted accounting principles and so report.

As to lack of disclosure of the uncertainty, the third reporting standard specifies that "informative disclosures in the financial statements are to be regarded as reasonably adequate unless otherwise stated in the [auditor's] report."[6] It is clear that this standard applies to all financial statements, even those that do not present financial position in conformity with generally accepted accounting principles. Thus, it seems that many auditors believe that a specific disclosure of such an uncertainty is not necessary in 5A statements. Possibly these auditors believe that the statement format itself, or the fact that the company is in the development stage, should give sufficient warning to the reader that deferred costs may not be recoverable.

TRANSITION PROBLEMS

When a company passes from the development stage to the operating stage it encounters several transition problems. Three of the most common of these problems are discussed below.

Determining when operations begin. If a company defers material preoperating costs which it would be required to charge off if it were operating, its financial statements are not fairly presented unless the company is truly in the development stage. How can management and the independent auditors make a determination of this condition?

The only authoritative body which has dealt with this question is the SEC. The SEC has stated that Form S-2, which may be used only by development-stage companies, may be used by companies which have not had, among other things, substantial gross returns from the sale of products or services or any substantial net income from any source for any fiscal year ended during the preceding five years.[7] The logical inference is that a company is operating if it exceeds these limits. The term "gross returns" is not defined, but it seems clear that it should be interpreted in practice to mean "gross earned revenues, computed in conformity with generally accepted accounting principles." Otherwise, a company could be considered to be operating when it has only unearned revenue (e.g., from the sale of franchises). During informal discussions, staff members of the SEC

---

[6]"The third and fourth reporting standards are applicable to special reports." Statement on Auditing Procedure No. 33, page 88, paragraph 3.

[7]Instructions to Form S-2, Securities and Exchange Commission.

have agreed with this interpretation. It also is reasonable to assume that the word "substantial" should be used in a relative sense — i.e., an amount which is substantial for a small company may not be so for a large company.

Beyond these guidelines it is difficult to generalize, and the answer to the question of when a company has begun operations is best left to management, subject to review by its independent auditors. Examples of some of the factors to be considered in answering this question are: the amount and trend of sales, sales backlog, the relationship of sales prices to related direct costs, the overall state of development of the company's production, marketing and administrative capabilities, and budgets and projections of future operating results.

Valuing capital shares. When assets other than cash or services are acquired by the issuance of capital shares, the transaction should be valued at the fair value of the consideration or of the shares, whichever is more clearly evident,[8] or in some cases at the cost of the consideration to the promoters. As previously mentioned, a company may issue capital shares under conditions which preclude an objective determination of the fair value of the shares or the consideration. In my own view, an objective valuation is one that is based on sufficient competent evidential matter and, as such, is not within the control of persons who are in control of the company before or immediately after the stock issue in question.

When the transaction cannot be objectively valued, the shares and consideration are expressed in number of shares issued instead of dollars. Since this procedure causes capital and assets to be understated, a balance sheet prepared on this basis would not present fairly the company's financial position in conformity with generally accepted accounting principles if the understatement were material. This is no problem for a company in the development stage — it simply uses the 5A format. It may become a problem, however, when operations begin and the company must submit a balance sheet and statement of operations. In many cases, the maximum probable amount of undervaluation — and, if applicable, amortization — is determinable and will not be material by the time the company begins operations. In such cases, the shares may remain unvalued (although this is not recommended) or they may be assigned a reasonable, albeit arbitrary, value without causing the financial statements not to be fairly presented. However, when the amount of undervaluation is or could be material, the shares must be assigned a value which is not materially

---

[8]Accounting Research Bulletin No. 48, paragraph 8.

different from the fair value at the date on which the shares were issued, or the financial statements will not be fairly presented. Companies, especially those which are publicly held, should anticipate this problem and take whatever action is necessary to enable them to obtain an objective valuation as of the date the shares were issued. Some examples of methods which have been used are described below.

When a significant number of capital shares is issued to promoters of the company in exchange for an asset, present practice usually requires that the shares be valued at an amount not in excess of the cost of the asset to the promoter. In determining cost, only actual expenditures are considered. In other cases, the following are among the valuation methods which may be used to objectively determine fair value:

1. Replacement cost of the consideration being valued (marketable securities, prepaid expenses, deposits, etc.).

2. Bona fide offers to purchase the consideration or the capital shares being valued, or to purchase identical or similar consideration or capital shares.

3. Actual sales of consideration or capital shares similar or identical to the consideration or capital shares being valued.

Appropriate adjustment should be made to the offer or sales price upon which the valuation will be based for the economic effects, if any, of differences in (1) the terms of the offer or sale and those of the transaction being valued, (2) attributes of the consideration or shares involved in the offer or sale and those of the consideration or shares being valued, and (3) the time lag between the date of the offer or sale and the date of the transaction being valued.

Other valuation methods have been used in practice (e.g., valuation by the board of directors) or have been discussed in accounting literature (e.g., appraisals and the present value of future income expected from the consideration), but it is questionable whether such methods are "objective" or would be acceptable.

Changes in accounting principles or methods. Companies in the development stage may elect to defer general and administrative costs and research and development costs. Such companies are usually required to charge off general and administrative expenses incurred after operations begin, but may elect to continue to defer research and development costs or write them off as incurred. This requirement and election raise two questions: (1) Does either change constitute a change in application of an accounting principle, thus requiring mention of a consistency change? (2) Is it a violation of generally accepted accounting principles to "double up" charges to operations by amortizing costs which were deferred in the development stage while also charging operations for the same type of cost in the period in which incurred? No authoritative body has issued a statement which specifically covers these two questions, and I have never seen an audit report which was qualified for either of these two reasons — but that, of course, is not conclusive.

The second standard of reporting requires that the audit report state whether accounting principles, practices, or methods of their application have been consistently observed during the current period in relation to the preceding period. This standard was adopted to ensure that, if comparability of financial statements is affected by changes in accounting principles, this fact is disclosed. A company that uses in a balance sheet (which purports to present financial position) accounting principles that differ from those used in special-purpose statements it has previously issued has changed its accounting principles. This change, however, reflects changed circumstances. Two sets of statements were prepared under different conditions and do not purport to present the same information. Therefore, the change is not in the consistency of application under static conditions, but in the accommodation of *different* conditions.

Thus, the answer to both of the questions raised above clearly appears to be "No" with respect to a company that has deferred the costs in 5A statements, assuming its 5A statements did not purport to present financial position. In fact, even if statements it issued while in the development stage purported to present financial position (as would be the case in balance sheet statements and might be the case in some 5A statements), the answer to both questions still seems to be "No" with respect to general and administrative costs. The change appears to meet the criteria of a type B change as described in Statement on Auditing Procedure No. 33, because it is required by changed conditions (the transition from the development stage to the operating stage) rather than resulting from a choice on the part of management.[9] As such, the change requires disclosure in a note to the financial statements but does not require a qualification in the auditor's report. Moreover, since it is a requirement of generally accepted accounting principles that such a company make the change, the resulting "doubling up" does not appear to be a violation of GAAP.

If the company has issued statements that purported to present financial position, the answer to the first question seems to be "Yes"

[9]Statement on Auditing Procedure No. 33, page 43.

with respect to research and development costs. The change appears to be a type A change as described in SAP No. 33 — that is, a change in accounting principles employed — because it involves a choice on the part of management, which could have elected to continue the deferral of research and development costs. As for the second question, since the change as to research and development costs is not required by generally accepted accounting principles, it appears that the change should be accounted for retroactively, thus avoiding a "doubling up," (The Accounting Principles Board has suggested this treatment in an exposure draft issued on February 16, 1970, entitled "Changes in Accounting Methods and Estimates.") Retroactive treatment has the same effect as if the company had used the full write-off method during its development stage. Since this method is generally accepted at present, retroactive treatment is not a violation of generally accepted accounting principles. However, if the full deferral method were required in the future, as recommended by the author, retroactive treatment would not be proper because it would have the effect of restating the accounts during the development period on an unacceptable basis. Under these conditions, the proper treatment would appear to be a write-off of these deferred costs in the first year of operations.

WEAKNESSES IN PRESENT PRACTICE AND RECOMMENDATIONS

Thus far we have concentrated on the description and analysis of present practice. In the following pages, I will describe what I believe to be weaknesses in present practice and make recommendations for improvement.

STATEMENT FORMAT

The balance sheet format is clearly more desirable than the 5A format because (1) it presents financial position, a concept widely understood by users of financial statements, (2) it is prepared on the basis of generally accepted accounting principles, (3) the auditor is required to express an opinion as to conformity with generally accepted accounting principles, and consequently must face the problem of recoverability, (4) the 5A format may be misleading, and (5) use of the 5A format may permit companies to "go public" which could not do so if they used the balance sheet format. Points 4 and 5 are discussed in the following two paragraphs.

Financial position has been defined[10] as "the assets and liabilities of an organization as displayed on a balance sheet, following customary practices in its preparation." The 5A statements differ from a balance sheet in only two, or occasionally three, respects:

1. They present the assets, liabilities, and capital in three or four statements instead of in two sections of one statement.

2. The "debit" section is usually described as presenting "assets and deferred charges" instead of "assets."

3. Some 5A statements express capital shares and related consideration in numbers of shares instead of dollars.

In my opinion these differences, particularly the first two, will go unnoticed by the average reader. He is used to seeing assets and liabilities presented in a balance sheet and will probably conclude that 5A statements, which contain almost all the same captions and other elements as a balance sheet, are essentially the same as a balance sheet. If he does so conclude, he will probably also believe that 5A statements present the same information as a balance sheet — namely, financial position. The three differences cited above are simply too subtle for any but a highly trained accountant to recognize, or at any rate to properly assess. Thus, when 5A statements actually do not present financial position — e.g., when assets do not equal the sum of liabilities and capital or when capital shares and related consideration are not expressed in dollars — the reader may be misled because, to him, they purport (i.e., seem or appear) to present financial position. He also may be misled if he is not informed that deferred costs are of uncertain recoverability, as is often the case when 5A statements are used.

It is typical of development-stage companies that there will be uncertainty as to the recoverability of deferred costs. If the uncertainty is so material that the independent auditor must disclaim an opinion on the balance sheet,[11] a registration statement under the Securities Act of 1933 will not be allowed to become effective. It is possible that a company facing this situation can merely change from a balance sheet to a 5A format and thereby avoid a disclaimer of opinion by the auditor and, in some cases, any disclosure of the uncertainty as well. Thus, a company may be in a position to attempt to sell securities

---

[10]Eric Kohler, *A Dictionary for Accountants*, Fourth Edition (Englewood Cliffs, N.J.: Prentice-Hall, 1970).

[11]"In some instances where the outcome of a matter is uncertain, the amount concerned may be so material that a qualified opinion is inappropriate. . . . In such cases [a disclaimer of opinion is required]." Statement on Auditing Procedure No. 33, page 73, paragraph 47.

to the public by simply replacing a balance sheet with separate statements which, for the reasons discussed in the preceding paragraph, readers may think is the same as a balance sheet. It is hard to believe that the use of the 5A format in such a case is in the public interest.

In view of the above considerations, it seems apparent that the balance sheet format should be required when all, or almost all, capital shares can be objectively valued. When a significant number of capital shares cannot be objectively valued, so that 5A statements are required, the statements should be prepared in conformity with generally accepted accounting principles and contain a note which will make it clear that (1) the statements are not intended to present financial position but do present the assets and deferred charges, liabilities, capital, and cash transactions of the company on that basis, (2) deferred costs are of uncertain recoverability, if that is the case, and (3) a significant number of capital shares which have been issued for assets or services have not been valued or reflected in the monetary amounts appearing in the statements.

GENERALLY ACCEPTED ACCOUNTING PRINCIPLES

I believe that the arguments in support of the full deferral method are sound and that those advanced for the partial and full write-off methods are largely fallacious.

I further believe that generally accepted accounting principles for companies in the development stage *should require* the deferral of all preoperating costs, with the sole exception of costs for specific projects which have been abandoned and which are clearly unrelated to other continuing projects. Present generally accepted accounting principles *permit* deferral of preoperating costs but require that the cost be recoverable if they are deferred. The generally accepted accounting principles which I recommend go beyond present practice in that they would require deferral of all costs except for those that are clearly not recoverable. An uncertainty as to the recoverability of deferred costs should be disclosed under both present and recommended generally accepted accounting principles.

The first argument in support of the two write-off methods is based on the assertion that generally accepted accounting principles for operating companies should be used by so-called "development-stage companies" because such companies are actually operating by virtue of the fact that they are incurring costs. To be sure, costs are one aspect of operations, but only a secondary aspect; the primary aspect is revenues. Costs are incurred in the hope of generating revenues and net income. A company could not "operate" long if it merely incurred costs and did not generate revenues. Thus, the essential element of "operations" is revenues, and a company is not really operating until it has significant revenues. This fundamental distinction between companies that have such revenues and those that do not should be reflected by different accounting principles for the two stages — and in fact this appears to be the case at present, since the vast majority of the companies in the development stage use the full deferral method.

The second argument in favor of the two write-off methods is based on (1) the alleged difficulty of identifying preoperating costs with the future in general and the admitted difficulty of identifying them with specific future revenues or periods and (2) the assertion that conservatism requires that pre-operating costs of uncertain recoverability be written off. The first part of this argument is fallacious, in my opinion, because all preoperating costs which are prudently incurred are necessarily identified with the future unless they are clearly unrecoverable. They are so identified because the benefits (sales and, hopefully, net income) for which the costs were incurred have yet to be realized. Identification with specific future revenues or periods is admittedly difficult, but no more so than for many other costs which are permitted to be deferred under generally accepted accounting principles — e.g., organization costs and goodwill. There is usually sufficient identification for a reasonable matching, but even if there is not, deferral achieves at least some degree of matching, whereas immediate write-off results in a complete mismatching. As to the second part of the argument, conservatism requires the write-off only when the loss is known, and an uncertainty as to recoverability is not a *known* loss. Indeed, how can a company take the position that its preoperating costs should be written off as unrecoverable when, as many are, it is attempting to raise additional capital to continue the selfsame development projects?

As for amortization policies, it seems clear that they should be designed to achieve the objective which was sought by deferring the preoperating costs — namely, as good a matching as is possible under the circumstances. Policies designed to "get the costs behind us" which do not meet this criterion should not be used.

REPORTING BY INDEPENDENT AUDITORS

Reports on statements in the balance sheet format appear to comply with generally accepted standards of reporting, but some reports on 5A statements may not. Reports which say that 5A statements "present fairly the information required to be stated therein" are certainly cryptic, to say the least, even if we are prepared to assume that readers know what information is "required." Such reports, as well as others which do not disclose the basis on which the statements were prepared, also appear to be a violation of Statement on Auditing Procedure No. 33 unless this information is clearly shown in the statements. This SAP says that "In reporting on statements which do not [purport to present financial position], the independent auditor should make sure that there is a clear representation of what they do present and of the basis on which they have been prepared. He should express his opinion as to whether or not the statements fairly present the data on the basis indicated."[12]

Considering today's investor-oriented environment, it is interesting to speculate on whether a typical investor would agree with the position that auditors do not need to express an opinion as to the conformity of 5A statements with generally accepted accounting principles because the *auditor* believes that the statements do not purport (i.e., seem or appear) to present financial position. For the reasons discussed above, the author believes that 5A statements probably do so purport[13] to practically everybody *except* the experienced auditor and analyst. In fact, when all issued shares are valued so that all assets, liabilities, and capital are shown, 5A statements not only purport to present financial position, they actually do present all of its elements.

It is interesting to note that the first audit report on 5A statements, developed by the subcommittee on mine accounting of the American Institute of Accountants (predecessor of the AICPA), did contain an expression of opinion as to the conformity of 5A statements with generally accepted accounting principles,[14] as did about one-third of the reports included in my own study of 1968 and 1969 prospectuses. If generally accepted accounting principles apply, the major question is obviously: What *are* generally accepted accounting principles for companies in the development stage? In the absence of any available source material for such an inquiry, a reader might conclude that the auditor should have qualified his opinion or disclaimed an opinion when a material uncertainty as to recoverability is present. If the statements or audit report did not even disclose such uncertainty, the auditor might be considered to be in violation of the third reporting

---

[12]Statement on Auditing Procedure No. 33, page 88, paragraph 4.
[13]"Purport" is defined as: "1. to profess or claim often falsely; 2. to convey to the mind as the meaning or thing intended; express or imply." *The Random House Dictionary of the English Language*, Unabridged Edition (New York: Random House, 1966).
[14]Journal of Accountancy, Feb.49, p. 140.

standard relating to adequacy of informative disclosures. In my own opinion it is unlikely that an investor would agree that such information is not material or that the uncertainty is obvious from either the use of the 5A format or the fact that the company is in the development stage. What is obvious to the experienced auditor should not be presumed to be obvious to the average prudent investor.

The generally accepted accounting principles which I recommend would require deferral of all preoperating costs unless they were clearly not recoverable, in which case they would have to be written off. Since even preoperating costs of uncertain recoverability would be required to be deferred under these recommended principles, the auditor would not qualify his opinion or disclaim an opinion because of such an uncertainty. (Present generally accepted accounting principles require a qualification or disclaimer for such an uncertainty, at least for companies not in the development stage.) However, the uncertainty should be disclosed to alert the reader to the fact that deferred costs may not be recoverable and also to the consequences of the fact that the company will have to change to different generally accepted accounting principles when it reaches the operating stage. One consequence of such a change is that the auditor may have to qualify his opinion or disclaim an opinion at some future date if the company continues to defer costs of uncertain recoverability after it reaches the operating stage. The reader should also be put on notice that special generally accepted accounting principles — those for companies in the development stage — have been followed in the preparation of the statements. This should be done by adding the phrase "for companies in the development stage (Note X)" following the phrase "generally accepted accounting principles" in the opinion paragraph of the auditor's report and by describing those principles in the note.

Figure 3, page 373, summarizes the consensus of present practice and describes the changes in reports of independent auditors which would be required in the future if my recommendations as to format, generally accepted accounting principles (GAAP), and reporting were adopted.

Summary

In light of the large number of development-stage companies presently issuing prospectuses and financial statements which are used in part by the general public to make investment decisions, it is essential that the problems of statement format, generally accepted accounting principles, and reporting practices be resolved promptly.

The American Institute of Certified Public Accountants has recently taken the first step toward solving the problems discussed above. It has formed an *ad hoc* committee to assist the Accounting Principles Board in the accounting problems, and a sub-committee of the committee on auditing procedure to tackle the auditing and reporting problems. In my view, these committees should take the following actions:

1. Develop guidelines as to when a company should be considered to be in the development stage.

2. Require the use of the balance sheet format when all, or almost all, capital shares have been or can be objectively valued.

3. Require that 5A statements be based on generally accepted accounting principles and that they disclose the following:
a. Information the statements present — i.e., assets and deferred charges, liabilities, capital, and cash transactions.
b. The fact that the statements are not intended to present financial position.
c. Any material uncertainty as to the recoverability of deferred charges.
d. The amount of any current and accumulated write-off of preoperating costs.

4. Provide guidance on how to objectively value capital shares issued for consideration other than cash.

5. Study the three alternative methods of accounting for preoperating costs and amortization policies and issue an Opinion to define generally accepted accounting principles in this area for companies in the development stage. As previously stated, I favor deferral of all costs except those which are clearly not recoverable, and amortization policies which are designed to achieve the best possible matching under the circumstances.

6. State that the first reporting standard applies to 5A statements. If it does apply, the auditor would be required to express an opinion as to conformity of the statements with generally accepted accounting principles for development-stage companies. Under present generally accepted accounting principles the auditor has to qualify his opinion or disclaim an opinion when a material uncertainty as to recoverability exists. Under the recommended generally accepted accounting principles, the uncertainty would have to be disclosed but a qualification or disclaimer would be inappropriate.

	Reports on balance sheet format		Reports on 5A format	
	Present practice	Future practice	Present practice	Future practice
Information which the statements are or will be described as presenting		Financial position and results of cash transactions (no change)	Various	Assets and deferred charges, liabilities, capital, and results of cash transactions
Basis on which the statements are or will be prepared	GAAP	GAAP for companies in the development stage	Various	GAAP for companies in the development stage
Applicability of the reporting standards:				
First: Expression of opinion as to compliance with GAAP		Required (no change)	Optional	Required
Second: Expression of opinion as to consistency of application of accounting principles		Required (no change)	Optional	Required
Third: Adequacy of informative disclosures		Required (no change)	Required(no change)	
Fourth: Expression of opinion as to fairness of presentation of statements, as a whole		Required (no change)	Required(no change)	
Disclosure of a material uncertainty as to recoverability of deferred costs		Required (no change)	Optional	Required
Effect on opinion when there is a material uncertainty as to recoverability of deferred costs	Qualification or disclaimer required	No effect; opinion will be unqualified, if otherwise appropriate	No effect unless statements are prepared in conformity with GAAP, in which case a qualification or disclaimer is required	No effect; opinion will be unqualified, if otherwise appropriate

**Present Practice vs. Future Practice
as Recommended in This Article**

Figure 3

Only the AICPA can implement the above recommendations. The SEC can help, but it can control only financial statements and audit reports which are filed under its jurisdiction. An independent public accountant — whether an individual or a firm — is simply not in a position to require that his clients use the format or accounting method which he prefers so long as the alternative format or accounting method which he considers undesirable has substantial authoritative support. Under these circumstances his only recourse is to refuse the engagement, knowing that other public accountants who honestly disagree with his views will approve the format or accounting method which he believes to be undesirable. The public accounting profession should act promptly to clarify accounting and reporting problems for companies in the development stage.

27. Audit Reports for Not-for-Profit Organizations*

Emerson O. Henke†

The content of the audit report for not-for-profit organizations has troubled the auditor for a number of years. One of the earlier official pronouncements regarding this matter is contained in the *Statement on Auditing Procedures, No. 28*, issued by the committee on Auditing Procedures of the American Institute of Certified Public Accountants in October 1957. A special report was issued in 1960 elaborating upon the application of Statement No. 28. In the special report the circumstances typically associated with financial statements of non-profit organizations were described as follows:

> If the statements are those of a non-profit organization, they may reflect accounting practices differing in some respects from those followed by business enterprises organized for profit. It is recognized that in many cases, generally accepted accounting principles applicable to non-profit organizations have not been as clearly defined as have those applicable to business enterprises organized for profit. In those areas where the auditor believes generally accepted accounting principles have been clearly defined, he may state his opinion as to the conformity of the financial statements either with generally accepted accounting principles, or (alternatively but less desirably) with accounting practices for non-profit organizations in the particular field, and in such circumstances he may refer to financial position and results of operations; in either event it is assumed that the auditor is satisfied that the application of such accounting principles and practices results in a fair presentation of financial position and results of operation or that he will state his exceptions thereto.[1]

The statement cited above was incorporated with only slight modifications into *Statements on Auditing Procedures, No. 33*. (See paragraph 8, Chapter 13) The following sentence has been added to clarify the position which should be taken by the auditor in those instances where he judges that generally accepted accounting principles have not been clearly defined.

---

*From *The Texas CPA* (April, 1972), pp. 20-24. Reprinted by permission of the Texas Society of Certified Public Accountants.

†Emerson O. Henke, DBA, CPA, is Dean of Hankamer School of Business, Baylor University.

[1]American Institute of Certified Public Accountants, *Special Reports — Application of Statement on Auditing Procedure No. 28*, 1960, pp. 41-42.

"In those areas where he believes generally accepted accounting principles have not been clearly defined, the provisions concerning special reports as discussed under cash basis and modified accrual basis statements are applicable.[2]"

If we refer to the pronouncements in *Statements on Auditing Procedures, No. 33* relating to cash basis and modified accrual basis statements, we find the following pertinent provisions:

In reporting on statements prepared on a cash basis, (or substantially so) which may appear to but do not present financial position and results of operations, disclosure should be made in the statements or their footnotes, or less preferably, in the independent auditor's report: (a) of the fact that the statements have been prepared on a basis of cash receipts and disbursements, and (b) of the general nature of any material items omitted; and where practical, of the net effects of such omissions on the statements.

Where the independent auditor thinks that misleading inferences may still be drawn from the statements, he should include an explanation in his report that the statements do not present financial position and results of operations.

In reporting on statements prepared on a modified accrual basis of accounting which purport to present financial condition and results of operations, the independent auditor may conclude that the resulting statements are materially incomplete or were prepared in accordance with accounting practices materially in apparent variance with those customarily followed in preparing accrual basis statements. In such cases, the nature and where practicable the amounts of the major variances should be disclosed and the independent auditor should qualify his opinion or express an adverse opinion.[3]

Referring now to another American Institute publication entitled *Audits of Voluntary Health and Welfare Organizations*, we find the following comments relating to bases of accounting.

The accrual basis is ordinarily necessary for fair presentation of financial position and operating results of voluntary health and welfare organizations. The independent auditor should carefully consider the propriety of expressing an unqualified opinion on financial statements prepared on the cash basis which purport to present financial position and results of operations in accordance with generally accepted accounting principles. Such an expression of opinion is appropriate only if the

---

[2]American Institute of Certified Public Accountants, *Auditing Standards and Procedures Statement on Auditing Procedure No. 33*, 1963, p. 90.
[3]Ibid., pp. 88-89.

financial statements do not differ materially from statements prepared on an accrual basis.

An additional basis of accounting known as the modified accrual basis has been in use by certain types of voluntary health and welfare organizations. Under this method, such items as receivables, inventories, and payables may be accounted for on an accrual basis while other items such as income from investments, insurance, rent, salaries, etc., may be accounted for on the cash basis. Financial statements prepared on this basis may not fairly present financial position and results of operations depending on the materiality of the items omitted.[4]

These quotations from official publications of the American Institute may well cause the critical thinker to raise certain questions regarding the appropriateness of the present position of the accounting profession with regard to the audit reports of not-for-profit organizations, generally.

A SEARCH FOR THE MEANING OF TERMS

An analysis of the statements included in the standard short-form audit report raises a question as to whether the auditor is misleading the users of the audit data when that report is used with the statements of many not-for-profit organizations. More specifically, we may inquire as to what the terms "fairly presents," "financial condition," and "results of operations" really mean to persons who analyze and interpret the published financial reports of not-for-profit organizations.

Reference to literature in the not-for-profit area discloses that municipalities, colleges and universities, hospitals, school districts, and health and welfare agencies all have developed statements of generally accepted accounting practices for economic enterprises operating within each of those respective areas. Some of these statements call for the use of the accrual basis of accounting. However, further analysis of the interpretations which these organizations give to that term discloses that they are really referring to what is more nearly a modified accrual basis than the true accrual basis as that basis is ordinarily understood. The one exception to this is the statement of accounting principles published by the American Hospital Association for the hospital area. That statement insists upon the use of the full accrual basis as normally interpreted. Colleges and universities describe their recommended basis of accounting as the modified accrual

---

[4]American Institute of Certified Public Accountants, *Audits of Voluntary Health and Welfare Organizations*, 1967, pp. 18-19.

basis. Thus, for all practical purposes, the auditor, within the provisions of presently accepted reporting practices, can use the standard short-form report in expressing an opinion on the financial statements of most of these organizations, even though the statements do not distinguish between capital and revenue expenditures, and, in other respects, do not adhere to the accrual basis of accounting as we normally interpret it in the profit area.

Words and phrases are used as communicating devices but they serve as effective communicating devices only when the reader interprets them to mean what the writer intended them to mean. This is the point at which some of the phrases used in the standard short-form report may be misleading when they are used in conjunction with the financial statements produced within the frame-work of generally accepted accounting practices of most of the segments of the not-for-profit area.

Let us begin by asking what the crucial terms "fairly presents," "financial condition," and "results of operations" would mean to the person who would typically be reading the published financial reports of not-for-profit organizations. The public and the governing boards of these organizations should be some of the more important users of these data. If we recognize the fact that accounting education is heavily oriented in the direction of profit enterprise accounting practices, we can logically conclude that those groups will be interpreting the data from a profit oriented accounting background. Few students develop any significant degree of familiarity with fund accounting techniques and fewer still are exposed to the statements of accounting principles followed by various segments of the not-for-profit area. Therefore, it appears that we may presume that the public and governing boards of not-for-profit organizations can have a reasonable knowledge of accounting without specific knowledge of the principles and procedures followed by the reporting not-for-profit organizations. If such is the case, would it not be logical to conclude that "fair presentation," to the average user of these statements, would mean that there had been an appropriate distinction between capital and revenue items and that the emphasis in making this distinction had been on the points of earning and consuming rather than upon the points of acquisition and disposal of resources? The overpowering orientation of our economic structure in the direction of profit motivation and profit oriented accounting suggests that such would be the case.

Let us now turn our attention to the second critical phrase in the standard short-form audit report. What may we conclude that the average reader of not-for-profit organization financial reports interprets the term "financial condition" to mean? Is it not again reasonable to conclude that most persons with a reasonable knowledge of accounting would interpret the term "financial condition" to mean a statement showing all resources and obligations of the entity valued on the basis of generally accepted accounting practices? For example, would they not expect the fixed assets of the enterprise to be included and valued at cost, less accumulated depreciation? If such is the case, they would often be misled in this conclusion because the accounting practices followed by many not-for-profit organizations permit the omission of significant fixed assets from the financial statements. Even where the fixed assets are included they generally are valued at original cost rather than original cost less accumulated depreciation.

"Results of operations" is another critical term in the audit report. It seems likely that the average reader with a reasonable knowledge of accounting practices would interpret this term to mean a statement showing accrual based revenues and expenses for the period. If so, this conclusion generally would be misleading because insofar as most not-for-profit organizations are concerned the so-called operating statement is actually a statement displaying the sources from which appropriable resources were acquired and the ways in which those resources were expended during the operating period.

Regardless of how careful the accounting profession may be in spelling out what it intends to say in rendering audit reports for not-for-profit organizations, it is difficult to conclude that these reports are not significantly misleading to many of the persons who read and interpret them. It seems that the accountants should critically evaluate the words and phrases which they use in the audit report by giving special consideration to what readers with reasonable accounting orientation will presume those terms to mean. Generally speaking, this suggests that, unless the financial statements are prepared by using a basis of accounting which is not significantly different from the full accrual basis, the accountant should not use the terms "fairly presents," "financial condition," and the "results of operations" without explanatory comments.

SUGGESTIONS FOR IMPROVEMENT

Quite obviously, one answer to the problem which we have discussed would be for the accounting profession to insist that not-for-profit organizations use the full accrual basis of accounting, including a distinction between capital and revenue expenditures and an appropriate provision for depreciation, before a completely unqualified audit report would be given. Up to this point, however, the public accounting profession has not really exercised the prerogative of being independently critical of the so-called generally accepted accounting practices developed within the various segments of the not-for-profit area. In the judgment of the author, the public accounting profession should specifically evaluate and appraise these statements of principles from the point of view of whether they provide for the fair presentation of the financial condition and the results of operation.

Another possibility would be to develop a special short-form audit report format which would describe more specifically the financial data that were being presented. In some instances, this would necessitate changing the statement of financial condition to a statement of appropriable resources and obligations against those resources. It would certainly call for changing the "statement of operating results" to a statement of revenues and expenditures with perhaps some explanation as to the meanings of those terms. As an example, Howard A. Withey has suggested that the following reporting format might be used for colleges and universities:

> We have examined the balance sheet of the ABC College as of ...., ... and the related statements of changes in funds for the year then ended. Our examination was made in accordance with generally accepted auditing standards, and accordingly included such tests of the accounting records and such other auditing procedures as we considered necessary in the circumstances.
>
> In our opinion, the accompanying balance sheet and statements of changes in funds present fairly the financial position of ABC College at ...., ... and its changes in the resources for the year then ended in conformity with generally accepted accounting principles appropriate for non-profit organizations reporting on a fund basis applied on a consistent basis.[5]

Mr. Withey also suggest that the auditor might include a statement such as:

> ABC College is a non-profit organization which follows the practice of reporting on the use of resources by specific fund groups. On the basis of these practices, certain fixed asset acquisitions have been charged as a use of unrestricted current funds and related assets added to the equity in plant facilities.[6]

---

[5]Howard A. Withey, "Financial Reporting for Non-profit Organizations," *Journal of Accounting* (December, 1967), p. 41.
[6]Ibid.

In examining the proposed audit report form, one still might question whether the use of the term "balance sheet," without explanatory comments, might be misleading. Nevertheless, a reporting format carefully developed along these lines for the various types of not-for-profit organizations could do much to prevent the auditor from misleading the users of financial statements of not-for-profit organizations.

Conclusion

It is the contention of this paper that the present provisions governing audit reports for not-for-profit organizations can allow the published financial statements of those organizations to be misleading to many reasonably informed persons using them. The author's preferred solution to this problem would require the financial statements to be presented on a full accrual basis. However, if the profession feels that it cannot insist upon use of the full accrual basis of accounting, it should at least make the statements less misleading by requiring auditors to use appropriately worded audit reports in expressing their opinions on them.

SECTION B

Auditor Oriented

As noted in an earlier section, recent court rulings have heightened the auditor's awareness of his responsibility in the client-auditor relationship during and after the audit period. Three items were selected to provide a sampling of auditor-related type problems.

The first article by Robert C. Holsen discusses some of the problems encountered in the development of Statement on Auditing Procedure No. 41, "Subsequent Discovery of Facts Existing at the Date of the Auditor's Report." In this statement the auditor is given something in the professional literature to serve as support in situations where he concludes that other considerations override the Code of Ethics and state laws regarding confidential client-auditor relations.

In the same vein, Joseph Bencivenga and D. R. Carmichael explain the reasoning involved in the development of SAP No. 42, "Reporting When a Certified Public Accountant is Not Independent." This statement concludes that only a disclaimer of opinion is appropriate when a lack of independence has been established.

In the closing article, Dennis S. Neier reviews and analyzes the provision of SAP No. 45, "Using the Work and Reports of Other Auditors." The objective of this SAP is to clarify the responsibilities of the principal and secondary auditor(s) thus resulting in better disclosure and reporting practices.

28. Case History in Development of "Subsequent Discovery" Statement* Robert C. Holsen†

". . . When our subcommittee began deliberations we believed that revised financial statements arising from subsequent discovery of facts would be extremely rare. In fact, we were unable to find any examples. But the extreme rarity may be a thing of the past as four or five companies have issued revised financial statements in the last couple of years.

Some of our early conclusions later turned out not to be as good as we first believed, so we shifted gears and started off in a new direction. Sometimes we found our way back to where we started and other times we found new answers which led to new questions. Through it all we kept consulting with the full committee in meetings and by correspondence. Each draft of the Statement — and seven were given to the full committee — evoked a letter from each member of the committee. And each letter was considered carefully in the writing of the next draft. . . .

We discussed the effect on the financial statements of the newly discovered information. Yet on reflection we realized that we should be concerned only with the effect this information would have on our reports and that is the pitch of the final Statement.

We used the term "newly discovered information" in a few of the drafts. But as we progressed, it seemed that the word "discovered" had the connotation of some work by the auditor so that he could discover or find the things we have in mind. This was something we did not mean so we went to the words "the auditor becomes aware of facts." This solved the one problem but raised others as to the source of the new information. Did we now mean graffiti on the wall in the men's room? Or idle gossip in a bar? We hoped not, but one of the most difficult problems we faced was limiting the information that the auditor should investigate. We tried any number of combinations of words and at last came to the idea that the auditor would investigate a new fact only if it is of such a nature and from such a source that he would have investigated it had it come to him during the course of

*From *The Journal of Accountancy* (February, 1970), pp. 70-71. Copyright (1970) by the American Institute of Certified Public Accountants, Inc. Reprinted by permission of the AICPA.
†Robert C. Holsen, CPA, is a partner in Ernst & Ernst in Cleveland, Ohio.

his examination. We felt that these words would effectively rule out any action on his part when the auditor read a message on the men's room wall. On the other hand, if during his usual examination, the auditor paid attention to such messages he would continue to do so for new facts so set out. But we think the language keeps the auditor from investigating every bit of trivia that he hears or sees.

Throughout our work we have been painfully aware of the existence of the Code of Professional Ethics and certain state laws regarding the confidentiality of auditor-client communications. However, some attorneys have advised us that the auditor's responsibility may override the Code and the state laws. Inasmuch as the laws of the states differ considerably, we obviously could not take a position that would be equally acceptable in each state. As a result we suggest that the auditor consult his attorney whenever he encounters the circumstances to which this Statement applies.

Much of what I have said related to matters we considered and discarded so I would like to devote just a few minutes to talk about what is in the Statement. The purpose of the Statement, and here I quote, "is to establish procedures to be followed by the auditor who, subsequent to the date of his report, becomes aware that facts may have existed at that date which might have affected his report had he then been aware of such facts." I have already mentioned that he may become aware of such facts, but the Statement bluntly says that the auditor, once he has issued his report, has no "obligation to make any further or continuing inquiry or perform any other auditing procedure with respect to the financial statements covered by that report unless new information which may affect his report comes to his attention" except for audited financial statements included in registration statements between the date of the auditor's report and the effective date.

Let's assume that some of this new information comes to the auditor's attention and that he wants to investigate it.

To make a proper investigation the co-operation of the client is a necessity so let's take the case of a co-operative client who assists in determining that the newly discovered information is both reliable and existed at the date of the auditor's report. The auditor must then decide (1) whether his report would have been affected if the information had been known to him prior to the date of his report and had not been reflected in the financial statements and (2) whether he believes there are persons currently relying or likely to rely on the financial statements who would attach importance to the information. If he decides the answers to both (1) and (2) are in the affirmative, the Statement says "he should advise his client to make appropriate disclosure of the newly discovered facts and their impact on the financial statements." If the client is still co-operating, he can meet the disclosure requirements by issuing revised financial statements with a new auditor's report and the matter, hopefully, will be ended.

But what if the client agrees with everything but refuses to make disclosure? The Statement discusses this situation and concludes that unless the auditor's attorney recommends a different course of action, the auditor should, to the extent applicable, notify the client, any regulatory agencies having jurisdiction over the client, and each person known to the auditor to be relying on the financial statements that his report should no longer be associated with the financial statements nor be relied upon. In the larger companies notification to the persons relying on the financial statements becomes impracticable because the auditor rarely knows the names of shareholders or investors at large. Here notification to the regulatory agency having jurisdiction over the client may be the only way the auditor can provide for appropriate disclosure.

The Statement also sets out some procedures for the auditor to follow in the horrible situation where the client refuses to help in investigating the information or to make any kind of disclosure, and closes with the idea that while the Statement is written as though it applies solely to corporations, its concepts apply in all cases where financial statements have been examined and reported on by independent auditors.

One of the important aspects of the Statement is that it gives the auditor something in the professional literature to support him in those situations when the auditor concludes, after a consultation with counsel, that other considerations override the Code of Professional Ethics and state laws regarding confidential relations between auditor and client. . . .

29. Reporting on Lack of Independence*

Joseph Bencivenga and
D. R. Carmichael†

Generally accepted auditing standards are benchmarks for judging the quality of an auditor's performance. The personal or general standards require that the profession's services be undertaken with professional competence by properly trained persons. They concern the qualifications of the auditor and the quality of his work. In other words, they govern both field work and reporting.

INFLUENCE OF INDEPENDENCE STANDARD ON OPINION

The second general standard states:

"In all matters relating to the assignment an independence in mental attitude is to be maintained by the auditor or auditors."

The independence standard has generally been considered the hallmark of the profession. It is the auditor's independence which makes his opinion valuable to third parties.

If the auditor is not independent he cannot perform an audit in accordance with generally accepted auditing standards. The auditor's inability is unequivocal, for the auditing standards are not mutually exclusive. Further, the nature of the general standards is such that they permeate the standards of field work and reporting. It follows that when the auditor is not independent, no aspect of his examination can be in accordance with generally accepted auditing standards. Under these circumstances, the auditor is precluded from expressing an opinion on financial statements. However, to comply with the fourth reporting standard the auditor must issue a report and, when he lacks independence, that report must be a disclaimer.

In these circumstances, a disclaimer is, essentially, a denial of an opinion. The message such a disclaimer should carry to the reader of the financial statements is that the auditor is not assuming any responsibility for the statements and that the auditor's association with the statements should not add any credibility to them. However,

*From *The Journal of Accountancy* (March, 1970), pp. 68-71. Copyright (1970) by the American Institute of Certified Public Accountants, Inc. Reprinted by permission of the AICPA.

†Joseph Bencivenga, CPA, is the National Director of Quality Control for Harris Kerr, Forster & Company. D. R. Carmichael, Ph.D., CPA, is Assistant Director, Auditing & Reporting, American Institute of Certified Public Accountants.

there is an implication that the auditor is unaware of any deficiencies in the statements.

The message intended by the report should be the guiding factor in determining appropriate report language. To achieve that goal, when the auditor lacks independence, the report must not add any credibility to financial statements. With the issuance of Statement on Auditing Procedure No. 42, "Reporting When a Certified Public Accountant Is Not Independent," the official position concerning the reporting requirements applicable when a CPA lacks independence moves closer to meeting this objective. This article explains the major points of change and the reasons for the adoption of the new position.

PREVIOUS OFFICIAL POSITION

Opinion No. 15 of the committee on professional ethics, which was issued with the concurrence of the committee on auditing procedure in 1964, suggested the following disclaimer of opinion when the auditor lacks independence.

"Inasmuch as we have a direct financial interest in XYZ Company [or for other reason] and therefore are not considered independent, our examination of the accompanying financial statements was not conducted in accordance with generally accepted auditing standards. Accordingly, we are not in a position to and do not express an opinion on these financial statements."

This suggested disclaimer fell short of the goal of not adding credibility to the financial statements in a number of respects.

The first question that might be asked is: "Of what use is this opinion?" If someone is not independent, the best opinion he can give is a disclaimer which says, in effect, that the opinion should not be relied upon. The role of the attest function in our society is, succinctly, to add credibility to financial statements. If the auditor cannot fulfill this function, why should he accept an engagement? Should he be barred from accepting such engagements? There are at least two good reasons for not prohibiting this type of engagement.

First, the lack of independence may occur after the engagement is well under way and prohibition of an unforeseen impairment of independence would invoke a severe hardship on both the auditor and his client. One possible circumstance of this type could result if a close relative of the auditor, without his knowledge, acquires a significant financial interest in the client. If he learns of this financial interest before issuing his opinion, the auditor might conclude that others would question his independence. Since he could not have foreseen the impairment of independence, the requirement of issuing a disclaimer in such circumstances seems burdensome enough.

The second situation involves a foreseeable impairment of independence, but with the consequences of prohibition of association being more onerous than the issuance of a disclaimer. A CPA practicing in a town of less than average size in an area rather isolated geographically may be the only qualified accountant available to many of the business enterprises in the area. For these businesses, the choice may be between receiving a disclaimer because of lack of independence or not receiving any accounting services at all. A business enterprise in this situation should not be deprived of qualified accounting service.

Once the basic existence of the disclaimer for lack of independence is accepted, attention can focus on the limitations in the report recommended in Opinion No. 15. The following questions were considered in the development of SAP No. 42.

1. Should the reason for lack of independence appear in the report?

2. Should the language describing the work of the auditor imply that any type of examination was performed?

3. Should each page of the financial statements carry some type of warning to the reader in the manner that unaudited statements are marked?

4. If the auditor is not independent and, in addition, the scope of his examination has been severely limited, what type of report should be issued?

DESCRIPTION OF REASON

Obviously, the disclaimer must specifically state that the auditor lacks independence. However, stating the reason for lack of independence allows the report reader to impute credibility to the report. If the auditor adjudged himself to be not independent, care must be taken to avoid allowing the report reader to dismiss that lack of independence as unimportant. If the reason for lack of independence is explained in the report, there is an increased chance that the reader may judge, without any appropriate basis for doing so, that the matter is a mere technicality. Whether or not the auditor is independent is something he must decide and the reader should not be given any basis for making another judgment on his own. For this reason, the report should state flatly and simply that the auditor is not independent with no additional explanation.

REFERENCE TO EXAMINATION

The reference to the auditor's work in the disclaimer recommended in Opinion No. 15 clearly implies that some type of examination has been made. The wording is:

". . . our examination of the accompanying financial statements was not conducted in accordance with generally accepted auditing standards."

This report language is undesirable because the nature of the examination performed is not at all clear. A possible alternative wording is:

"We have not examined the accompanying financial statements in accordance with generally accepted auditing standards."

However, this language is ambiguous as to whether or not any type of examination was performed. A reader might conclude either that no examination was made at all, or that an examination was made, but not one in accordance with applicable standards. Report language should be clear and definite and not offer a reasonable possibility of misunderstanding.

The committee on auditing procedure concluded that if the CPA is not independent he cannot perform an audit. Another way of expressing this position is that a CPA in public practice has only one set of standards governing his work as an auditor — generally accepted auditing standards. He cannot follow some other group of standards when he functions as a CPA in public practice. Therefore, for a CPA offering his services to the public, an audit not in accordance with generally accepted auditing standards is not an audit. Lack of independence negates compliance with all other auditing standards. This interpretation does not seem to be an undue appropriation of the term "auditing." Certainly, an internal auditor can use evidence gathering methods similar to those used by a CPA and the internal auditor is then "auditing." However, the CPA, as a professional offering the attest function as a service to the public, cannot forsake generally accepted auditing standards and choose to follow other undefined standards. If the CPA is not independent, every evidence gathering procedure he applies and every judgment he makes is tainted by his lack of independence. Under these circumstances the financial statements are for all practical purposes unaudited and the disclaimer of opinion should not imply otherwise. Only such a report meets the objective of not adding any credibility to the financial statements. Of course, if the CPA concludes on the basis of facts known to him that the statements are not fairly presented, he should either insist on appropriate revision, set forth his reservations in his disclaimer, or refuse to be associated with the statements.

WARNING ON STATEMENTS

Another improvement which was made in reporting practice when the auditor lacks independence is a requirement to mark each page of the financial statements with a warning to the reader. Some CPA firms follow the practice of including a reference to the auditor's opinion on each page of the financial statements whenever an unqualified opinion cannot be expressed. However, this practice, although desirable, is not a reporting requirement. On the other hand, some auditors' reports so critically affect the reliability of the statements that a warning should be placed on the statements. Whether or not reliability is critically affected is a matter of judgment, but the profession has decided that certain types of disclaimers are always critical and always require a warning on the statements. Statement on Auditing Procedure No. 38, "Unaudited Financial Statements," requires that unaudited financial statements be clearly and conspicuously marked as unaudited. A disclaimer caused by lack of independence is also critical enough to require a warning on each page of the statements.

The warning could quite simply refer the reader to the disclaimer of opinion by a reference such as "see accompanying disclaimer of opinion." The reader may, however, attach a certain degree of importance to the statement because of the absence of the warning "unaudited."

As mentioned previously, the CPA's objective in attesting to financial statements is to add credibility to the statements. If the objective is unattainable because his lack of independence critically affects the value of any opinion, then the statements are unaudited and the CPA should label them as such.

This position has drawn criticism from some members of the profession. They argue that a nonindependent CPA can confirm and reconcile cash, observe the taking of inventories, review tax accruals and perform auditing procedures just as reliably as an independent CPA. They concede that the reader should not derive any benefit from the performance of the above procedures because traditionally the CPA's role has been to serve the public first and foremost, which necessitates independence. Therefore, the accountant's disclaimer, according to them, should simply state his lack of independence and disclaim for the reason that an examination has not been performed in accordance with generally accepted auditing standards.

Other CPAs feel that when a non-independent CPA is associated with financial statements the situation is equivalent to, or perhaps worse than, the situation where the statements are unaudited. They believe this because the lack of independence takes the statements and the auditor's work out of the frame of reference which users traditionally apply and puts it into a category somewhat on the same level as financial statements which are prepared by a company's own accountant. In addition, not only can the non-independent auditor not perform an audit, but his disclosure of information pursuant to his discovery of lack of adherence to generally accepted accounting principles cannot be relied upon because he is not an independent observer.

The committee on auditing procedure favored the latter position. If the CPA is not independent, the statements are unaudited because the only type of audit a CPA in public practice can perform is an audit in accordance with generally accepted auditing standards. Consistent with this position, each page of the financial statements should be clearly marked "Unaudited — see accompanying disclaimer of opinion." Language which is ambiguous as to whether or not an examination was performed, such as "we have not examined the accompanying financial statements in accordance with generally accepted auditing standards," should be avoided in the disclaimer.

One thorny problem which may arise when the CPA lacks independence and should issue the recommended disclaimer occurs when the auditing procedures employed by the CPA constitute significantly less than a full scope audit.

THE DUAL BASIS DISCLAIMER

If the CPA has performed a limited examination and SAP No. 38 on unaudited financial statements applies, how should his disclaimer be affected by the additional complication of lack of independence? Either situation alone would be sufficient to regard the financial statements as unaudited. Which disclaimer should be used?

Chapter 10, paragraph 16 of SAP No. 33 requires that "whenever the independent auditor disclaims an opinion, he should give *all* the substantive reasons for doing so." When the scope of the examination is severely limited and the CPA also lacks independence his disclaimer should convey that information. However, if this disclaimer were to differ from the type applicable when only independence is lacking there would be an obvious danger. Three situations, all of which would lead to a disclaimer of opinion intended to avoid adding any credibility to the financial statements, would be reported upon differently. These situations are:

1. The auditor lacks independence.

2. The scope of the examination is severely limited.

3. The auditor lacks independence and the scope of the examination is severely limited.

If each situation leads to a differently worded disclaimer, report readers could distinguish the different situations and impute differing degrees of credibility to the associated financial statements, when none of the disclaimers should add any creditiblity to the statements.

Perhaps an auditor who lacks independence and who has not performed a full scope audit should seriously consider disassociating himself from the financial statements. An independent auditor even though he does not perform a full scope audit may perform an important service by objectively reviewing the financial statements and accounting records. On the other hand, an auditor who lacks independence may still provide important accounting services by acting effectively as controller for a company that would otherwise go without any accounting services. However, an auditor that fulfills neither function may be doing a disservice to his client, the public, and his profession. If the auditor in such a position chooses to remain associated with the statements, the best alternative would seem to be a requirement that he clearly state the substantive reasons for his disclaimer.

THE PRECEDENCE ISSUE

However, in recognition of the inherent danger of unwarranted imputation of credibility to financial statements that are essentially unaudited, a decision was made to forestall undue reliance in one or more of the three possible situations. The required decision was: Which factor — lack of independence or severe scope restrictions — should take precedence? If the scope limitations take precedence, in any situation in which the statements are unaudited, whether or not the CPA is independent, the type of disclaimer recommended in SAP

No. 38 would be issued. On the other hand, if lack of independence is deemed to take precedence, the type of disclaimer recommended in SAP No. 38 would be issued only when the auditor is independent and has not performed significant auditing procedures. The committee concluded that the type of disclaimer appropriate in any situation in which the auditor lacks independence, regardless of the extent of procedures performed, should not add any more credibility to the financial statements than the type of disclaimer recommended in SAP No. 38. Therefore, the following disclaimer is recommended for any lack of independence situation, because this is the only type of disclaimer which clearly and unequivocally will not add any undue credibility to financial statements.

"We are not independent with respect to XYZ Company, and the accompanying balance sheet as of December 31, 19-- and the related statement(s) of income and retained earnings for the year then ended were not audited by us; accordingly, we do not express an opinion on them."

Since neither a disclaimer for lack of independence nor a disclaimer for insignificant auditing procedures should add any credibility to financial statements, lack of independence should be given precedence. For only in such circumstances will the recommended disclaimers achieve the objective of not adding credibility to financial statements and not allowing unwarranted imputation of differing degrees of credibility to differently worded disclaimers.

SUMMARY

The four questions raised for consideration in the development of SAP No. 42 were resolved as follows:

1. The disclaimer must specifically state that the CPA is not independent, but the reason for lack of independence should not be disclosed.

2. The language of the disclaimer should not imply that any type of examination was performed and the financial statements should be described as unaudited.

3. Each page of the financial statements should carry the warning "Unaudited — see accompanying disclaimer of opinion."

4. If the auditor is not independent and, in addition, the scope of his examination has been severely limited, lack of independence takes precedence and the disclaimer recommended in SAP No. 42 should be issued.

30. Using the Work and Reports of Other Auditors*

Dennis S. Neier†

In July 1971, the Committee on Auditing Procedure of the American Institute of Certified Public Accountants issued Statement on Auditing Procedure (SAP) No. 45: "Using the Work and Reports of Other Auditors." This SAP establishes guidelines for reporting on financial statements when the independent auditor (referred to herein as the principal auditor) utilizes the work and reports of other auditors who have examined the financial statements of one or more subsidiaries, divisions, branches or other components included in the financial statements on which the principal auditor is reporting.

This article reviews and analyzes the provisions of SAP No. 45. It points out their implications and compares the new provisions with those set forth in Paragraphs 32 to 36 of Chapter 10 of SAP No. 33, the paragraphs which are superseded by the new Statement. It also discusses the reporting requirements set forth in SAP No. 45.

Because of the complexity of the subject and the limitation of space no attempt has here been made to cover all aspects of the new provisions; and, because the kinds of arrangements that can be made between the principal auditor and other auditors are almost endless, and since the circumstances in each case will be different, no attempt has been made to cover all the possible variations and questions that might arise. Since the concerned auditor should fully understand and comply with its provisions, it is worth emphasizing the importance of actually reading and working with the new SAP itself. What the principal auditor should do in a particular situation and what he should say in his report is a matter of professional judgment but should be based on the guidelines contained in this SAP as they apply to the circumstances in his particular case. Some embarrassments have resulted from laxity in "other auditor" services and the Statement is directed to their future avoidance.

PRINCIPAL AUDITOR'S COURSE OF ACTION

It is not unusual for a public accountant, as the principal auditor, to report on financial statements where part of the examination has

*From *The New York Certified Public Accountant* (October, 1971), pp. 721-725. Reprinted by permission of the New York State Society of Certified Public Accountants.
†Dennis S. Neier, CPA, is a manager with Oppenheim Appel Dixon & Company.

been made by other public accountants. The principal auditor may have performed all but a minor portion of the work, or significant parts of the examination may have been performed by other auditors. This form of collaboration between two or more public accountants for the purpose of reporting on one set of financial statements gives rise to several courses of action available to the principal auditor.

He must first decide whether his own participation is sufficient to enable him appropriately to serve as the principal auditor and to report as such on the financial statements taken as a whole. Among other things, this decision should be based on the materiality of the portion of the financial statements he has examined in comparison with that examined by other auditors, the extent of the knowledge he has of the overall financial statements and the importance of the components examined by him in relation to the enterprise as a whole.

Once he decides, based on the above considerations, that it is appropriate for him to serve as the principal auditor, he has to decide whether or not he will make reference in his report to the examination made by the other auditor or auditors. The guidelines upon which this decision should be made, and the effect that such reference or lack thereof would have on the responsibility assumed by the principal auditor are discussed later in this article.

RECOMMENDED PROCEDURES

Before the principal auditor utilizes the report of another independent auditor, regardless of whether or not he has decided to make reference to the examination of the other auditors, he should carry out certain procedures. He should make inquiries concerning the independence and professional reputation and standing of the other auditor. In this respect he could make inquiries of professional societies, other practitioners, bankers and credit grantors. He could obtain written representation from the other auditor that he is independent as defined by the American Institute of CPAs, and if appropriate, as defined by the Securities and Exchange Commission.

The principal auditor should take whatever action he deems essential to ascertain that the coordination of his activities with those of the other auditor is sufficient to permit a proper review of the matters affecting consolidation of the financial statements or combining of accounts in the financial statements. In this respect he could ascertain through communication with the other auditor:

That he is aware that the financial statements of the component which he is to examine are to be included in the financial statements on which the principal auditor will report and that the other auditor's report thereon will be relied upon (and, where applicable, referred to) by the principal auditor.

That he is familiar with accounting principles generally accepted in the United States and with the generally accepted auditing standards promulgated by the American Institute of Certified Public Accountants, and will conduct his examination and will report in accordance therewith.

That he has knowledge of the relevant financial reporting requirements for statements and schedules to be filed with regulatory agencies such as the Securities and Exchange Comission, if appropriate.

That a review will be made of matters affecting elimination of intercompany transactions and accounts and, if appropriate in the circumstances, the uniformity of accounting practices among the components included in the financial statements.

In addition to satisfying himself as to the matters described above (and especially when the principal auditor assumes responsibility for the examination of the other auditor to the same extent as though he had performed the work himself, as discussed later), the principal auditor may want to undertake measures to satisfy himself that the scope of the other accountant's examination was adequate. Some of the measures are as follows:

Visit the other auditor and discuss the audit procedures followed and the results thereof.

Review the audit programs of the other auditor. In some cases it may be appropriate to issue instructions to the other auditor as to the scope of his audit work.

Review working papers of the other auditor, including his evaluation of internal control and his conclusions as to other significant aspects of the engagement.

Participate in discussions with management personnel of the component whose financial statements are being examined by the other auditor regarding any significant or contentious aspects of the audit or financial statements.

Make supplemental tests of a portion or all of the accounts examined by the other auditor.

THE ASSUMPTION OF TOTAL ATTESTATION RESPONSIBILITY

If the principal auditor is satisfied, based on the procedures discussed above, as to the independence, professional reputation, and adequacy of the other auditor's examination he may be willing to assume the responsibility for the examination of the other auditor to the same extent as though he had performed the work himself. When he so decides, he *should not* make reference to the other independent auditor in his report. In this respect, SAP No. 45 is stronger and more definite than was SAP No. 33. Paragraph 36 of Chapter 10 of SAP No. 33 states that when the principal auditor is willing to assume the responsibility for the examination of the other auditor to the same extent as though he had performed the work himself, the principal auditor "need make no reference to the other independent auditor in . . . his report. If reference is made, he should state that he is assuming the responsibility for such work." SAP No. 45 holds that such reference, when the principal auditor is assuming full responsibility, may cause a reader to misinterpret the degree of responsibility being assumed, and should not be made.

THE ASSUMPTION OF LIMITED ATTESTATION RESPONSIBILITY

In many cases the principal auditor is unwilling to assume responsibility for the performance of the other auditor's work (to the same extent as though he had performed that work himself) but is willing to utilize the report of the other independent auditor for the purpose of expressing his opinion on consolidated or combined statements. In such cases the principal auditor may utilize other reports, and may appropriately express an unqualified opinion on the fairness of the consolidated or combined financial statements without assuming responsibility for the report or work of the other independent auditor, provided the basis for his opinion is adequately described. The principal auditor should indicate clearly in *both* the scope and opinion paragraphs of his report the division of responsibility between that portion of the financial statements covered by his own examination and that covered by the examination of the other auditor.

Here again, SAP No. 45 is stronger than the superseded paragraphs of SAP No. 33 which required disclosure in the scope *or* opinion paragraphs of the principal auditor's report as to the division of responsibility.

In making reference in his report to the work performed by the other auditor, the principal auditor may name the other auditor, but only with his express permission and provided that the report of the other auditor is presented together with that of the principal auditor.

DISCLOSURE OF MAGNITUDE OF EXTERNAL SERVICE

When the principal auditor decides that he will make reference to the examination of another auditor, he is required to disclose, in his report, the magnitude of the portion of the financial statements examined by the other auditor by stating the dollar amounts or percentages of the appropriate criteria that most clearly reveal the extent of participation by the other auditor. This requirement was found nowhere in Chapter 10 of SAP No. 33.

An example of appropriate reporting by the principal auditor indicating the division of responsibility when he makes reference to the examination of the auditor follows:

We have examined the consolidated balance sheet of X Company and subsidiaries as of December 31, 197-- and the related consolidated statements of income and retained earnings and of changes in financial position for the year then ended. Our examination was made in accordance with generally accepted auditing standards and accordingly included such tests of the accounting records and such other auditing procedures as we considered necessary in the circumstances. We did not examine the financial statements of B Company, a consolidated subsidiary, which statements reflect total assets and revenues constituting 20% and 22%, respectively, of the related consolidated totals. These statements were examined by other auditors whose report thereon has been furnished to us and our opinion expressed herein, insofar as it relates to the amounts included for B Company, is based solely upon the report of the other auditors.

In our opinion, based upon our examination and the report of other auditors, the accompanying consolidated balance sheet and consolidated statements of income and retained earnings and of changes in financial position present fairly. . . .

When two or more auditors in addition to the principal auditor participate in the examination, the percentages covered by the others may be stated in the aggregate.

The mention of work performed by other auditors in the report of the principal auditor, under the guidelines established in SAP No. 45, is only a factual explanation of the manner in which the examination was performed and an indication of the divided responsibility between the auditors and should not be considered a qualification of the opinion.

Inability to utilize the work or report of the other auditor. A situation might arise in which the principal auditor concludes, based on the results of the inquiries and procedures outlined above, that he can neither assume responsibility for the work of the other auditor insofar as that work relates to the principal auditor's expression of an opinion on the financial statements taken as a whole, nor report in the manner set forth under "The Assumption of Limited Attestation Responsibility" above. In such situations, he should appropriately qualify or disclaim an opinion on the financial statements taken as a whole stating his reasons and the magnitude of the portion of the financial statements to which his qualification extends. Superseded paragraph 35 of Chapter 10 of SAP No. 33, which dealt with this situation, recommended the use of "except for" when the intention was to qualify the opinion. This recommendation is not repeated in SAP No. 45 as it was realized that situations of this kind could exist where a "subject to" qualification might also be appropriate.

AUDITORS' RESPONSIBILITIES

Whether or not the principal auditor makes reference in his report to the examination made by the other auditors, the other auditors remain responsible for the performance of their examinations and for their own opinions.

In order to avoid confusion, this point warrants some discussion. One might wonder if it contradicts the idea expressed earlier that the principal auditor *can* assume responsibility for the report and work of other auditors. These two points, in my opinion, are not contradictory but are rather complementary, one really clarifying the other. Where the principal auditor assumes responsibility for the report and work of the other auditor, he does so only insofar as the other auditor's report and work affects the consolidated or combined financial statements taken as a whole. The other auditor remains responsible for the performance of his own examination and for his own opinion when the financial statements (or the part of the financial statements) upon which he is reporting are considered individually.

The principal auditor who utilizes the work and report of another auditor for the purpose of expressing his opinion on consolidated or combined statements, and assumes responsibility for the performance of the work and for the opinion of the other auditor to the same extent as though he had performed that work himself, is solely responsible to third parties who rely on the opinion of the principal auditor with respect to the consolidated or combined financial statements. The other auditors are solely responsible to third parties (including the principal auditor) who rely on the opinion expressed by them as to the individual financial statements (or part thereof) examined by them.

OTHER ASPECTS

Qualifications in the report of the other auditor. If the report of the other auditor is qualified, an additional burden is placed on the principal auditor. He must decide whether the subject of the qualification is material in relation to the consolidated statements taken as a whole. If the subject of the qualification is material, a qualification in the report of the principal auditor would be required *whether or not* the report of the other auditor is presented.

It is interesting to note the terminology used in paragraph 14 of SAP No. 45 when stating the reporting requirements of the principal auditor with respect to referencing a qualification, contained in the report of the other auditor, which is not considered material in relation to the consolidated financial statements taken as a whole. There is an ever-so-slight difference in the terminology depending on whether or not the other auditor's report, containing such a qualification, is presented. The SAP states that if the subject of a qualification in the report of the other auditor is not considered material in relation to the consolidated financial statements taken as a whole "and the other auditor's report is not presented, the principal auditor *need not* (emphasis added) make reference in his report to the qualification; if the other auditor's report is presented, the principal auditor *may wish* (emphasis added) to make reference to such qualification. . . ." The terms "need not" and "may wish" both imply that it is not required that the principal auditor make reference to a qualification contained in the report of the other auditor which is not considered material in relation to the financial statements taken as a whole, but, the principal auditor can, if he so wishes, make reference to such qualification in his report in either case. Why, then, the difference in terminology? The slight difference implies that if the other auditor's report is presented it would be more appropriate for the principal auditor to make reference to such qualification than if the report of the other auditor was not presented; however, if reference is made in either case, the principal auditor should state that the subject and nature of the qualification in the report of the other auditor is not material in relation to the consolidated statements taken as a whole.

Reporting on financial statements of prior years following a pooling of interests. The question as to what the principal auditor's function and responsibilities are when he is called upon to report on the related financial statements of one or more prior years following a pooling of interests transaction when other auditors have examined one or more of the entities included in such financial statements was not covered in Chapter 10 of SAP No. 33 but is discussed in SAP No. 45.

In these situations, the auditor may decide that, based on the guidelines discussed above, he cannot serve as principal auditor, in which case he would be unable to render an opinion as to the fairness of the financial statements taken as a whole. Also, in such cases, it is often impossible, inappropriate or unnecessary for the auditor to perform sufficient auditing procedures to enable him to express an opinion on the restated financial statements taken as a whole. However, his review may have been sufficient in scope (i.e.: checking the compilation for mathematical accuracy and for conformity of the compilation methods with generally accepted accounting principles) to enable him to express an opinion solely with respect to the compilation of such statements. SAP No. 45 indicates, however, that the auditor should not even issue an opinion as to compilation unless he "has examined the statement of at least one of the entities included in the restatement for at least the latest period presented." In reporting on the compilation of such restated financial statements the auditor does not assume responsibility for the work of other auditors nor the responsibility for expressing an opinion on the related financial statements taken as a whole.

Predecessor auditor. When an auditor examines financial statements for the first time, he must either satisfy himself as to the account balances at the beginning of the period under examination and as to the consistency of the application of accounting principles in that period as compared with the preceding period, or he must appropriately qualify his opinion or disclaim an opinion and state his reasons for so doing. The auditor, in applying auditing procedures to the account balances at the beginning of the period under examination may consult with the predecessor auditor and may review the predecessor auditor's working papers, but the auditor cannot rely solely on the work performed by the predecessor auditor and relieve himself of responsibility for such work by making reference to the report or work of the predecessor auditor in his report.

CONCLUSION

As the concepts of accountants' legal liability are changing, there is a great deal of question and concern regarding the extent of the responsibility of both the principal and the secondary auditor when the principal auditor reports on financial statements where part of the examination has been made by other auditors. The new SAP should clarify the responsibility of both the principal and secondary auditor and should lead to better reporting practices and a clearer understanding as to the meaning of the disclosure of the use of the work of other auditors in an audit report.

SECTION C

Report Oriented

A few of the more important aspects of audit report writing are given consideration in this section. The selections include writings which present a fresh look at some reporting issue or treat a controversial element of reporting.

A member of the former Accounting Principles Board, and current chairman of the Financial Accounting Standards Board, Marshall S. Armstrong, suggests in the first article that determination of how "substantial authoritative support" is established might lead to an acceptable operational definition of this term. Acceptance or rejection of an accounting principle or method requires the highest degree of professional judgment and in all cases the auditor must have supporting evidence in the application of such judgment.

Eric L. Kohler, in the second article, presents conditions which must be met in order to report that financial statements are presented "fairly." Mr. Kohler concludes that the concept of "fairness" is still in the developmental stage.

In the final article, Leopold A. Bernstein discusses the need for guidelines for materiality. The profession has avoided setting clear-cut quantitative standards by which one may measure materiality and the auditor must still rely on his "professional judgment."

31. Some Thoughts on Substantial Authoritative Support*

Marshall S. Armstrong†

A few weeks ago, I received a telephone call from a practicing certified public accountant who was trying to decide whether he should accept a change in an accounting principle proposed by one of his clients for use in preparing year-end financial statements. He explained that his client had just returned from a convention where a competitor had told how he intended to improve earnings merely by adopting the proposed accounting method. The acceptability of the new method was in doubt.

I asked whether any authoritative support had been found for the proposed principle and he replied, "Well, I looked for an example in *Accounting Trends & Techniques* but found none, so, I thought I should give you a call."

Obviously, he was thanked for the expression of confidence and then I proceeded to comment on his failure to undertake a more thorough search for substantial authoritative support concerning the proposed accounting principle.

Certainly this experience was not unique. Many practicing CPAs have had similar phone calls or discussions during their professional lives. My friend should be complimented, since a CPA should always counsel with his partners or with other experienced colleagues whenever a serious question of professional judgment is involved. The exercise of professional judgment can be put to no stronger test than in a case which requires acceptance or rejection of an accounting principle, practice or method of application. My comments in this case concerned the need for a more complete search for authoritative support, rather than placing reliance upon such a limited "one publication" type of search.

It is important, in my view, for the CPA to be able to produce evidence in support of all professional judgments which he makes in his capacity as the independent auditor of financial statements. Furthermore, since the corporate financial executive normally initiates accounting principles and practices for his company, he must find support for his accounting decisions by reference to authoritative

*From *The Journal of Accountancy* (April, 1969), pp. 44-50. Copyright (1969) by the American Institute of Certified Public Accountants, Inc. Reprinted by permission of the AICPA.

†Marshall S. Armstrong, CPA, is the managing partner of Geo. S. Olive & Company in Indianapolis, Indiana.

sources. Where the acceptability of an accounting principle or practice is in doubt, the financial executive and the auditor may have difficulty in satisfying their respective responsibilities in this regard.

Present accounting and auditing literature does not provide adequate guidelines on how auditors or financial executives should proceed in developing evidence to support judgments in this area. While I believe it would be inappropriate for our profession to develop a list of specific rules to be followed, some general guidelines should be helpful to practicing CPAs and to business financial management.

The purpose of this article, therefore, is to present some thoughts on substantial authoritative support and, also, to consider the question of whether the profession should define that term specifically or merely develop guidelines to help the practitioner and financial executive find adequate support for accounting principles. By following the latter approach an acceptable definition may evolve.

STATEMENT OF THE PROBLEM

It is well known that the Council of the American Institute of Certified Public Accountants is an elected body of about 230 members, established for the principal purpose of serving as the governing board of the Institute. Decisions of Council influence the actions of all Institute members as well as many segments of the business and financial community.

Those elected to serve on Council are experienced, intelligent and astute professional men. Their decisions are usually sensible and objective. However, on occasion a decision of Council makes one wonder to what extent implementation techniques were considered before the issue was resolved.

Take for example the action of Council in October of 1964, which included these three statements:

1. "Generally accepted accounting principles" are those principles which have substantial authoritative support.
2. Opinions of the Accounting Principles Board constitute "substantial authoritative support."
3. "Substantial authoritative support" can exist for accounting principles that differ from Opinions of the Accounting Principles Board.

As a result of this 1964 action, Institute members are required to see to it that departures from Opinions of the Accounting Principles Board are disclosed, either in footnotes to financial statements or in the audit reports of members in their capacity as independent auditors.[1] When the auditor is faced with such a situation, he is required to determine that substantial authoritative support exists for the alternate principle before he is permitted to express an unqualified opinion on the financial statements.

Obviously, if substantial authoritative support can exist for accounting principles that differ from APB Opinions, the auditor must be able to find such support for the alternate principle being used. In fact, it is necessary for the auditor to determine whether substantial authoritative support exists for all principles used in financial statements, particularly in those areas on which the APB has not expressed Opinions or which are not dealt with in Accounting Research Bulletins.

Council's 1964 edict seems ambiguous, particularly the first statement previously quoted — " 'Generally accepted accounting principles' are those principles which have substantial authoritative support."

Recently a prominent certified public accountant stated his objection in these words:

> I doubt that any member of the Council . . . could have given an adequate explanation of what was meant by the adopted recommendation. . . . It sounded good and was not controversial even if it was not understood. It was a compromise between the two opposing viewpoints expressed in the Council. However, an undefined term was used to describe another undefined term, and the problem was merely deferred.

Another recent comment by a leading accounting authority is apropos. He said:

> It seems to me, we are putting the cart before the horse. How can we say that a particular principle has substantial authoritative support without first setting forth which principles are generally accepted accounting principles? We must start with something more basic — the purpose or purposes of financial statements.

Even though this 1964 action of Council represents a step forward in the continuing effort to define generally accepted accounting principles, it certainly creates many questions of substance. For example, what is the source of substantial authoritative support on a brand-new development? Is the practice of any one industrial firm or the extensive

---

[1]AICPA, "Disclosure of Departures From Opinions of Accounting Principles Board," *Special Bulletin* (October, 1964).

practice of a group of firms sufficient to constitute substantial authoritative support for an accounting principle? Is one financial report or a small number of reports a source of substantial authoritative support where the nature of the item is such that it is not likely to arise frequently? If there are several authoritative sources of support, what weight should be given to each source? What source is sufficiently authoritative to be on a par with an Opinion of the Accounting Principles Board? These are only a few of the questions that come to mind.

In any case, it did not take Council long to recognize some of the difficulties involved in the situation. In the spring of 1965, Council gave the Accounting Principles Board several recommendations. The first one is very important in any consideration of substantial authoritative support. It reads thus:

1. At the earliest possible time, the Board should:
   a. Set forth its views as to the purposes and limitations of published financial statements and of the independent auditor's attest function.
   b. Enumerate and describe the basic concepts to which accounting principles should be oriented.
   c. State the accounting principles to which practices and procedures should conform.
   d. Define such phrases in the auditor's report as "present fairly" and "generally accepted accounting principles."
   e. Consider, with the committee on auditing procedure, the possibility of improving the terminology of the auditor's report, and in particular the words "generally accepted" in the expression "generally accepted accounting principles."
   f. Define the words of art employed by the profession, such as "substantial authoritative support," "concepts," "principles," "practices," "procedures," "assets," "liabilities," "income," and "materiality."

At this time, the Board is hard at work on most of the points contained in that recommendation. For example, an exposure draft of a statement or an Opinion entitled "Basic Concepts and Accounting Principles Underlying Financial Statements of Business Enterprises" is currently being developed. The present draft deals with many of the matters contained in Council's first recommendation. It considers purposes of financial accounting, basic concepts of accounting, generally accepted accounting principles, and purposes of financial statements — just to name a few of the subject items. These are not easy matters to delineate. They are complex, controversial and very elusive.

The Board and the accounting research division of the Institute have been working about three years on this project. Completion prospects look good at the moment.

How can we define words of art such as substantial authoritative support? One way would be to construct a definition based on deductive reasoning. Such reasoning would probe the fundamental meanings of the terms *substantial, authoritative,* and *support.* These meanings would be analyzed and combined into a definition of the term that would serve as a guide to practitioners and financial executives. The definition would then be confirmed or altered via its repeated testing in practice. In this way, the definition would be rooted in logic and made operational.

A second way, the one chosen here, would be to scrutinize practice to see how substantial authoritative support is now discovered in the light of present-day standards of accounting practice and financial reporting. In a way, we will inventory the state of the art with respect to substantial authoritative support. By describing "how substantial authoritative support is found" rather than pinpointing "what substantial authoritative support means" in an airtight, logical sense, we will better appreciate the complexity of the term and why the problems of implementation must play a major part in the evolution of an acceptable *operational* definition.

BRIEF HISTORICAL BACKGROUND OF THE TERM

One of the historical landmarks which outlines the problem inherent in defining or searching for substantial authoritative support is contained in 1932 correspondence between a committee of the American Institute of Accountants (now AICPA) and a companion committee of the New York Stock Exchange.

In one part of this correspondence, the American Institute committee made these points:

> In considering ways of improving the existing situation (i.e., improving financial reporting for listed companies), two alternatives suggest themselves. The first is the selection, by competent authority out of the body of acceptable methods in vogue today, of detailed sets of accounting rules which would become binding on all corporations of a given class. The arguments against any attempt to apply this alternative to industrial corporations generally are overwhelming.
>
> The more practicable alternative would be to leave every corporation

free to choose its own methods of accounting . . . but require disclosure of the methods employed and consistency in their application from year to year. . . .

Thus started the debate — should the profession write a rule book of accounting principles for all business enterprises or should business management be free to choose principles and practices from various alternatives? Obviously, the "rule book" approach would eliminate the need to search further for substantial authoritative support. In my judgment, most people today are seeking the middle ground between these two extremes. The goal should be to eliminate alternative accounting principles which are not justified by different circumstances.

In 1936, another historical landmark appeared. The American Institute revised and published a bulletin entitled "Examination of Financial Statements." The following extract is relevant:

It is an important part of the accountant's duty, in making his examination of financial statements, to satisfy himself that accounting practices are being followed which have *substantial recognition* by the accounting profession. This does not necessarily mean that all companies will observe similar or equally conservative practices. Accounts must necessarily be largely expressions of judgment, and the primary responsibility for forming these judgments and preparing the financial statements in which they are reflected must rest on the management of the corporation. But unless the difference is of minor importance the accountant must assume the duty of expressing his dissent through a qualification in his report or otherwise, if the conclusions reached by the management are, in his opinion, *manifestly unsound*, though he is not entitled to substitute his judgment for that of the management when the management's judgment has *reasonable support* and is made in good faith. (Emphasis added.)

You will note the bulletin contained terms which implied a need to measure the acceptability of accounting practices; e.g., "substantial recognition," "manifestly unsound," and "reasonable support." Although management was free to choose the accounting principles which it considered applicable, and also the method of their application, the independent auditor was required to express his opinion on the financial statements. The same general pattern of responsibility of management and of the auditor has continued from 1936 to the present time. Accounting practices which do not have "substantial recognition" will not receive an unqualified opinion from the auditor.

The term "substantial authoritative support" appeared in accounting literature in 1938 in Accounting Series Release No. 4, issued by the Securities and Exchange Commission. This release expresses a fundamental concept:

> In cases where financial statements filed with this Commission pursuant to its rules and regulations, under the Securities Act of 1933 or the Securities Exchange Act of 1934, are prepared in accordance with accounting principles for which there is no *substantial authoritative support*, such financial statements will be presumed to be misleading or inaccurate despite disclosures contained in the certificate of the accountant or in footnotes to the statements, provided the matters involved are material. In cases where there is a difference of opinion between the Commission and the registrant as to the proper principles of accounting to be followed, disclosure will be accepted in lieu of correction of the financial statements themselves only if the points involved are such that there is *substantial authoritative support* for the practices followed by the registrant and the position of the Commission has not previously been expressed in rules, regulations, or other official releases of the Commission, including the published opinions of its chief accountant. (Emphasis added.)

In effect, ASR No. 4 takes the position that accounting principles *with* substantial authoritative support will be accepted by the Commission, and those *without it* will be presumed to be misleading or inaccurate. However, the release is silent with regard to the source of such support. The implication seems to be that support can originate outside of the Commission itself.

Clearly, the crux of the matter is where and how to find substantial authoritative support.

When we look for guidance in publications of our own profession, we find little comfort. For example, the first standard of reporting requires that the auditor's report "shall state whether the financial statements are presented in accordance with generally accepted principles of accounting."

A discussion of adherence to generally accepted accounting principles is found in Chapter 7 of Statements on Auditing Procedure No. 33. Maybe that discussion will give us guidance. This is what it says:

> The determination of whether financial statements are presented in accordance with "generally accepted accounting principles" *requires exercise*

of judgment as to whether the principles employed in the statements have found general acceptance. The determination further requires a familiarity with alternative principles, sometimes more than one, which may be applicable to the transaction or facts under consideration, and a realization that *an accounting principle may have only limited usage but still have general acceptance.* (Emphasis added.)

Frankly, little help comes from that statement. The only expressed guideline here is to exercise our own professional judgment. Does it really assist in solving the problem of finding substantial authoritative support? On the other hand, as professional men, do we *need* more than this?

Based on observations of current practice, which have shown some lack of knowledge as to how one should proceed in an attempt to find support, it is obvious that we *do* need something more.

A Suggested Approach to Finding Substantial Authoritative Support

In my judgment, we need guidelines to assist in organizing the search for evidence which will justify decisions of financial executives or practicing CPAs as to whether, in fact, substantial authoritative support does exist in those cases where the acceptability of an accounting principle is in doubt. Bear in mind, we should be searching for present-day standards of practice — we would not be attempting to write a new set of principles.

Possibly most of the problems in this area can be resolved by systematically proceeding through five basic steps: (1) define the problem, (2) survey relevant literature, (3) survey present practice, (4) evaluate the information so developed and (5) reach a conclusion. Obviously, search for support should not be done in isolation. Group investigation and discussion are essential to the success of such a process. As to practicing CPAs, counseling with partners in their own firms or with other experienced and knowledgeable practitioners is implicit in the "five basic steps" approach.

The summary of this approach, which appears on page 411 and 412, is not all-inclusive as to details of each step in the proposed process since it is intended only to be suggestive. Obviously, the circumstances of each case will dictate both the sources and the depth of search that may be required in various phases of the process.

Five Basic Steps in Searching for Substantial Authoritative Support

I. DEFINE THE PROBLEM

(1) This step includes preparation of a complete description and documentation of the business event or transaction in question. The memorandum should describe the economic and other objectives sought by the various parties as well as all pertinent facts relating to the event or transaction.

(2) In addition, there should be set forth a complete description of the proposed accounting practice or alternative practices that are to be considered. Describe the timing and amounts of entries to be recorded, the financial statement presentation of the various elements and the facts which would be disclosed in notes to the financial statements.

II. SURVEY RELEVANT LITERATURE

Having defined the problem in complete detail under Step I, a thorough survey of relevant literature should be undertaken. Hopefully, this second step will provide evidence of what may be standards of acceptable practice currently in use. Without attempting to produce an exhaustive list of reference points, the following are representative but will vary on a case-by-case basis:

(1) Pronouncements of the American Institute of Certified Public Accountants — for example:
   (a) Opinions of the Accounting Principles Board.
   (b) Accounting Research Bulletins, including Terminology Bulletins.
(2) Other publications of the AICPA:
   (a) Statements of the APB.
   (b) Accounting research studies.
   (c) Industry audit guides.
(3) Pronouncements of other professional societies, including those of foreign countries in some circumstances.
(4) Rules and regulations of the Securities and Exchange Commission.
(5) Written views of individuals.

Accounting textbooks, reference books, accounting articles and speeches are a vital part of professional literature. Care must be taken to distinguish between those that describe accounting which is presently regarded as sound and acceptable in the financial community and those which strive to describe a logical theory of accounting for the future regardless of its present use or acceptance.

(6) Federal, state and local laws.
(7) Pronouncements of industry regulatory authorities, which may provide some acceptable evidence. (See Addendum to APB Opinion No. 2 for guidance in this area.)
(8) Publications of industry associations such as those for colleges and

universities, hospitals, health and welfare organizations, retail merchants, and the petroleum industry. (These frequently contain descriptions of principles of accounting that are appropriate for such specialized endeavors.)

III. SURVEY PRESENT PRACTICE OF ORGANIZATIONS WITH SIMILAR PROBLEMS

In searching for substantial authoritative support, the importance of knowing "what is going on in practice today" cannot be overemphasized. In fact, many practitioners, and financial executives as well, believe that "generally accepted" when used in the phrase "generally accepted accounting principles" literally means that the majority of companies are using the particular principle or practice in preparing their financial statements. On the other hand, this "head count" interpretation of the phrase is rejected by many. They prefer to view the phrase "generally accepted accounting principle" to mean a "sound accounting principle," which may not be the principle in predominant use.

It is the author's view that "generally accepted" principles should always be "sound" principles in the sense that results of financial transactions must be presented in financial statements without defect as to truth, justice or reason.

However, regardless of one's own preference, the search for substantial authoritative support must include a careful survey of present practice. The American Institute of Certified Public Accountants annually publishes **Accounting Trends & Techniques.** This study is based upon a review of 600 published financial reports of publicly held companies and is a good starting point for the survey of present practice. Also, several industry studies are published by industry groups or associations. They may provide good information relevant to the accounting question under consideration.

In addition, a practitioner can usually receive for his own files copies of published reports by any publicly held company, merely by asking to be placed on its mailing list.

IV. EVALUATE THE INFORMATION DEVELOPED

and

V. REACH A CONCLUSION

The responsibility for evaluating the information developed under the first three steps of this process, and that of determining the precise weight of evidence necessary to constitute substantial authoritative support in a given situation rests with the individual practitioner or financial executive. He must make these determinations in each instance by exercising his best judgment on the matter after examining all facts relevant to the particular case.

In my view this five-step decision-making process is not unlike that of the auditor as he searches for and evaluates evidential matter in other areas in his examination of financial statements. The suggested approach is neither new nor unique — I believe it is being followed frequently by financial executives and practicing CPAs today.

As previously stated, most of the cases encountered can be solved by proceeding through the five basic steps enumerated; the real test of finding substantial authoritative support, however, may come in the remaining few but difficult cases. How does one find substantial authoritative support for a brand-new development or, in other cases, where there is no recorded evidence in support of, or in opposition to, the proposed accounting treatment? On the other hand, it may be that the available material is out of date or obsolete and indicates a position the opposite of that which the CPA or financial executive feels is proper in the particular circumstances, possibly in the light of recent refinements in accounting thought.

Obviously, different CPA firms or individual practitioners may approach these special cases in different ways. The "special case" approach varies from the "basic five-step" process only in the source of substantial authoritative support as will be noted in the following brief summary:

As the first step, a thorough search is made into all aspects of the particular situation and a written statement of the problem and of the proposed solution is prepared.

Second, this material, which would mention all references, pro and con, is subjected to intense scrutiny by a group of firm partners with wide experience whose opinions on the matter are usually documented in a memorandum for the files.

As the third step, considered reactions are obtained from experienced members of other prominent CPA firms, and, if the consensus of the parties supports the proposed accounting position, no further action is taken.

One exception might exist. If the principle in question were one on which the SEC had previously taken an informal position contrary to the present consensus, discussions would take place with the staff of the SEC, particularly if the company were subject to SEC regulations.

Finally, since existing literature is silent as to authoritative views on the particular practice in question, or fails to reflect recent refinements in accounting thought, these proceedings and memorandums become a part of the firm's record and thus constitute "substantial authoritative support."

In the instance of a new development, which requires origination of an accounting treatment, the importance of analogy should not be overlooked. Here, the search for substantial authoritative support should include an analysis of situations which are similar to the new development and for which sound accounting has been established.

THE WEIGHT OF AUTHORITY

Much could be written on the relative weight that should be given to various sources of authority. In the minds of some people, if the Accounting Principles Board has not spoken on an issue, widespread use by industry is the main source of authority. On the other hand, rare usage of such an accounting principle creates something of a negative presumption that needs to be overcome. *Previous use* of a principle is insufficient evidence if there are indications that a large part of the accounting profession no longer accepts the principle. Others believe that industry practice should be viewed as the most authoritative support for an accounting principle in every instance. Obviously, pronouncements by the Securities and Exchange Commission carry great weight for those companies that are required to file their financial statements with the Commission.

In my own judgment, the most objective and unbiased source of authority, and therefore number one in authoritative weight, is found in publications of the American Institute of Certified Public Accountants. In an *amicus curiae* brief filed recently in a United States District Court case, the Institute clearly supported its "number one weight position" in these words —

The Institute is the oldest and foremost professional organization of public accountants in the United States. Founded in 1916, it now has a membership of more than 64,000 certified public accountants in the country. The Institute has throughout its existence assumed a principal responsibility for the development, promulgation and enforcement of the professional standards which guide and govern the practice of public accounting in the United States. The formal Opinions of the Institute's Accounting Principles Board and its predecessor constitute the most authoritative and comprehensive statements of generally accepted accounting principles; and the series of Statements on Auditing Procedure, issued by the Institute's committee on auditing procedure, sets out in definite form the generally accepted auditing standards and furnishes guidance in the application of those standards. Such generally accepted accounting principles and auditing standards are incorporated by reference in a code of ethics dealing with relations between the Institute's members and their clients, and public and fellow members of the profession, which is enforced by the Institute through disciplinary proceedings. Although governmental agencies, principally the Securities and Exchange Commission, and others also exercise authority to establish and enforce professional standards for accountants as to matters within their respective jurisdictions, the Institute, as principal spokesman for the profession itself, has long borne and exercised the primary responsibility in this field. The Commission has itself recognized the primacy and the importance of the Institute's role in this regard.

While an attempt should not be made to substitute inflexible rules for good judgment or to reduce the determination of substantial authoritative support to a mechanical exercise, some guidance as to the relative importance of various types of support should be helpful to all practitioners and to the business community in general. It has been suggested that sources of authority could be divided into two classes.

Class 1 should include those sources of support for accounting principles which would be sufficient evidence in themselves to constitute substantial authoritative support — for example:

- Opinions of the Accounting Principles Board.

- Accounting Research Bulletins of the committee on accounting procedure.

- Industry audit guides of the AICPA.

- Regulation S-X and accounting series releases of the SEC.

- In the absence of the first four items, predominant practice within an industry if peculiar to that industry, or of business enterprises in general if not peculiar to a particular industry.

Class II would include sources of support which in themselves would not be sufficient evidence to constitute substantial authoritative support but which, in combination with other such sources, may contribute toward sufficient evidence. Further, all Class II sources might not be accorded the same relative importance. If this thought were to be accepted, Level A sources would be considered more significant than Level B sources; Level B sources would be considered more significant than Level C sources, etc. Without attempting to indicate levels of relative importance, Class II sources of support might include:

- Pronouncements of industry regulatory authorities.

- Substantial practice within an industry.

- Accounting research studies of the AICPA.

- Published research studies of authoritative professional and industry societies.

- Federal, state and local laws.

- Accounting textbooks and reference books of individuals whose views are generally respected.

- Publications of recognized industry associations.

- Published articles and speeches of distinguished individuals.

If our profession were to adopt such a classification of authoritative support, changing circumstances undoubtedly would warrant the addition of new sources of support for accounting principles or perhaps the deletion or reclassification of some of the sources of support currently suggested.

In any event, the question of proper weighting of authoritative sources needs careful consideration and final resolution if guidelines in the area of substantial authoritative support are to be meaningful and helpful to practitioners and to financial executives.

Throughout this article, an attempt has been made to justify the earlier premise that it would seem to serve no useful purpose to concern ourselves at this time with a deductively reasoned definition of substantial authoritative support. Hence, some thoughts have been offered on how a practicing CPA or a financial executive might proceed in determining whether substantial authoritative support exists for a particular accounting principle or practice. As is usual in our profession and in the financial community, one must exercise his best judgment in the face of each circumstance.

It is my hope that our profession and others will eventually come to the conclusion that substantial authoritative support rests in the considered opinions of experienced practicing certified public accountants, experienced objective corporate officials and learned academicians which, as you have seen, is the foundation for the suggested five-step approach to finding substantial authoritative support.

This concept was expressed well by a subcommittee of the Accounting Principles Board during its preliminary work on a Board project entitled Basic Concepts and Broad Accounting Principles. They put it this way:

Generally accepted accounting principles are primarily conventional in nature. They are the result of decisions; they represent the consensus at any time as to how the financial accounting process should operate and how financial statements should be prepared from the information made available through the financial accounting process.

Inasmuch as generally accepted accounting principles embody a consensus, they depend heavily on notions such as "general acceptance" and "substantial authoritative support," which have not been and probably cannot be precisely defined.   There is concurrence, however, that the notions of "general acceptance" and "substantial authoritative support" relate to the propriety of the practices, as viewed by informed, intelligent, and experienced accountants in the light of the purposes and limitations of the financial accounting process.

Finally, by having described in this article "how substantial authoritative support is found" rather than pinpointing "what substantial authoritative support means" in a purely logical sense, I trust an acceptable *operational* definition of the term has been developed.   If financial executives and practicing CPAs will be helped thereby in their search for support, indeed it will be gratifying.

32. "Fairness"*

Eric L. Kohler†

In 1959, I think it was, a certain member of this association and myself were seated in the lobby of the hotel in which the American Institute of CPAs was holding its annual meeting. My recollection is that we were in the process of disposing, at a lofty level, of all the difficulties with which the Institute was then plagued — including its perennially avowed aspiration of wanting to produce something that could be called *the* principles of accounting. Postulates had been bruited about for a year or so, most of them readily identifiable with practices to which, for one reason or another, their proponents had long been addicted — this notwithstanding the common assumption that postulates could be formulated that would be precursors rather than by-products of principles.

Well, in the midst of this esoteric dialogue we were joined by George O. May — for whom I am sure all of us have had a great affection, though now in memory. Mr. May was attending what proved to be, I believe, his last Institute meeting; he had been and had continued to be much exercised over the profession's feverish preoccupation with postulates and principles. His mood at the moment was decidedly bellicose. Having made quite clear his opinion of previous strivings for principles, including those of the American Accounting Association, he concluded: "There is but one principle of accounting." At this point, without disclosing the "principle," he left us.

But within hours thereafter, Mr. May, his subject unannounced, was vigorously championing his thesis at a middle-of-the-floor microphone before an open forum of the Institute. There he brought to the fore what he had been referring to in his talk with us: that between the investor and the object of his investment the public accountant stands as a beacon; versed in the language of both, the accountant as auditor assumes the responsibility for backing management's representation of financial position and operating results that portray one to the other. A large portion of the auditor's function

*From *The Journal of Accountancy* (December, 1967), pp. 58-60. Copyright (1967) by the American Institute of Certified Public Accountants, Inc. Reprinted by permission of the AICPA.

†Eric L. Kohler, CPA, is Consulting Accountant, Chicago, Illinois.

is to broaden the path of communication between the two.   The auditor's consuming ambition, therefore, must be, he continued, *not* to guide the investor but to project the image of the investment. Recognizing that since 1934 the auditor had been bound by the phrase "present fairly" in his short-form report, Mr. May ended by proposing to install "fairness" as the one guiding principle of accounting.   Unhappily, his proposal was lost on his hearers, for at that time the compulsive drive for "principles" was in full cry.   An endemic itch to progress from the obvious to the obscure had infected the profession and its leaders, and it could not be alleviated by so simple a formula.

Since this episode the auditor's audience has steadily increased and it has occurred to me on several occasions that Mr. May's thesis deserves exploration — not, however, as a substitute for principle, but in recognition of the need for a minimal reporting level between such areas of human endeavor as a business corporation and the public it serves.

In 1950, nine years preceding this incident, shortly before the publication of a certain dictionary with which some few of you may have had a passing acquaintance, I had essayed a definition of "fairness" which was continued in the second and third editions of this book. It read as follows:

"(in or of a financial statement) The condition of financial-statement propriety to which an auditor attests in his *report* by employing language similar to the following: 'In our opinion, the accompanying balance sheet and income statement present *fairly* the financial position of the AB Company at December 31, 19-1, and the results of its operations for the year then ended, in conformity with generally accepted accounting principles applied on a basis consistent with that of the preceding year.' The term signifies not only that in the building and form of the financial statements consistent, customary accounting practices have been incorporated, but that the presentation, often giving effect to any special facts or conditions not covered by such practices, conforms to overall tests of truth, justness, equity, and candor. Where an accounting practice has not attained uniformity, as in methods of inventory pricing, the test of fairness is regarded as having been complied with when the financial statement is accompanied by a *disclosure* of the particular practice followed."

Now, involved in the business of preparing copy for a fourth edition of the dictionary, I have been experimenting with what seems to be the current necessity for an expanded definition of "fairness." This experiment lies before you.. It embraces the notion one may infer from the earlier definition: that it is not the auditor who assesses fairness but the reader of financial statements; that the investment analyst, or one whose exposure to financial statements has endowed him with the analyst's perceptivity, looks for and presumably hopes to find a certain minimum reliability reflected in them. He assumes that without a disclosure to the contrary certain standards have been met in the presentation, these being of two sorts: the invisibles or procedural standards adhered to in the auditor's examination — the quality of which he infers from the auditor's report — and the visibles — the body of disclosures that constitute the financial statements.

Fairness and reliability in all situations ought at least to be reciprocal terms: the one, the auditor's asseveration, the other, the reader's judgment. But they may diverge. It has seemed, therefore, that an inventory of the elements of convergence (see pages 421 and 422) would shed light on the present state of the auditor's art as well as lend some degree of realism to the attempt to build a more comprehensive understanding of the notion of "fairness."

You will note that this project of defining "fairness" contains 25 propositions referred to as "conditions" on which a reader of financial statements may be expected to bank whenever the statements are accompanied by the present form of unqualified short-form report. I would anticipate very little professional disagreement with these propositions. Some of them echo pronouncements of the Institute's committee on auditing procedure: others indicate well-seeded practices that are universally if not consciously followed and quite generally assumed by readers of financial statements. It is not suggested that the 25 propositions or any part of them be regarded as a standard; as a definition, the objective is simply to reflect current practices in reporting — conditions an outsider may justifiably assume the auditor has met.

Proposition 25 refers to the modified language encountered on occasion in the auditor's report; one would expect the cause of the "departure" to lie in some imperfection associated with one or more of the other 24 propositions. The custom of calling attention to and identifying a limited fault is presumed to make possible the expression of an unqualified opinion on the balance of the presentation — "taken as a whole" as the saying goes — provided the detail supplied is sufficient to enable the reader to determine for himself the relative importance of the item and its effect on the total presentation, and provided, of course, that the auditor himself has concluded that the overall view intended by the financial statements has not been seriously impaired.

Conditions Which Have Been Met in an Unqualified Short-Term Report

The phrase "present fairly" in the public accountant's unmodified short-form report means that no less than the following conditions have been met:

As to the auditor's examination

1. His independence, reflected in the conduct of his audit and affirmed by the character of his report, is unquestioned.

2. No limitation, natural or imposed by the client, has reduced the scope of his audit below the level he considers minimal.

3. Records and other supporting evidence required by him have been available to and utilized by him.

4. He has tested receivables by correspondence and substantiated opening and closing inventories by observation, or he has satisfied himself with respect to these items by other means of his choice.

5. He has accepted responsibility for the report of another auditor (e.g., on a branch or subsidiary) which has been combined or consolidated in the financial statements accompanying his report, or he has submitted the other's report collaterally with his own.

6. Contingencies and other uncertainties affecting present and future interpretations of financial statements have been evaluated by him and reported as he judges necessary.

7. His short-form-report language follows the current professional standard, on occasion modified by him to express a qualified, adverse, or disclaimer of opinion; or he prepares no report and dissociates himself from the financial statements he has examined.

8. In general, he has exercised professional care and judgment throughout his examination.

As to the client's internal controls and accounting methods

9. Internal controls have been adequate.

10. Accounting principles have been observed and the client's applied accounting policies and procedures have been acceptable.

11. Accounting policies and applications have been consistent throughout the audit period and the period preceding.

12. The books of account have been brought into agreement with the financial statements.

As to the financial statements and appended notes

13. Terminology common to financial statements is employed or notes defining unfamiliar terms are provided.

14. The arrangement of financial statement items follows the conventional pattern.

15. The financial statements are comparable in form and item with those of similar organizations.

16. Unexpired acquisition cost is the basis of asset valuation; any other basis is described and the amount by which it differs from acquisition cost less accumulated-depreciation acquisition cost appears.

17. Depreciation methods for both accounting and tax purposes, and current provisions and accumulations, are revealed.

18. More-than-minor differences between net income and taxable income are explained.

19. Annual rentals, and other provisions of general interest in long-term leases, pension plans, compensation agreements, and stock-option and bonus plans are set forth.

20. An unusual large-scale transaction, an important change in activities, or other major post-balance-sheet event or condition is disclosed.

21. No misstatement or misrepresentation known to the auditor is reflected in the financial statements.

22. Facts and conditions are included without which the financial statements might be interpreted as misleading.

23. Information that may contribute to the reader's better understanding is provided, even though without it the statements cannot technically be regarded as misleading.

24. Financial statements and their attached notes are management's although prepared by the auditor, or added to or modified at his instance; any item omitted from them judged by the auditor to be of importance appears in his report.

As to any departure, deemed by the auditor to be material in character or amount, from any of the preceding conditions

25. His report identifies the item with the accompanying financial statements (and attached notes) and provides information designed to aid an outsider's appraisal of its significance.

The first eight of these propositions have to do with the conduct of the auditor's examination: the limiting environment within which he has labored and the conditions that have led to his report, unqualified or qualified. Item 4, a harkback to the *McKesson & Robbins* case, would not deserve mention except that readers who underwent shock in 1938 are presumed still to expect mention of any exception to these indicated practices, even where the "other means" employed remain unexplained. Where an exception to the audit coverage indicated by these items has been noted by the auditor one must recognize that the analyst or other reader is quite likely to conclude that the general validity of the financial statements has in no way been affected.

Items 9-11 are accorded a major classification because they are so often regarded both within and without the profession as determinants of the range, depth and acceptance of the auditor's examination.

They constitute the essence of management's controls over transactions; by some accountants they could be regarded as suggesting the minimum coverage of a management audit. As for item 12 one would expect that the exception would carry with it an explanation of the omission.

The next dozen items (13-24) relate to the expectation of comprehensibility by readers of financial statements. The importance to readers of items 13-15 is often underestimated by auditors and management alike. Structure and form are emphasized here.

Items 16 and 17 call for a disclosure of differences, if any, between fixed-asset costs and reported values and between depreciation provisions and accumulations and the reported amounts of these items. Accelerated depreciation permitted for tax purposes and the basis that has been followed or normally would have been followed are never the same except by coincidence or after the lapse of a substantial number of years, even though the tax allowances for depreciation may have been expressed on the books of account and in the report. In most situations the disclosure called for here would be the amounts by which reported cost and depreciated-cost provisions and accumulations differ from original cost and straight-line depreciation based on original cost. The absence from the books of account of straight-line depreciation poses a problem for both management and auditor, for their contribution to a full comprehension by readers of financial position and operating results is an obvious one.

The next five items (18-22) call for disclosure practices now well accepted by most accountants. However, no standard has been commonly agreed to concerning the capitalization or expensing of such items as research and development costs, and the reader of financial statements must fend for himself with respect to their significance and future effect; consequently, among the conditions lying before you, you will find no mention of these items. The same may be said of any common agreement on the nature and recognition of liabilities: there is none. If we are to give credence to the American Institute's Accounting Research Study No. 8 ["Accounting for the Cost of Pension Plans"] and ARS No. 9 ["Interperiod Allocation of Corporate Income Taxes"], we must admit that there is no universally applicable test that will identify a liability; in fact, in these pronouncements, the application of "liability" has been stretched to a point that may again embrace provisions for so-called "special" contingencies as having at least a quasi-liability status, whether arising from charges to current expense or accumulated earnings. For the reader of financial statements we have no liability concept to offer; he must continue to be on his guard concerning the items mentioned, relying on disclosures to furnish him with details that he may wish to add or deduct from financial statements as they have been reported.

Item 23 has been generally recognized as accepted in principle, but in practice the evidence indicates widely varying practices as to the constitution of "helpful" information. The auditor in these days finds it necessary to be on the alert as to the possibility of an outsider's drawing wrong inferences from ostensibly correctly drawn financial statement detail. In some instances this has been remedied by an elaboration of titles and sideheads; in others, by interpretative footnotes in which technical language has been as far as possible expurgated. The auditor, in the final phases of his audit, imagines himself in the shoes of the intelligent reader — regardless of whether that reader is an old-time stockholder or a new-time, unidentified, inquisitive outsider.

Item 24 is an iteration of the theme encountered in numerous American Institute pronouncements: that the financial statements and their footnotes are management's, addressed nominally to stockholders but also intended for public consumption, although often prepared by the auditor himself or modified in accordance with his recommendations. Many readers are now well aware of this relationship.

Finally, item 25, already commented on, says in essence that in his short-form report the auditor asserts fairness of presentation and leaves to the judgment of the reader of his report whether his sense of fairness has had its intended effect.

The concept of fairness is still in the making. Its development has been impeded by our failure to put first things first. We still profess an ability to solve topical problems unrelated to any central core of principles.

Mr. May's thesis has merit. In the light of present-day audit objectives, we, as practitioners of the art, might profitably cultivate a fuller awareness of the inferences to which it gives rise.

33. Materiality — The Need for Guidelines*

Leopold A. Bernstein†

The concept of materiality is part of the wisdom of life. It means basically that there is no need to be concerned with what is not important or with what does not matter. Man's work is burdensome enough without his having to pay attention to trivia.

This concept has special significance in accounting for two main reasons:

1. Most users of accounting information do not understand it easily. Introducing additional or immaterial data can make that understanding even more difficult to reach. Furthermore, the mixing of significant with insignificant data can mislead. For clarity, immaterial items should not be given separate disclosure.

2. The process of auditing aims at achieving a satisfactory level of assurance regarding the fairness of presentation of financial statements at a point in time. This assurance is never complete, nor is it economical or feasible for it to be. Consequently, the limited time the auditor can appropriately devote to obtaining this assurance must be spent on matters of substance. He must always strive to avoid spending time on trivia or on what is known to be immaterial. This is not always simple, since it sometimes takes great effort to discover what, indeed, is consequential.

The concept of materiality thus permeates the entire field of accounting and auditing. The following statement appears in the introduction to the *Accounting Research Bulletins:*

> The committee contemplates that its opinions will have application only to items material and significant in the relative circumstances. It considers that items of little or no consequence may be dealt with as expediency may suggest. However, freedom to deal expediently with immaterial items should not extend to a group of items whose cumulative effect in any one financial statement may be material and significant.[1]

---

*From the *Lybrand Journal* (April, 1968), pp. 11-20. Reprinted by permission of Lybrand, Ross Bros. & Montgomery.

†Leopold A. Bernstein, Ph.D., CPA, is Professor of Accounting, Baruch College of City University of New York; Consultant to Lybrand's Accounting and Auditing Research Department.

[1]American Institute of Certified Public Accountants, *Accounting Research and Terminology Bulletins*, Final Edition, 1961, p. 9.

The Securities and Exchange Commission, in its accounting regulations, is also concerned with materiality. In trying to define the limits within which required information is to be furnished, the SEC wants to shield the reader of financial statements from being swamped with unimportant information that may be indiscriminately commingled with significant information. The agency, moreover, does not want to burden the filing company and its accountant with a requirement to disclose immaterial items. Its requirement is stated in Regulation S-X:

> The term "material," when used to qualify a requirement for the furnishing of information as to any subject, limits the information required to those matters as to which an average prudent investor ought reasonably to be informed before purchasing the security registered.[2]

The concept of materiality, when generally expressed, is simple to understand. However, when materiality is made a central concept in the *application* of accounting principles, a lack of specific definition converts it into a prime problem area. Nowhere is the impact of this application more important than in its effect on reported net income. The following statement, taken from a recent Canadian study, substantiates this view. It says:

> An accounting error (or a total of accounting errors) is material if the distortion affects or should affect the decisions of an intelligent reader of the financial statements. Since the prime concern of most readers is the earning power of the enterprise, the most obvious type of error affecting the reader is one which distorts reported net profit. In this study, therefore, materiality will be considered as it relates to the total of known and unknown errors distorting the net profit figure.[3]

EXTRAORDINARY ITEMS

The theory, as well as the practice, of the treatment and presentation of extraordinary items of gain and loss was one aspect of a research study I recently completed.‡ This study showed unmistakably that the absence of agreement on materiality criteria within the accounting profession has been, more than any other single factor, responsible

---

[2]U.S. Securities and Exchange Commission, Regulation S-X, Paragraph 1.02.

[3]The Canadian Institute of Chartered Accountants, *Materiality in Auditing* (Study Group on Audit Techniques: October, 1965), p. 3.

‡Bernstein, Leopold, *Accounting for Extraordinary Gains and Losses* (The Ronald Press: 1967).

for a complete lack of uniformity of practice in this area. While Accounting Principles Board Opinion No. 9, *Reporting the Results of Operations*, represents a significant improvement over the profession's prior pronouncement on this subject, it nevertheless retains "materiality" as a critical operational concept. No guidelines, however, have been provided to ensure a minimum of uniformity in the application of this extremely important concept. (See Figure 1 for current examples of practice.)

The concept of materiality has found its way into many other aspects of disclosure. Thus, in professional pronouncements, we find it applied to income tax allocation, renegotiation refunds, disclosure of unamortized discount and accounting for leases.

LACK OF GUIDES

What is material? *The Accounting Research Bulletins*[4] and subsequent APB pronouncements offer no concrete guidance. Interpretations in much of the literature indicate that this lack arises from the fact that assessment of materiality is purely a matter of judgment. The association of materiality with professional judgment results in the elevation of a simple, common-sense concept to a position of cardinal importance in accounting practice.

A well-known writer on materiality has expressed this as follows: "The concept of materiality is among the most important of the basic ideas by which an auditor is guided in reporting on his examination of financial statements and in the formulation and application of his audit procedures. . . ."[5] The questions that immediately come to mind are these: Has the importance of materiality been overrated? Is it really of such great importance? Does it rank as a *basic* idea in accounting?

THE NEED FOR CRITERIA

The need for some guides on materiality is evident from a just-published and eminently practical work which records the replies of the AICPA's Technical Services Department to member inquiries.[6] After

---

[4]American Institute of Certified Public Accountants, op. cit., p. 63.
[5]E. L. Hicks, "Some Comments on Materiality," *The Arthur Young Journal* (April, 1958).
[6]E. F. Ingalls, *Practical Accounting and Auditing Problems* (AICPA: 1966), Vol. 1, pp. 289-293.

Lack of Materiality Criteria

APB Opinion No. 9 states that extraordinary items are ". . . events and transactions of material effect. . . ." How large in relation to net income should an item be before it is designated as material? Conversely, how small a percentage relationship would make the item not material? The following examples are indicative of the lower end of the wide range of practice that can exist in the absence of spelled-out materiality criteria and guidelines:

United Air Lines, Inc., in its 1967 annual report, considers a "gain on sale of aircraft after tax" as extraordinary even though it is only slightly above 1% of earnings before this gain.

Western Union International, Inc., designates a 1967 gain on sale of stock, net of tax, as extraordinary even though it represents but 3% of income before extraordinary items.

Oneida Ltd., in its income statement for the year ending 1/31/1968, considers as extraordinary a "loss on devaluation of English pound . . .," amounting to less than 4% of income before extraordinary items.

Figure 1

receiving less than full satisfaction on a question involving materiality, one inquirer wrote, "If materiality is to be measured by net income, at which point does an item become or cease to become material? . . . Please understand that this letter . . . is intended to help us establish some guidelines for use in the future." In answer to the follow-up inquiry, the Technical Services Department closed the correspondence by saying, in part, that "it goes without saying, the question of 'materiality' is an elusive matter." In a similar response to a request for guidance in this area, Carman G. Blough (former research director of the American Institute) maintained that the committee on accounting procedure did not consider it feasible to set down any general criteria on the subject.[7] Mr. Blough's reply revealed that the alternatives available to an accountant faced with a decision on materiality are quite varied.

An item should be considered in relation to only one year, not to a number of years, of income. At present, however, this is an extremely flexible concept. There seems no reason why an average of five years is better than, say, eight years, or 10 or even 15. Surely, the results could be substantially different, depending on the number of

---

[7]"Some Suggested Criteria for Determining Materiality," *The Journal of Accountancy* (April, 1950), pp. 353-54.

years used. Actually, the income figure used should be representative of a recent (say, five-year) earnings level if the current earnings figure differs markedly from it. It should also be recognized that to the decision-maker the most recent years are far more important than those of the more distant past.

Once the percentage relationship of an item to net income has been determined, further variation is possible. Some consider 10 percent material enough to justify excluding an item from income, while others go as high as 20 percent to 25 percent. Mr. Blough believes, further, that percentages can change between items.

The above deviations are only examples, for the suggested considerations extend to many more variables. One writer has suggested that the effect on the analytical measurements employed by security analysts when judging whether an item is material or not should be considered.[8] Here, too, the focus on one type of relationship may yield conclusions differing from those resulting from concentration on a different type of relationship.

The Importance of Judgment

All this suggests the existence of a serious dilemma. In a profession where objectivity is a cardinal requirement, the definition of materiality seems to be in urgent need of improvement. If materiality is really such an important concept — and it certainly plays a dominant role in a number of pronouncements — then how is the profession to achieve consistent or uniform treatment of it? How are new entrants to the profession to be trained? What are they to be told about the judgment processes leading up to materiality decisions?

We are told that the determination of materiality is a matter of judgment. What kind of judgment? Professional judgment, of course, is the answer. And here it ends. Nowhere is the term "judgment" defined — let alone described — in the sparse literature on the subject.

In few other areas of accounting practice is "judgment" invoked so categorically as in the area of materiality determination. Judgment is, of course, a vital aspect of any professional's work. In accounting it plays an important role every step of the way — but that does not mean that it is a mysterious process, indefinable and inexplicable. The following are three main reasons why analysis and description of judgment processes are important:

---

[8]D. Rappaport, "Materiality," *The Journal of Accountancy* (April, 1964).

1. An undefined and all-embracing process described as "judgment" does not inspire the confidence of thinking men.

2. The mere assertion that a vital professional process depends on "judgment" is useless in educating and training entrants to the profession.

3. Such an undefined approach is conducive to the kind of practice most likely to discredit the profession.

Judgment is of course not peculiar to accounting. It plays a vital role in management, where in recent years it has come increasingly under study. The advent of the electronic computer, which has displayed a remarkable capability for simulating our thought processes, has encouraged this study. Yet, to program a computer properly, the thought and judgment processes of managers had to be analyzed and understood, which led to increasing dissatisfaction with the all-inclusive description of the manager's work as "the exercise of judgment." This dissatisfaction was described by a leading student of decision theory in these words: "When we ask how executives make nonprogrammed decisions, we are told that they 'exercise judgment' and that this judgment depends, in some undefined way, upon experience, insight and intuition."[9] Professor Simon maintains that this is like describing a sedative as something possessing a dormitive property.

As the judgment process was more thoroughly examined in relation to the computer, it resulted in such specialized computer applications as operations research, linear programming, PERT and other techniques comprising modern management science. Judgment has also been systematically dissected in connection with security analysis.

The increasing complexity of managerial decision-making plus the shortage of managerial talent has also focused attention on the need for studying judgment processes for training purposes. The same consideration applies to the accounting profession. It is not sufficient to say that a determination of materiality requires the exercise of professional judgment.

Nearer to the discussion of materiality, the auditor, recognizing the advances in these related areas, no longer completely relies on a haphazard judgment faculty. He now utilizes sophisticated techniques requiring more complete examination and descriptions of his work and lending themselves to more objective evaluation.

This does not mean that all these processes can be defined, that there is a full substitute for experience, or that wisdom can be taught.

---

[9]H. A. Simon, *The New Science of Management Decision* (Harper & Brothers: 1960), p. 11.

Without some description, however, we cannot establish those norms that must guide and circumscribe this quality. Right now the undefined concept of professional judgment in accounting, especially as it relates to materiality, can only result in a proliferation of loose standards and practices. This obtains especially where, as in the treatment and presentation of extraordinary items, practice as a whole shows a substantial lack of uniformity.

A REASONABLE DEGREE OF UNIFORMITY

Why is uniformity necessary? The answer is by no means self-evident. Moreover, the need for more uniformity is an important reason why the processes of the accountant's judgment cannot remain obscure. The debate about the uniformity-diversity dichotomy has been going on for many years. Often, unfortunately, the positions under attack are characterized in too extreme a fashion. It is obvious that no accountant who believes in a free society would strive for the dictation of his discipline by a book of rigid rules, or that such a system could really work to society's benefit. On the other hand, no supporter of "diversity" can possibly mean, by that, that judgment and practice can be cut off from all clearly defined concepts and standards. Those who do believe that professional judgment should not be restricted are not thinking about the profession's standing; they are merely convinced of the unimpeachability of their own judgment and integrity.

Surely the substance of the entire debate lies between these extremes. Greater uniformity is necessary for two major reasons: It (1) facilitates comparability, and (2) acts as a regulator of quality. Comparison is a vital analytical tool; no decision involving the use of accounting information can be made in a vacuum or by considering just one variable. Thus, investment decisions are made by comparing one investment with another, a decision to lend is made by contrasting one loan application with another, and so on. Many factors make comparisons among companies difficult, and the accountant must do his part in facilitating comparison as much as he can.

Given vague guides or no guides at all for applying the concept of materiality, the result must be widely varied practice in an area where a reasonable degree of uniformity and comparability is essential. Without a common frame of reference, uniformity of practice is impossible. Adherence to a set of principles and their consistent application will give the user of financial statements a degree of assurance that minimum standards are being applied to the accountant's work.

FREEDOM AND DISCIPLINE

The accountant is naturally disinclined to accept restrictions on his judgment. He feels that, having firsthand knowledge of all the circumstances of a case, he can best decide what is material and what is not. This is of course true. But, at the same time, he may apply to a given situation criteria different from those applied by his colleagues or criteria differing from those the reader assumes to have been applied. The strong influences of management's viewpoint, as well as the absence of any clear standards, make this all the more likely.

The free exercise of judgment by a professional man in his field is important, and, if possible, this freedom should not be restricted. Some, however, would lead us to believe that this is the paramount "value" to be considered.[10] Yet, public confidence in and understanding of the auditor's work are also important; in fact, without them, auditing cannot serve as a profession. Public confidence is the "value" which justifies the profession's giving up some of its freedom of action. Complete liberty of action and choice, not governed by any defined criteria of materiality, can be achieved only at the cost of a serious lack of uniformity in practice.

What is material and what is not cannot be left to the undefined realm of "judgment." The debate over which criteria are applicable is useless if the resulting practice produces greatly diverse results under similar conditions.

MATERIALITY GUIDELINES

It is therefore recommended that we establish definite standards which, given similar circumstances, will help accountants to arrive at meaningfully similar conclusions on questions of materiality. Such standards must be operative in areas where quantification is not possible. Establishing a border zone between what is material and what is not is a feasible solution in this area. Such border zones have proved workable in the case of accounting policy regarding stock dividends. The SEC, where the need for clear directives demanded a decision, has also clearly indicated the borderline of materiality.[11]

Such a suggested border zone is not meant to be a rigidly delineated area, but rather an area of strong presumption from which an accoun-

---

[10]For example, see D. E. Browne, "Cost of Imposing Uniform Accounting Practices," *Financial Executive* (March, 1966).

[11]For example, Rule 1.02 of Regulation S-X indicates that a significant subsidiary (for purposes of the regulations) is one whose assets exceed 15% of the consolidated assets or whose sales and revenues exceed 15% of the consolidated sales and revenues. (One can well imagine the practice which would result from leaving decisions in this area solely to "judgment.")

tant can depart only for compelling reasons known to him and *disclosed* by him. There cannot be an assumption that circumstances are so complex that an accountant cannot disclose them. Communication of complex economic facts is his principal function, and one to which he can give the full rein of his judgment and skill.

A border zone has the advantage of meeting the arguments of those who will always point out that 10 percent is not so different from 10.1 percent. It brings the cutoff point closer to the level of a concept and removes it from the numbers game, while leaving room for appropriate discretion.

A widely known and accepted border zone has other great advantages. It places the burden of proof on those who would deviate from it, and provides the profession and the users of financial statements with a known and explicitly stated norm. Professional accountants can use it as a guide and as an assurance that some degree of consistent practice is being followed. Users of financial statements can rely on substantial adherence to the border-zone limits and can expect to be alerted to any significant deviations from them.

What should the limits of such a border zone be? The modal area of practice revealed by the empirical study mentioned previously suggests a border zone of 10 percent to 15 percent of net income after taxes as the line of demarcation between what is and what is not material. As already indicated, what is meant by net income is a figure typical of recently experienced (five-year average) earning power. A border zone of this nature could be a starting point towards progress in defining materiality; and such a zone is probably one on whose dimensions the accounting profession could agree.

It must be recognized, however, that, while the 10 percent to 15 percent border zone may represent the thinking of many accountants, it does not necessarily coincide with that of many other serious users of the income statement. Discussing materiality with regard to the treatment of "nonrecurrent items," Graham, Dodd and Cottle state that "small items should be accepted as reported. For convenience we may define 'small' as affecting the net results by less than 10 percent in the aggregate."[12]

EFFECT ON NET EARNINGS

According to the 1957 Statement of the American Accounting Association, "an item should be regarded as material if there is reason to

---

[12]B. Graham, D. Dodd and S. Cottle. *Security Analysis* (McGraw-Hill: 1962), p. 112.

believe that knowledge of it would influence the decisions of an informed investor."[13] Many security analysts would probably consider items that affect net results by as little as 5 percent to be significant and hence material. The compound annual growth rate of earnings of a great many corporations is around 5 percent; an influence on net earnings as great as the annual change due to growth must generally be deemed significant.

The compound annual growth rate of all manufacturing corporations varies greatly, depending on the period selected. A recent study shows that during the postwar period, 1947-1964, it was at the rate of 2 percent.[14] Taking the longest period, 1935-1964, we find a 7 percent annual growth rate. The latter period starts at or near a major cyclical bottom and includes a major war. Another study of the compound annual growth rates of the earnings of 127 large and successful companies shows that for 1947-1963 it was 6.0 percent.[15] Thus, a change considerably lower than 10 percent to 15 percent is significant in many instances. While a company's individual experience can be expected to vary from an average of the aggregates, we must, in designating the border zone between what is and what isn't material, take the average experience into account (see Figure 2).

The Effect of a 5% Change in Earnings

The following examples of compound annual growth rates in earnings per share for the years 1953-1964 for some well-known and well-managed corporations point out the importance of a 5% change in earnings:

American Telephone & Telegraph Co.	4.8%
American Tobacco Co.	5.3%
General Motors Corp.	6.6%
Gulf Oil Corp.	6.4%
Sears Roebuck & Co.	7.3%

Figure 2

The border zone of 10 percent to 15 percent is a broad guideline at best, but its establishment would at least be a start. Many situations

---

[13]American Accounting Association Committee on Accounting Concepts and Standards, *Accounting and Reporting for Corporate Financial Statements and Preceding Statements and Supplements*, (American Accounting Association: 1957), p. 8.

[14]Sidney Cottle, "Corporate Earnings: A Record of Contrast and Change," *Financial Analysts Journal* (November-December, 1965).

[15]Edmund A. Mennis, "Perspective on 1965 Corporate Profits," *Financial Analysts Journal* (March-April, 1965).

exist where items of a much smaller percentage impact on net income would require disclosure because of the intrinsic significance of the item itself. Conflict-of-interest cases are one example.

Regulations S-X of the SEC provides an instance of low materiality criteria in the case of loans and advances to directors, officers and principle holders of equity securities other than affiliates. Rule 5-04 stipulates that an aggregate indebtedness to the filing corporation, by such parties, of $20,000, or 1 percent of total assets, whichever is less, which is owed or was owed during the period covered by the profit and loss statements must, with certain exceptions, be shown in a separate schedule. Obviously, disclosure of such relatively small amounts is governed by the significance of the transactions themselves.

AVENUES OF IMPROVEMENT

When the accountant assesses materiality he looks backward to evaluate relationships, but he must also look forward to assess the probabilities of future and cumulative effects. Not everything is subject to quantification, and some guiding, qualitative judgment criteria affecting materiality decisions must be spelled out. Those should lower rather than lift the border zone-percentage range.

Deciding on specific materiality criteria is difficult and complex. This article suggests that a beginning must be made in defining the concept of materiality and in establishing more objective criteria of measurement. Another way of tackling the problem may be to de-emphasize the importance of "materiality," and, by extending the degree of overall disclosure in financial statements, to make the impact of its application less critical. The accounting profession, however, is not moving away from attaching great importance to the concept of materiality. On the contrary, a recent special bulletin,[16] which represents a milestone in efforts to strengthen the authority of APB pronouncements, increases the importance of decisions involving "materiality." The Special Bulletin states:

5. If an accounting principle that differs *materially* in its effect from one accepted in an Opinion of the Accounting Principles Board is applied in financial statements, the reporting member must decide whether the principle has substantial authoritative support and is applicable in the circumstances. . . .

---

[16]Special Bulletin, *Disclosure of Departures from Opinions of Accounting Principles Board* (October, 1964).

6. Departures from Opinions of the Accounting Principles Board which
have a *material* effect should be disclosed in reports. . . . (Emphasis added.)

The significance of the change instituted with the publication of
the special bulletin should not be underestimated. Yet, most of its
practical effect will depend on how freely it is interpreted. As in other
important areas, leeway exists in large measure because the concept
of "materiality" remains undefined.

The preceding discussion was made with full cognizance of the
complexities facing the practicing accountant. This is an attempt not
to underestimate the difficulties of defining and describing the accountant's judgment processes, but rather to point out that a degree of definition is essential. Similarly essential is the setting of a border zone
between what is material and what is not. The zone will certainly not
be perfect, nor will it meet all situations equally well, but without it
the concept of materiality cannot be useful, either to the profession
or to the users of financial statements.

RECENT COMMENTS ON MATERIALITY

"Since no one knows what moves or does not move the mythical 'average
prudent investor,' it comes down to a question of judgment, to be exercised
by the trier of the fact as best he can in the light of all the circumstances. It
is my best judgment that the average prudent investor would not have cared
about these [comparatively minor] errors in the 1960 sales and earnings
figures,* regrettable though they may be. I therefore find that they were
not material within the meaning of Section 11 [of the Securities Act of 1933].

". . . As per balance sheet, total current assets were $4,524,021, and total
current liabilities were $2,413,867, a ratio of approximately 1.9 to 1. This
was bad enough, but on the true facts, the ratio was worse. As corrected,
current assets, as near as one can tell, were approximately $3,924,000, and
current liabilities approximately $2,478,000, a ratio of approximately 1.6
to 1.

"Would it have made any difference if a prospective purchaser of these
debentures had been advised of these facts? There must be some point at

---

*	1960		1959
	As Originally Reported	As Corrected	Correct Original Reporting
Sales	$9,165,320	$8,511,420	$3,320,121
Earnings Per Share	.75	.65	.33

which errors in disclosing a company's balance sheet position become material, even to a growth-oriented investor. On all the evidence I find that these balance sheet errors were material within the meaning of Section 11."

         — Judge McLean in Escott v.
         BarChris Construction Corp.

     "Materiality can only be considered in relative terms. In a small business £ 100 may be material whereas £ 1 million may not be material in classifying the expenditure of a very large undertaking, especially as too much elaboration could obscure the true and fair view. Those responsible for preparing and auditing accounts have to decide which, out of the many facts available to them, are the ones that have a real bearing on the true and fair view which the accounts must give. In some circumstances a difference of about 10 percent might be acceptable but in other circumstances a difference as low as 3 percent might be too much. While percentage comparisons can, properly used, constitute useful broad guides, it must be kept in mind that they are no more than rough rules of thumb, and should not be applied indiscriminately without regard to particular circumstances.

     ". . . The view given by accounts may sometimes be affected by the trend of profit, or turnover, and of various expense items. An inaccuracy which might not otherwise be judged to be material could have the effect of reversing a trend, or turning a profit into a loss, or creating or eliminating the margin of solvency in a balance sheet. When an item affects such a critical point in accounts, then its materiality has to be viewed in that narrower context."

     — From a statement by the Council of the Chartered Accountants in England and Wales for the guidance of members on the meaning to be attached to the expression "material."

MATERIALITY CASE STUDIES SUGGESTED

"A way must be found to make information about materiality decisions more accessible to the interested practitioners, teachers and researchers. As a solution to this dilemma, it is suggested that a series of case studies be produced in which emphasis is placed on the details and circumstances surrounding typical and also unusual materiality decisions. These cases should not be "arm-chaired," but should be written up from actual data, altered only if necessary to conceal the identities of the firms and people involved. The case studies in auditing, produced by the American Institute of CPAs, serve as an example, although the envisioned studies on materiality would be shorter, more numerous. Little development and improvement of the materiality concept can be made until some orderly way is established for relevant facts to be made available to everyone interested. — WARREN REININGA, "The Unknown Materiality Concept," <u>The Journal of Accountancy</u>*, February 1968.*

PART FIVE

Extensions of the Attest Function and Future Horizons

The attest function has developed over many years to meet the needs of clients, creditors, stockholders and others. The auditor clearly performs a vital function in his role of attestor of the fairness of client's financial statements and his competence in this role is not seriously challenged. It is the extension of the audit function beyond its traditional bounds which offers new avenues of service and correspondingly raises the most serious hazards.

Extension of the audit function to several new areas is receiving the current attention of the profession and other affected parties. This part brings together several differing views on extending the attest function in the areas of forecasts, internal control, audit of management and client compliance with legal and regulatory requirements. The concluding selections focus on the futuristic role to which the auditor must look.

Forecasting by business organizations is an essential and widely accepted practice. The future cannot be controlled but planning and forecasting serve to help reduce some of the uncertainty. Thus events demand a look at the issue of what the auditor's role should be in forecasting. The Willingham, Smith, and Taylor article discusses the experience of Chartered Accountants in England and Wales and advocates extending the CPA's opinion to include forecasts. The authors maintain that the English experience has not created undue difficulties and that attesting to forecasts is within the auditor's competence.

There is contention that the auditor should attest to more than the fairness of the financial statements. Many have observed that stockholders and others should be provided with information regarding the effectiveness of the internal control of the firm. It seems natural to ask, why not have the auditor attest to how well management is discharging its responsibility of maintaining an effective internal control system. D. R. Carmichael has considered this issue and poses several questions which must be faced before resolving the issue. Although not reproduced here, the AICPA Committee on Auditing Procedures has also addressed itself to the issue and has announced its position in SAP No. 49 which is now part of Statement on Auditing Standards No. 1.

The issue of the propriety and feasibility of an audit of management is not a new topic but it is nevertheless still very current. T. G. Secoy in his article distinguishes between an audit of management performance and an audit of financial statements to determine fairness. He also includes an example of a report which might be issued by an auditor upon completion of a management audit.

Business organizations must comply with numerous laws and regulations. The noncompliance with such laws and regulations may impinge upon the fairness of the financial reports, directly or indirectly, and in addition these violations may affect the long term success and survival of the firm. As the firm becomes more dependent on and more responsible to the social and legal constraints of society, one inevitable question is the impact of this development on the audit function. Two brief entries are provided in this section to emphasize the growing awareness of the profession to the changes in the business environment. Two recent developments, namely, wage-price regulations and pollution control requirements are treated by D. R. Carmichael and T. D. Wood, respectively.

A viable profession must constantly look to the future. The hazards of predicting the future are great but a profession must contemplate and plan for events ahead. J. G. Birnberg and Nicholas Dopuch have advanced an alternative to the conventional accounting framework of disclosure. Their ideas for expanding the bounds of disclosure continue to deserve serious consideration. In the concluding article, F. S. Capon, president of the Canadian Institute of Chartered Accountants at the time of writing, points to the broadening of the accounting function into a total information system. Capon calls for extended vision to guide us through a period of great transition.

34. Should the CPA's Opinion be Extended
to Include Forecasts?*

John J. Willingham,
Charles H. Smith and
Martin E. Taylor†

The American Institute of Certified Public Accountants specifically prohibits its members from attesting to the accuracy of management's forecasts of future accomplishment of a business entity. The following is taken from the AICPA's *Code of Professional Ethics* (1967): "A member or associate shall not permit his name to be used in conjunction with any forecast of the results of future transactions in a manner which may lead to the belief that the member or associate vouches for the accuracy of the forecast."

Contrast this statement with one recently issued by the Council of the Institute of Chartered Accountants in England and Wales concerning revised guidelines on reporting by accountants and auditors on profit forecasts by companies. English accountants can, with some limitations, ". . . properly undertake a critical and objective review of the accounting bases and calculations for profit forecasts, and can verify that the forecasts have been properly computed from the underlying assumptions and data and are presented on a consistent basis." (*Accountants' Reports on Profit Forecasts:* 1969.)

It appears that the AICPA is implying that attesting to forecasts is not part of auditing. The Institute in England and Wales seems to be taking the opposite tack.

This difference of opinions raises the important question of whether accountants' reports on profit forecasts can be considered within the boundaries of auditing discipline.

Whether audits of forecasts *should* be included among the services offered by CPAs can be argued pro and con from many practical perspectives. On the other hand, it is quite a different matter to determine whether auditing of forecasts *is theoretically* consistent with the usual services offered by CPAs. It is this latter consideration which is addressed here. Briefly, this article argues that attesting to forecasts is within the purview of CPAs.

The argument assumes that a close relationship exists between accounting and auditing; i.e., an auditor attests to the results of the

*From the *Financial Executive* (September, 1970), pp. 80-89. Reprinted by permission of the Financial Executive Institute.

†John J. Willingham, Ph.D., CPA, is Professor of Accounting, The University of Houston. Charles H. Smith, Ph.D., is Associate Professor, University of Texas at Austin. Martin E. Taylor is Assistant Professor, University of Maryland.

accounting process. Consequently, we will examine two areas of accounting theory in order to gain insight into the nature of forecasts: first, the entity concept and, second, the concept of exchange transaction. Finally, we will look more closely at the English practice of giving opinions on forecasted profit statements.

A BEHAVIORAL SYSTEM

Most writers in accounting consider the entity as an essential requisite in accounting. Paton and Littleton, in *An Introduction to Corporate Accounting Standards* (AAA, 1940) stated ". . . it has become almost axiomatic that the business accounts and statements are those of the entity. . . ."

However, accountants have regarded the entity more as a frame of reference from which to report the results of transactions than as a social system with all its attendant interpersonal interaction. For example, Gilman said that "Accounting . . . is founded upon the viewpoint of an entity separate and distinct from its owners or other sources of capital." (*Accounting Concepts of Profit*, Ronald Press, 1939).

Some valuable insights and implications for accountants might be found if the entity could be thought of as a complex social organization rather than as simply a frame of reference for accounting. Formal organizations can be viewed as patterns of relationships between people. Interaction is guided by norms determined by behavioral prescriptions and proscriptions. The norms extant in any complex organization are composed of a blending of societal and cultural values with the unique circumstances of the particular organization. They determine how participants ought to think, feel, and behave. To a significant extent, the view of an accounting entity as a complex social organization serves to clarify the nature of one basic concept — the entity itself — with which accountants deal.

The entity, in and of itself, has no goals or objectives. It is incapable of emotion, pleasure, pain, and consumption of wealth. For an entity to have goals and objectives, they must be imposed upon it by the interaction of the participants in the organizational structure (formal and informal). These participants include stockholders, customers, employees, and the general public. As Herbert Simon said in *Administrative Behavior* (Macmillan, 1958) ". . . The organizational objective is indirectly a personal objective for all the participants. It is a means whereby their organizational activity is bound together to achieve a satisfaction of their own personal motives."

What are the objectives common to all participants? An objective common to all participants is survival. "The tendency to expand and to secure the bailiwick of the organization permeates all the sets and subsets of the organization structure." (Kuhn, *The Study of Society: A Unified Approach*, Irwin, 1963).

As the entity moves through time, it needs information to insure its survival and growth. Such information is provided to enable the prediction of behavior and thereby lessen uncertainty. The American Accounting Association, in its *Statement of Basic Accounting Theory* (1966), stated "Accounting information must be useful to people acting in various capacities both inside and outside of the entity concerned. It must be useful in the formulation of objectives, the making of decisions, or the direction and control of resources to accomplish objectives. The utility of information lies in its ability to reduce uncertainty about the actual state of affairs of concern to the user."

Viewing the accounting entity as a complex social organization brings the usefulness criterion into sharper focus. Many accountants have extolled the virtues of usefulness as a guiding precept, but few have demonstrated its applicability to choices between accounting alternatives. While usefulness is to some extent dependent upon the perception of individual humans, it can be applied if human objectives are stripped down to levels common to all participants in an endeavor.

The corporation in 1970 is a complex social system that includes perhaps thousands of participants with differing personal goals and aspirations. The participants can be sub-divided into broad classes — labor, management, owners, suppliers, creditors, and customers. These classes of participants *may* hold general values in common. Each of the broad participant classes can be further subdivided (e.g., lower, middle, and top management) and more precise goal statements can be obtained. Finally, at the individual levels of analysis, it may be possible to isolate very specific individual aspirations.

If one were to undertake a study of a specific organization that aimed at listing the verbalized goals of the participants, consensus among individual participants, sub-classes of participants, classes of participants, and the aggregate of the participants would be limited to survival, and perhaps growth, of the corporate organization. In order to insure the attainment of this minimal corporate goal, estimates of future accomplishment are necessary.

Most businesses prepare budgets in order to satisfy the need for information about the future. Traditionally, budgeting has been the responsibility of accountants, and auditors attest to the fairness of the results of the historical accounting function. It would be a natural extension of the auditors' responsibility to attest to the results of the extrapolative accounting function.

Subject Matter of Accounting

That the exchange transaction, or simply transaction, is the input to the accounting system permeates much of accounting literature. Paton and Littleton in their *Introduction to Corporate Accounting Standards* (already cited) state that "The activities of the specific business enterprise, with respect to which the accountant must supply pertinent information, consist largely of exchange transactions with other enterprises. Accounting undertakes to express these exchanges quantitatively. The basic subject matter of accounting is therefore the measured consideration involved in exchange activities, especially those that are related to services acquired (cost, expense) and services rendered (revenue, income)."

Their conclusion has been confirmed by Schrader in a study which revealed that "The 'debits' have in common that they are *values received* in exchange. The 'credits,' by way of observable apposition, are *values given* in exchange. ("An Inductive Approach to Accounting Theory," *The Accounting Review*, July 1964). The entity, being a system, exists in a dynamic environment and inevitably interacts with other systems in the environment. Willingham, in a study of interactions between social organizations, identifies this interacting activity as that of exchange. ("The Accounting Entity: A Conceptual Model," *The Accounting Review*, July 1964.) If it is accepted that exchanges are the basic subject matter of accounting, the question still to be answered is, does exchange theory apply solely to past or actual exchanges, or could it possibly include anticipated exchanges?

Accounting literature does not state categorically that the exchanges with which accounting should be concerned relate only to past transactions. Budgeting, for example, seems to be concerned primarily with the anticipated future exchanges of the entity. It would appear that budgeting could legitimately be termed part of accounting only if anticipated future exchanges are regarded as part of accounting. While we concede that there might be a problem in measuring anticipated exchanges accurately, we feel that this is not sufficient ground for excluding management forecasts from accounting. In fact, this is not much different from present accounting practice in regards to depreciation: allocation of depreciation is dependent upon the estimate of the future life of the fixed asset. Lack of verifiability appears to be the main reason why the American Accounting Association has expressed reservations about attesting to forecasts. The *AAA's Statement of Basic Accounting Theory* states: "Accountants generally refrain from reporting budgets relating to future periods to external users, on the ground that the information is not sufficiently verifiable, although it might be highly relevant to external users' needs. Failure to observe the standard of verifiability to a minimum degree would place the accountant, in some cases, in the role of forecaster and would reduce the confidence of the user and thereby diminish the usefulness of accounting reports. We believe that a substantial level of verifiability is most important for externally reported accounting information."

Budgets have been reserved traditionally for internal (management) uses. In fact, it might be argued that accountants have restricted forecasts to internal use because of presumed lack of verifiability. If this argument is valid, it represents a circumstance unique to the accounting discipline; the norms of auditing are constraining accounting practice in this instance.

The question arises as to what course of action CPAs would take if corporations began to include budgets in published annual reports. Figure 1, page 445, shows the annual report of a small public corporation which chose to disclose sales budgets. The forecasted statements show alternative sales outcomes with probabilities attached to each outcome. The budgets, which are not audited, represent a definite departure from traditional reporting practice.

Obviously, different assumptions were made to cast the statements. While these assumptions are mentioned, the likelihood (probability) of attaining each is not discussed. All alternatives listed are dependent upon the consummation of specific exchange transactions which are, as we have attempted to demonstrate earlier, the basic raw materials of accounting. At this point, we ask who is best equipped to attest to the probabilities of occurrence of these events? The Institute of Chartered Accountants in England and Wales has determined that auditors are the best qualified to accomplish this task.

ENGLISH INSTITUTE'S CERTIFICATE

Figure 2, page 446, contains a sample of the unqualified form of the "Accountants' Report on Profit Forecasts" now used by the Institute of Chartered Accountants in England and Wales. This form is altered to reflect any reservations of the auditor. According to the report, the auditor attests to two items: (1) the bases for the forecasts and (2) the calculations.

Attesting to the bases on which the forecasts are made seems to present no special problem of verifiability. For example, to test the method of inventory valuation used in a forecast, the accountant

MICRO-TOL ENGINEERING CORPORATION
SALES FORECAST

Product	Probability	68/69 FY	69/70 FY	70/71 FY
1. Resolution	O*	$300,000.	$ 600,000.	$1,300,000.
Multiplier	M	150,000.	300,000.	650,000.
	P	75,000.	150,000.	350,000.
2. High Vacuum	O	55,000.	110,000.	150,000.
System	M	27,500.	55,000.	75,000.
	P	11,000.	27,500.	35,000.
3. Electron	O	8,000.	12,000.	18,000.
Optics Kits	M	5,000.	7,000.	10,000.
	P	3,000.	4,000.	6,000.
4. Detector	O		250,000.	650,000.
System	M		125,000.	350,000.
	P		50,000.	200,000.
5. Engrg. & Mfg.	O	260,000.	405,000.	425,000.
Contract Work	M	150,000.	250,000.	250,000.
	P	100,000.	175,000.	175,000.
6. Totals	O	$623,000.	$1,377,000.	$2,543,000.
	M	332,500.	737,000.	1,335,000.
	P	189,000.	406,500.	766,000.
7. Profit Potential	O	62,300.	137,700.	254,300.
(10% after taxes)	M	33,250.	73,700.	133,500.
	P	18,900.	40,650.	76,600.

*Optimistic (70%)
Median (93%)
Pessimistic (99%)

Source: Micro-Tol Engineering Corporation, *Annual Report*, Fiscal Year 1967-68.

Figure 1

would have to determine only whether the method used in the forecast is consistent with the method adopted by the company in its published historical financial statements. Neither verifying calculations would present a problem to the accountant. An important aspect of the certificate is that the accountant is not responsible for reporting on the assumptions upon which the corporation based its forecast, which would exclude the accountant from the role of "forecaster," a role regarded as alien by many accounting organizations and individual CPAs.

Important as well is the fact that the report specifically states that the directors are solely responsible for the forecast. The report must

---

A SPECIMEN ACCOUNTANTS' REPORT ON THE ACCOUNTING BASES AND CALCULATIONS OF PROFIT FORECASTS

To the directors of X Ltd.:

We have reviewed the accounting bases and calculations for the profit forecasts of X Ltd. (for which the directors are solely responsible) for the periods _____ as set out on pages _____ of this circular. The forecasts include results shown by unaudited interim accounts for the period _____. In our opinion the forecasts, so far as the accounting bases and calculations are concerned, have been properly compiled on the footing of the assumptions made by the Board set out on page _____ of this circular and are presented on a basis consistent with the accounting practices, normally adopted by the company.

Source: *Accountants' Reports on Profit Forecasts*, Institute of Chartered Accountants in England and Wales (July, 1969) p. 7.

Figure 2

also include the assumptions the directors have used in the forecast, and the user of the information is thus able to decide for himself whether the assumptions are valid.

SUMMARY AND CONCLUSION

The business entity is a complex behavioral system that requires information useful in meeting the needs of the various participants as they try to determine where the entity should be and is headed. Forecasts simulate future behavior, and, by introducing some measure of predictability, help reduce uncertainty.

The basic subject matter of accounting appears to be exchange transactions. We suggest that forecasts consist of anticipated exchanges and, as such, should be considered within the boundaries of the accounting discipline. It seems that the main objection to accountants attesting to forecasts is the lack of verifiability of future transactions.

Extant CPA practice in the United States would not be altered radically by the adoption of report requirements similar to those adopted by the Institute of England and Wales on profit forecasts. The "Report on Profit Forecasts" is a small step, but a step in the right direction. As measurement techniques are developed to make more accurate predictions, the accountant might consider including in his opinion some of the assumptions underlying the forecasts.

Extending the CPA's opinion to forecasts is within the present competence of the profession. As the needs of society change, accounting and auditing must evolve to meet these changing needs; the question becomes one of the demand for audited forecasts.

35. Opinions on Internal Control*

D. R. Carmichael†

With increasing frequency, auditors hear the suggestion that they should express an opinion on the effectiveness of a client's internal control system. Advocates of this extension of the attest function are quick to point out that there are already instances in which independent auditors are reporting publicly on the effectiveness of their clients' systems of internal control and that some government agencies, including the Securities and Exchange Commission in some cases, require a report. Opponents of attestation-type reports counter that any report on internal control effectiveness would be misleading to the public and they believe that there is a significant difference between present regulatory agency reporting requirements and an opinion on internal control. This article reviews the present reporting practices, considers the desirable features of the reports as well as the associated hazards, and, finally, proposes some of the questions which must be answered before any final judgment can be made.

THE CURRENT STATUS OF REPORTS

Although auditors' reports do in several circumstances contain references to internal control, the nature of the representations made concerning effectiveness differ significantly.

Large banks. Opinions on internal control are, in fact, given in the case of a few large banks and the opinions do appear in published annual reports. These opinions are sometimes requested by the board of directors. For example, the following opinion appears in the 1969 annual report of a large New York bank, as a third paragraph in the independent accountant's standard short-form report:

> Our examination included an evaluation of the effectiveness of the bank's internal accounting controls, including the internal auditing. In our opinion, the procedures in effect, together with the examinations conducted by the bank's internal audit staff, constitute an effective system of internal accounting control.

*From *The Journal of Accountancy* (December, 1970), pp. 47–53. Copyright (1970) by the American Institute of Certified Public Accountants, Inc. Reprinted by permission of the AICPA.

†D. R. Carmichael, Ph.D., CPA, is Assistant Director, Auditing & Reporting, American Institute of Certified Public Accountants.

Opinions are rendered for a few other banks, but they are essentially the same as the quoted opinion.

SEC requirements. SEC Form X-17A-5, which requires that the independent auditor make certain representations concerning internal control, must be filed annually by most members of national securities exchanges and every broker or dealer registered pursuant to Section 15 of the Securities Exchange Act of 1934.

In addition, the SEC's Rule 17a-5(g) requires that the independent auditor's report contain "a statement as to whether the accountant reviewed the procedures for safeguarding the securities of customers." Moreover, many exchanges require that the report indicate that a review has been made of "the accounting system, the internal accounting control and procedures for safeguarding securities including appropriate tests thereof for the period since the prior examination date," and, evidently, the SEC staff prefers that the accountant include language similar to that required by the exchanges in all reports filed with the SEC. The scope paragraph of the report usually reads as follows:

> We have examined the statement of financial condition of (name) as of (date). Our examination was made in accordance with generally accepted auditing standards, and *accordingly included a review of the accounting system, the internal accounting control and procedures for safeguarding securities and such tests thereof since the prior examination date, (date)* and of the accounting records and such other auditing procedures as we considered necessary in the circumstances. (Emphasis added.)

To avoid confusion as to the type of review made, it is related to "generally accepted auditing standards" by the word "accordingly." Note that the requirement is met without the expression of an opinion on adequacy since the report merely states that a review has been made.

If there are material inadequacies in internal control, the independent auditor is required to report them to the SEC, but according to Rule 17a-5(b)(3) inadequacies may be reported in a confidential supplementary report. If no material inadequacies are found, a representation to that effect is neither required nor expected. Therefore reports to the SEC do not constitute the expression of an opinion on internal control effectiveness and, in this respect, differ significantly from the reports issued for a few large banks.

Other government agencies. Government agencies differ widely in the type of report required on internal control. Perhaps the most stringent requirement is that administered by the Office of Economic Opportunity. Section 243 of the Economic Opportunity Amendments of 1967 requires an auditor's appraisal of a grantee's accounting system and internal controls before a substantial amount of OEO grant funds have been expended (see JofA, Sep. 70, pp. 78-82). The auditor's report must include the following opinion:

> The accounting system and internal controls of the (grantee and delegate agencies) are considered (adequate, inadequate) to safeguard the assets of the grantee, check the accuracy and reliability of accounting data, promote operational efficiency and encourage adherence to prescribed management policies.

Some agencies require a report very similar to that required by the SEC for brokers. The Federal Home Loan Bank Board, for example, requires that the auditor's report indicate that internal control has been reviewed and requires submission of a copy of the management letter containing comments about any weaknesses in the system and recommendations for their correction.

THE DESIRABILITY OF REPORTING ON INTERNAL CONTROL

Those who believe that reports on internal control are desirable do so primarily for two reasons. First, they believe such reports would be useful to the public in evaluating management's performance in this area of its responsibility. Some regard such reports as a feasible and logical first step toward reports on management's performance in other areas.

The second reason advanced by advocates of reports on internal control is that these reports would provide an additional basis for reliance on unaudited interim financial statements. In view of the increasing importance of quarterly and other interim statements, the advocates believe that such reports would provide a useful public service. Opponents, on the other hand, are concerned that such reports would be a disservice to the public because of the risk of misunderstanding and unwarranted reliance. Thus, the crux of the question concerning desirability of reporting on internal control turns on an evaluation of the potential benefits and hazards to the readers of such reports.

HAZARDS OF REPORTING ON INTERNAL CONTROL

If reporting on internal control holds potential benefit for the profession and report users, what has impeded wholehearted assumption of responsibility for reporting on internal control?

First, there is really no such thing as an overall evaluation of internal control. An auditor views internal control in terms of specific types of errors and irregularities which may occur because of weaknesses in the procedures concerning specific classes of transactions and related assets. Unless internal control is excellent in every respect, generalizations about the adequacy of the overall system are extremely difficult to make. Strengths in one area of internal control do not normally offset weaknesses in another area. Weaknesses in cash receipts procedures are not mitigated by strength in handling of cash disbursements, and adequate collection procedures cannot substitute for ineffective control over billing procedures.

Second, and closely related to the difficulties of an overall evaluation, there is the incomparability of an opinion on the financial statements taken as a whole and an opinion on the internal control system taken as a whole. Weaknesses in internal control can have a potential material impact on operations, but their materiality cannot be evaluated in the same manner that a known dollar amount of error can be with respect to the financial statements taken as a whole. Therefore, it is difficult to formulate the language of a standard report from which deviations could be considered as having a special and known significance.

Third, there are many inherent limitations on the effectiveness of any system of internal control. Certain actions are not subject to control within the scope of internal control systems. Control procedures that depend primarily on the separation of incompatible duties can be circumvented by collusion. Management officials who are charged with administering the internal control system are in a position to perpetrate intentional errors and irregularities in spite of the controls that might prevent similar actions by lower ranking employees. Perhaps the most critical inherent limitation is the fact that performance of many control procedures is dependent on human judgment and volition and there are many possibilities for error arising from misunderstandings, mistakes, carelessness, distraction or fatigue.

Finally — partially as a consequence of the other problems — reports on internal control create a significant possibility of unwarranted and misleading inferences on the part of users. Prominent among possible misunderstandings is the unwarranted projection of the opinion into future periods and the concomitant undue reliance on unaudited financial information. The review and tests of internal control pertain only to the period covered during the examination. In the future, conditions, procedures and compliance may change. Many changes may occur to cause variations in compliance with established procedures, including new employees or employees taking over new responsibilities, unusual fluctuations in business volume that cause employees to take short cuts, and innovations in operations which introduce new types of transactions. Further, the reliability of financial statements is significantly influenced by management judgments which are not subject to control by the system.

In view of the significant hazards associated with opinions on internal control, such opinions should be expressed with care and caution. At present there is an absence of field work and reporting standards for expressing an opinion on internal control, and the CPA who renders a report is exposing himself to an undefined responsibility.

Many questions must be answered before opinions on internal control should be issued on a regular basis. These questions may be divided into fundamental questions and reporting guideline questions.

FUNDAMENTAL QUESTIONS

DOES AN OPINION ON INTERNAL CONTROL CONTAIN INFORMATION IMPORTANT TO ANYONE OTHER THAN MANAGEMENT?

Letters to management recommending improvements in the internal control system are a traditional by-product of independent audits. While the value of these reports on internal control is acknowledged as an important service to management, opponents of opinions on internal control question their importance to parties other than management.

Advocates of opinions on internal control hold that the report does, to a limited extent, increase the reliance which can be placed on unaudited financial information in the future even though reliability is unaffected. At the present time, an unqualified opinion on financial statements may be based on an examination which includes a significant extension of auditing procedures necessitated by poor internal control, but the reader of the auditor's report has no way of knowing this. A report on internal control would highlight the weakness and the reader would know that substantially less reliance should be placed on the unaudited financial information issued during the period between audited statements. In addition, and of more importance, is the fact that an opinion on internal control reports on management's significant fiduciary obligation to devise, install and supervise an adequate system of internal control.

WOULD REPORTING ON INTERNAL CONTROL SIGNIFICANTLY EXTEND THE AUDITOR'S LIABILITY BEYOND THAT ASSUMED WHEN ISSUING AN OPINION ON FINANCIAL STATEMENTS?

Any suggested extension of the attest function raises apprehensions concerning a concomitant extension of legal liability. Although a definitive answer to the extent of legal liability assumed cannot be obtained prior to litigation, there are several lines of speculation.

One view is that the most likely cause of action will arise when an unreported weakness in internal control causes a material misstatement in financial position or in the results of operations in the period covered by the opinion. Under these circumstances the deficiency in the report is likely to receive widespread attention and people relying on the report are likely to be damaged thereby. In this situation, the auditor would probably be involved in litigation anyway because of his opinion on the financial statements.

There is also a possibility of material errors or irregularities caused by deliberate management misrepresentation or employee collusion, which no system of internal control can prevent. The auditor's responsibility for these items should be similar to his responsibility when the financial statements on which he renders an unqualified opinion are materially misleading because of deliberate management misrepresentation or employee collusion. As long as he complied with generally accepted auditing standards, he would not be responsible.

Another view on legal liability is that the expression of an opinion on internal control will draw attention to present responsibilities and also increase those responsibilities. Plaintiffs in a case against auditors will have a new alleged deficiency with which to charge the auditor. In addition, if the subject of internal control review and evaluation becomes a point of litigation, juries may have even more difficulties evaluating this technical subject than they do evaluating testimony concerning financial statement presentation.

SHOULD A REPORT ON INTERNAL CONTROL BE REQUIRED OR SHOULD IT BE VOLUNTARY AND ISSUED AT THE DISCRETION OF MANAGEMENT?

It does not seem to be within the auditor's province to require a report on internal control. The report does not add any credibility to audited financial statements and, thus, is not required for a fair presentation of financial position and results of operations. Those opposed to opinions on internal control contend that only "positive" opinions that internal control is adequate will be issued. Management would have a natural reluctance to have significant inadequacies in internal control exposed to public view and, consequently, would not allow unfavorable opinions to be issued.

Those favoring opinions on internal control counter that new reporting practices must start somewhere. Voluntary reporting disclosures — if they contain significant information — have a way of becoming required either by public pressure or the force of custom.

CAN A REPORT BE PREPARED WHICH WILL NOT BE MISLEADING TO REPORT USERS?

Whether a report will be misleading is a function of both the accuracy and clarity of the report and the knowledge and understanding possessed by the users of the report. One of the most significant hazards of reporting on internal control is the possibility of unwarranted and misleading inferences on the part of users. Experience with the short-form report on financial statements indicates that it may be as important for a report on internal control to say what the report does not represent as it is to accurately state what is represented. Actually, the answer to this question depends, to a large extent, on the answers obtained from the reporting guideline questions.

REPORTING GUIDELINE QUESTIONS

SHOULD THE REPORT ON INTERNAL CONTROL BE A SEPARATE REPORT DISTINCT FROM THE OPINION ON FINANCIAL STATEMENTS?

Although there is a definite relationship between the evaluation of internal control and the opinion on the financial statements, there is a significant distinction between audited financial statements and internal control evaluation. In forming his opinion on the statements, the auditor's evaluation of internal control is only an intermediate step in his examination. The opinion on internal control adds no further credibility to the financial statements and any implication that this is true should be avoided.

Of course, internal control evaluation must be mentioned in the report on the financial statements when internal control is so inadequate that compliance with generally accepted auditing standards is impossible. In the extreme case when internal control is virtually nonexistent, a disclaimer of opinion on the statements is appropriate. In these circumstances there is a significant probability of unrecorded transactions, documentary evidence examined is highly suspect, and post balance sheet events cannot be adequately reviewed.

If the distinction between the opinion on financial statements and the opinion on internal control is to be made forcefully, the opinion on internal control should be a separate report. If the reports are not separated, the opinion on financial statements should precede the report on internal control to avoid implication that the latter is necessary for fair presentation of the financial statements.

WHAT IS THE APPROPRIATE SCOPE OF AUDIT WORK NECESSARY TO SUPPORT AN OPINION ON INTERNAL CONTROL?

There are no standards of field work for determining the scope of work necessary to support an opinion on internal control. An adequate description of the work performed in a scope section of the report could serve the same function as the scope paragraph in the report on financial statements. An auditor should be responsible for failure to disclose a weakness in internal control only if his review and evaluation should have uncovered that weakness. The scope of audit work for opinions on internal control has two aspects — breadth of coverage and depth of investigation.

SHOULD THE SCOPE OF THE REVIEW BE CLARIFIED BY INCLUDING A CONCISE DEFINITION OF INTERNAL CONTROL IN THE REPORT?

The breadth of coverage could be as broad as a special investigation of a management information system or as narrow as the accounting controls which must be reviewed to comply with the second standard of field work. No matter what breadth of coverage was, the scope paragraph could include a concise definition of the internal control system reviewed. Although a number of definitions would probably be equally suitable, some definition should be given to describe concisely the subject of the report. A phrase at the end of the definition introduced by the work "including" could be used to identify any aspect of controls requiring specific mention. For example, the board of directors may feel that evaluation of the internal auditing department is especially important.

IS THE SCOPE OF THE EXAMINATION NECESSARY TO SUPPORT AN OPINION ON INTERNAL CONTROL THE SAME AS THAT REQUIRED TO SATISFY THE SECOND STANDARD OF FIELD WORK?

The second standard of field work states:

There is to be a proper study and evaluation of the existing internal control as a basis for reliance thereon and for the determination of the resultant extent of the tests to which auditing procedures are to be restricted.

If the breadth of coverage of the opinion is the same as that required for an opinion on financial statements, then the depth of the investigation may be related to compliance with the second standard of field work. This aspect may be covered in a scope section of the report as follows:

> Our examination of the financial statements performed in accordance with generally accepted auditing standards, *accordingly* included a review and evaluation of the accounting system and internal controls. (Emphasis added.)

In a large company with a high volume of clerical work, any degree of audit coverage beyond tests of a small percentage of total transactions would be prohibitively costly. Consequently, the auditor must review and test the internal controls and be satisfied with the adequacy of the system. In a small company this may not be true. In addition, accountants are not in complete agreement on the amount of audit work necessary to perform a review and evaluation of internal control which meets the second standard of field work. For these reasons, there is disagreement on the depth of investigation necessary to support an opinion on internal control.

SHOULD AN OPINION ON INTERNAL CONTROL BE EXPRESSED IN TERMS OF AN OVERALL MEASURE SUCH AS ADEQUACY OR EFFECTIVENESS?

Several characteristics of internal control systems are relevant to this question. Weaknesses in internal control are not offsetting, all systems have inherent weaknesses, and cost acts as a constraint on the effectiveness of all systems. One view is that these characteristics are "understood" in a comprehensive expression such as adequacy or effectiveness. "Effective" in this context means appropriate for the particular situation, with each company regarded as a unique situation.

Another view holds that experience with the short-form report on financial statements indicates that very little should be presumed to be "understood" and that, since the "adequacy" of the system is the auditor's representation, great care should be exercised in clearly stating what "adequate" means.

SHOULD AN OPINION ON PRESCRIBED METHODS AND PROCEDURES BE SEPARATED FROM AN OPINION ON COMPLIANCE WITH THOSE PROCEDURES?

One suggested alternative to a comprehensive representation on effectiveness is the division of the opinion between the adequacy of prescribed internal control procedures and the adequacy of compliance with those procedures. A proper study and evaluation of internal control includes two distinct phases. According to the American Institute of CPAs' Statement on Auditing Procedure No. 33 (p. 32):

> Adequate evaluation of a system of internal control requires (1) knowledge and understanding of the procedures and methods prescribed and (2) a reasonable degree of assurance that they are in use and operating as planned. (Numerals added.)

Knowledge and understanding of the prescribed procedures are gained by a review of the system accomplished by inquiry, observation and review of documentation. On the other hand, assurance that the procedures are in use and operating as planned requires tests of compliance. By observation of personnel and examination of documentary evidence, the auditor determines, for the entire period covered by the examination, whether the necessary procedures were performed and, if so, by whom. Thus, the auditor may form different conclusions concerning the adequacy of the prescribed procedures and the degree of compliance with those procedures.

Separation of the opinion on prescribed procedures from the opinion on compliance serves the further purpose of alerting the reader to some of the limitations inherent in any internal control system by giving notice that the existence of adequate procedures does not automatically assure satisfactory compliance.

IF A SEPARATE OPINION IS EXPRESSED ON COMPLIANCE, WHAT PERIOD OF TIME SHOULD BE COVERED?

Since one of the significant hazards of expressing an opinion on internal control is unwarranted projection of the representations to the future, the opinion should be expressed with respect to a point in time or a span of time. An opinion could be expressed on the internal control system in effect at the time of the completion of the review, which would normally coincide with the completion of field work. On the other hand, the opinion might be expressed for the period of time in the company's operations covered by the examination, which would normally coincide with the period covered by the financial statements. Another variation would limit the period of time for which the opinion was expressed to the time span of the review and evaluation of the internal control system which could be limited to a few months.

SHOULD ADDITIONAL CAUTIONARY LANGUAGE BE ADDED TO THE OPINION TO CLARIFY THE NATURE OF THE OPINION AND EXPLAIN WHAT IT DOES NOT REPRESENT?

Two hazards of reporting on internal control are especially relevant to this question: (1) The effectiveness of any system is subject to inherent limitations and (2) there is a danger that the system may change in the future, which makes projection of the opinion to the future unwarranted.

An opinion on internal control could include a denial section which concisely explains the limitations of the opinion. Wording such as the following might be included in such a section: (1) The continuing effectiveness of the system as designed requires constant surveillance on the part of management and periodic review. (2) The effective functioning of any system of internal control depends on whether individuals continue to conform to prescribed policies and procedures. (3) We do not express an opinion on future compliance with prescribed procedures. (4) The system of internal control cannot prevent collusion or prevent intentional irregularities by the administrators of the system.

WHAT CRITERIA SHOULD BE USED IN DETERMINING WHETHER EXCEPTIONS TO EFFECTIVE INTERNAL CONTROL SHOULD BE REPORTED?

There are two alternative, existing criteria which could be used as a basis for reporting exceptions. One criterion relates effectiveness or adequacy of internal control to financial statement presentation. Under this criterion an exception would be reported if controls would not, with reasonable promptness, prevent or detect material errors and irregularities, i.e., those which have a potential material impact on the financial statements. The other criterion would report exceptions on the same basis used to recommend improvements in internal control to management.

HOW SHOULD EXCEPTIONS BE REPORTED?

This question is not so much one of format as it is a matter of degrees of opinions. Under one view exceptions would be introduced into the report by adding the phrase "except as noted below" to the appropriate opinion sentence. Exceptions would be listed after the opinion paragraph and classified by major class of transaction or asset and the relation to adequacy or compliance. If the exceptions were sufficiently material, the opinion would be expressed that internal control was inadequate. In other words, there would be three types of opinions equivalent to the unqualified, qualified and adverse types of opinions rendered on financial statements.

Another view would limit the types of opinions to either "adequate" or "inadequate." Under this view, weaknesses not considered sufficient to regard the system as inadequate might be included in a report on internal control. Further, some controls outside the scope of the review for internal control report purposes might be included in a report to management, which might very well be different from the report to others. This situation is analogous to the situation which exists for long-form and short-form reports. The recommendations to management not contained in the report on internal control should not warrant reporting in the opinion on internal control, i.e., they should not support a contention that the report on internal control was misleading.

How should the auditor comply with internal control reports prescribed by regulatory agencies?

If the regulatory agency requirement is for a statement that the internal control system was reviewed as part of the examination and a copy of the recommendation letter to management, the requirement does not expose the auditor to the hazards of expressing an opinion on internal control previously outlined. However, if the regulatory agency requires a positive expression of opinion on internal control effectiveness and, in addition, prescribes the form of report, the auditor should give careful consideration to whether the prescribed form sufficiently recognizes the reporting hazards.

If the prescribed form is unacceptable to the auditor, he has two basic alternatives. He could attempt to persuade the agency to accept a substantially different report, which could take a variety of forms. On the other hand, he could modify the prescribed opinion to reduce the reporting hazards in a manner which meets the specific requirements of the agency.

Consider the reporting requirement administered by the Office of Economic Opportunity, which is that "the auditor's appraisal regarding the accounting systems and internal controls *must include* the following words [previously quoted opinion] in order to be acceptable to OEO." (Emphasis added.) In other words, their opinion paragraph must be used, but they do not say that the opinion has to be confined to their wording. A possible modification of the prescribed form would be the addition of a scope paragraph to clarify the basis supporting the opinion and another paragraph to explain what the opinion does not include, which might be called a denial paragraph. (See *JofA*, Sept. 70, p. 78 for a more comprehensive analysis.)

SHOULD AN OPINION ON INTERNAL CONTROL BE EXPRESSED WHEN AN AUDIT IS NOT PERFORMED?

When the auditor is associated with financial statements which are unaudited, a report on internal control is not in accordance with paragraph 8, SAP No. 38, which states that "any auditing procedures that may have been performed in connection with unaudited financial statements ordinarily should not be described. . . ." When the statements are unaudited, the review and tests of internal control are among the incomplete procedures which should not be reported because of the risk of misunderstanding their significance.

Situations may arise in which only a report on the adequacy of prescribed procedures is desired. Such a report would be appropriate as a result of a special assignment when the auditor is not associated with financial statements. If an opinion is rendered on the adequacy of prescribed procedures alone, the opinion should explicitly exclude responsibility for representations concerning present and future compliance with those procedures.

CONCLUSION

Although reports concerning internal control are issued in numerous circumstances, with rare exceptions these reports are not attestations on internal control effectiveness. In the absence of established auditing standards for internal control reports, issuance of attestation-type reports is fraught with significant hazards. This article proposes several questions concerning reporting guidelines which must be answered before opinions on internal control are issued with any frequency. However, even when the questions of report form are answered, several fundamental questions must still be resolved.

36. A CPA's Opinion on Management Performance*

T. G. Secoy†

Should a certified public accountant express an independent attestation on management performance for the benefit of third parties? This question is the subject of some controversy. Proponents of this extension of the attest function believe it is feasible and would aid stockholders, creditors and other third parties in their assessment of corporate management.[1] Opponents question its practicability.[2]

A report on a management audit expressing an independent attestation on management performance raises some fundamental questions. First, what are the nature and wording of the attestation which an auditor can, and should, include in his report? Second, what are the content and structure of the report? Other significant questions concern: (1) the lack of an established body of generally accepted auditing standards and procedures for management audits; (2) the kinds of financial data and other informational materials to be covered in such audits; (3) the lack of an established body of standards for the evaluation of managerial abilities and performance; (4) the competence of auditors to conduct and report on such audits; (5) the auditor's independence and objectivity in management auditing; and (6) the legal liability of auditors with regard to such audits.

In a recent article, Douglas R. Carmichael made the following comments about expressing an independent attestation on management performance:

> In all of the many articles written on management auditing not one author has suggested an appropriate report for expressing an independent attestation on management. Some have suggested that the management audit report would need to be longer and have a less standard format

*From *The Journal of Accountancy* (July, 1971), pp. 53-59. Copyright (1971) by the American Institute of Certified Public Accountants, Inc. Reprinted by permission of the AICPA.

†T. G. Secoy, Ph.D., CPA, is Professor of Accounting, Illinois State University, Normal, Illinois. The author wishes to acknowledge the assistance of Bruce W. Breitweiser, a graduate student, in the initial research for this article.

[1]See, for example, John C. Burton, "Management Auditing," *Journal of Accountancy* (May, 1968), p. 41; Robert W. Clarke, "Extension of the CPA's Attest Function in Corporate Annual Reports," *Accounting Review* (October, 1968), p. 769; and Harold Q. Langenderfer and Jack C. Robertson, "A Theoretical Structure for Independent Audits of Management," *Accounting Review* (October, 1969), p. 777.

[2]See, for example, Douglas R. Carmichael, "Some Hard Questions on Management Audits," *Journal of Accountancy* (February, 1970), pp. 72-74; and Howard F. Stettler, "CPAs/Auditing/2000±," *Journal of Accountancy* (May, 1968), p. 58.

than the report on financial statements. That makes sense. *But why has not one example of such a report been given?*

Could it be that the management audit is such a loosely defined and abstract concept that the *actual writing of a concrete report* has not been attempted? The time has come for the advocates of management auditing to be specific. *A report should be proposed so that it can be evaluated on its merits.*[3] (Emphasis added.)

The purpose of this article is to propose an example of a report on a management audit expressing an independent attestation on management performance which can be evaluated on its merits. The report proposed here is admittedly tentative and is submitted with the hope that it will help stimulate discussion of this important accounting matter.

NORMATIVE ASSUMPTIONS AND CONDITIONS

The proposed report is necessarily based on a set of normative assumptions and conditions regarding the various questions relating to management audits mentioned earlier. First, it is taken for granted that a management audit had been made — specifically, an audit of the XYZ Manufacturing Corporation (a medium-sized company). It is also assumed that the same firm of certified public accountants audited and rendered a standard short-form report on the company's financial statements.

Second, it is assumed that the audit staff was able to develop and apply a set of *management auditing standards and procedures* which were found to be appropriate and satisfactory in the circumstances. It may be noted that these standards and procedures included: (1) some of the generally accepted auditing standards and procedures for financial audits and (2) established standards, procedures and techniques used in applied research in business and the behavioral sciences.

Third, it is taken for granted that a wide variety of financial data (in addition to that in the audited financial statements) and other informational materials were available for audit without restriction by management. Such data and other materials covered the following areas: the organizational structure of the company; the information system; the system of managerial controls[4] (including the system of internal financial controls); management procedures; and the various

---

[3]Carmichael, *op. cit.*, p. 72. Mr. Carmichael is auditing research consultant for the AICPA.
[4]Burton, *op. cit.*, p. 42, has listed five possible areas of managerial control: organization control; planning and information systems; asset management; marketing system; and production system.

operating projects and managerial plans, policies and goals for the year under investigation. Further, it is assumed that such data and other materials, together with that covered in the financial audit, were sufficient for an evaluation of management.

Fourth, it is assumed that the audit staff was able to develop and apply standards for the evaluation of management which were found to be appropriate and satisfactory in the circumstances. These standards included, among others, the following "possible measures of success" listed by Burton:

1. Ratio of operating return on sales earned by the company compared to the return earned by the industry.
2. Ratio of operating return on long-term capital earned by the company compared to the return earned by the industry.
3. Comparative variability in return compared to average industry variability.[5]

These standards also included the following "seven reported indicators of managerial ability," listed by Langenderfer and Robertson, which are based on the results of a study made by Mautz:

1. Return on common equity.
2. Ratio of net income before interest to invested capital.
3. Financial condition.
4. Net income.
5. Growth of company.
6. Reputation of key personnel.
7. Market performance of stock.[6]

Fifth, it is assumed that the members of the audit staff were competent in view of their training and experience to perform the management audit and provide an attestation on management performance. Further, the audit staff is assumed to have consisted of four persons from the management services staff of the accounting firm (a systems analyst, a financial analyst, an industrial psychologist and a production analyst) and three members of the audit staff (a senior and two assistant auditors).

Sixth, it is assumed that there was no question as to the independence and objectivity of the auditors — there being no conflict of interest between management and the auditors, and management did not attempt to influence the conduct of the audit or the report on its performance. The firm was engaged by a corporate audit committee consisting of outside board members, none of whom were officers

---

[5]*Ibid.*, p. 43.
[6]Langenderfer and Robertson, *op. cit.*, p. 779, citing R. K. Mautz, *Financial Reporting by Diversified Companies* (Financial Executives Research Foundation, 1968).

of the firm or directly active in its management. The report on the management audit was to be directed to the audit committee and to the stockholders and was to be included in the annual report to stockholders in a special section following the financial statements and the standard short-form report on these statements.

Seventh, it is assumed that the express terms of the engagement were such that the partner-in-charge believed, on the advice of legal counsel, that he, the firm and the staff members were assuming no unusual or untoward legal liability with regard to management or the stockholders and other third parties.

Finally, it is assumed that the audit revealed only one major operational deficiency that could be fairly and reasonably attributed to management — a lack of effective communication of operational information from the supervisory level to the higher levels of management planning and controls. On all other counts the performance of management was found to be reasonably satisfactory, evaluated on the basis of the audited materials and measured in terms of the standards developed and used by the audit staff.

The Report

As mentioned earlier, the formulation of a report on a management audit involves two crucial questions concerning, first, the nature and wording of the attestation which an auditor can, and should, render on management performance and, second, the content and structure of the management audit report.

There are two positions that can be taken with regard to these questions. First, it can be held that the report should be similar to the standard short-form report on an examination of financial statements. That is, there would be a statement regarding the "scope of the management audit," including a representation that it was conducted in accordance with a body of "generally accepted auditing standards for management audits," followed by an "opinion" that "managerial representations" regarding its performance were "fairly presented" in conformity with a body of "generally accepted standards of management performance." This view seems to be implicit in much of Carmichael's criticism of the concept of a report on a management audit.[7]

Alternatively, the position can be taken that such a report should differ in several important respects from the standard short-form

---

[7]Carmichael, *op. cit.*, pp. 72-73. See, in particular, his discussion of question No. 3, "Just exactly what are management representations?" and No. 4, "Can the notion of 'fair presentation' be applied to representations other than the basic financial statements?"

report. In this view, some of the essential elements and characteristics of the short-form report would not be appropriate in a report on a management audit and thus would have to be altered or omitted. Further, such a report would contain elements and characteristics not present in the short-form report.

The first position is untenable because the nature and consequent methodology of a management audit and the objective of the report on such an audit are essentially different from those of a financial audit and the short-form report. Specifically, the two essential elements of the short-form report — namely, the representation regarding the *scope* of the audit in the scope paragraph and the attestation in the opinion paragraph — are not applicable in a report on a management audit in the technical and traditional senses in which they are used in a report on a financial audit. Further, in view of its fundamental objective — an independent attestation on management performance — the report necessarily must contain information which is not required in a short-form report and the information in the report must be arranged differently from that in the short-form report. Therefore the format of the two reports must differ.

SCOPE OF THE AUDIT

The auditor's conventional representation regarding the *scope* of his audit is based on a body of ten generally accepted auditing standards and related procedures which has developed over the years to meet the requirements of financial audits. That is, his representation is based on a set of standards and procedures comprising an audit methodology which is generally taken to apply only to an examination of financial statements. Further, these generally accepted auditing standards have been codified and have an òfficial status through action of the AICPA.[8]

Kohler has described these standards as follows:

General standards: (a) The audit must be conducted by a person of adequate technical training and experience who must (b) maintain an independent mental attitude throughout, and (c) exercise due professional care during the audit and in his report. *Fieldwork standards:* (d) The work must be adequately planned, and assistants, if any, properly supervised; (e) internal controls must be studied and evaluated as a basis for reliance and for determination of the extent to which audit tests may be restricted; and (f) adequate evidence must be obtained through inspection, observation, inquiries and confirmations that will supply the basis for the audit report. *Reporting standards:* The report must indicate

---

[8]See AICPA committee on auditing procedure, *Generally Accepted Auditing Standards* (New York: AICPA, 1954).

(g) whether the financial statements conform to "generally accepted principles of accounting," (h) whether these principles have been followed consistently and conform to those of the preceding period, and (i) any exceptions to the adequacy of disclosures appearing in the financial statements; (j) it also must contain an opinion, qualified where necessary, on the financial statements.[9]

The question here, as Carmichael has indicated,[10] is whether the standards and procedures of financial auditing can be transferred to management auditing and, if so, to what extent.

Some of the ten standards and their related procedures are presently applicable to management auditing and can be used as readily and competently there as they are in financial auditing. These standards are the second and third of the general standards and all three of the field-work standards as listed and described on page 464. A careful reading of the descriptions[11] of these five standards reveals no apparent reasons why these standards and the requisite related procedures cannot be transferred to management auditing and appropriately modified to fit the nature and objectives of such auditing. It is these standards and their related procedures which are assumed to be a part of the set of management auditing standards and procedures which were found to be appropriate and satisfactory in the audit of the XYZ Manufacturing Corporation.

While there is no doubt that some auditors are fully qualified to perform all phases of the work in a management audit, it is questionable whether most auditors, with little special training[12] or experience in management auditing, are qualified to perform a management audit in its entirety. For this reason, there is a question of whether the first general standard, regarding "the training and proficiency of the auditor," can be transferred to management auditing without qualification. However, when the accountants on the audit staff are not fully qualified to perform all phases of the management audit, other experts can be added to the audit staff (such as financial analysts, systems analysts, production analysts, industrial psychologists) who are qualified to perform the requisite work under the supervision of the accountant-in-charge. This is presently done in some management advisory services engagements. As was mentioned earlier, it is assumed that four such persons were included on the audit staff for the engagement with the XYZ Corporation.

---

[9]Eric L. Kohler, *A Dictionary for Accountants* (Englewood Cliffs, N. J.: Prentice-Hall, Inc., 1970), p. 42.

[10]Carmichael, *op. cit.*, p. 73.

[11]*Generally Accepted Auditing Standards, op. cit.*, pp. 20-43.

[12]See Arthur E. Witte, "Management Auditing: The Present State of the Art," *Journal of Accountancy* (August, 1967), pp. 57-58, for a description of the special staff training provided by his firm.

As for the four reporting standards, it is evident from a review of Kohler's description[13] that they are not applicable to management auditing. They are related specifically and exclusively to a report on an examination of financial statements and thus cannot be transferred to management auditing under any circumstances. It follows that other standards must be developed for reports on management audits.

In short, five of the ten standards, and their related procedures, are presently applicable to management auditing. Another applies on a qualified basis, while the four reporting standards are not applicable under any circumstances.

In view of the nature of the informational materials to be covered in a management audit and the evidence to be gathered as a basis for an evaluation of management, it is apparent that none of the standards and procedures transferred from financial auditing is sufficient alone to comprise a complete body of audit methodology for management auditing. What, then, are the additional standards and procedures required and how may they be developed? Many of them will be well-established standards, procedures and techniques presently used in applied research in business and the behavioral sciences. In addition, it is likely that combinations and modifications of various auditing and research procedures, such as statistical techniques, which are peculiarly suited to management auditing will be developed. In time, the accounting profession will develop a set of standards and procedures for management auditing which is comparable to the present body of generally accepted auditing standards and related procedures for financial auditing. Until this is done, however, the individual management auditor must develop and apply a set of standards and related procedures that are appropriate for each of his management auditing engagements. As stated earlier, it is assumed that this was done by the auditors of the XYZ Corporation to complete the set of management auditing standards and procedures they found appropriate and satisfactory in the circumstances.

In sum, therefore, auditors are not in a position to make a representation regarding the scope of a management audit, in the technical and traditional senses of that term as it is used in the scope paragraph of the standard short-form report, for the following reasons:

1. The representation in the scope paragraph is based on a body of generally accepted auditing standards and procedures, which are applicable only in part to management auditing.

---

[13]See *Generally Accepted Accounting Standards, op. cit.*, pp. 44-54, for a fuller description.

2. This representation is technically and authoritatively restricted by the reporting standards solely to a report on an examination of financial statements.

3. The scope of a management audit involves the use of standards and procedures not applicable to financial audits.

4. The scope of a management audit covers informational materials and data not covered in financial audits.

This being the case, what kind of a representation can an auditor make regarding the scope of a management audit and how should its wording differ from that of the short-form report?

First, the auditor should include a description at the beginning of his report of the areas of managerial activities, functions and controls and the related informational materials and data covered in his audit. He also should include a direct disclaimer of any coverage of, or responsibility for, managerial forecasts or projections pertaining to future years not covered by his audit. Second, he should include a direct reference to the "management auditing standards and procedures" he found appropriate for the audit and his evaluation of management performance.

As for its wording, the auditor should avoid any terminology which might be ambiguous and lead the reader to confuse his representation with a traditional representation regarding a financial audit. Thus, terms such as: audit or examination; scope of our audit; and generally accepted auditing standards should be avoided. In their place, terms such as: investigation, review, or study; objective research procedures and available standards; and the like should be used.

The Attestation

The attestation (opinion) in the opinion paragraph of the standard short-form report has generally been interpreted as the assumption of responsibility by the auditor for the credibility of management representations as embodied in the basic financial statements.[14]   In other words, technically speaking, the opinion is viewed as a representation by the auditor as to the fairness of management's representations regarding the financial position and results of operations of the enterprise.[15]

While this concept of attestation is valid with regard to an opinion on financial statements, it cannot be taken to apply by extension to an "opinion on management performance."   In the first place, there

---

[14]Carmichael, *loc. cit.*

[15]See Kohler, *op. cit.*, pp. 39 and 304 for definitions of "attest" and "opinion," respectively.

is a question of whether management representations regarding management performance are even involved in a management audit. Carmichael has questioned the concept of management representations, and particularly its application in the area of management audits.[16] More fundamentally, however, the point is that management does not make representations about its own performance which are the subject of representations by the auditor in his report on the management audit. Rather, the auditor makes his own evaluative representations regarding management performance based on the results of his audit.

In the second place, there is a question of whether the technical concept of fairness, as it is used in the traditional sense in the short-form report, applies in the case of an opinion on management performance. Thus, Kohler has defined *fairness* in the technical sense as: "The ability of *financial statements* to convey unambiguous, adequate information, particularly when accompanied by the *representation* (in a short-form *audit report*) of a public accountant to 'present fairly' the detail required by *convention* for depicting *financial position* and *operating results*."[17] Since fairness as so defined relates to a quality of the financial statements, and an opinion on management performance is not expressed on the statements, fairness in the technical sense relates *only* to financial statements and the auditor's representation regarding such statements. In brief, the concept of fairness as technically conceived and used in an opinion on financial statements does not apply to an opinion on management performance.

In the third place, the opinion on the financial statements is based upon and expressed in accordance with the four reporting standards. Since these standards apply exclusively to an opinion on financial statements, they cannot be extended to an opinion on management performance. Here, then, is additional evidence that the traditional concept of attestation is not valid for the report on a management audit.

If the traditional concept of attestation is not valid in an opinion on management performance, what is the nature of the concept of attestation which may be taken to apply in a report on management performance? The answer to this question can be found in the definitions of the terms: "opinion," "testify" and "attest function."

Webster's definition of "opinion," which is relevant here, is: "A view, judgment or appraisal formed in the mind about a particular

---

[16]Carmichael, *op. cit.*, pp. 72-73.
[17]Kohler, *op. cit.*, p. 186.

matter."[18]   The pertinent definition of "testify" is "to make a statement based on personal knowledge or belief."[19]   And Kohler has
defined the "attest function" as ". . . the extension of the public accountant's role to any situation where he may be called upon for an
objective statement of fact or opinion that may assist in the making
of judgments by others."[20]   Thus, putting these definitions together,
we can define the concept of attestation in the sense in which it applies
in a report on a management audit as an *affirmation by the auditor
regarding his appraisal of management, based on his personal knowledge and belief.*   As so defined, the attestation is in the nature of
an *evaluation* of the *quality* of management performance.   As such,
it is not based on absolute certainty but on what seems true and valid
to the auditor in the light of his audit findings.   In other words, it is
judgmental, a subjective assessment of management performance —
a conclusion the auditor has reached as a result of his audit.   It is, in
sum, an opinion only in the general sense of that term as a "view,
judgment, or appraisal formed in the mind about a particular matter."

It follows that, in reporting on management performance, the
auditor is not expressly professing or implying infallibility or freedom
from error.   It should be clear that another auditor might reach a
different conclusion from the same evidence, and consequently express
a different opinion on the basis of his judgment of that evidence.   It
also should be clear that with hindsight a critic may later find fault
with the auditor's judgment in the light of information which was not
available at the time of the audit.

This concept of the nature of the attestation on management performance provides an insight into the nature of a management audit
and the standards and procedures required for such audits.   It is
perceived to be essentially similar to a research project — that is,
a study involving a careful investigation or systematic inquiry regarding
managerial performance in which the auditor gathers evidence by means
of objective research standards and procedures (including any applicable auditing standards and procedures), reaches a conclusion based
on that evidence and then expresses an opinion, as his considered
judgment, on management performance.

In view of the previous discussion, it will be recognized that the
word "fairness" is inapplicable and should not be used in the attestation on management performance.   Similarly, the word "opinion"

---

[18] *Webster's Seventh New Collegiate Dictionary* (Springfield, Mass.:   G. & C. Merriam
Co., 1970), p. 592.
[19] *Ibid.*, p. 912.
[20] Kohler, *op. cit.*, p. 39.

should be avoided and a word such as "judgment" should be used, since it is likely that many readers would interpret the word opinion in the technical sense in which it is used in the opinion paragraph of the short-form report.

THE FORMAT

The content, structure and length of the report will vary from case to case depending upon such factors as the business conditions prevailing during the audit period, the competency of management, the explicit terms of the engagement and the results of the audit.

In any case, it should contain certain essential elements arranged, ordinarily, as follows:

First, there should be a section containing a description of the nature and purpose of the engagement, including the description of the areas of managerial functions, controls and activities covered in the audit. As indicated earlier, areas of management activity not covered and for which the auditor should assume no responsibility, express or implied, also should be described. These include managerial forecasts of cash flows, earnings and the like, and projections of the results of plans and policies in future years.

The next section, as previously described, should contain a statement describing the "management auditing standards and procedures" the auditor found appropriate and used in the engagement. In view of the indicated nature of these standards and procedures, phrases other than "generally accepted auditing standards" should be used to describe them. This section might be no more than a concise assertion that standards and procedures the auditor considered appropriate were used. On the other hand, it might contain a detailed description of these standards and procedures and their application if this were called for in the circumstances.

The third section should contain the attestation, presented as a brief statement setting forth the auditor's evaluation of management performance during the period under audit. It should be worded so that it is quite clear that his evaluation is a matter of judgment, and is based on the evidence obtained in his investigation. This section also should include a reference to the short-form report on the examination of financial statements when the latter report accompanies the management audit report—the case assumed here.

The fourth section should contain a description of the major findings of the investigation. Typically, this would be the longest section of the report, varying in length from a few concise paragraphs to several pages, depending upon the number and significance of the findings.

The next section should consist of a concise description of any major deficiencies in management discovered during the audit. The nature of each deficiency and its effects should be described in non-technical language. The auditor would have informed management of any deficiencies, of course, together with his recommendations for overcoming them. A statement to this effect also should be included in this section. It may be noted that Burton has suggested that the report might be supplemented by a separate report to management and directors containing ". . . . a more detailed discussion of corporate results and controls and recommendations for improvement in the management system of the corporation."[21]

The last essential element of the report is a denial of any responsibility for the activities of the management of the company or the results of its operations — past, present or future. Further, the report should be so structured and worded as to avoid even the appearance of any acceptance of responsibility for management's activities or the results of its activities.

Several caveats regarding the wording of the report are worth noting here. First, there should be no names or other identification of officers, employees or other personnel in the report. Necessary criticisms should be presented on an impersonal basis, in factual language and without any emotional coloration. If the criticisms are thoughtlessly worded, they may defeat their purpose, and, moreover, even expose the auditor to legal action. Second, where the auditor expresses a favorable judgment of management, he should avoid laudatory language and express his opinion with restraint and moderation — terms such as adequate and satisfactory being preferable to excellent, superlative and the like. This is to avoid any inference on the part of third parties that he is trying to curry the favor of management. The management auditor, in particular, must maintain an appearance of independence and objectivity as well as be independent and objective in fact.

Set forth below, for evaluation on its merits, is the proposed report on the management audit of the XYZ Manufacturing Company.

THE PROPOSED REPORT

TO THE AUDIT COMMITTEE OF THE BOARD OF DIRECTORS AND THE STOCKHOLDERS OF XYZ MANUFACTURING CORPORATION

We have investigated the management of XYZ Manufacturing Corporation for the year ended December 31, 1970. In carrying out our investigation, we focused on the following areas: the organizational structure

---

[21]Burton, *op. cit.*, p. 43.

of the company; the information system; the system of managerial controls and procedures; and the managerial plans, policies and goals for the year under investigation. Our investigation did not include managerial forecasts of earnings and cash flows, or the projected results of planned projects, operations and financial position in future years.

In conducting our investigation and evaluating managerial performance, we used objective research procedures and available standards, both absolute and comparative, which we considered necessary and appropriate in the circumstances.

In our judgment, XYZ Manufacturing Corporation was managed with reasonable efficiency during the year ended December 31, 1970, judged in the light of our findings and the circumstances in which the company operated during that year.

Your attention is called to the report on our examination of the financial statements of the company for the year ended December 31, 1970, on page 10 of this annual report.

A summary of the major findings of our investigation follows. First, the systems of informational, financial and operational controls and procèdures were found to be well established and working on a basis consistent with the organizational structure of the company. There were good relationships among the various levels of management, and the management personnel displayed mutual respect and empathy in their work. There was convincing evidence of a satisfactory degree of motivation at all levels of management.

Second, the plans, policies and goals of management for the year were evaluated and found to be reasonable and attainable. The organizational structure fostered the attainment of the goals, while the plans and policies were found to be efficiently designed and implemented.

Third, the most important opportunity for improving management was found in the areas of the information system. We found several cases in which information communicated from lower supervisory levels was either incomplete, irrelevant or so classified and summarized that it did not provide an adequate basis for decision-making. As a result, additional costs were incurred to obtain adequate information, decisions were often delayed and faulty decisions were made. We have provided management with a detailed description of this deficiency, a list of the actions we recommend to overcome it, and have been assured that they will be implemented immediately.

It will be understood that our firm assumes no responsibility for the activities of the management of the company or the results of such activities.

John Doe & Company
Certified Public Accountants

February 21, 1971

37. Investigation and Disclosure of Compliance with Laws and Regulations*   D. R. Carmichael†

From time to time, the Institute has received inquiries from practicing CPAs and others concerning the independent auditor's responsibility for investigation and disclosure of clients' compliance with laws and regulations. Most businesses are subject to a multitude of legal requirements which are accompanied by penalties of varying severity for failure to comply; the wage-price regulations are only a recent — though notable — example. The purpose of this article is to present some guidelines for the investigation and disclosure of compliance with laws and regulations in an examination made for the purpose of expressing an opinion on financial statements.

INVESTIGATION OF COMPLIANCE

Recently, attention has focused on the auditor's need to concern himself with his client's compliance with governmental wage-price regulations. While the auditor would not ordinarily be expected to search for isolated changes in the compensation of individual employees or the prices of individual products, especially when their number is large, he should take cognizance of those items which come to his attention and general changes in the compensation of large groups of employees or the overall pricing structure. In such cases, he should obtain competent evidence as to whether the changes have been authorized by the appropriate governmental body or are of a nature which under the regulations do not require such authorization. Though currently prominent, wage-price regulations are only one example of matters with which the auditor should be concerned.

The auditor's concern with compliance with laws and regulations is directly related to the bearing these matters have on the fair presentation of the statements. The effect of noncompliance on the financial statements is the primary consideration and the likelihood of the statements' being affected materially will influence the auditor's course of action.

Failure to comply with various laws and regulations may create liabilities in the form of fines, damages, other financial penalties or

---

*From *The Journal of Accountancy* (January, 1972), pp. 76-77. Copyright (1972) by the American Institute of Certified Public Accountants, Inc. Reprinted by permission of the AICPA.

†D. R. Carmichael, Ph.D., CPA, is Assistant Director, Auditing & Reporting, American Institute of Certified Public Accountants.

restraints on the company which may affect future operations. If the effect of noncompliance could reasonably be expected to have a material impact on the financial statements, the auditor should recognize this possibility. He is expected to have general knowledge of the existence and general nature of the laws and regulations under which his client operates.

In the absence of knowledge of noncompliance, the independent auditor's examination, made for the purposes of expressing an opinion on financial statements, does not include a specific search for violations, but should probably include the following procedures. The usual examination includes inquiries as to the system of internal control and the accounting procedures of the company. In addition, the auditor should usually make general inquiries of the management as to the safeguards, procedures and organizational steps which have been adopted to insure compliance with applicable laws and regulations. It is also customary to obtain a statement, preferably in writing and signed by a responsible official of the client, indicating that all outstanding liabilities are reflected in the accounts and setting forth the status of any contingent liabilities. Possible penalty for violation of laws and regulations is one of the matters to be considered for specific coverage in such a statement.

On the other hand, the auditor should make further inquiry if, in the course of his usual examination, he encounters evidence which leads him to believe that violations have occurred which might result in liabilities or penalties materially affecting the financial statements. The nature of any further inquiry will necessarily vary in the circumstances of each case. Since the applicable laws and regulations may be quite complex and technical, their interpretation may be outside the scope of the auditor's expertise. In these cases, the auditor may find it necessary to obtain legal counsel's opinion as to the interpretation and effect of the laws and regulations in question and he is ordinarily entitled to rely on opinions of legal counsel for these matters.

The need for extending the usual procedures will vary with the circumstances, depending upon the relative importance of the consequences of violation on the financial statements, the safeguards provided by the client and the nature of the evidence coming to the attention of the auditor.

DISCLOSURE OF NONCOMPLIANCE

When the auditor in the course of his usual examination, comes upon information which leads him to believe that the client may have violated laws or regulations and, as a result of further inquiry, he has reason to believe that a violation has occurred, the matter should be brought to the attention of the management with a recommendation that adequate provision be made in the financial statements for the resulting liability with appropriate disclosure. Inadequate provision or omission of a provision when the amount is material should cause the auditor to take exception in his opinion on the financial statements.

38. A New Reporting Problem for Auditors — The Impact of Pollution Controls on Financial Statements*

Thomas D. Wood†

It has become increasingly obvious that the pollution of natural resources will be one of the most pressing problems of the next few years. What is not yet so obvious, but what, in the author's opinion, will become a fundamental issue, is the significance of pollution and pollution control costs for financial statements. The problem for independent auditors will be twofold. One is relatively simple — how are pollution control costs to be accounted for? This question involves consideration of capitalizing versus expensing outlays, capitalizing of leased facilities, the adequacy of depreciation allowances, etc.

The more serious problem — and the one to which this article is addressed — is the auditor's response when pollution control is inadequate or nonexistent. There are two possible circumstances: (1) a responsible government agency has by general statute or specific injunction required pollution control to attain a pre-determined level of efficiency by a given date, or (2) the firm under audit is polluting but no government sanctions have been issued. While these two situations are not unrelated, the former will likely have an easier solution than the latter.

POLLUTION CONTROLS IMPOSED

When the firm has been given a directive to comply, the auditor should determine that full disclosure has been made of all significant information, which may be simply discharged by a footnote to the balance sheet stating the deadline date. However, in some cases a more complex approach may be required. Achieving full disclosure may be, necessarily, expanded to include a report of the progress of the firm toward its imposed goal, which may include engineering estimates of: (1) expectations with respect to whether the firm will meet the date, and (2) costs to date and expected future costs.

The significance of meeting the deadline date will hinge largely on penalties for noncompliance. If, for example, the penalty is pecuni-

---

*From *The Journal of Accountancy* (March, 1972), pp. 75-76. Copyright (1972) by the American Institute of Certified Public Accountants, Inc. Reprinted by permission of the AICPA.

†Thomas D. Wood, Ph.D., CPA, is Associate Professor of Accounting, University of South Alabama, Mobile.

ary, and the date will clearly not be met, the financial statements may need to disclose information concerning the size of the expected penalty. In fact, the question arises as to whether the penalty should be accrued and deducted from income when the likelihood of meeting the deadline is past.

If, however, the penalty is loss of license, or other impositions which threaten the continued existence of the company, the auditor must make sure this fact is disclosed in the financial statements, and appropriately qualify his opinion.

The need for drawing attention in the financial statements to the costs to date and expected future costs to meet the control standard will depend on the materiality of the costs. When the costs have been, or are expected to be, material, disclosure and appropriate adjustment will be required or the financial statements may be misleading.

No Controls Imposed

The auditor faces a more perplexing situation when the firm under audit is polluting and no governmental controls have been imposed. Once the extremely difficult question of by what standard the extent of pollution is to be evaluated has been answered, consideration must be given to the following factors: (1) there may be no future date by which the pollution can be expected to be controlled, therefore period allocation of expected costs is difficult; (2) no plans may be underway to control the firm's pollution; and (3) neither management nor the auditor may be able to estimate the probability that the government will intervene, or the extent of its intervention.

If management is enlightened and has a self-imposed target date for controlling pollution the auditor's task is rendered simpler, and adequate disclosure may be achieved as previously suggested when government controls have been imposed. In the absence of a target date, the auditor may be faced with either simply attesting the write-off of expense as incurred or acquiring engineering estimates of the earliest possible completion date, along with expected costs.

When the firm is not controlling its pollution and has no plans to do so, the auditor's recourse is less clear. When management clearly does not intend to control its firm's pollution, the possible effects of such a course of action (or inaction) are: (1) loss of image by the firm as the public becomes aware of the firm's inactivity; (2) much greater costs in the future if pollution is delayed; and (3) the social costs of continued pollution. Any one of the listed possible outcomes could have an adverse effect on the firm. The auditor should assess the potential impact of adverse events and the likelihood of their occurrence.

The inability to predict government intervention may be a temporary frailty. Government can be expected to continue to play an expanded role in pollution control. Thus, in due time, government intervention may be imminent when pollution occurs. At present, however, the problem exists and makes reporting difficult. For example, sudden unanticipated government intervention may have grave implications. One implication is raised costs because of the need for quick action. Another implication is the very real possibility that the firm may simply not be able to act expeditiously enough to prevent possible shut-down, fine, or loss of license.

Summary

In summary, auditors face a serious and imminent need to consider the impact of pollution control on financial statements. This author recommends that: (1) auditors should consider the adequacy of the pollution control of the firm under audit; (2) when no control exists, the auditor should consider his alternatives in light of possible adverse effects on the firm; (3) the auditor should determine that management has made appropriate disclosure of pollution control matters either in footnotes to the financial statements, or in monetary terms in the body of the financial statements, or both; and (4) the auditor should be prepared to modify his opinion when circumstances warrant. These circumstances could include the inapplicability of the going-concern assumption or the possibility that the firm has materially overstated its income by not accruing the cost of controlling pollution.

39. A Conceptual Approach to the Framework for Disclosure[*]

Jacob G. Birnberg
and Nicholas Dopuch[†]

Implicit in the fiduciary relation between property management and property ownership is the right of the owners of the property to secure an accounting of the stewardship from their managers. The significance of the stewardship report may vary, however, according to the economic organization prevalent at the time. In the earliest instances of stewardship, the value of formal reports was minimized by the fact that the owners of property were personally able to observe the handling of their property. In the present day, however, the operations of the enterprise have become so diverse that the formal report is often the only means available to owners to secure information on the management of their capital. Indeed, it may well be that "without assurance of reliable economic data, the remote investor or creditor would probably not supply capital to the enterprise."[1]

While initially the report is the responsibility of the management, the processing of economic data for remote external groups has become a responsibility of the accounting discipline. Accordingly, part of the function of the internal accountant and the CPA has been the determination of various sets of economic data which might be disclosed to the interested outsiders and the manner in which these data might best be presented.

It is not surprising, therefore, that many accountants have concerned themselves with the problem of the boundaries of disclosure — the question of what constitutes, in any given situation, adequate disclosure — and the extent of the CPA's attest responsibilities.[2] These boundaries may never be final, however, for the economic conditions which affect the stewardship relationships are in a constant state of flux, thus requiring a constant revaluation of the extent to which the formalized reporting structure actually discloses the appropriate economic data.

A consideration of the recent literature in accounting theory indicates that we have reached a stage where such a revaluation seems necessary.[3]

[*]From *The Journal of Accountancy* (February, 1963), pp. 56–63. Copyright (1963) by the American Institute of Certified Public Accountants, Inc. Reprinted by permission of the AICPA.

[†]Jacob G. Birnberg, Ph.D., is Professor of Business Administration, University of Pittsburgh. Nicholas Dopuch, Ph.D., is Professor of Business Administration, University of Chicago.

[1]Herman W. Bevis, "The CPA's Attest Function in Modern Society," *The Journal of Accountancy*, Vol. 113, No. 2 (Feb., 1962), p. 31.

[2]For example, see Charles T. Horngren, "Disclosure — 1957," *The Accounting Review*, Vol. 32 (October, 1957), p. 598; and Bevis, *op. cit.*, p. 30.

[3]See R. K. Mautz and Hussein A. Sharaf, *The Philosophy of Auditing* (Madison, Wisconsin,

PURPOSE

The purpose of this discussion is to investigate the question of which economic data should be disclosed to the remote external groups. The framework which is developed, though broader than the usual accounting interpretation of disclosure, is geared to the responsibilities which the accountant will be called upon to fulfill in the future.

Specifically, the discussion is divided into four parts:

1. A consideration of the present framework of disclosure (as implied in the present scheme of reporting).

2. A presentation of a conceptual framework within which the accountant can organize relevant data.

3. A consideration of several of the advantages and limitations of the proposed framework.

4. A reconciliation of the proposed framework with various facets of current practice.

PRESENT APPROACH TO DISCLOSURE

As implied earlier, the purpose of the accountant's report is to convey to the investors of capital a report on the status and management of corporate properties. Traditionally, this report has included the balance sheet and the income statement, supplemented perhaps by supporting schedules. Essentially, the purpose of these statements is to communicate data concerning the results of the past year's operations — the income statement; and the financial position achieved — the balance sheet.

Implicit in the choice of these statements for financial reporting is the assumption that the efficiency of management's actions can be determined from a study of the economic data the statements reveal. But because the balance sheet has been relegated to a position of supplementing the determination of periodic income, we must conclude that, in fact, a single standard of managerial efficiency has evolved. This standard is the level of periodic income. "In large measure it is on the basis of the reported net earnings that we label this corporation successful, that a failure, or . . . cite this management as progressive and that as ineffective."[4] Thus the current framework for disclosure accepts as its basis the classical conception of the enterprise and the entrepreneur — the maximization of wealth via the periodic income stream.

American Accounting Association, Monograph No. 6, 1961); Alan Cerf, *Corporate Reporting and Investment Decisions* (Berkeley, California, University of California, Institute of Business & Economic Research, Public Accounting Research Program), Chs. 1 and 2; Bevis, *op. cit.* and John L. Carey, "The Next 50 Years," *The Ohio Certified Public Accountant*, v. 18, Winter, 1959 p. 7

[4]Norman S. Buchanan, *The Economics of Corporate Enterprise* (New York, Henry Holt, 1940), p. 227.

CURRENT ENVIRONMENT

The development of the proposed framework is based upon explicit consideration of the following conditions of the economic environment:

1. The presence of uncertainty suggests a needed modification in our concepts of rational actions by managers.

2. The effect of uncertainty is made even more critical by the fact that modern enterprise is characterized by long-run projects which extend over many years or income periods from planning to project completion.

3. The scope and the extent of corporate enterprises have become so broad that the limits of the stewardship obligation of management have expanded to include additional classes of interests, e.g., customers and employees.

4. These, and other factors, have led to the possibility that managements may attempt to achieve other goals, in addition to profit maximization.[5]

The existence of uncertainty may require a modification in our concept of managerial effectiveness in the sense that uncertainty may lead to the pursuit of diverse or multiple goals. This possibility develops when managements, in an attempt to decrease the likelihood of or the adverse effects of unexpected events, strive for flexibility and security. Flexibility, the ability to change to alternative plans, reduces the consequence of adverse events. The necessary investments to achieve flexibility may, however, require the foregoing of greater profits.[6]

COMPLETION OF PROJECTS

Common examples of this manifestation are found in the market share consciousness of many managements, in the quest for stable profits, in the trends toward diversification, in investments in research, and in the over-all concern over competitive positions.

This concern is heightened by the fact that many commitments by managements involve several years for completion. Profits may be forthcoming only if the planned projects can be completed, which places a premium on maintaining flexibility and securing the competitive position. In fact, there is some speculation that concern over the completion of these projects, in

---

[5]The validity of assumptions one and three is becoming more and more evident. For example, see K. E. Boulding and W. Allen Spivey, *Linear Programming and the Theory of the Firm* (New York, Macmillan, 1960), Chapters 1, 6, and 7; Albert Lauterbach, *Man, Motives and Money*, 1st and 2nd edition (Ithaca, New York, Cornell University Press, 1954 and 1959); *Management's Mission in a New Society*, Ed. by D. H. Fenn, Jr. (New York, McGraw-Hill Book Co., 1959); A. A. Berle, Jr., *Power Without Property* (New York, Harcourt, Brace & Co., 1959); *Management and Corporations 1985*, Ed. by Melvin Anshen and George Leland Bach (New York, McGraw-Hill Book Co., 1960).

[6]Flexibility is often achieved at the expense of profit maximization. See A. G. Hart, *Anticipations, Uncertainty,* and *Dynamic Planning* (New York, August M. Kelley, 1951); also J. Fred Weston, "A Generalized Uncertainty Theory of Profit," *American Economic Review,* Vo. XL — Part I (March, 1950), p. 43; M. Shubick, "Information, Risk, Ignorance and Indeterminacy," *Quarterly Journal of Economics,* Vol. 68 (November, 1954). p. 635.

the light of uncertainty, is a factor accounting for the expansion of the stewardship contract to include other interests, since managements must maintain a proper social as well as economic climate. In any respect, however, the existence of alternative goals requires an extension of the framework of disclosure if a proper evaluation of enterprise operations is to be achieved.[7] This is necessary, regardless of the motive or source of multiple goals.

The commitment to long-run projects has an additional bearing on the framework of disclosure since this practice renders suspect the usefulness of any given income figure as an indication of managerial effectiveness. In fact, Drucker suggests that the present reliance on a measurement of periodic income is more akin to a "trading economy" where each transaction is an event in itself.[8] And as Papandreou observes ". . . in the absence of knowledge concerning the enterpreneur's horizon and expectations, the profit maximization construction becomes an empirically irrelevant tautology."[9]

Any new criteria for disclosure must give rise to an information system which is appropriate to the conditions outlined above. It must be realized, however, that all the criteria will not be equally applicable to all firms in all situations. In some instances it will not be possible to include certain measurements and classifications because of considerations of materiality and feasibility.

The framework proposed here divides the appropriate data into three broad categories:

1. A section of the report which describes in terms of the goals of management the relevant changes which occurred during the previous periods.

2. A section which indicates those of management's expectations which are necessary for a better understanding of the enterprise's future operations.

3. A section which describes in both financial and economic terms the current stores of service potentials available to the enterprise.

This is an appropriate framework for the environment described above since it recognizes the need to include, as elements of an evaluative framework in an uncertain, incomplete, and risky world, the nature of the economic situation, the contemplated acts of the enterprise, and the various changes which have occurred.[10] Specifically, the concept of disclosure

---

[7]H. A. Simon, D. W. Smithburg, and V. A. Thompson, *Public Administration* (New York, Alfred A. Knopf 1950), p. 488.

[8]Peter F. Drucker, *The New Society* (New York, Harper and Brothers, 1950), p. 54.

[9]Andreas G. Papandreou, "Some Basic Problems in the Theory of the Firm," in *The Survey of Contemporary Economics* — II, Ed. by B. F. Haley (Homewood, Illinois, Richard D. Irwin, 1952), p. 208.

[10]The inclusion of goals or objectives is a fundamental element in a world where the *best* action is difficult or even impossible to define. For a nonaccountant's comments here, see Dwight P. Flanders, "Accountancy, Systematized Learning, and Economics," *Accounting Review*, V. 36 (October, 1961), p. 576, ff.

assumes that the appropriate framework should follow a classification and measurement scheme based upon the goals adopted by the enterprise, the expectations underlying the acquisition and utilization of means of accomplishing these goals, and a comparison of results anticipated to the results actually achieved. A failure to supply these data would require interested parties to interpolate the motives and expectations of management to evaluate the results obtained in any period of operation.

In the following sections, an attempt will be made to elaborate on the methods by which this concept of disclosure can be made operational.

PERIODIC CHANGES

The inclusion of a discussion of periodic changes, i.e., the results of past activities, is not a departure from existing practice. Fundamentally, the income (and funds) statements perform this function within the present framework.

In the proposed framework, however, the function is expanded to include alternative and additional goals which managements may define for their enterprise. These goals would include both income- and nonincome-oriented goals. They can include profit maximizing or, alternatively, the achievement of satisfactory rather than maximum profits, securing market positions, developing new products and processes and developing the work force.[11] The exact set of goals (or, if appropriate, specific goal) will vary from firm to firm, being itself an element of the reporting framework.

The periodic changes reported must, therefore, be evaluated in the context of the goals adopted. They must be measured and communicated within a classification scheme depicting the acquisition and utilization of service potentials in attempts to accomplish the given firm's goals.

It should be noted that this proposal will require the extension of the accountant's framework into nonmonetary areas. The extent of these data will be determined by the portion of the firm's goals that represent values not subject to pecuniary measurements.[12]

EXPECTATIONS

In order to inform the external parties of what they anticipate the future to hold for the entity, management must provide the investor with information on three types of expectations.

---

[11]For one such list, see Lewis E. Lloyd, "The Origin of the Objectives of Organization," in *Organization Theory in Industrial Practice*, Ed. by Mason Haire (New York, John Wiley and Sons, 1962) p. 35.

[12]There is much speculation as to management's function relative to human resources. Nevertheless Likert offers some variables for measurement which ought to be investigated by accountants. See Rensis Likert, *New Patterns of Management* (New York, McGraw-Hill Book Co., 1961). Also see James G. March and others, *Organizations* (New York, John Wiley & Sons, 1958).

1. Prospects for the economy

2. Prospects for the industry and the enterprise as a member of that subset

3. The specific expectations which underlie the *major* investments made in resources and the projects undertaken in attempting to achieve the enterprise's goals

Of the three classifications of data, the least important in the managerial report is that pertaining to the economy as a whole. However, the inclusion of such data serves two very general functions:

1. It provides the general setting which management must take into consideration when formulating the latter two sets of expectations and planning future operations.

2. It permits the reader to compare his expectations with those of management.

The conditions anticipated for the industry are more specific than the first set of expectations. They involve projections of the effects of events which are more immediate to the enterprise and therefore will have a greater impact on the management's attempts to achieve the enterprise's goals.

These expectations include the generally accepted sales projection of the industry, the trend of input and output prices, and any other relevant events of an economic or social significance which will *probably* affect the enterprise's plans and actions.

EXAMPLE OF THE FRAMEWORK FOR EXPECTATIONS

The third group of expectations appears to have the greatest degree of significance to the external parties. These expectations concern the particular results which management anticipates from investments in resources and the undertaking of particular projects by the enterprise.

A method for including these expectations in an enterprise's report could utilize the following specific categories:

(a) Expectations implicit in the acquisition and storage of resources

(b) Expectations underlying investments in major projects

(c) General expectations, including expectations of the economy, industry, and general environment[13]

The measurement of expectations is best performed in class (a). Class (b) expectations constitute a more ideal and much more difficult state of

---

[13]The inclusion of managerial expectations in the framework for disclosure is not as unique an innovation as it may appear. It has been suggested by many that the proper matching of costs and revenues in the income statement requires a decision on the expectation of service potentials. See David Green, Jr., "A Moral to the Direct Costing Controversy?" *Journal of Business*, Vol. 33 (July, 1960), p. 218; also George H. Sorter and Charles T. Horngren, "Asset Recognition and Economic Attributes — The Relevant Costing Approach," *The Accounting Review* (July, 1962), p. 391; and Bevis, *op. cit.*

reporting. The class (c) expectations were discussed above.

With respect to class (a) expectations, the discussion will be facilitated if they are considered in reference to commitments to particular types of resources or endeavors.

INVENTORIES

The acquisition and storage of inventories is predicated on the assumption that they can be formed into more valuable outputs. This expectation is implicit in the acquisition of inventories, and its disclosure can be limited to the measurement of alternative prices of the inventories. This would indicate the extent to which the expectations are in fact being realized. The desired prices would include the present prices of raw materials which indicate the gain or loss from holding them and the probable value of the finished goods.[14] Assuming that the historical costs of these inventories are disclosed, the data would be available to permit an evaluation of the likelihood of realizing the manager's expectations.

WORK FORCE

Similar to the above case, most of the expectations underlying investments in the work force are implicit in the very acquisition of these resources, the payment plans adopted, and the investments in training and development programs (supplemented by efficiency trends). Measurements of turnover, morale, absenteeism, and of other "intervening variables" may be accepted as indications of these labor force characteristics.

PLANT AND EQUIPMENT ON HAND

Expectations concerning fixed assets are presently included in the form of their expected uses (outputs), expected length of life and probable replacement conditions.[15]

The degree to which these expectations will be realized is a function of many variables. Progress in the realization of these expectations can, however, be indicated by measurements of trends in outputs, and value in the next best alternative use.

INVESTMENTS IN SECURITY

(A) Research and development: Expectations underlying research and development revolve around the purpose of the research — basic research,

---

[14]While, ideally, we would also include changes in the value of work-in-process, there exist extreme problems of feasibility.

[15]A proposed method cf measuring changes in the value of plant and equipment which is consistent with our suggestions is offered by David Green, Jr. and George H. Sorter, "Accounting for Obsolescence — A Proposal," *Accounting Review*, Vol. 34 (July, 1959), p. 433.

new products, product improvement, or efficiency. The measurement and inclusion of these expectations might parallel this classification and be confined to a span of time where actual results could be delineated and the rewards from the research and development program thereby indicated.

(B) Charitable and community investments: Expectations in this category are more generally suited to qualitative measurements, i.e., whether they are directed toward scientific, educational, or community needs. To the extent that tangible results are expected, these investments can be reported in quantitative terms. Thus they may be compared later to the actual benefits accruing to the enterprise.

MAJOR PROJECTS

Expectations underlying investment in major projects are the most difficult to summarize and give precision so that they can be included in the accounting report. Nevertheless, with the capital budgeting developments, management's expectations are more and more becoming amenable to quantification. These expectations include cash receipts and disbursements, length of the time span, etc. To the extent these can be included, they serve as the bench marks for subsequent evaluation of the results obtained.

During the year of the acquisition, it seems feasible that the flows of benefits and outlays expected relative to major projects could be measured and included in a special schedule. During the initial or critical years, the results actually forthcoming could then be compared to these expectations so that future trends could be extrapolated.[16]

Whether or not data on expectations concerning major projects can be reported, however, may be a function of a basic restriction — the need for secrecy by the enterprise. This is a problem that can be solved only by actually analyzing each situation.

CURRENT STATUS OF THE ENTERPRISE

The discussion of the current status of the enterprise is closely related to the previous section dealing with the expectations. The current position of the enterprise will condition its expectations of future events. It is, therefore, not surprising that these two facets of enterprise reporting involve a degree of overlap.

16It is conceivable that such information as this would have proved valuable in the anticipation of the future course of actions of the Convair Division of General Dynamics. Including these expectations in the report may also be beneficial to an analysis of the effects of uneven cash flows on annual earnings. See "How a Great Corporation Got Out of Control — Part I and Part II," *Fortune*, Vol. 65 (January and February, 1962), p. 64 and p. 120.

In the current framework of reporting, the status of the enterprise is reflected by the balance sheet. Its assets and its liabilities are mirrored in the dollar amounts which the balance sheet discloses.

Such an approach, when it is considered in light of the environment cited earlier, suffers from three serious defects:

1. The balance sheet fails to include characteristics of assets and liabilities of the enterprise which merit disclosure.

2. The historical cost representation of intangible assets fails to disclose much important data about them.

3. The balance sheet does not include data with respect to the nonfinancial goals of the enterprise, e.g., security, general welfare.

In an attempt to solve these problems, the suggested framework utilizes those features found in the previous section on expectations — nonaccounting data, nonmonetary data, and explicit disclosure of managerial expectations.

INVENTORIES

The data discussed in the previous section on expectations will provide the external groups with all the relevant data needed on the nature and value of the enterprise's inventory.

PLANT AND EQUIPMENT ON HAND

Various characteristics of the plant and equipment must be indicated as well as management's expectations about their utilization. Typically, the relevant characteristics will be indexes of the plant's and equipment's remaining life, efficiency, and capacity as well as any other aspects of the plant and equipment which in any unique situation is of value to the external groups.

It should be noted that these data differ from the indexes of managerial expectations in that they are absolute (i.e., how much *could* the facilities produce?) rather than conditional (i.e., given management's expectations of the market, how much *will* the facilities produce?). In this respect the discussion of the status differs from the expectation of the enterprise.

WORK FORCE

Among the many nonaccounting assets (i.e., those service potentials which the enterprise possesses but which are not disclosed in the traditional balance sheet) is the work force which the enterprise has recruited. The data cited in the previous section on the expected utilization of the work force will also indicate the status of the work force.

SECURITY OF THE ENTERPRISE[17]

The current status of the enterprise as described by its likelihood of economic survival is measured by a combination of many things. In the simplified world of certainty and perfect competition, the sole index of continued survival was profitability. In the current economic environment characterized by oligopolistic relationships and varying amounts of uncertainty, profitability or expected profitability is not enough. Any enterprise's managers must also be aware of the likelihood of the occurrence or set of occurrences which could jeopardize the existence of the firm.

The suitable index or indexes of the likelihood of such occurrences will vary from firm to firm and industry to industry. Some likely indexes are market share, position in the industry, level of operating efficiency, research and development position, and the stability of the market in which the enterprise competes.

BENEFITS OF UTILIZING SUCH A FRAMEWORK

The chief advantage which accrues from this framework is in a more complete evaluation of managerial performance. Under the current reporting framework, management's efficiency is ascertained by some measure of the previous period's profitability, e.g., profits or rate of return. In a riskless economy where the most logical decision is always rewarded and the poorest decisions result in losses, such a criterion would be acceptable. The level of profitability — or certainly the presence of profits rather than losses — would serve as an indicator of logical decision making. Losses would be the "failing grade" received by poor managers.

As was indicated earlier, however, we do not live in a riskless economy. Thus it is possible that managers who behave in a perfectly logical manner can, because of entirely unforeseeable factors, incur losses — or a lower than desirable level of profits. The converse is, of course, equally possible. It is, therefore, necessary that the interested external groups have data from which to ascertain not merely the level of profits, but the factors which led management to behave in such a manner. Only then can managerial efficiency truly be fully evaluated.

The framework outlined earlier incorporates disclosure in a sufficiently broad manner to provide the reader with the data which he needs to evaluate management's direction of the enterprise in the manner cited above. The report contains information on management's goals for the enterprise — what it is attempting to achieve. Data are supplied on the service poten-

---

[17]In this section security implies the idea of continued economic survival in a similar economic condition. Thus a firm may be considered to have undergone an unfavorable economic change tantamount to "death" when a large producer must contract its operations and exist as a smaller one. For example, Chrysler would not consider it true survival to continue to exist as a peer of American Motors or Studebaker.

tials available to management — what management has at its disposal to achieve its goals. Finally, data are also included on the various plans which management may utilize with some assessment of the risks involved.

Under these circumstances, management or the interested party can, in period two, refer to the period one report and assess the logic of the approach taken to solving the problem of achieving the enterprise's goals. If the approach taken to the problem, as indicated in the period one report, is apparently an acceptable one, then the failure to achieve these goals in period two may be ascribable to the risks inherent in the environment. The cause can be isolated and management praised instead of criticized.

The above approach to assessing managerial performance is also consistent with the current trends in cost control. It focuses the attention upon three factors: the goal(s), the discrepancy between the goals and their achievement, and an attempt to rationalize any significant discrepancy between the goal(s) and the level of achievement. By such a process, management's true responsibility for success or failure can be isolated.

This suggested framework has the additional benefit of permitting the accountant to meet the varying needs of interested classes of readers. Our present framework seems to suggest the disclosure of sets of data more relevant to a long-run evaluation of enterprise operations. While we recognize that individuals might select particular classes of data as more significant to a particular objective, we also recognize that the significance is likely to be transitory, for individuals possess a variety of interests and motives which, over a period of time, manifest themselves in a shifting system of priorities of needs. In this respect it is difficult to anticipate completely which data will be suitable to which particular class of interests. Each interested party must be considered as occupying an overlapping position with his actions being influenced by not only "*what* he anticipates . . . but by *where* he believes his choices will place him in respect to the remaining turns in the world."[18] This too might be considered a product of our uncertain environment. A decision based on *personal* assessments of the effects of the decisions in enhancing the conditions of opportunity at terminal dates may be a method of circumventing the uncertainty of final outcomes of actions.[19]

PROBLEMS OF THE FRAMEWORK

It is readily admitted that the types of data desired are not at present uniformly available for all firms nor is the available data of the highest

---

[18]George A. Kelly, "Man's Construction of His Alternatives," in *Assessment of Human Motives*. Edited by Gardner Lindzey (New York, Rinehart and Company) 1958, pp. 56, 57, 58–59.

[19]C. West Churchman, *Prediction and Optimal Decision* (Englewood Cliffs, N. J., Prentice-Hall Inc., 1961), p. 327.

quality. An examination of annual reports, which constitute the primary means of enterprise-external group communication, would disclose that many firms have made attempts in this direction.[20]

The weakness of this system, which has grown up to supplement the limited accounting data, is that it is both haphazard and entirely unverified. Thus many enterprises omit relevant data from the report because no attempt has previously been made to carefully evaluate the over-all approach to disclosure. It, like Topsy, has too often "just growed," and no one has been responsible for it.

The framework proposed here may have as its most serious limitation the ability to verify the data which it is recommended be included. It should be emphasized, however, that the traditional conception of the attest function is more and more being modified to lead to the acceptability of much of the data recommended here.[21]

On the other hand, the emphasis given here on uncertainty, risk and changes, and the inclusion of multivaluations may reduce the dangers which would be present in accepting and verifying only one measurement in isolation from all others. Indeed, even now, the accountant evaluates expectations in many of the measurements he certifies — depreciation, bad debts, inventories (cost or market), patents, good will, etc. The concept of the going concern is operationally determined by the accountant according to many of the expectations recommended for disclosure in this paper.

A second problem which faces any attempt to expand the amount of information provided and to increase the reliability of the data is the question of secrecy. How much data can management disclose to the external parties without jeopardizing the security of the firm?

Clearly there are limitations upon the type of data which can be provided. In part, however, these data are more detailed than the report visualizes. The true secrets of any company need not be revealed in any simplified report.

The most difficult aspect of the problem of secrecy may be the period of adjustment to the more complete framework of disclosure. However, a great deal of the data which are currently leaked via anonymous sources and via other indirect methods will be gathered together into the report. There is no reason to believe that, in the long run, the adjustment to fuller disclosure will harm the enterprise.

---

[20]For example, see the study of Alan Cerf, *Corporate Reporting and Investment Decisions* (Berkeley, California, University of California, 1961). In a different context, substantial support for the hypothesis that managements deliberately include nonbalance sheet or income statement data which they feel are particularly relevant can be obtained from a cursory examination of annual reports.

[21]See Mautz and Sharaf, *op. cit.* Also Herman Bevis, *op. cit.*

Finally, it should be reiterated that the approach here does not rule out profit maximization as a motive — either for managements or investors. If anything, this approach to disclosure facilitates an analysis of the situation which would be of much more benefit to a single-valued investor than the present report. The area of corporate goals is a complex one. Nevertheless, it has become necessary to recognize the fact that many managements accept other goals — e.g., market share, position in the industry, public and employee welfare — and allow these goals to influence their behavior.

40. The Totality of Accounting for the Future*

Frank S. Capon†

Accounting like any other discipline, is one of the many factors which constitute ongoing society. It performs an essential function within the economic, social, and even ecological environment in which society progresses, a function that is nevertheless of value only in terms of the contribution it makes to progress.

Our world has been through a truly fantastic two centuries of progress and change. And, in fact, over half the total economic progress has been achieved in the tiny span of the last three decades. The impact of change of this scope and speed upon all the systems and structures by which men govern themselves has inevitably been dramatic, and we should not be surprised at the stress cracks and signals of disintegration we see all around us. These same precursors of crisis are the red flags warning society of its needs for better, more complete, and more timely information to aid the complex task of planning and decision. They are also the signs to financial executives that society needs their expert services far more than at any time in the past.

I am greatly disturbed by the fact that technical accounting discussions today sound exactly as they did when I was in training 40 years ago. It seems to me that we are doing the same things essentially the same way, applying the same standards, rules, and principles. And we justify this by claiming that these same standards and principles are all generally accepted. But, since every other facet of ongoing society has changed drastically, any thinking accountant ought to be seriously disturbed about his relevance. However, the fact that all our organizations are currently involved with reappraisals of our functions is proof that we are still alive.

We can get some measure of the changing demands on accounting by glancing briefly at what is happening in other sectors. The awesome power of the computer to process information is the outstanding harbinger of the new world, and it is revolutionizing our capability to develop and to communicate new knowledge. The early local telephone has been replaced by a whole new worldwide communications network of voice and visual devices, using satelites, lasers,

*From *The Financial Executive* (July, 1972), pp. 28-34. Reprinted by permission of the Financial Executives Institute.

†Frank S. Capon is President of the Canadian Institute of Chartered Accountants.

and other mechanisms. The new technology of automated cybernetic systems will largely eliminate labor in the production of real wealth. Travel has moved from the train and automobile through piston aircraft into jet or even supersonic aircraft, and we are only now starting to understand the implications of space travel.

All our systems have accelerated so drastically that those in charge must now rivet their attention on the future rushing toward us, with no chance to relax for a backward glance at where we have been. And under such conditions there is little hope of achieving a rewarding future unless we have the most thorough plans for objectives and how to attain them. Without such plans there is no way of knowing how to make decisions for any kind of satisfying life. Thus, the demand we place on our systems — and the task of every separate sector such as accounting — are also different from those of only a few decades ago. Because accounting has meaning only in terms of the economic and social structures it serves, we cannot consider the future role of accounting without first understanding something of the direction in which society seems to be heading.

CHANGING DEMANDS OF SOCIETY

The function of society has always been the improvement of the quality and standard of human life. This takes place through the organization and progress of communities in which men live at peace and work cooperatively, each by means of his special talents or training, to achieve the most effective employment of resources. Our efforts are directed first to the generation and distribution of real wealth. And once we are assured of sufficient incomes to eliminate insecurity, we turn our attention to the quality factors in life.

Throughout the first 750,000 years of his existence, man, by his toil, produced only enough for bare subsistence. But in the next short 200 years of mechanization and automation we have suddenly learned to produce enough wealth for affluence. Once we commercialize the new technology we shall have eliminated most production jobs, even though our structures are built on the job as a man's status symbol, his place in the hierarchy or pecking order, and the means whereby he supports his family. By obsoleting work in the generation of physical wealth we shall have destroyed the validity of wages as the main basis for equitable distribution of incomes, even though we have no useful alternative to fill the gap. This lack of a viable alternative to income distribution is rapidly forcing the prosperous and progressive capitalist countries into the mediocrity and poverty of socialism, even though only the incentives of free enterprise can provide humanity as a whole with the world of prosperity and peace which is now possible.

Man has invented the mechanisms whereby he can assure prosperity and peace for every human, we have all the knowledge and skill needed to design the economic and social structures whereby these mechanisms can provide a way of life of the highest quality and standard, and our planet contains all the resources needed for the task. We are at that hinge point in time when we must decide on our future course simply because the technology for affluence now exists, and its initial use is already precipitating crises in income distribution, employment, monetary instability, trade imbalance, and economic warfare. The future is upon us, and its form must now be decided. We must choose between affluence and poverty, between leisure and toil, between individual freedom and state serfdom, between free enterprise and socialism. And because the democratic process requires that the will of the majority prevail, we shall choose the route perceived by the largest number as being useful to them.

FUTURE ROLE OF ACCOUNTING

Intelligent choices between alternatives can be based only upon good information. And this is why the role of accounting and financial people is so vital at this point in history. Society as a whole, and every separate unit of society, must now decide where it wants to go because the potential for the future is different from that of the past. The kind of world in which we can live, and the kind of lives we can live in it, can now be infinitely more rewarding than anything we have known. But we cannot attain such goals by our present policies or structures, by our existing economic and social systems. Never before have managements in all sectors — business, government, education, institutions, and others — had a greater need for objective total information. But only a tiny part of that information is the financial statements and reports now seen as the end product of the accounting function.

Accounting was developed as the mechanism for recording transactions to permit adequate regular reports on stewardship. Developing business and other activities required that capital owners delegate to managers the responsibility for employing their savings, and this process of delegation in turn called for a regular reporting to confirm both the honesty and the effectiveness of managers. And because the resources turned over to managers could be best expressed in money terms, as could also the countless diverse transactions undertaken by managers, money has always been the language of accounting.

The money language has trapped us in two major weaknesses: first, information that could not be readily expressed in money terms has been excluded from our reports, and second, we have become rigidly tied to numbers of monetary units rather than intrinsic values as the basis for our reports. These weaknesses were not important when we had no means for measuring the countless peripheral factors that affect results and when monetary unit values did not change frequently. But today non-monetary factors frequently have overpowering importance, and monetary units have become chronically unstable at both the national and international levels.

The stewardship reporting function remains essential because honesty and performance need to be watched and because statements of past transactions are required for tax and legal purposes. But such information is of little real significance to those who must formulate objectives and plan the strategies and policies for attaining these objectives. Forward planning managers, who are in fact making the essential decisions today for business, for government, and for all the institutions of society, have long since ceased to spend much time with traditional financial statements and reports that come from the accounting process.

Good information remains as crucial as ever to the planning and decision process. The great difficulty is that the information needed by those who must plan and decide today is of an entirely different order from that needed only a decade ago. To achieve our potentials of prosperity and leisure, we have to use the newest technology and we have to develop new mechanisms or structures for the distribution of wealth. The new technology of computers includes the ability to simulate our future environment in complete detail, to measure the relative values of alternative courses, and to select the most desirable plans or programs. But the information needed to construct such models is in large part subjective, judgmental, and non-quantifiable in the monetary sense. It cannot be classified as financial information; it will not fit within the standards of generally accepted accounting principles. Yet it is vital to the establishment of future objectives and to the formulation of strategies and policies needed to attain them.

All of this is not particularly comfortable for accounting people. Through the years we have developed a concept of financial information and forecasts, we have established rules or standards for expressing financial data, and we have argued that data which cannot be expressed in financial terms has no place in our reports. But new knowledge invalidates this approach. The factors which will have the most direct impact on our future course are not financial and cannot be expressed in financial terms, but we do have the techniques for building non-financial models and for including in them factors which were not previously quantifiable.

We know all about the weaknesses of forecasts or projections, but we also know that a forecast, no matter how inexact, has many times the value of an historical statement. We have a horror of releasing forecasts to shareholders, government, or the public, and our professional auditors shun any suggestion that they should certify such subjective data. Yet, since management can, and does, produce forecasts and plans upon which major investment or policy decisions are based, surely that same information is capable of review by outside professionals, and surely it is of infinitely greater significance to investors or other segments of society than is a glossy picture of past results.

If accounting and financial people intend to maintain their importance to society, if they expect to play a valuable role in the years ahead, if they hope to form an essential part of the teams which will plan and execute the future of society and its institutions, they need to reach out for the total information function which is waiting to be assumed. Total information is not financial. It has to do with the totality of what is happening — with financial, scientific, economic, social, ecological, and even political developments, with their measurement and inter-relationships, with an understanding of the impact of each on the course of events. The implications for future success or failure are immeasurable. The choices men must make will be made soon for the foreseeable future. Our opportunity, and thus our responsibility, to influence or to shape these choices is immense.

Future Replaces Past

It has always been true that the future is the only important decision area for humanity. The past is interesting, and we need to know how we did in order to learn from experience. But the past is past; it cannot be relived or altered. On the other hand, the future is what we choose to make it. Man is the only animal capable of establishing future objectives for his quality and standard of living and then controlling his total environment to attain those objectives. We can invent our future. We can make it happen. And because this is possible, leading thinkers or managers will undertake it.

In the past, change was so slow from year to year that the process of forward planning was really one of evolution, with the near-term future looking so much like the past as to allow the decision process to place great weight on history. But today our future can be so totally different from even the most recent past that we can attain our fullest potential only if we will turn virtually all our attention to the future. Such a change spells disaster for an accounting function based squarely upon the recording and interpretation of completed transactions.

We financial executives are, of course, oriented to the future as well as to the past. But our balance is wrong. We pay far too much reverence to past performance. Our standards and principles are locked into value systems which are rapidly becoming meaningless to the future development of society. And the most innovative or imaginative thinking or writing on what ought, in my opinion, to be the role of accounting and finance is coming from leaders who do not for a moment think of themselves as accountants. The future has already replaced the past as the basis for planning objectives and the strategies and policies needed to attain them, but I do not yet see many accountants out there on the frontiers of change.

It is not that accountants are insensitive to developing change. There is ample evidence that leading financial people in all countries have reacted to change, are questioning the value of our existing approaches in terms of ongoing society, are seeking to up-date their roles to restore the value of their contribution to the total development of national and international communities. The Trueblood and Wheat studies of the AICPA are examples of the most fundamental reappraisal of the purposes of accounting and its standards or principles. Recent membership bulletins of FEI bear eloquent testimony to the great amount of probing re-examination of our function being undertaken by financial leaders in industry. Task Force 2000 of the CICA was a model analysis of the next 30 years of accounting as seen by the most able young Canadian accountants we could put together as a study team. In the U.K. a new broad-gauge research institute has been formed at Lancaster University to undertake a critical reappraisal of all facets of accounting.

Much is indeed going on. And our most trusted and experienced leaders are deeply involved, testifying to their concern for maintaining a truly meaningful role for accounting. But results of these studies are now beginning to appear, at least in tentative form, and I for one am greatly disturbed by them. For the tenor seems to be that we must be careful to avoid damage to our function or image by adopting rapid change, that our traditional approaches are so intimately inter- twined in our economic and fiscal structures that basic change is im- practical. To illustrate what I mean, I will quote some phrases from recent authoritative statements.

"Business does not yet have the ability to make forecasts which have the degree of accuracy required for reporting to the public."

"The actual amount involved in a business transaction is a demonstrable fact, and all other bases of valuation are conjectural."

"Historical costing methods are more or less fully understood and generally accepted . . . whereas other methods of valuation are presently controversial."

"Financial analysts and others should recognize the limitations of accounting and place more reliance on non-accounting information to supplement their evaluation of reported financial results."

Such comments show a lack of commitment to the future and, in fact, a regression from authoritative accounting texts of many decades ago. Ever since man invented money, he has always recognized that currency as such has no intrinsic value — that it is nothing but a medium of exchange, a convenient way of eliminating the ponderous aspects of barter in the effective distribution of goods and services. The only factor of ongoing importance in economic development is the intrinsic value of goods or services. Such values are expressed in money terms so that they can be equated and recorded at the point of exchange, but it is always the effective purchasing power equivalent and not the number of dollars that matters.

Values change. They can change very quickly and for a variety of reasons. We have fallen for fiscal and monetary policies which make inflation a way of life. We have accepted the concepts of short-sighted economists who assure us that inflation is necessary for prosperity. But this is only another way of saying that savings put aside in terms of dollars will depreciate because the purchasing power of those dollars, when needed by the saver, will have dropped sharply. Interest costs have of course adjusted themselves to this condition because they function in an open market competitive situation, but we accountants refuse to allow production and investment costs to be corrected in the same way.

There are other reasons for changing values. Advancing technology can have an immense impact on the economic value of investment, and thus on real costs and revenues. Changes in the international competitive world can greatly affect relative monetary values and therefore the intrinsic values of investment or operations expressed in affected currencies.

The function of accounting is to provide meaningful, accurate, and timely information for the planning and decision process. Our present standards, principles, and concepts do not do that, which is why we have undertaken so many searching analyses of how we do our job.   In the face of this dissatisfaction, and particularly in view of the vast amount of new thinking by other disciplines in our general area, we need to look very critically at the conclusions which are emerging from our own studies.

Those in charge in any function are by definition the establishment. They are usually the most experienced and prestigious leaders, having achieved their positions by excelling over their confreres.   But they are too often wedded to their own concepts, which are by then traditional and generally accepted, and they naturally tend to avoid adoption of new systems with which others are more familiar.   It is always easy to think up reasons against change.   The comments I have quoted are eminently reasonable.   To go against them would indeed cause confusion, discomfort, and possibly even dismay for those who are comfortable in the rut of traditional financial statements and reporting.

But this insistence on adherence to tradition is not a viable option for accounting unless we decide that our role is to be limited to the bookkeeping function of recording past transactions.   Record-keeping is necessary, but it can be reduced to routine, it can be largely automated, and it has lost much of its significance in the vital task of formulating objectives, strategies, and policies for developing society. The future has already replaced the past as the arena for challenging activity, and those who insist on remaining in the comfortable world of the past have no choice but to move over and allow others to take their rightful place at center stage.   For us to call on financial analysts and others to use "non-accounting information to supplement evaluation of financial results" is to concede that we are interested only in a minor role, in partial information, and therefore that some discipline other than accounting must take over the task of total information systems.

PLANNING AND ACCOUNTING

Because he is blessed, or cursed, with his big brain, man is the only animal capable of developing new knowledge, of understanding and therefore controlling his total environment — in fact, of attaining his dreams or destroying his planet.   This awesome capability results entirely from knowledge.   And our leading thinkers in all sectors are constantly seeking to push back the boundaries of knowledge, to attain ultimate truth.

It is an uncomfortable, even terrifying, fact that we have already attained ultimate knowledge in some directions and are probably approaching it in many more. Let me give you just a couple of examples. In medicine, we know how to create life molecule by molecule, we can stimulate mental activity before and after birth, we know how to achieve cloning (the artificial reproduction of any required number of exactly duplicate animals or humans), we are close to new breakthroughs in control of the aging process, major organ transplant techniques cause us to question when death occurs and just what is the essential part of the body which determines the individual.

In weaponry, we now have ultimate weapons — those which can destroy all life on earth — and thus we dare not use them. And when one recognizes that almost all human history has resulted from advancing weapons technology, one suddenly realizes that past political mechanisms for developing man's communities and structures must now be replaced by some system whereby all men can work and progress together by voluntary cooperation.

Such ultimate knowledge is here or close, not just in medicine and weaponry, but in all sectors of total society. And because such knowledge does exist, it will be used, ethically or unethically, in the ongoing development of society. This is the real world in which we live, in which we must play our part as accountants.

It is a world of planning for the future and then attaining those plans. Development of knowledge has soared ahead of our ability to use the knowledge effectively, but we must now put it to use. And because it is new knowledge, it offers us potentials totally different from our limited achievements of the past, which in turn has to mean that the economic, fiscal, and social systems and structures by which we operate will almost certainly need major surgery if not total transplant.

Surely it is no coincidence that we have developed the machine systems for processing data of infinite volume and complexity at the very point in history when we need to process such data. Ten years ago we had no means for dealing with information of this type; we had no choice but to fly by the seat of our pants. But today the fantastic power of the computer and the mathematical simulation concepts opens up for us the ability to put together future plans which give due weight to every factor that can influence life on earth.

The leader in developing such techniques is probably Professor Jay Forrester of MIT, whose computer models of companies, cities, nations, or even the entire world have shown us graphically the interrelationships of forces or factors which have not previously been measured. He has brought into mathematical models factors so diverse that they have been ignored in the past because we had no means to cope with them. Those models, now that they exist, show us that any plans or decisions which failed to take into account all such factors were dangerously incomplete.

We now have the machine systems and the techniques to plan our economic and social future molecule by molecule, to develop infinite numbers of alternative models, to select the optimum plan from among viable alternatives, and to take into account every economic, social, or ecological factor in the formulation of strategies or policies needed to attain objectives. This is real. The knowledge, the techniques, the hardware needed all exist. And the principles are identical whether we are planning the future of a company, a community, a hospital, a nation, or even the world.

Surely the implications for the accounting function are obvious to all. With that kind of capability open to mankind, how can we expect society to place much importance on the bookkeeping function of recording past transactions and producing financial statements of past results. The true challenge now is, where are we going and how do we get there, not where have we been and what did we do right or wrong? We developed the accounting function as a bookkeeping task, we adopted money as its language, and we fenced it in with all the rigidities that were logical to a task that could be standardized within clearly defined rules and procedures. So long as change was gradual, so long as monetary units remained relatively stable, and so long as there was no means to quantify or assimilate into the measurement process diverse and subjective information on countless obtuse or indirect factors, this tidy world of accounting could play an important role. But it is no longer important. The new knowledge and data processing ability exist. To insist on working without them, to refuse to take advantage of new knowledge and technology for planning and decision, would be to deprive management of much of its new capabilities.

Only experienced accountants have the training, the carefully developed integrity and objectivity in dealing with information, which is so essential to the new technique of simulation and of planning through the use of complex mathematical modelling. Mathematicians can play with figures and produce any result you want because they have no depth of commitment to the integrity of financial information. Futurists can dream up all types of attractive alternatives and color them vividly to make them marketable, but they lack the objectivity so vital to the correct evaluation of alternatives. Accountants too often lack the knowledge or understanding of the innumerable complex non-financial factors in the equation of progress and prosperity, but this lack can be overcome probably more easily than we can instill objectivity and integrity into mathematicians, economists, and futurists.

PEOPLE MAKE PROGRESS

As has been true throughout history, people bring about progress by their restless imaginative probing and innovation, just as other people prevent progress by stubborn resistance against what they do not comprehend. Humanity has gone through its unbelievable two centuries of exponential development because those who reached out for the future were able to retain the balance of power. If we are faltering today it may be because the leaders are so far ahead that they are out of sight of the masses, who mill around without sound leadership. It may also be that we have already achieved as much new knowledge or technology as can be usefully digested in the next century or two, and that further pressure would cause our structures and systems to distintegrate unless we adapt them to our new potentials.

Regardless of the reasons, we are surely at the end of our two centuries of exponential growth. This thought should be consoling rather than frightening. Because what we have already developed is the potential for affluence, peace, and leisure for all humanity without the need for any further knowledge, skill, or technology. The remaining task of achieving such objectives is staggering, even though we already possess all the necessary means to do so.

It is now up to people to work with existing knowledge, skill, and resources to build this brave new world. They will have to be able, imaginative, and dedicated people capable of developing in detail the concept of such a world and of inventing the systems and structures needed for the efficient generation and equitable distribution of the wealth upon which success depends. And they will have to take into account all the diverse environmental factors which are so difficult to measure, yet which will, in the final analysis, determine the quality of life on earth.

Standing against them in opposition are the serried ranks of those who resist change, who defend traditional positions, who seek to preserve for the future values or systems which were designed for the much simpler and infinitely less productive periods of the past. It is not that our treasured standards and principles are without value. It is just that they are rapidly losing their relative importance because the purposes for which they were developed have been surpassed by new aspirations or objectives of infinitely greater significance to mankind.